JE CROIS EN MOI

MORIARTY
❧ THE PATRIOT ❧

BASED ON THE WORKS OF Sir Arthur Conan Doyle
STORYBOARDS BY Ryosuke Takeuchi
ART BY Hikaru Miyoshi

1

CONTENTS

MORIARTY THE PATRIOT

1

SHONEN JUMP Edition

BASED ON THE WORKS OF Sir Arthur Conan Doyle
STORYBOARDS BY Ryosuke Takeuchi
ART BY Hikaru Miyoshi

TRANSLATION (´･∀･`)ｻｧ?
TOUCH-UP ART & LETTERING Annaliese "Ace" Christman
DESIGN Joy Zhang
EDITOR Marlene First

First published in Japan in 2016 by SHUEISHA Inc., Tokyo.
English translation rights arranged by SHUEISHA Inc.

Printed in U.S.A.

Published by VIZ Media, LLC
P.O. Box 77010
San Francisco, CA 94107

10 9 8 7 6 5 4 3 2 1
First printing, October 2020

ratings.viz.com RATED T+ OLDER TEEN

PARENTAL ADVISORY
MORIARTY THE PATRIOT is rated T+ for Older Teen and is recommended for ages 16 and up for realistic violence, drug use and criminal activity.

VIZ MEDIA
viz.com

SHONEN JUMP
shonenjump.com

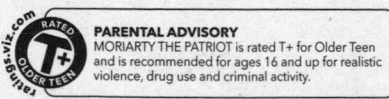

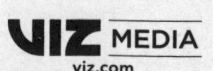

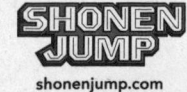

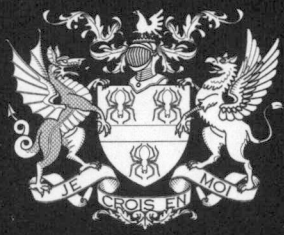

RYOSUKE TAKEUCHI

When I was a kid, I always loved main characters without really thinking too much about it. But as I grew up and understood more about how irrational the world is, I started to actually empathize with the villains. Colonel Muska, Master Archfiend Zoma... What motivated them to want to take over the world? I think it's fun to imagine all these things when a villain's motivations aren't explained in a story. Professor Moriarty is one of those villains.

HIKARU MIYOSHI

This all started around the end of my previous series when my editor asked me, "What do you think of drawing Sherlock Holmes next?" A year passed, during which I studied the British Empire like crazy. After much trouble, Holmes's archnemesis, Professor Moriarty, became the main character. I still have a lot to learn, but I hope you enjoy this series!

RYOSUKE TAKEUCHI was born November 20, 1980, in Hyogo, Japan, and is a manga artist and writer. He got his big break in 2011 with *ST&RS*, his first serialized *Weekly Shonen Jump* series. He later did the storyboards for *All You Need Is Kill*.

HIKARU MIYOSHI is a manga artist whose previous work includes *Inspector Akane Tsunemori*, which was based on the popular anime *Psycho-Pass*.

Takeuchi and Miyoshi began collaborating on *Moriarty the Patriot* in 2016.

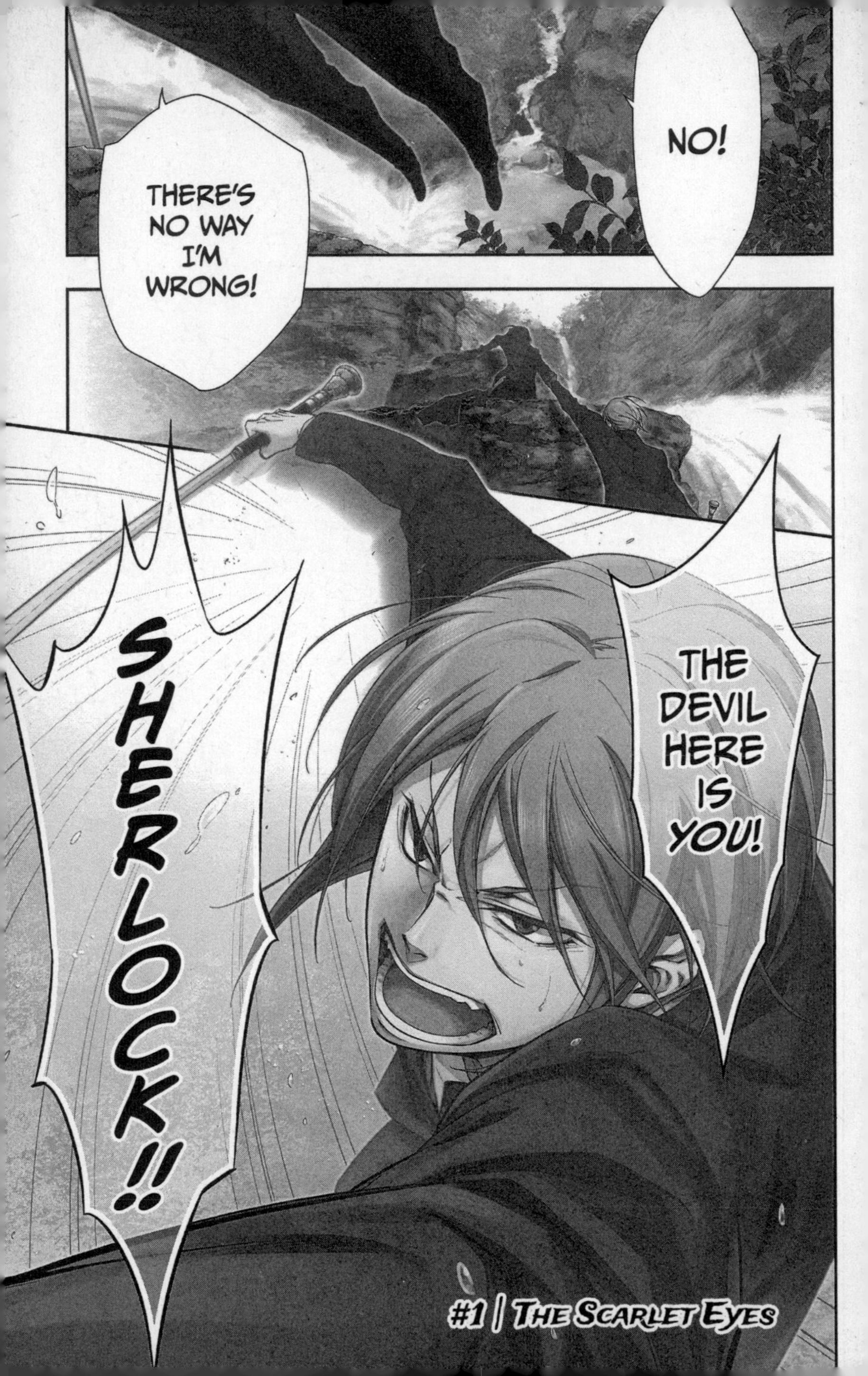
NO!
THERE'S NO WAY I'M WRONG!
THE DEVIL HERE IS YOU!
SHERLOCK!!
#1 | The Scarlet Eyes

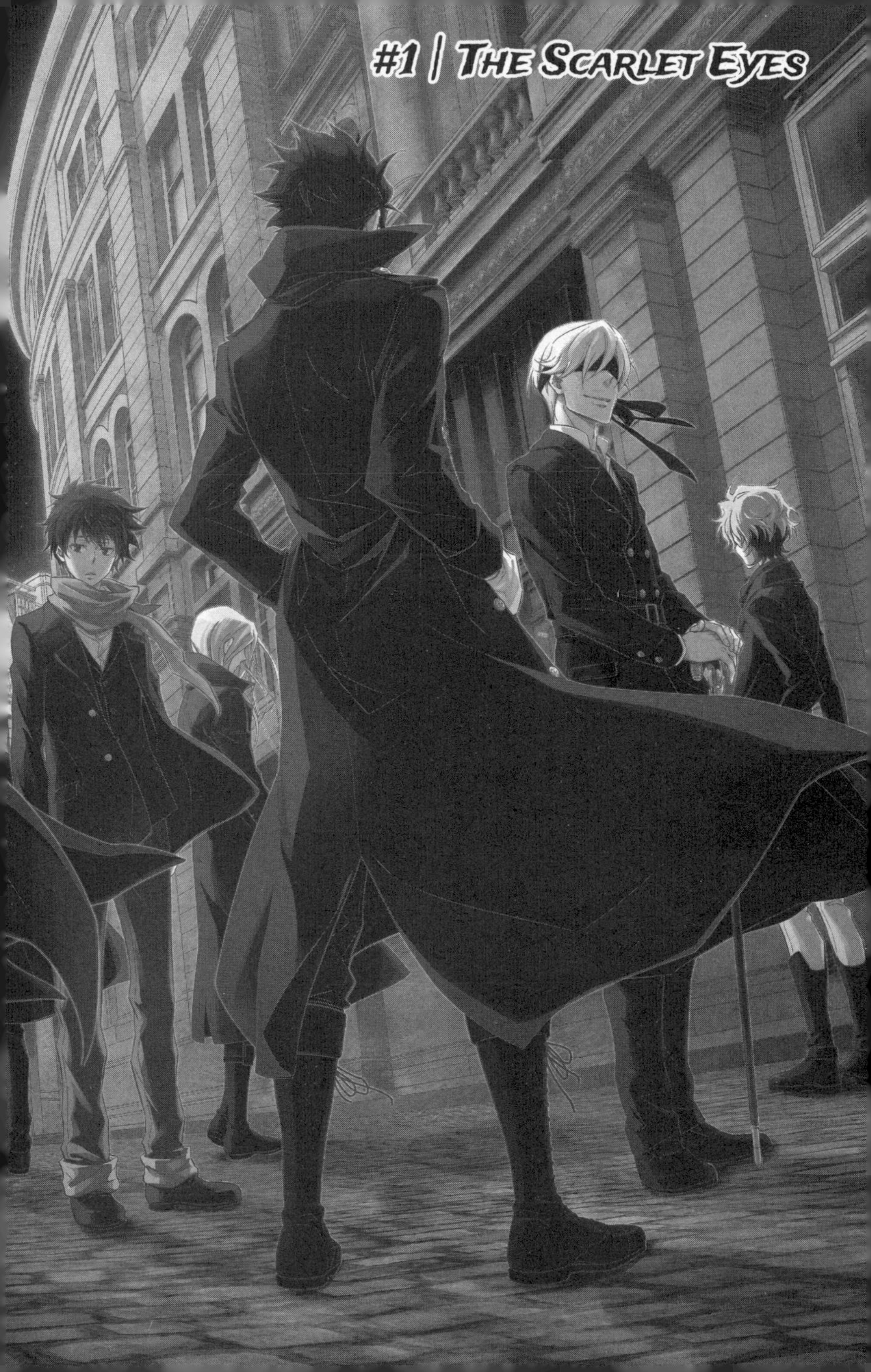
#1 | The Scarlet Eyes

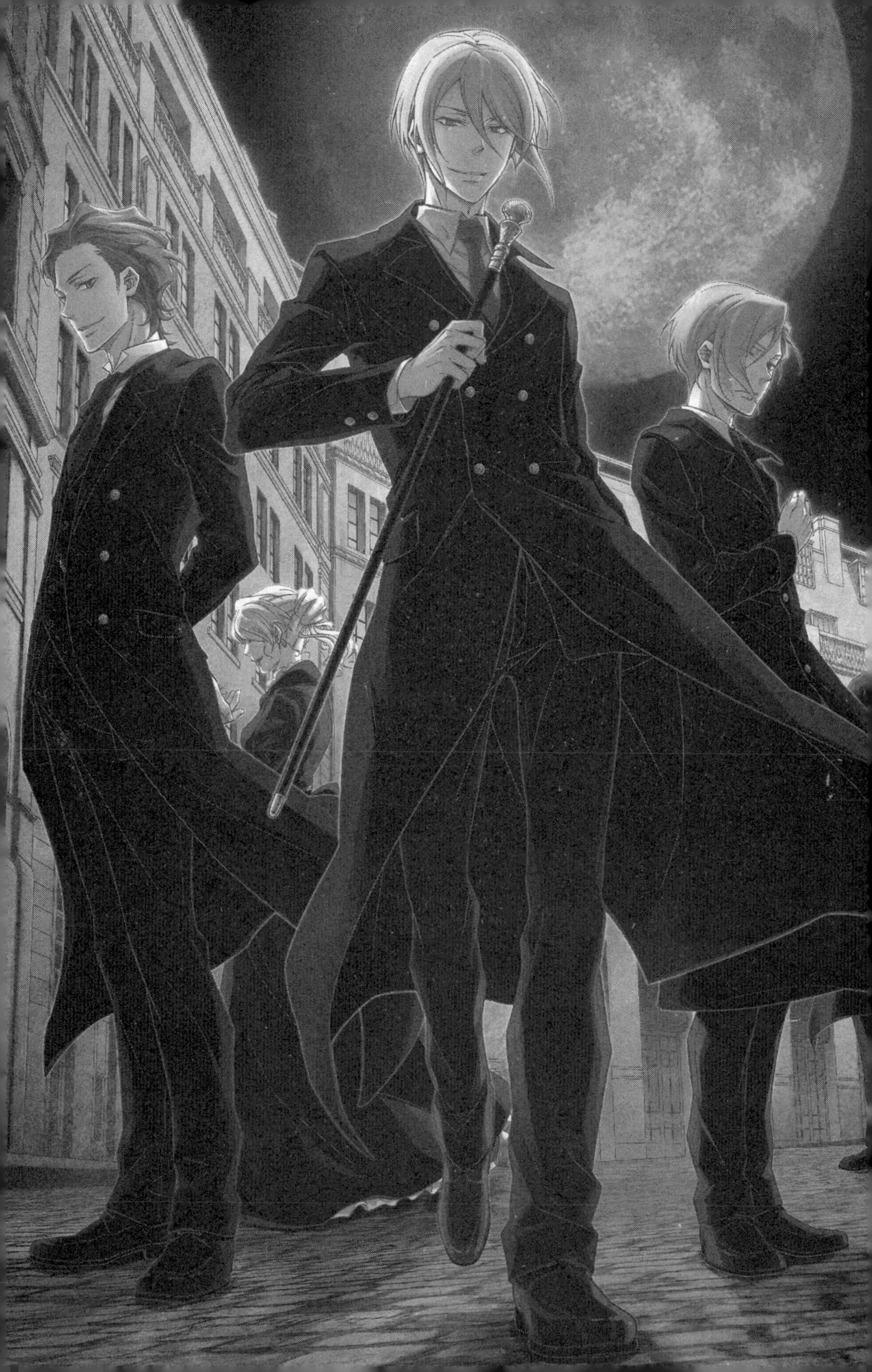

MORIARTY
THE PATRIOT

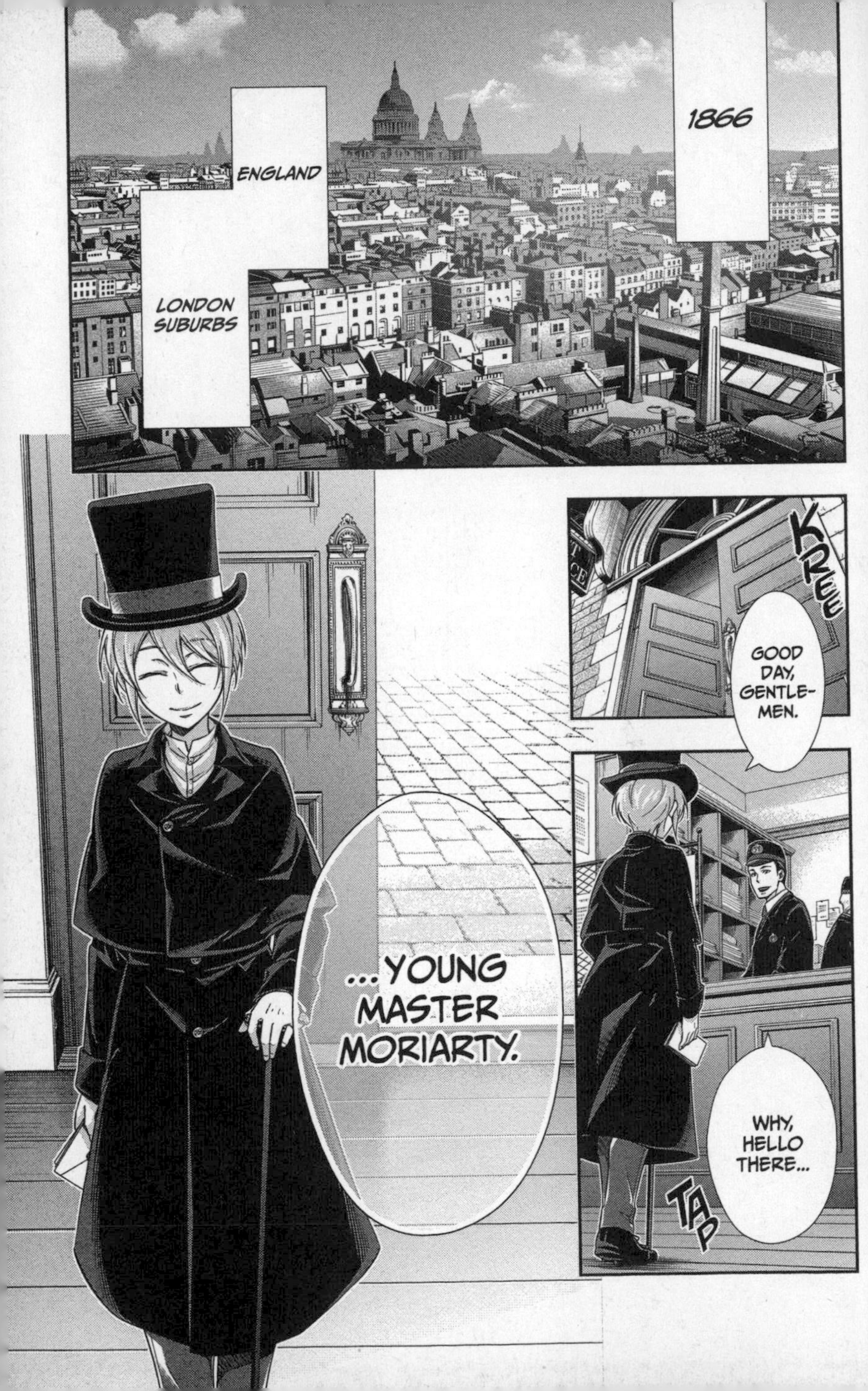
1866
ENGLAND
LONDON SUBURBS
KREE
GOOD DAY, GENTLEMEN.
WHY, HELLO THERE...
TAP
...YOUNG MASTER MORIARTY.

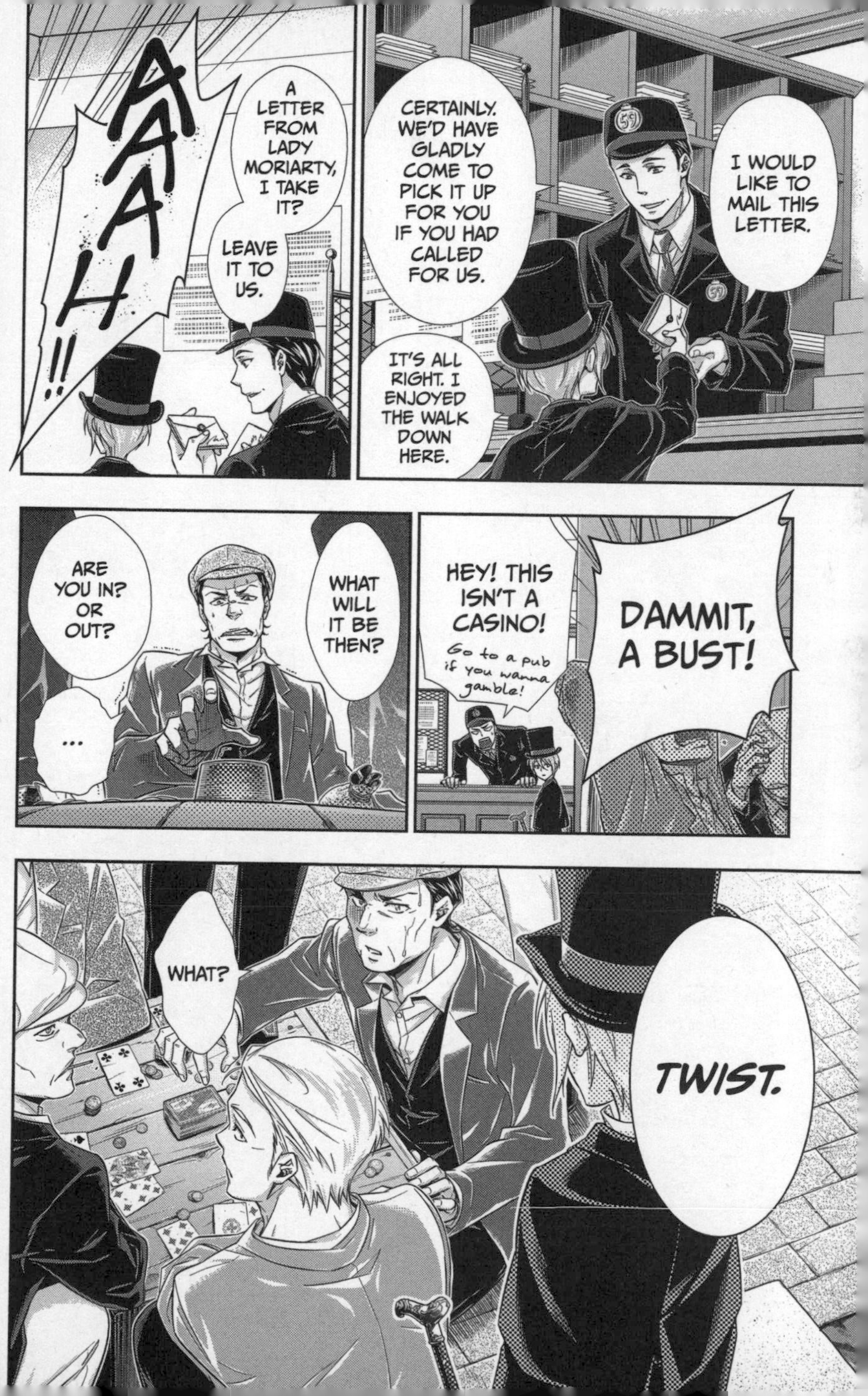
I WOULD LIKE TO MAIL THIS LETTER.
CERTAINLY. WE'D HAVE GLADLY COME TO PICK IT UP FOR YOU IF YOU HAD CALLED FOR US.
IT'S ALL RIGHT. I ENJOYED THE WALK DOWN HERE.
A LETTER FROM LADY MORIARTY, I TAKE IT?
LEAVE IT TO US.
AAAH!!
DAMMIT, A BUST!
HEY! THIS ISN'T A CASINO!
Go to a pub if you wanna gamble!
WHAT WILL IT BE THEN?
ARE YOU IN? OR OUT?
...
TWIST.
WHAT?

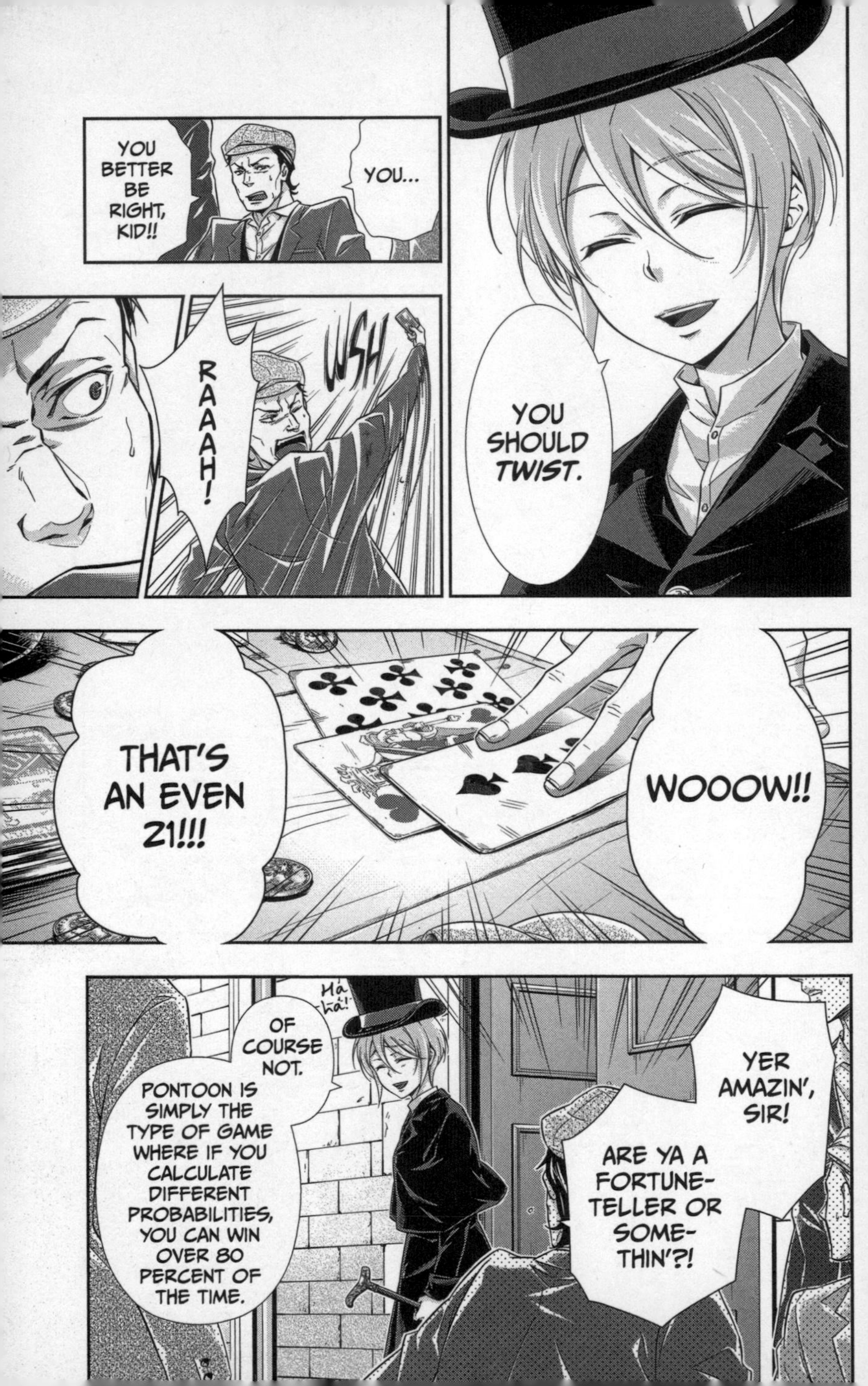
YOU SHOULD TWIST.
YOU...
YOU BETTER BE RIGHT, KID!!
WSH
RAAAAH!
WOOOW!!
THAT'S AN EVEN 21!!!
YER AMAZIN', SIR!
ARE YA A FORTUNE-TELLER OR SOME-THIN'?!
Ha ha!
OF COURSE NOT.
PONTOON IS SIMPLY THE TYPE OF GAME WHERE IF YOU CALCULATE DIFFERENT PROBABILITIES, YOU CAN WIN OVER 80 PERCENT OF THE TIME.

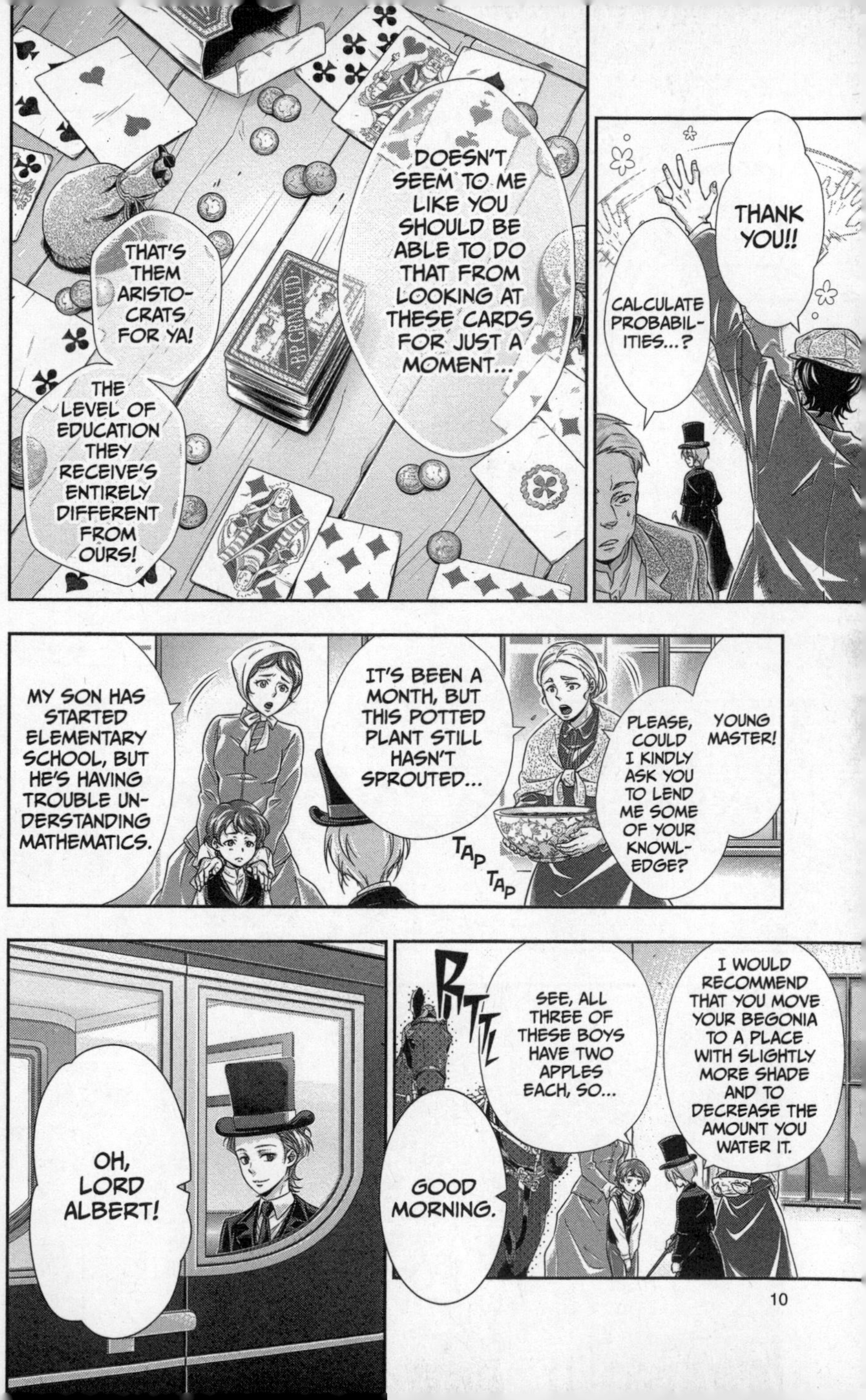
THANK YOU!!
CALCULATE PROBABILITIES...?
DOESN'T SEEM TO ME LIKE YOU SHOULD BE ABLE TO DO THAT FROM LOOKING AT THESE CARDS FOR JUST A MOMENT...
THAT'S THEM ARISTOCRATS FOR YA!
THE LEVEL OF EDUCATION THEY RECEIVE'S ENTIRELY DIFFERENT FROM OURS!
YOUNG MASTER!
PLEASE, COULD I KINDLY ASK YOU TO LEND ME SOME OF YOUR KNOWLEDGE?
IT'S BEEN A MONTH, BUT THIS POTTED PLANT STILL HASN'T SPROUTED...
TAP TAP
MY SON HAS STARTED ELEMENTARY SCHOOL, BUT HE'S HAVING TROUBLE UNDERSTANDING MATHEMATICS.
I WOULD RECOMMEND THAT YOU MOVE YOUR BEGONIA TO A PLACE WITH SLIGHTLY MORE SHADE AND TO DECREASE THE AMOUNT YOU WATER IT.
SEE, ALL THREE OF THESE BOYS HAVE TWO APPLES EACH, SO...
RTTL
GOOD MORNING.
OH, LORD ALBERT!

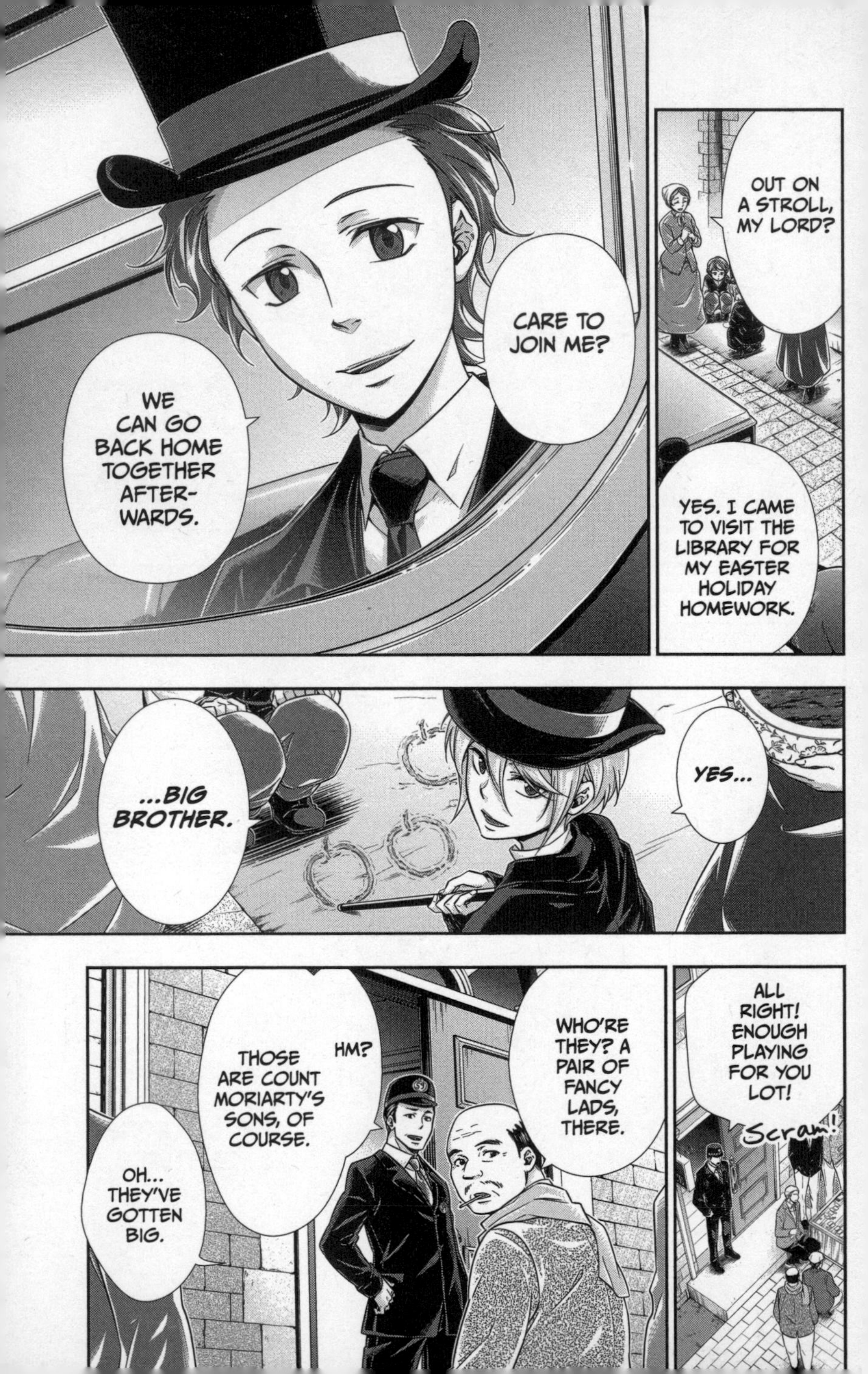
OUT ON A STROLL, MY LORD?
YES. I CAME TO VISIT THE LIBRARY FOR MY EASTER HOLIDAY HOMEWORK.
CARE TO JOIN ME?
WE CAN GO BACK HOME TOGETHER AFTER-WARDS.
YES...
...BIG BROTHER.
ALL RIGHT! ENOUGH PLAYING FOR YOU LOT!
Scram!
WHO'RE THEY? A PAIR OF FANCY LADS, THERE.
HM?
THOSE ARE COUNT MORIARTY'S SONS, OF COURSE.
OH... THEY'VE GOTTEN BIG.

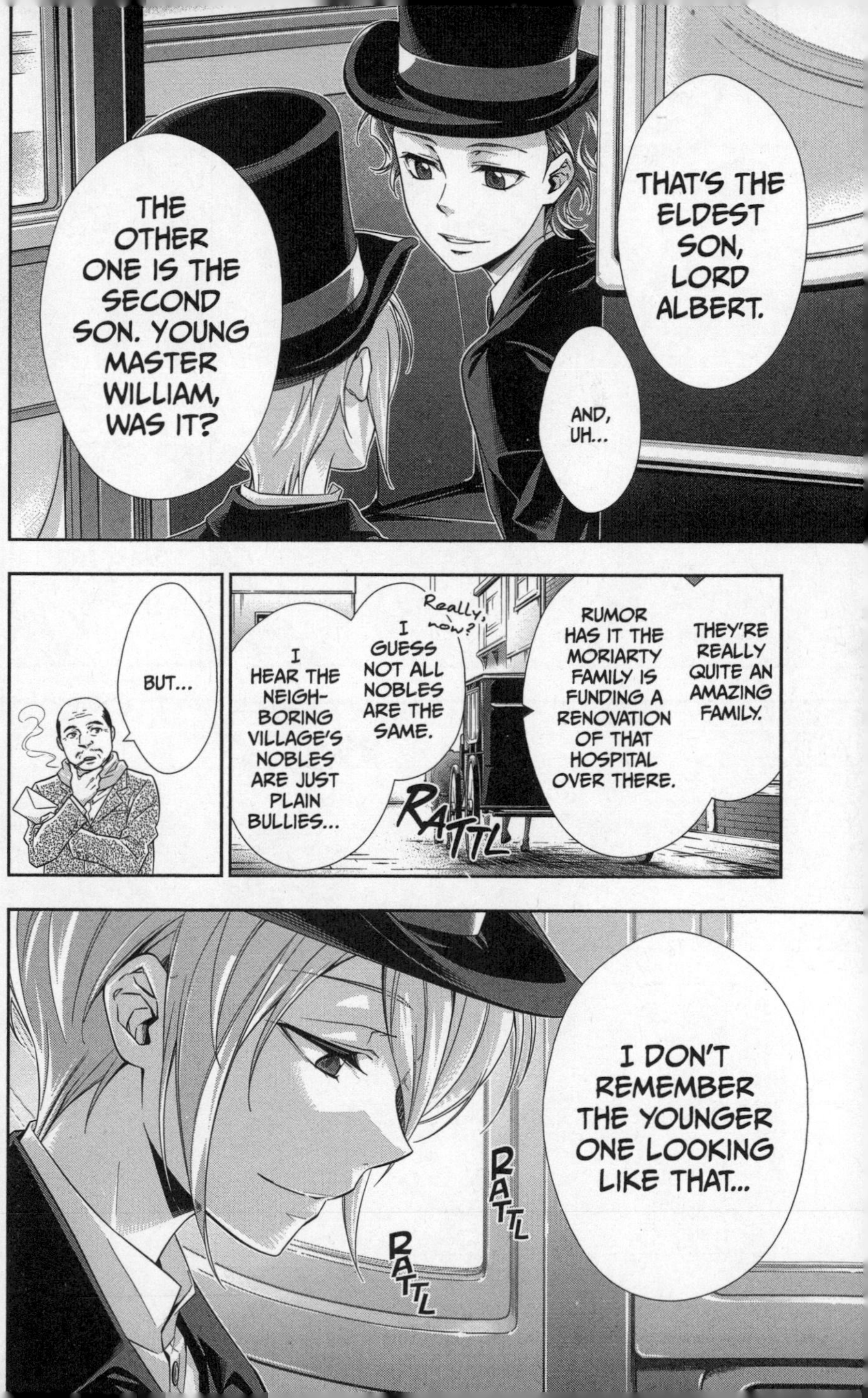
THAT'S THE ELDEST SON, LORD ALBERT.
AND, UH...
THE OTHER ONE IS THE SECOND SON. YOUNG MASTER WILLIAM, WAS IT?
THEY'RE REALLY QUITE AN AMAZING FAMILY.
RUMOR HAS IT THE MORIARTY FAMILY IS FUNDING A RENOVATION OF THAT HOSPITAL OVER THERE.
Really, now?
I GUESS NOT ALL NOBLES ARE THE SAME.
I HEAR THE NEIGH-BORING VILLAGE'S NOBLES ARE JUST PLAIN BULLIES...
RATTL
BUT...
I DON'T REMEMBER THE YOUNGER ONE LOOKING LIKE THAT...
RATTL
RATTL

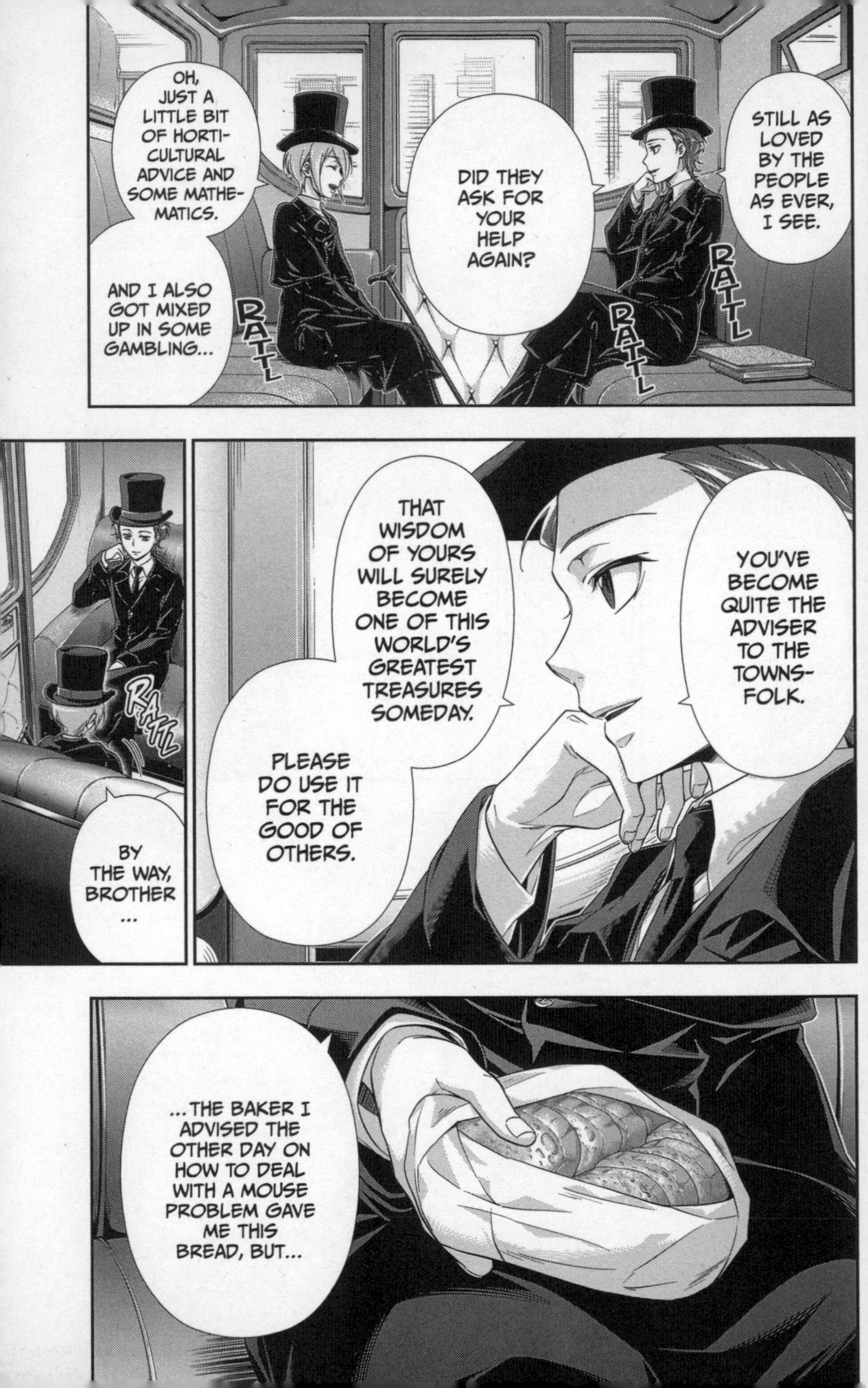
STILL AS LOVED BY THE PEOPLE AS EVER, I SEE.
RATTL
RATTL
DID THEY ASK FOR YOUR HELP AGAIN?
OH, JUST A LITTLE BIT OF HORTICULTURAL ADVICE AND SOME MATHEMATICS.
RATTL
AND I ALSO GOT MIXED UP IN SOME GAMBLING...
YOU'VE BECOME QUITE THE ADVISER TO THE TOWNSFOLK.
THAT WISDOM OF YOURS WILL SURELY BECOME ONE OF THIS WORLD'S GREATEST TREASURES SOMEDAY.
PLEASE DO USE IT FOR THE GOOD OF OTHERS.
RATTL
BY THE WAY, BROTHER ...
...THE BAKER I ADVISED THE OTHER DAY ON HOW TO DEAL WITH A MOUSE PROBLEM GAVE ME THIS BREAD, BUT...

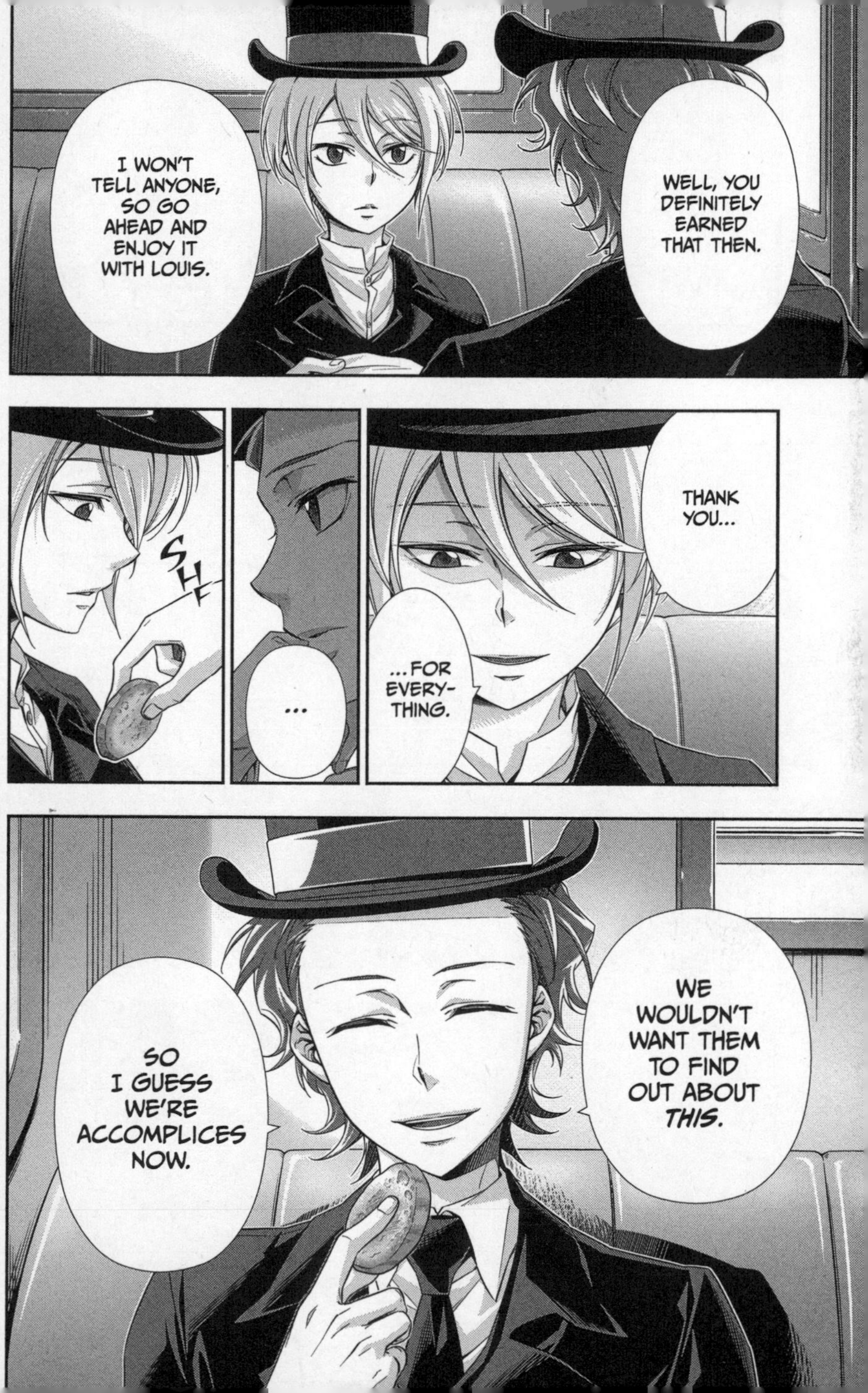
WELL, YOU DEFINITELY EARNED THAT THEN.
I WON'T TELL ANYONE, SO GO AHEAD AND ENJOY IT WITH LOUIS.
THANK YOU...
...FOR EVERYTHING.
...
SHF
WE WOULDN'T WANT THEM TO FIND OUT ABOUT *THIS*.
SO I GUESS WE'RE ACCOMPLICES NOW.

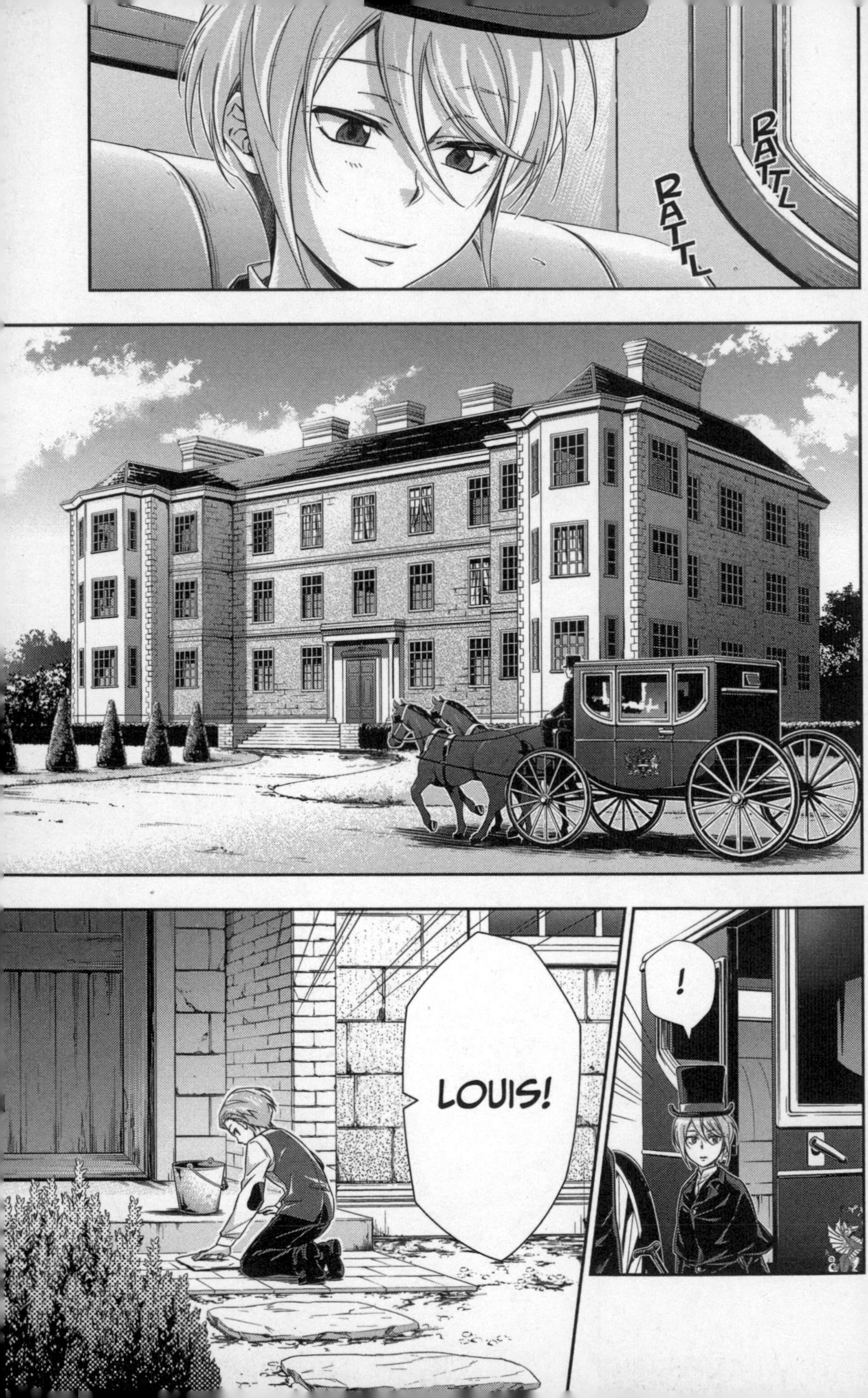
RATTL
RATTL
!
LOUIS!

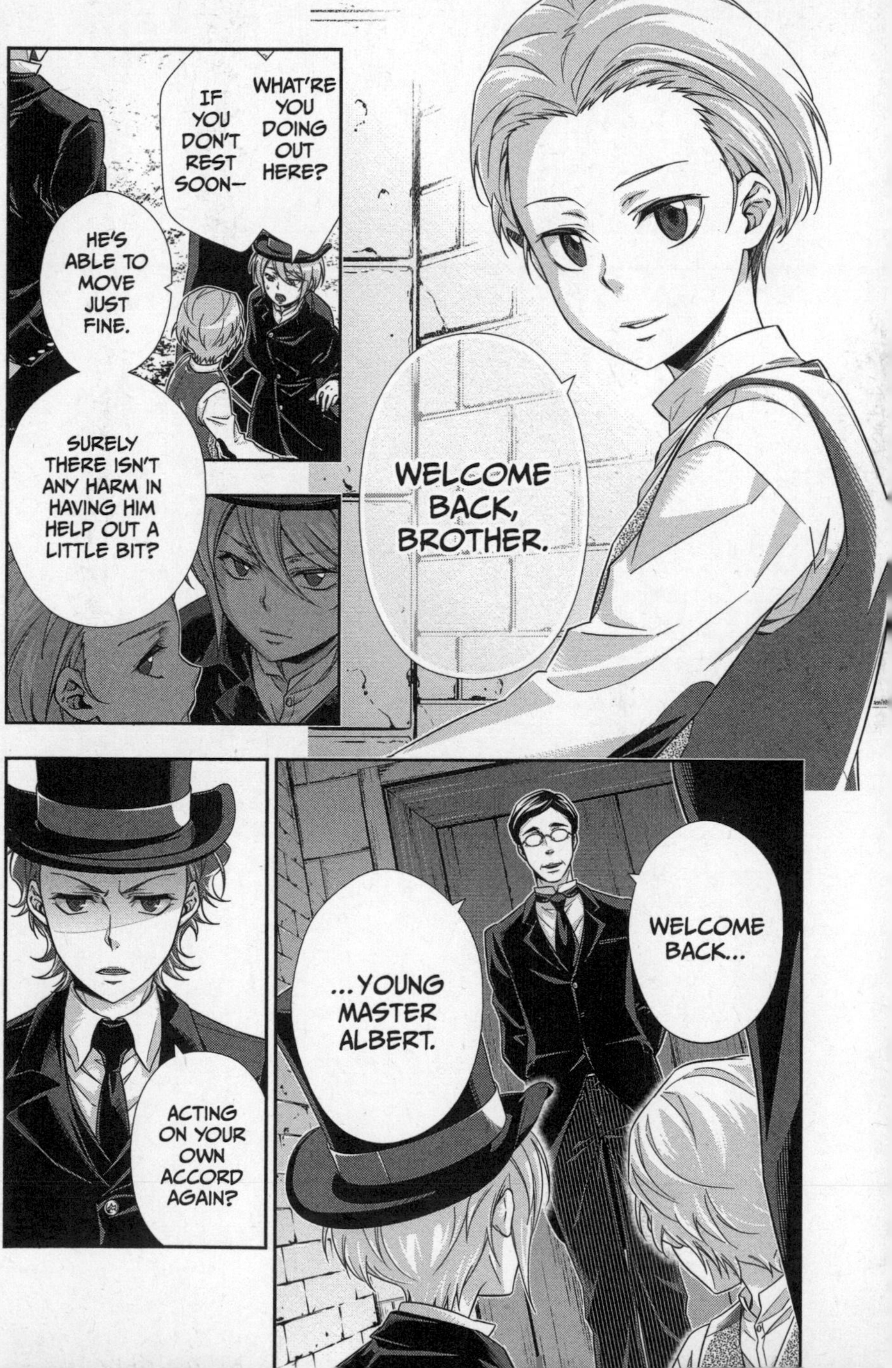
WELCOME BACK, BROTHER.
WHAT'RE YOU DOING OUT HERE?
IF YOU DON'T REST SOON—
HE'S ABLE TO MOVE JUST FINE.
SURELY THERE ISN'T ANY HARM IN HAVING HIM HELP OUT A LITTLE BIT?
WELCOME BACK...
...YOUNG MASTER ALBERT.
ACTING ON YOUR OWN ACCORD AGAIN?

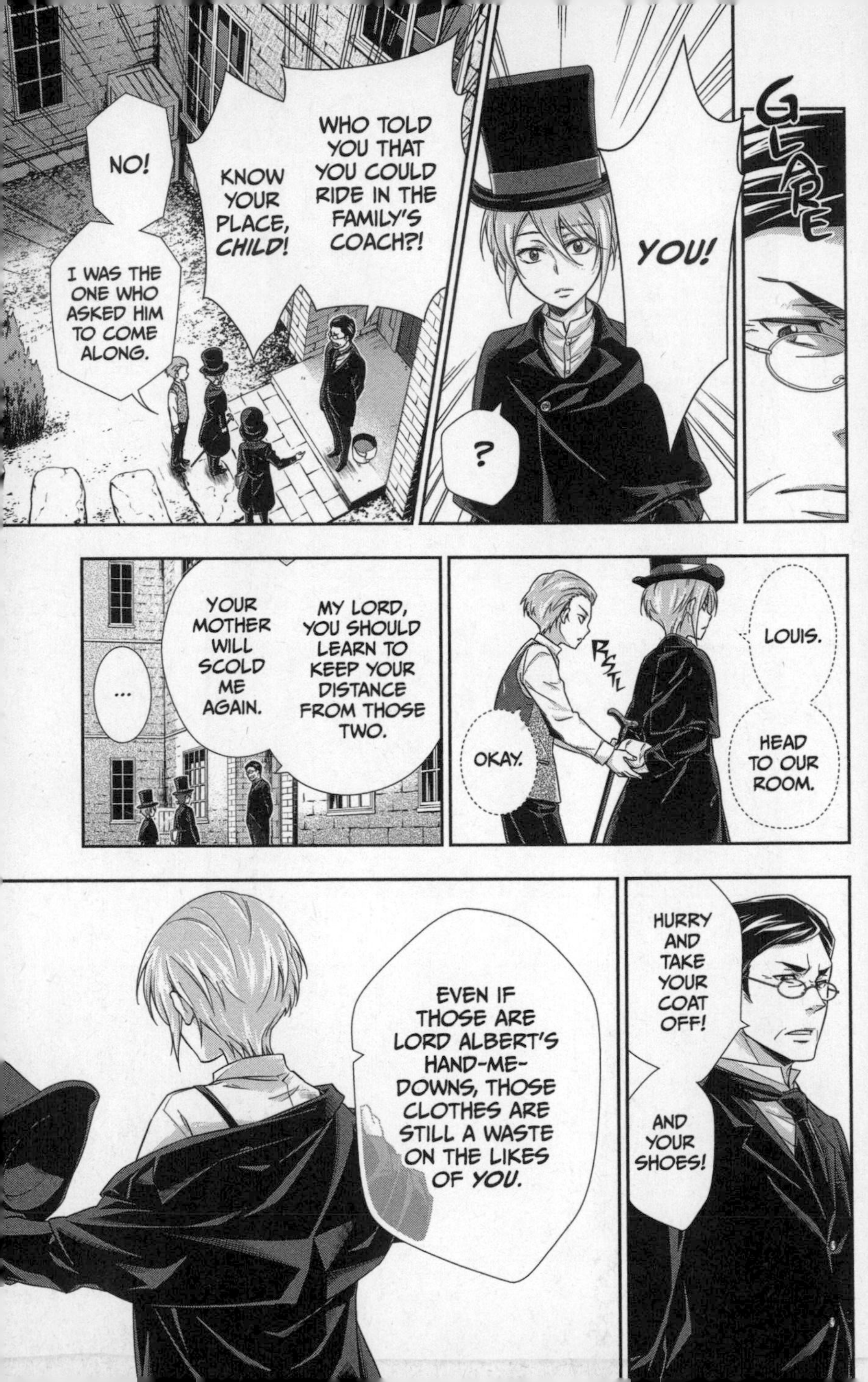
GLARE
YOU!
?
WHO TOLD YOU THAT YOU COULD RIDE IN THE FAMILY'S COACH?!
KNOW YOUR PLACE, *CHILD!*
NO!
I WAS THE ONE WHO ASKED HIM TO COME ALONG.
LOUIS.
HEAD TO OUR ROOM.
RSTL
OKAY.
MY LORD, YOU SHOULD LEARN TO KEEP YOUR DISTANCE FROM THOSE TWO.
YOUR MOTHER WILL SCOLD ME AGAIN.
...
HURRY AND TAKE YOUR COAT OFF!
AND YOUR SHOES!
EVEN IF THOSE ARE LORD ALBERT'S HAND-ME-DOWNS, THOSE CLOTHES ARE STILL A WASTE ON THE LIKES OF *YOU*.

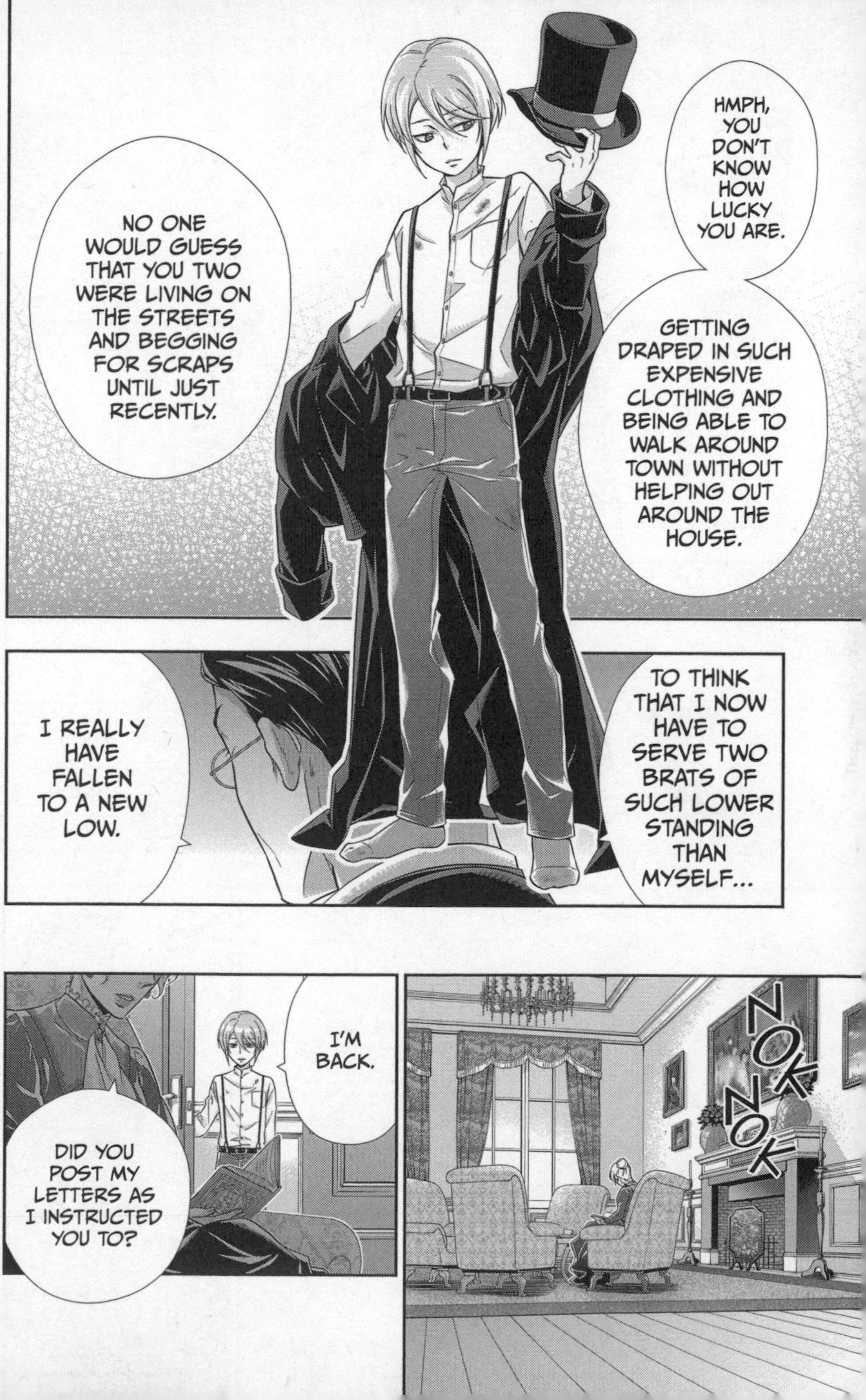
HMPH, YOU DON'T KNOW HOW LUCKY YOU ARE.
GETTING DRAPED IN SUCH EXPENSIVE CLOTHING AND BEING ABLE TO WALK AROUND TOWN WITHOUT HELPING OUT AROUND THE HOUSE.
NO ONE WOULD GUESS THAT YOU TWO WERE LIVING ON THE STREETS AND BEGGING FOR SCRAPS UNTIL JUST RECENTLY.
TO THINK THAT I NOW HAVE TO SERVE TWO BRATS OF SUCH LOWER STANDING THAN MYSELF...
I REALLY HAVE FALLEN TO A NEW LOW.
NOK NOK
I'M BACK.
DID YOU POST MY LETTERS AS I INSTRUCTED YOU TO?

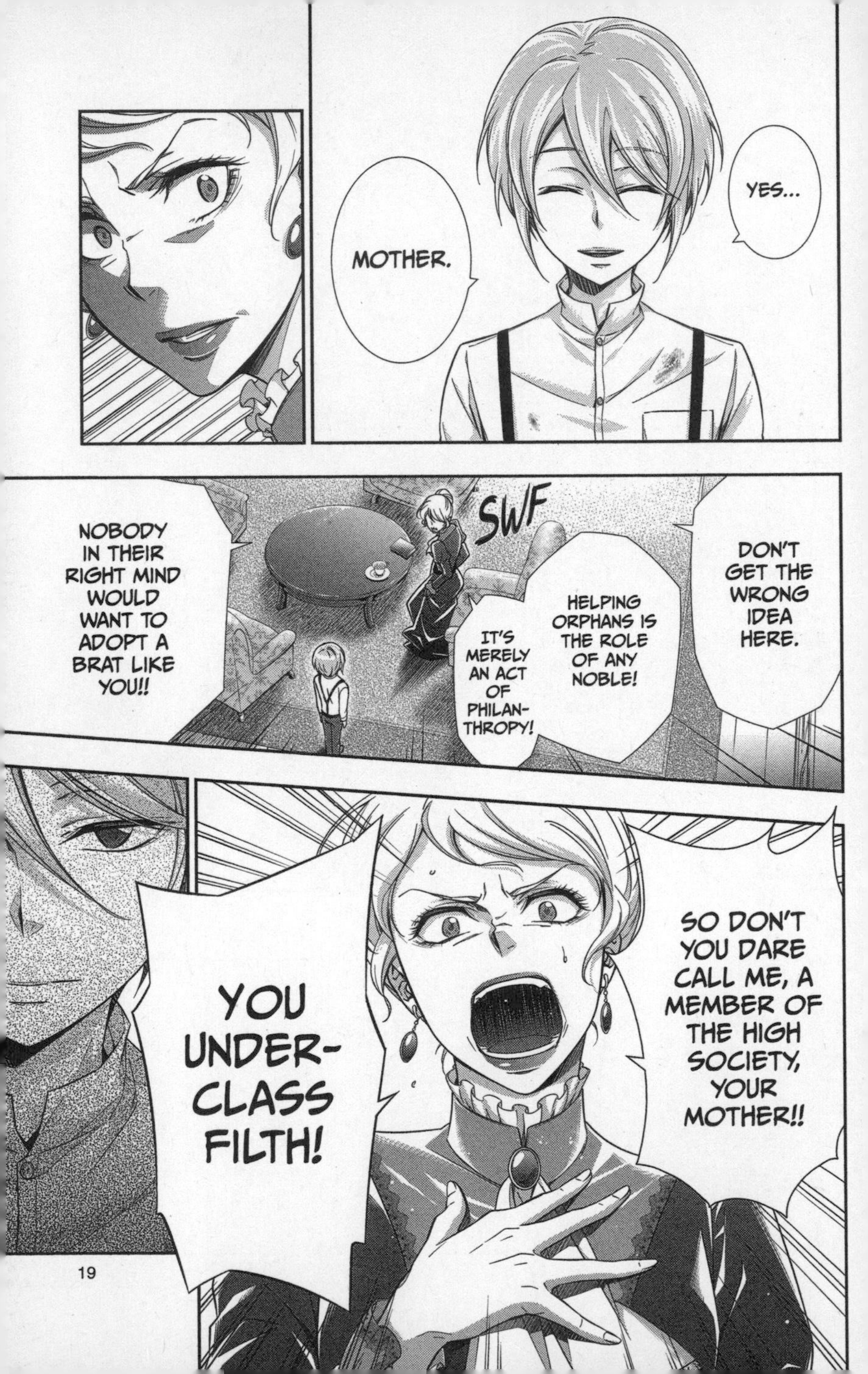
YES...
MOTHER.
DON'T GET THE WRONG IDEA HERE.
SWF
HELPING ORPHANS IS THE ROLE OF ANY NOBLE!
IT'S MERELY AN ACT OF PHILAN-THROPY!
NOBODY IN THEIR RIGHT MIND WOULD WANT TO ADOPT A BRAT LIKE YOU!!
SO DON'T YOU DARE CALL ME, A MEMBER OF THE HIGH SOCIETY, YOUR MOTHER!!
YOU UNDER-CLASS FILTH!

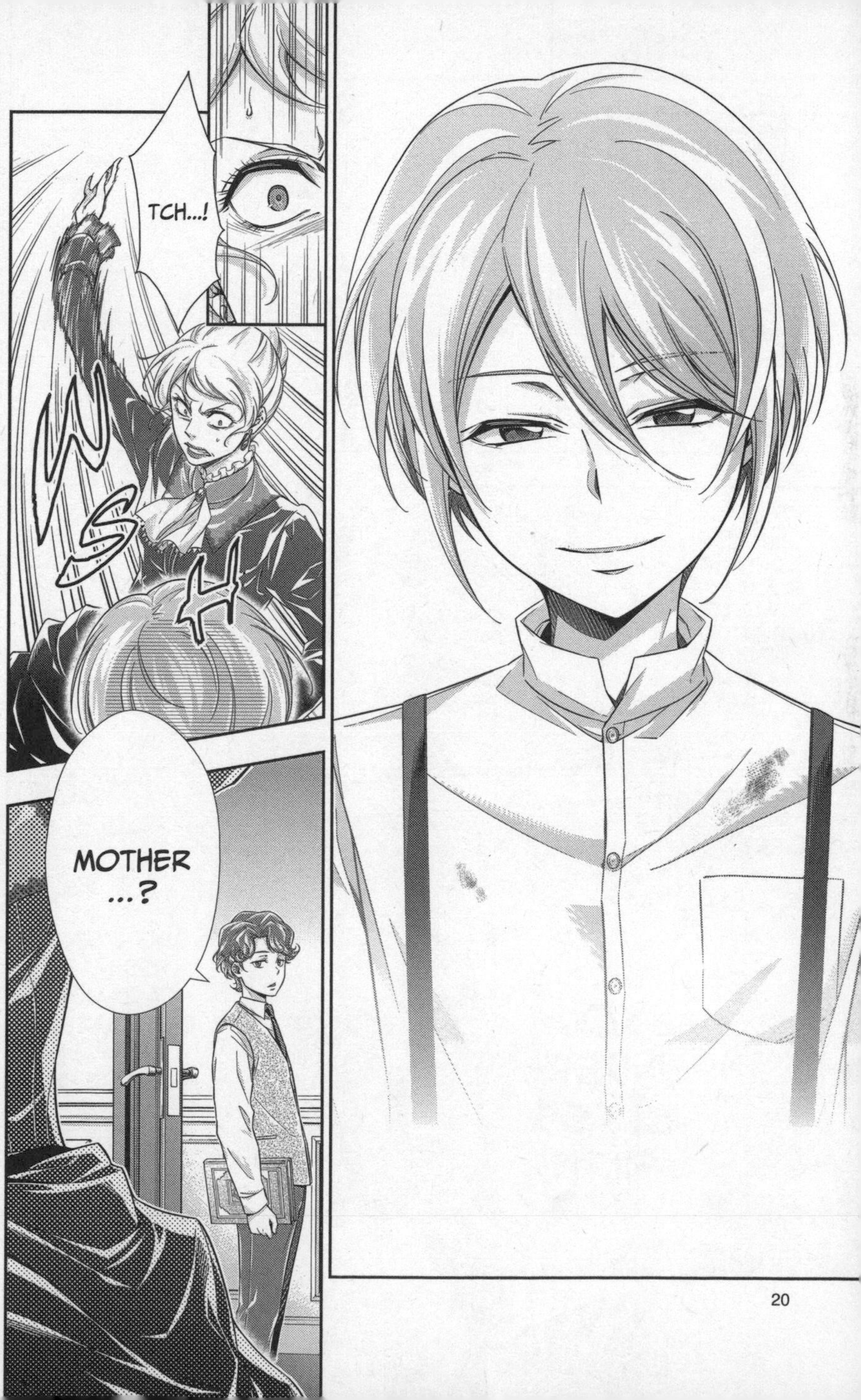

TCH...!
WSSH
MOTHER ...?

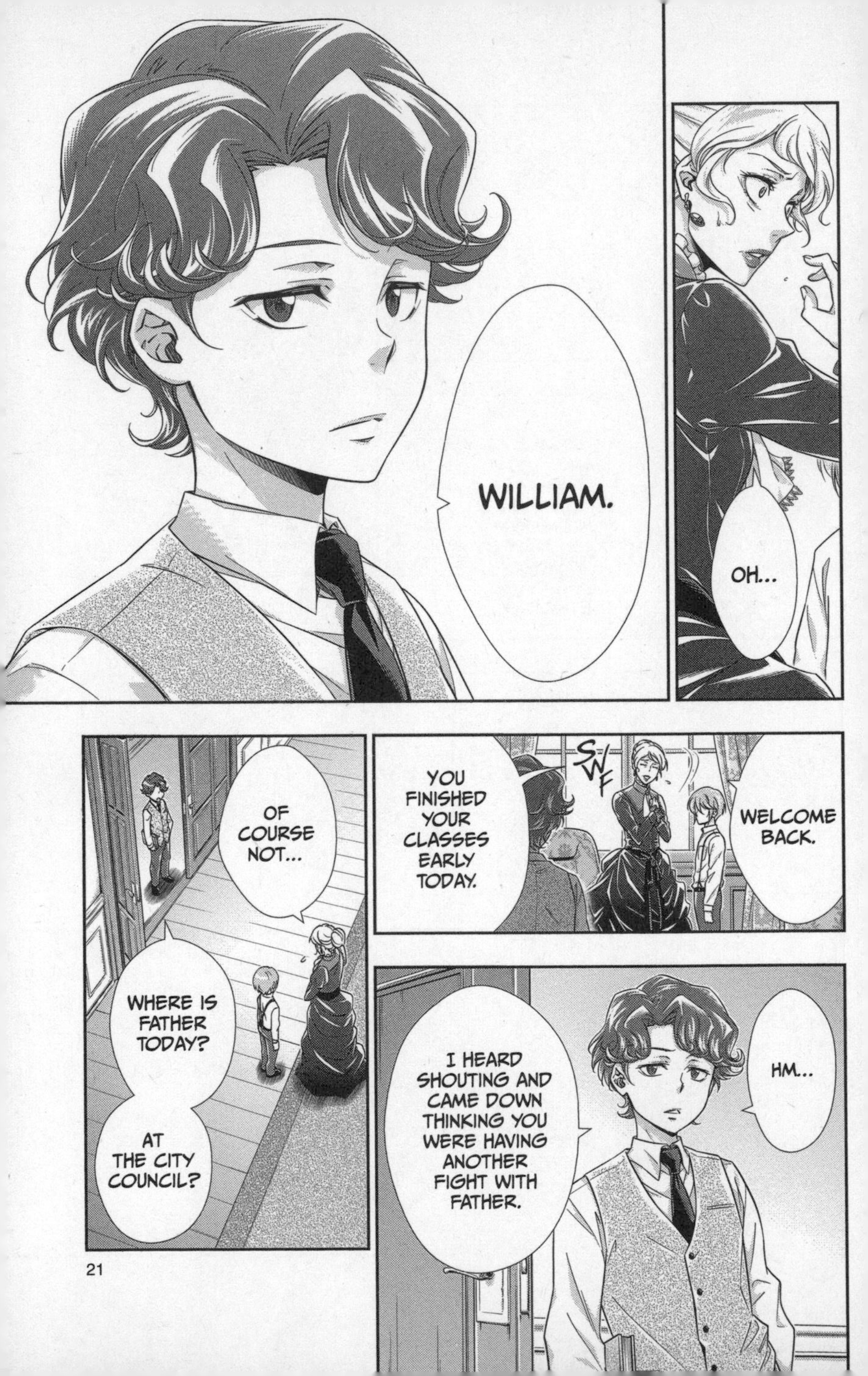
OH...
WILLIAM.
WELCOME BACK.
S-WF
YOU FINISHED YOUR CLASSES EARLY TODAY.
HM...
I HEARD SHOUTING AND CAME DOWN THINKING YOU WERE HAVING ANOTHER FIGHT WITH FATHER.
OF COURSE NOT...
WHERE IS FATHER TODAY?
AT THE CITY COUNCIL?

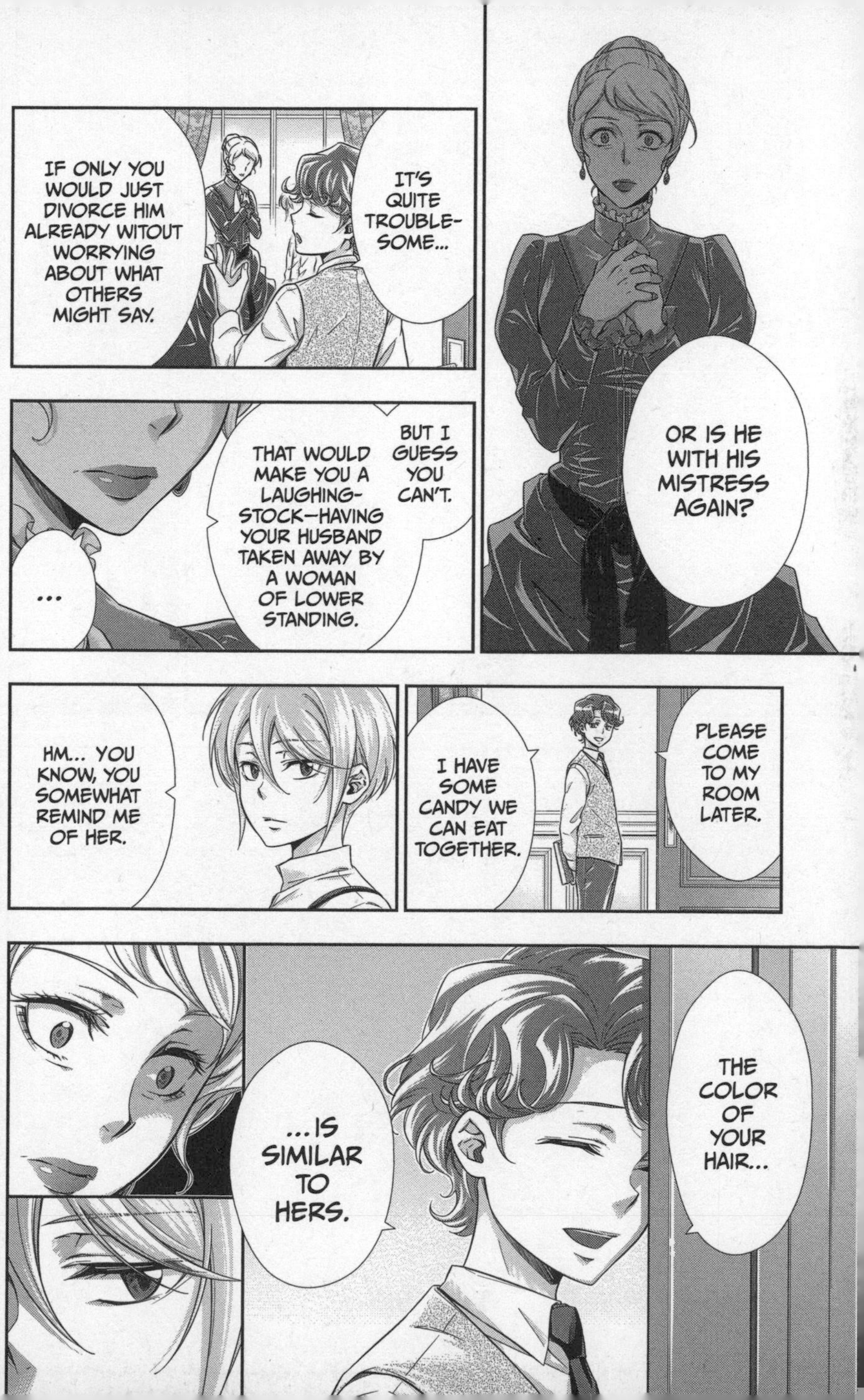
OR IS HE WITH HIS MISTRESS AGAIN?
IT'S QUITE TROUBLE-SOME...
IF ONLY YOU WOULD JUST DIVORCE HIM ALREADY WITOUT WORRYING ABOUT WHAT OTHERS MIGHT SAY.
BUT I GUESS YOU CAN'T.
THAT WOULD MAKE YOU A LAUGHING-STOCK—HAVING YOUR HUSBAND TAKEN AWAY BY A WOMAN OF LOWER STANDING.
...
PLEASE COME TO MY ROOM LATER.
I HAVE SOME CANDY WE CAN EAT TOGETHER.
HM... YOU KNOW, YOU SOMEWHAT REMIND ME OF HER.
THE COLOR OF YOUR HAIR...
...IS SIMILAR TO HERS.

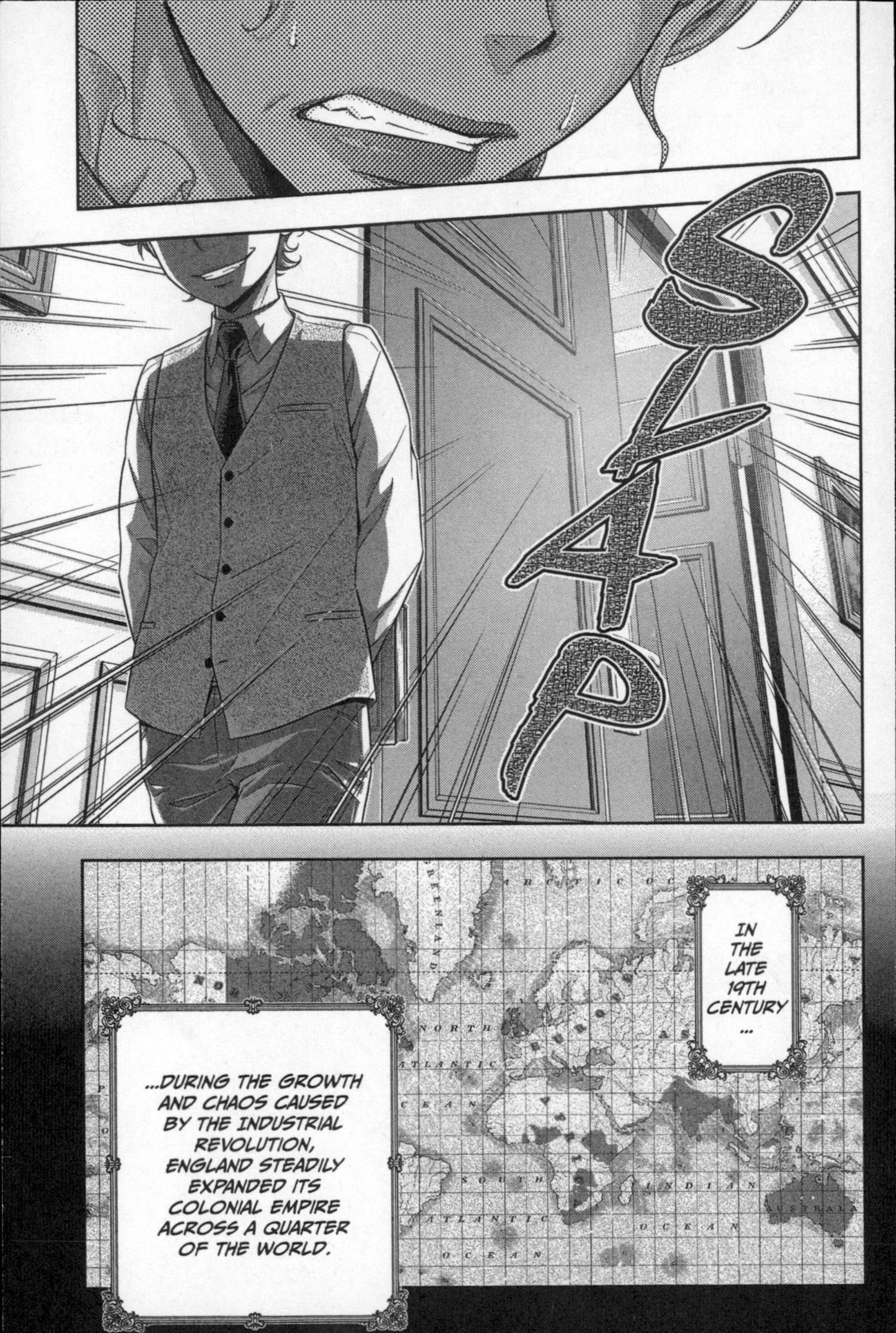
SNAP
IN THE LATE 19TH CENTURY...
...DURING THE GROWTH AND CHAOS CAUSED BY THE INDUSTRIAL REVOLUTION, ENGLAND STEADILY EXPANDED ITS COLONIAL EMPIRE ACROSS A QUARTER OF THE WORLD.
GREENLAND
NORTH ATLANTIC OCEAN
SOUTH ATLANTIC OCEAN
INDIAN OCEAN

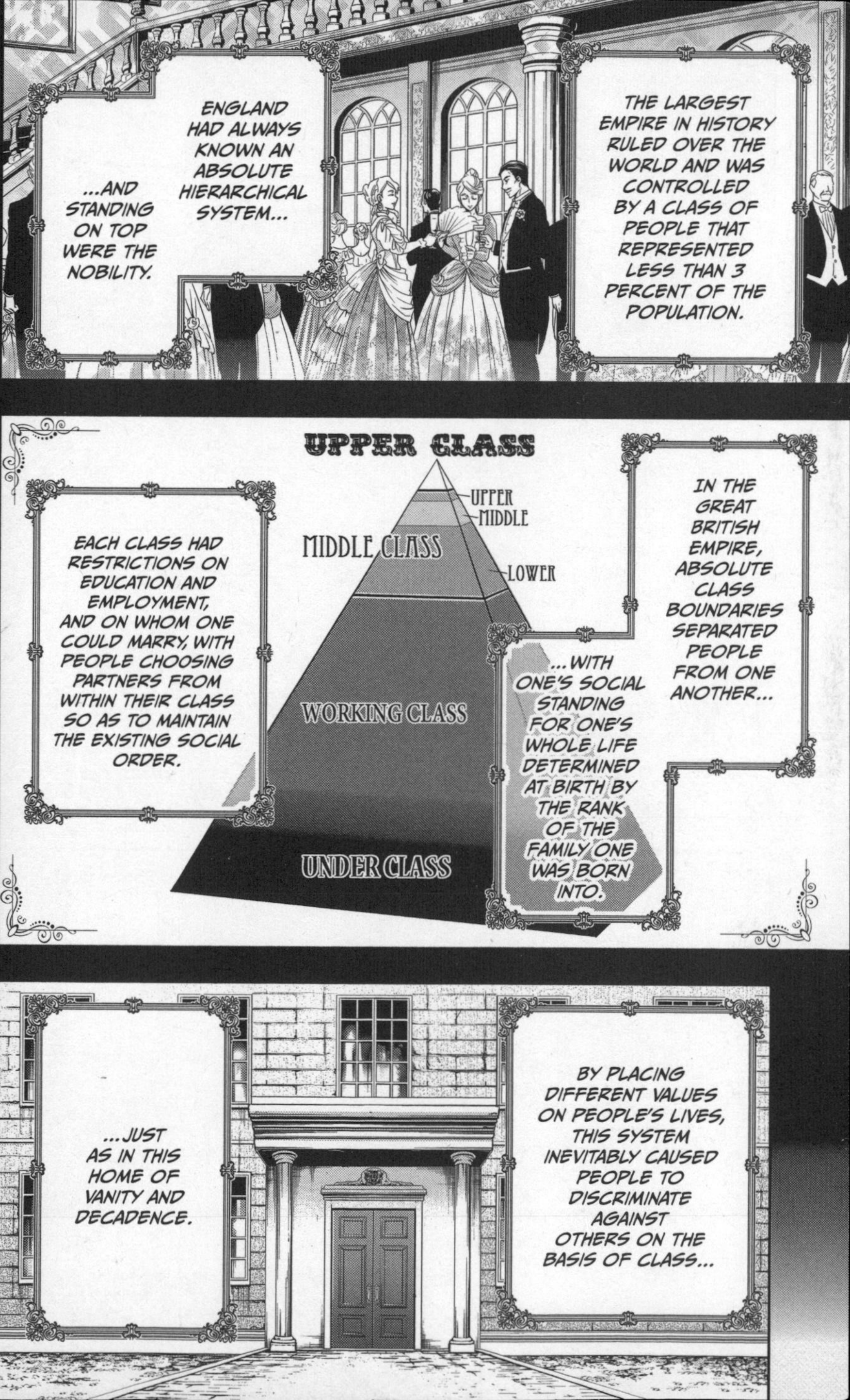
THE LARGEST EMPIRE IN HISTORY RULED OVER THE WORLD AND WAS CONTROLLED BY A CLASS OF PEOPLE THAT REPRESENTED LESS THAN 3 PERCENT OF THE POPULATION.
ENGLAND HAD ALWAYS KNOWN AN ABSOLUTE HIERARCHICAL SYSTEM...
...AND STANDING ON TOP WERE THE NOBILITY.
IN THE GREAT BRITISH EMPIRE, ABSOLUTE CLASS BOUNDARIES SEPARATED PEOPLE FROM ONE ANOTHER...
...WITH ONE'S SOCIAL STANDING FOR ONE'S WHOLE LIFE DETERMINED AT BIRTH BY THE RANK OF THE FAMILY ONE WAS BORN INTO.
UPPER CLASS
UPPER
MIDDLE
MIDDLE CLASS
LOWER
WORKING CLASS
UNDER CLASS
EACH CLASS HAD RESTRICTIONS ON EDUCATION AND EMPLOYMENT, AND ON WHOM ONE COULD MARRY, WITH PEOPLE CHOOSING PARTNERS FROM WITHIN THEIR CLASS SO AS TO MAINTAIN THE EXISTING SOCIAL ORDER.
BY PLACING DIFFERENT VALUES ON PEOPLE'S LIVES, THIS SYSTEM INEVITABLY CAUSED PEOPLE TO DISCRIMINATE AGAINST OTHERS ON THE BASIS OF CLASS...
...JUST AS IN THIS HOME OF VANITY AND DECADENCE.

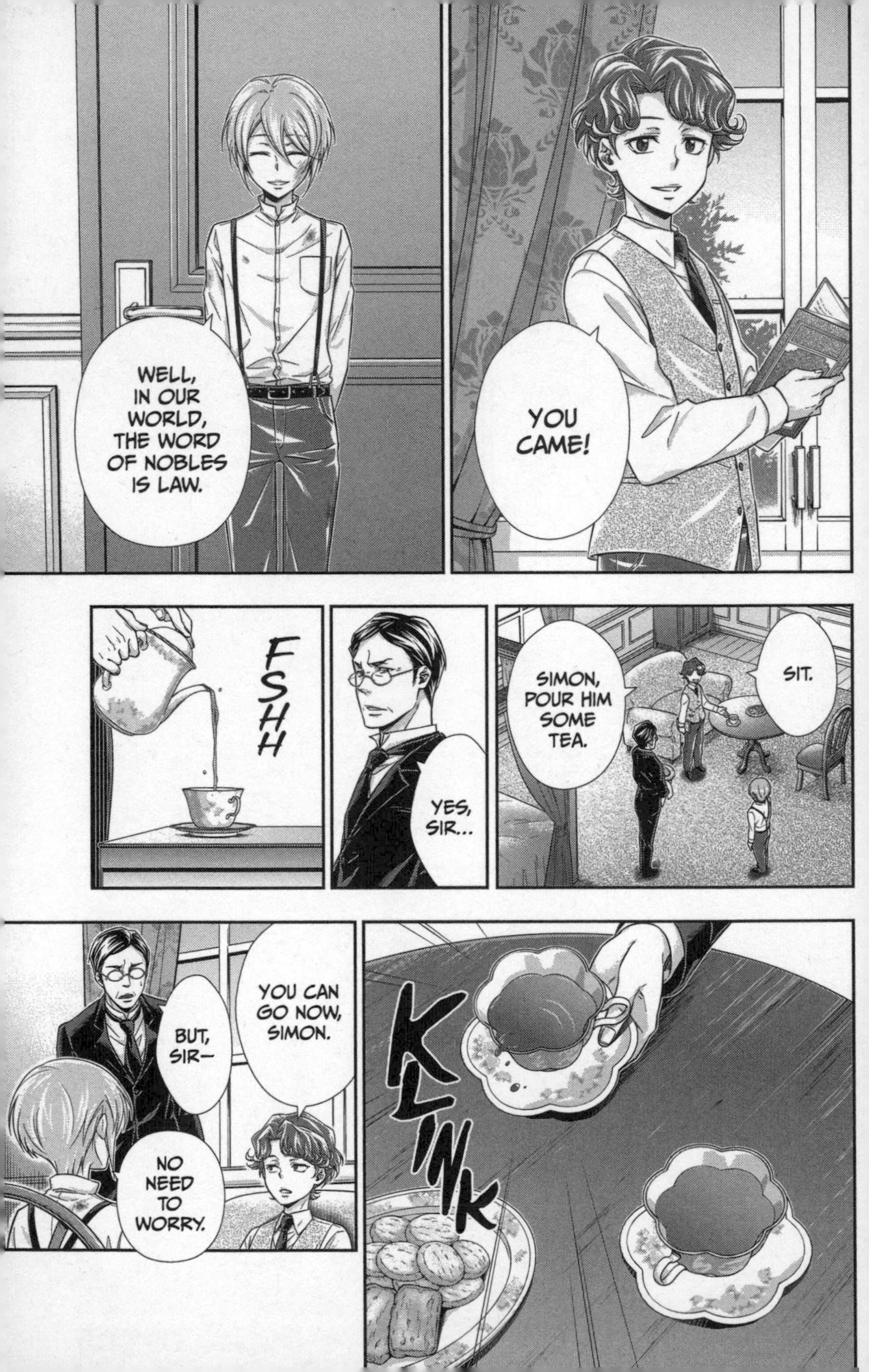
YOU CAME!
WELL, IN OUR WORLD, THE WORD OF NOBLES IS LAW.
SIT.
SIMON, POUR HIM SOME TEA.
YES, SIR...
FSHH
KLINK
YOU CAN GO NOW, SIMON.
BUT, SIR—
NO NEED TO WORRY.

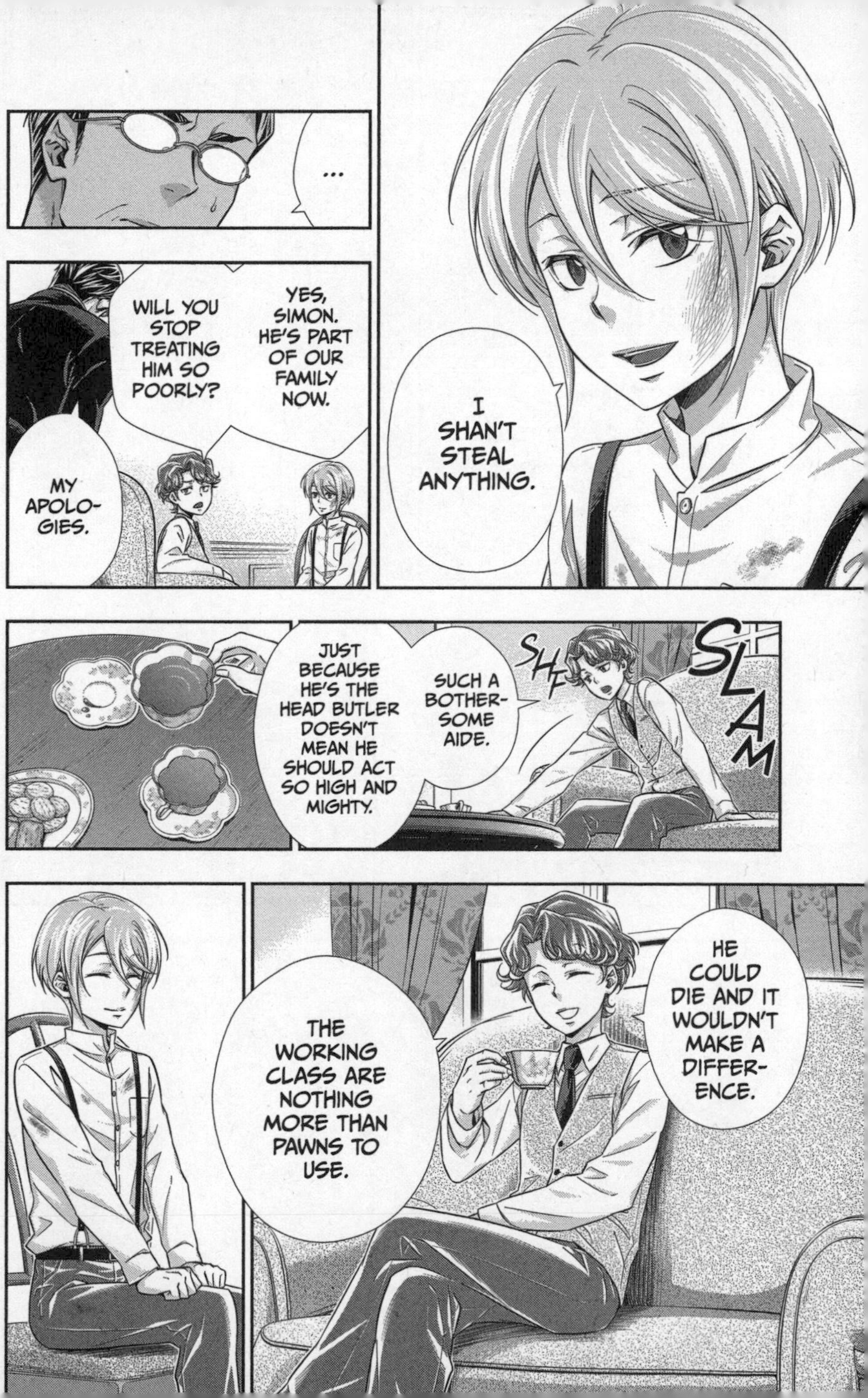
I SHAN'T STEAL ANYTHING.
...
YES, SIMON. HE'S PART OF OUR FAMILY NOW.
WILL YOU STOP TREATING HIM SO POORLY?
MY APOLOGIES.
SLAM
SHF
SUCH A BOTHERSOME AIDE.
JUST BECAUSE HE'S THE HEAD BUTLER DOESN'T MEAN HE SHOULD ACT SO HIGH AND MIGHTY.
HE COULD DIE AND IT WOULDN'T MAKE A DIFFERENCE.
THE WORKING CLASS ARE NOTHING MORE THAN PAWNS TO USE.

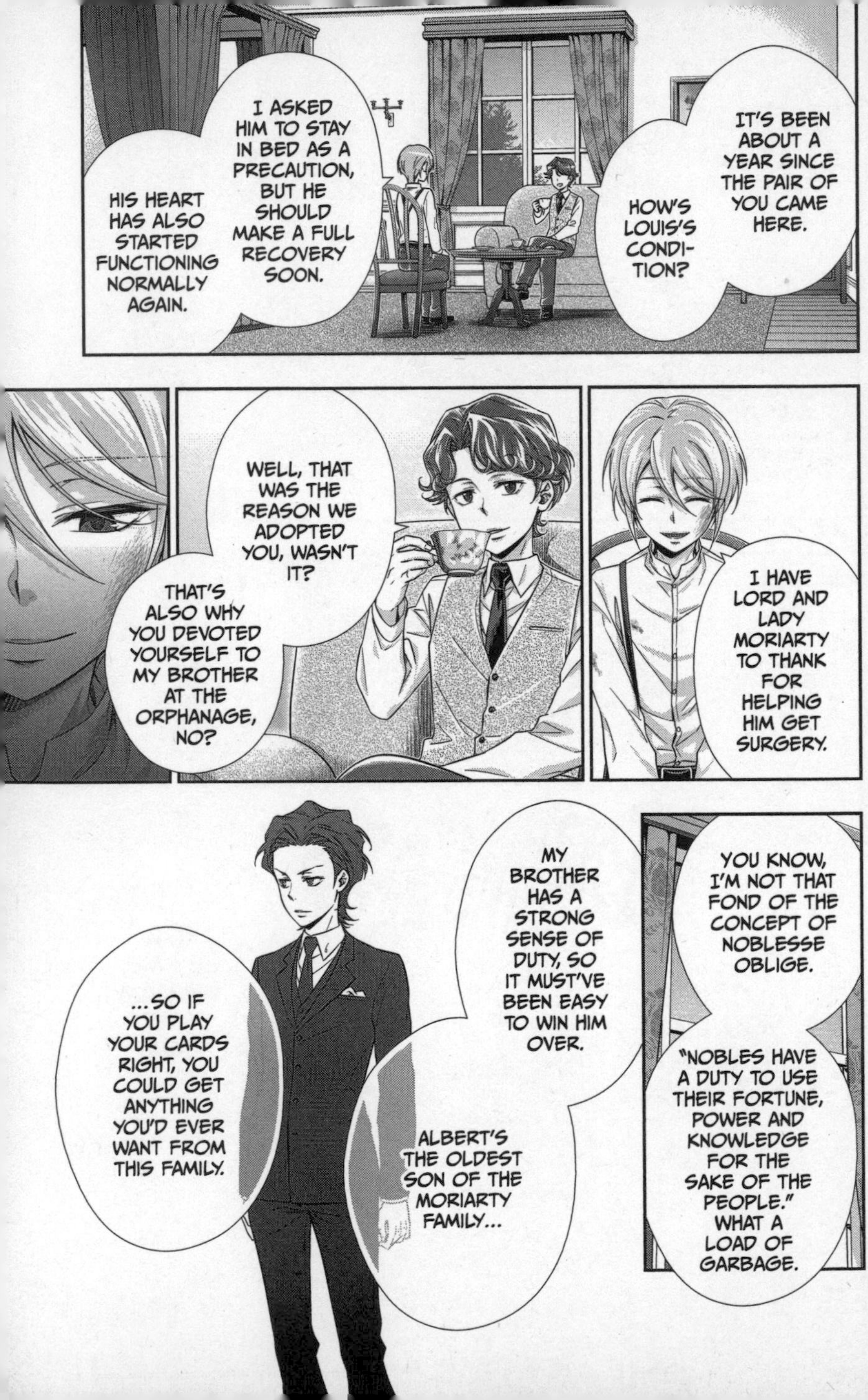
IT'S BEEN ABOUT A YEAR SINCE THE PAIR OF YOU CAME HERE.
HOW'S LOUIS'S CONDITION?
I ASKED HIM TO STAY IN BED AS A PRECAUTION, BUT HE SHOULD MAKE A FULL RECOVERY SOON.
HIS HEART HAS ALSO STARTED FUNCTIONING NORMALLY AGAIN.
I HAVE LORD AND LADY MORIARTY TO THANK FOR HELPING HIM GET SURGERY.
WELL, THAT WAS THE REASON WE ADOPTED YOU, WASN'T IT?
THAT'S ALSO WHY YOU DEVOTED YOURSELF TO MY BROTHER AT THE ORPHANAGE, NO?
YOU KNOW, I'M NOT THAT FOND OF THE CONCEPT OF NOBLESSE OBLIGE.
"NOBLES HAVE A DUTY TO USE THEIR FORTUNE, POWER AND KNOWLEDGE FOR THE SAKE OF THE PEOPLE." WHAT A LOAD OF GARBAGE.
MY BROTHER HAS A STRONG SENSE OF DUTY, SO IT MUST'VE BEEN EASY TO WIN HIM OVER.
ALBERT'S THE OLDEST SON OF THE MORIARTY FAMILY...
...SO IF YOU PLAY YOUR CARDS RIGHT, YOU COULD GET ANYTHING YOU'D EVER WANT FROM THIS FAMILY.

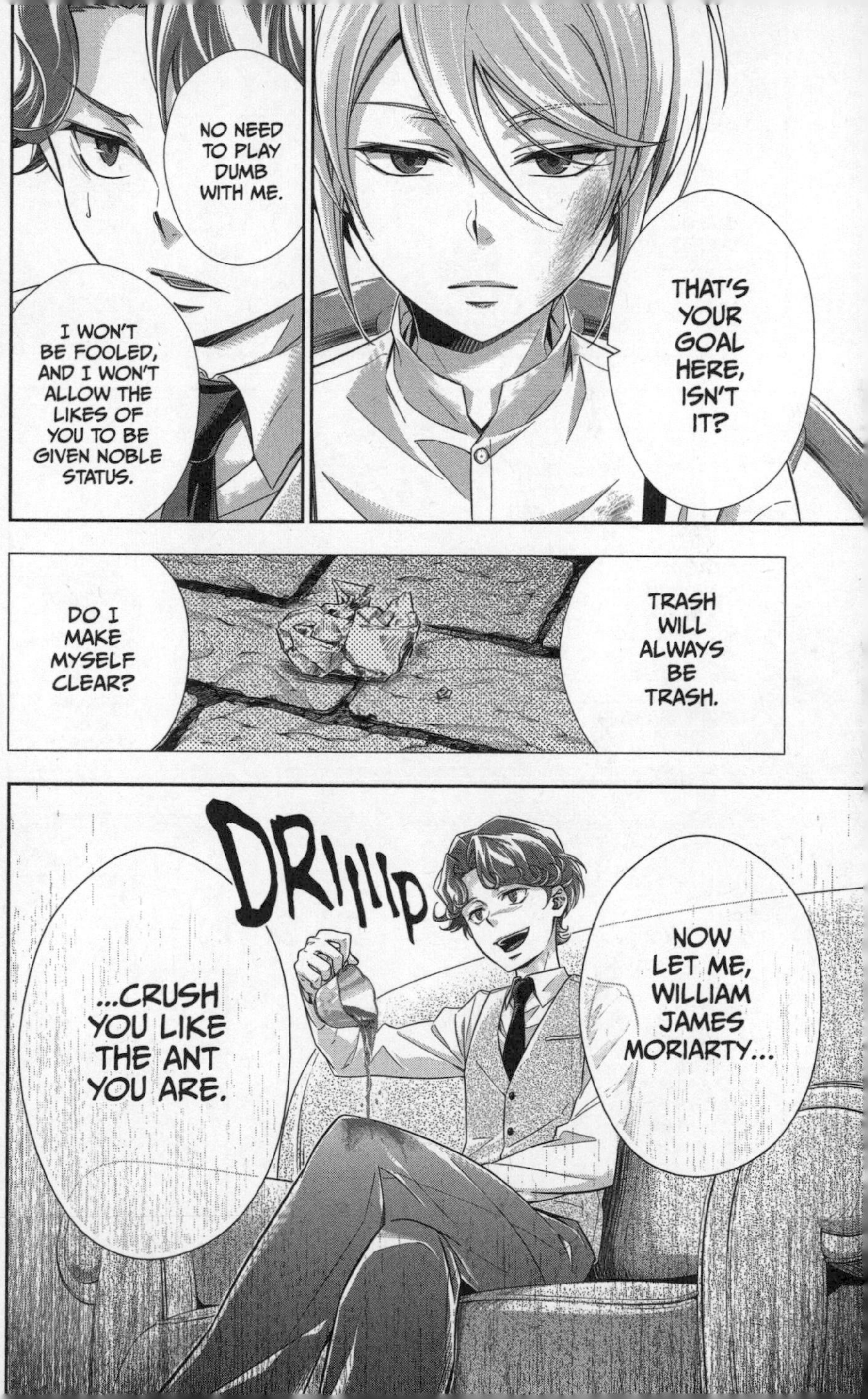
THAT'S YOUR GOAL HERE, ISN'T IT?
NO NEED TO PLAY DUMB WITH ME.
I WON'T BE FOOLED, AND I WON'T ALLOW THE LIKES OF YOU TO BE GIVEN NOBLE STATUS.
TRASH WILL ALWAYS BE TRASH.
DO I MAKE MYSELF CLEAR?
NOW LET ME, WILLIAM JAMES MORIARTY...
DRIIIP
...CRUSH YOU LIKE THE ANT YOU ARE.

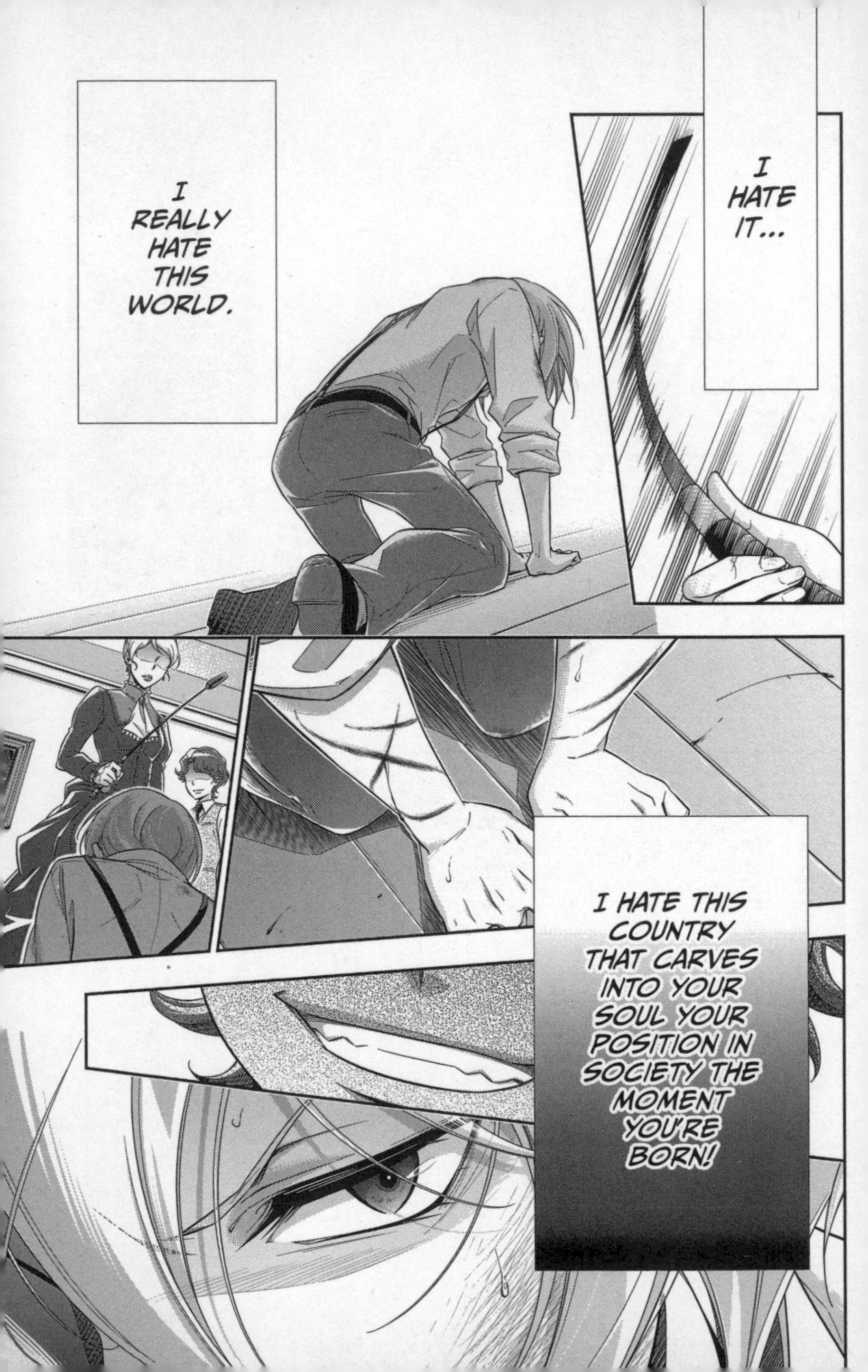
I HATE IT...
I REALLY HATE THIS WORLD.
I HATE THIS COUNTRY THAT CARVES INTO YOUR SOUL YOUR POSITION IN SOCIETY THE MOMENT YOU'RE BORN!

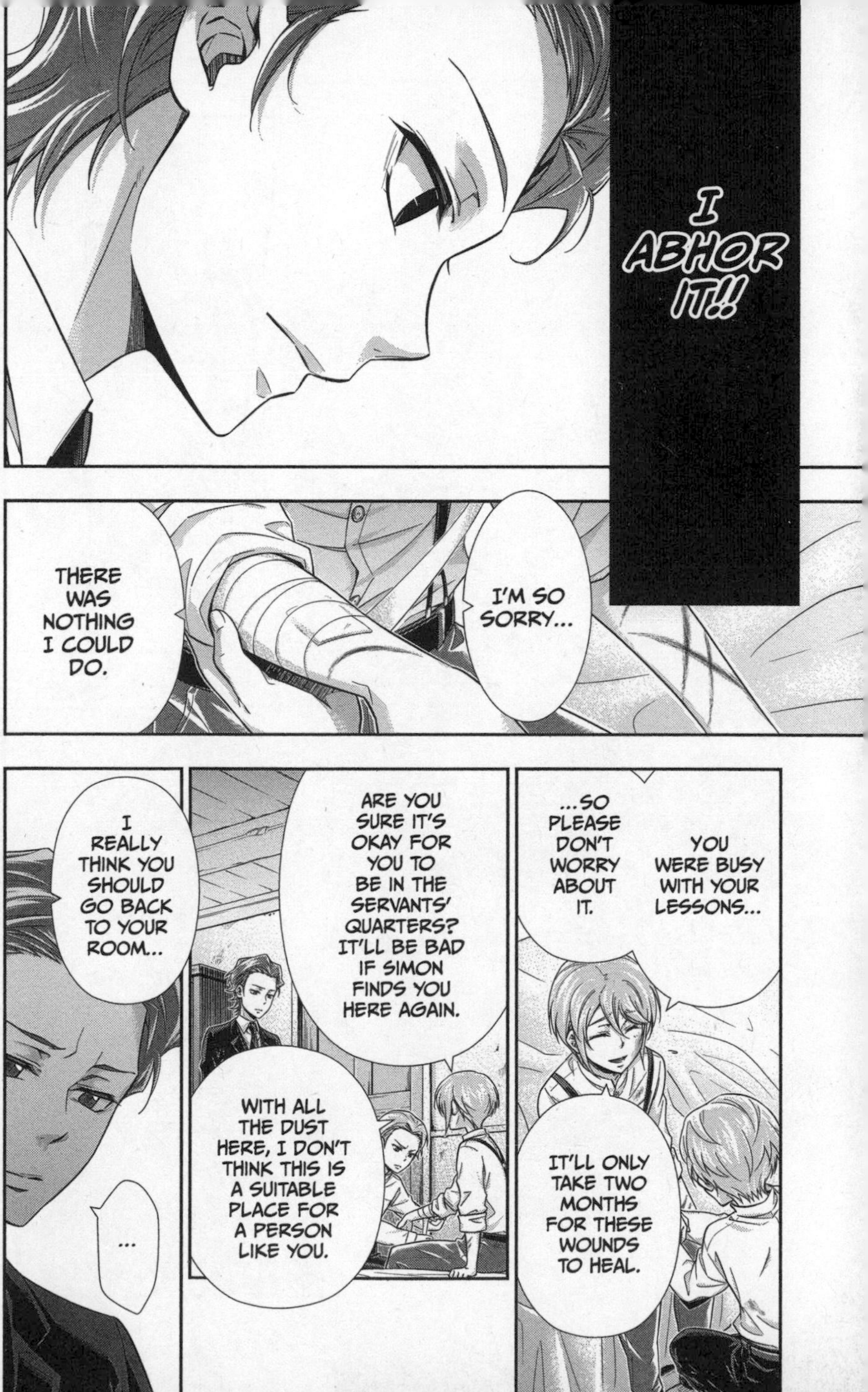
I ABHOR IT!!
I'M SO SORRY...
THERE WAS NOTHING I COULD DO.
YOU WERE BUSY WITH YOUR LESSONS...
...SO PLEASE DON'T WORRY ABOUT IT.
IT'LL ONLY TAKE TWO MONTHS FOR THESE WOUNDS TO HEAL.
ARE YOU SURE IT'S OKAY FOR YOU TO BE IN THE SERVANTS' QUARTERS? IT'LL BE BAD IF SIMON FINDS YOU HERE AGAIN.
WITH ALL THE DUST HERE, I DON'T THINK THIS IS A SUITABLE PLACE FOR A PERSON LIKE YOU.
I REALLY THINK YOU SHOULD GO BACK TO YOUR ROOM...
...

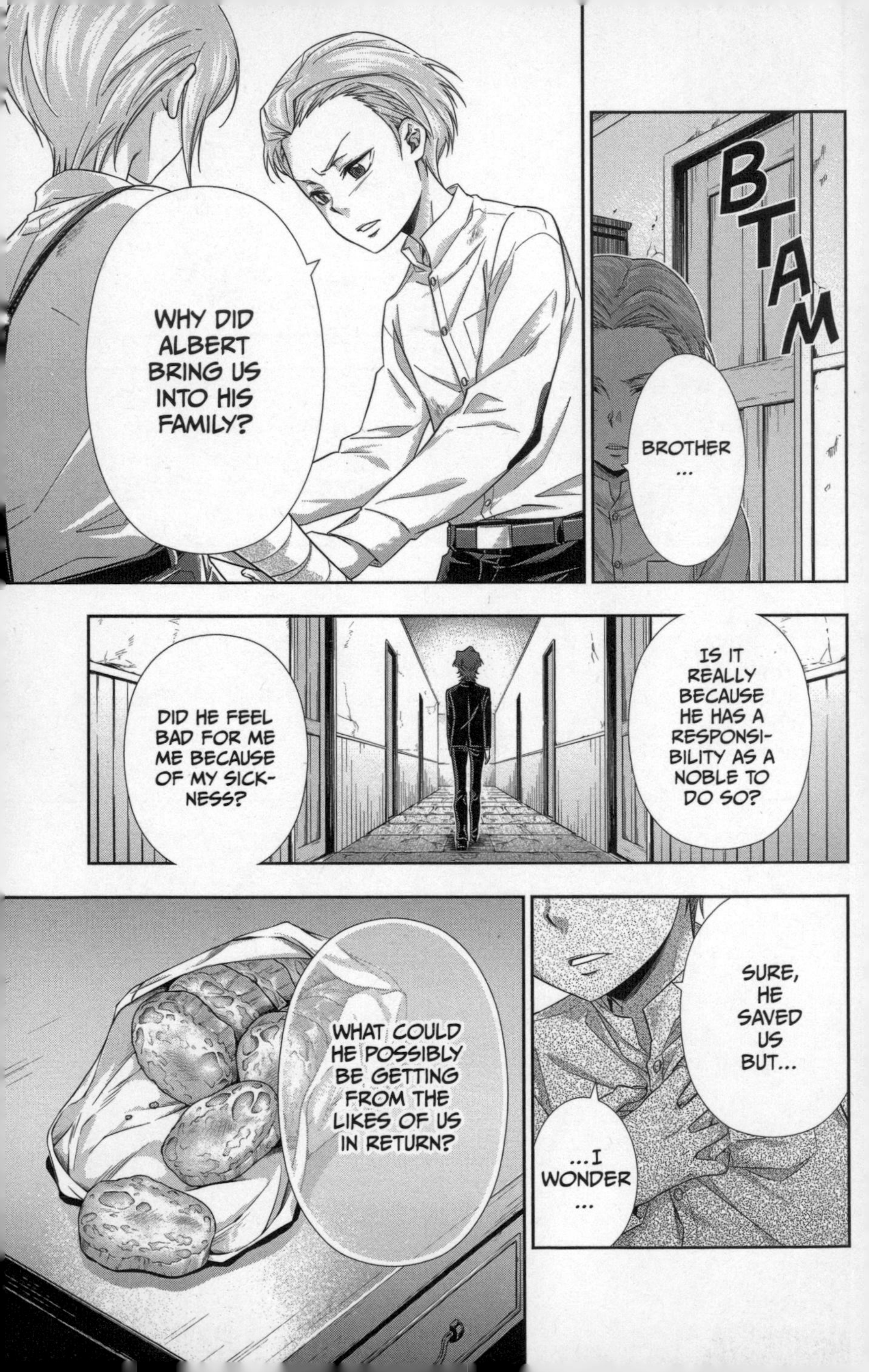
BTAM
BROTHER ...
WHY DID ALBERT BRING US INTO HIS FAMILY?
IS IT REALLY BECAUSE HE HAS A RESPONSI-BILITY AS A NOBLE TO DO SO?
DID HE FEEL BAD FOR ME ME BECAUSE OF MY SICK-NESS?
SURE, HE SAVED US BUT...
...I WONDER ...
WHAT COULD HE POSSIBLY BE GETTING FROM THE LIKES OF US IN RETURN?

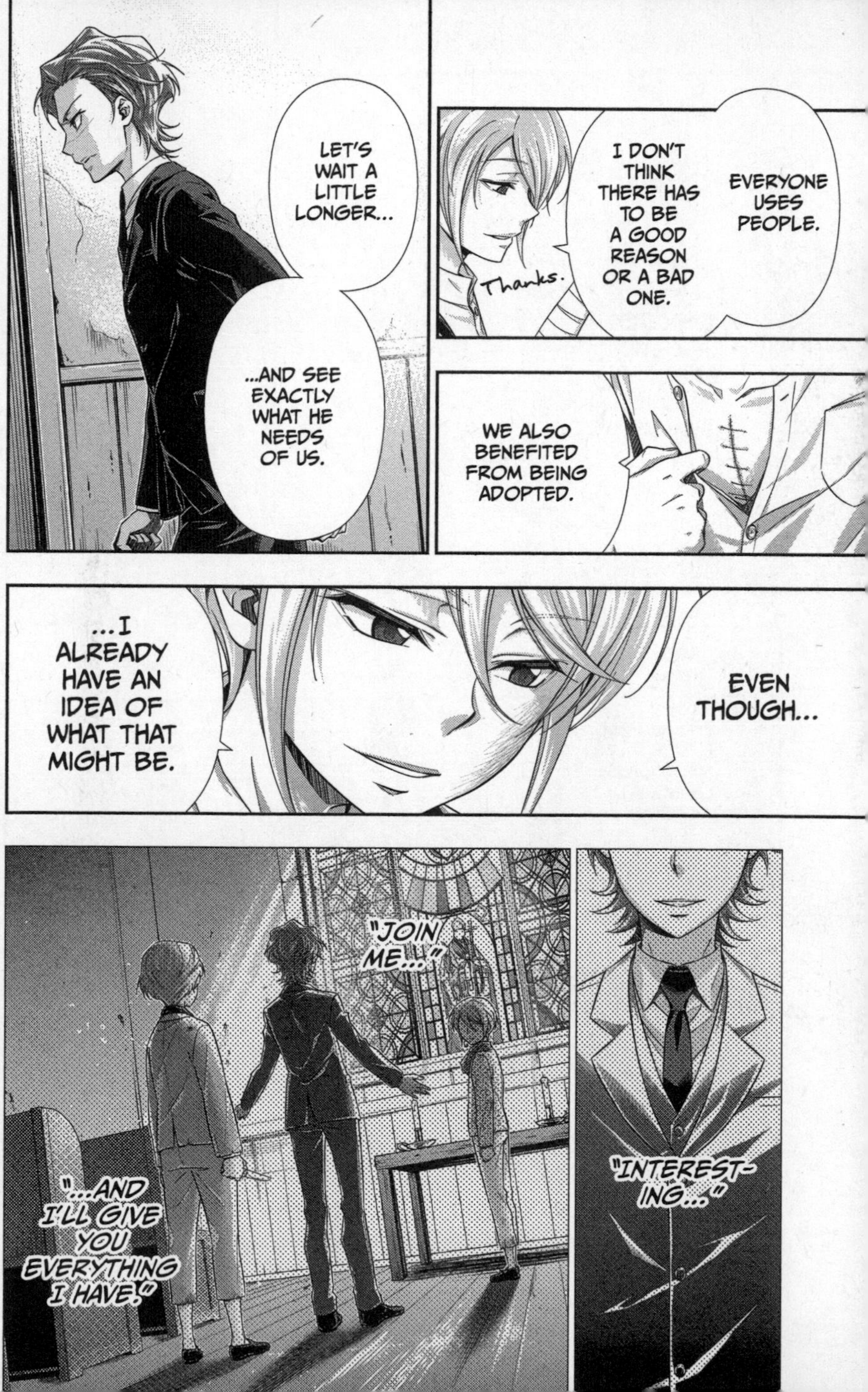
EVERYONE USES PEOPLE.
I DON'T THINK THERE HAS TO BE A GOOD REASON OR A BAD ONE.
Thanks.
WE ALSO BENEFITED FROM BEING ADOPTED.
LET'S WAIT A LITTLE LONGER...
...AND SEE EXACTLY WHAT HE NEEDS OF US.
EVEN THOUGH...
...I ALREADY HAVE AN IDEA OF WHAT THAT MIGHT BE.
"INTERESTING..."
"JOIN ME..."
"...AND I'LL GIVE YOU EVERYTHING I HAVE."

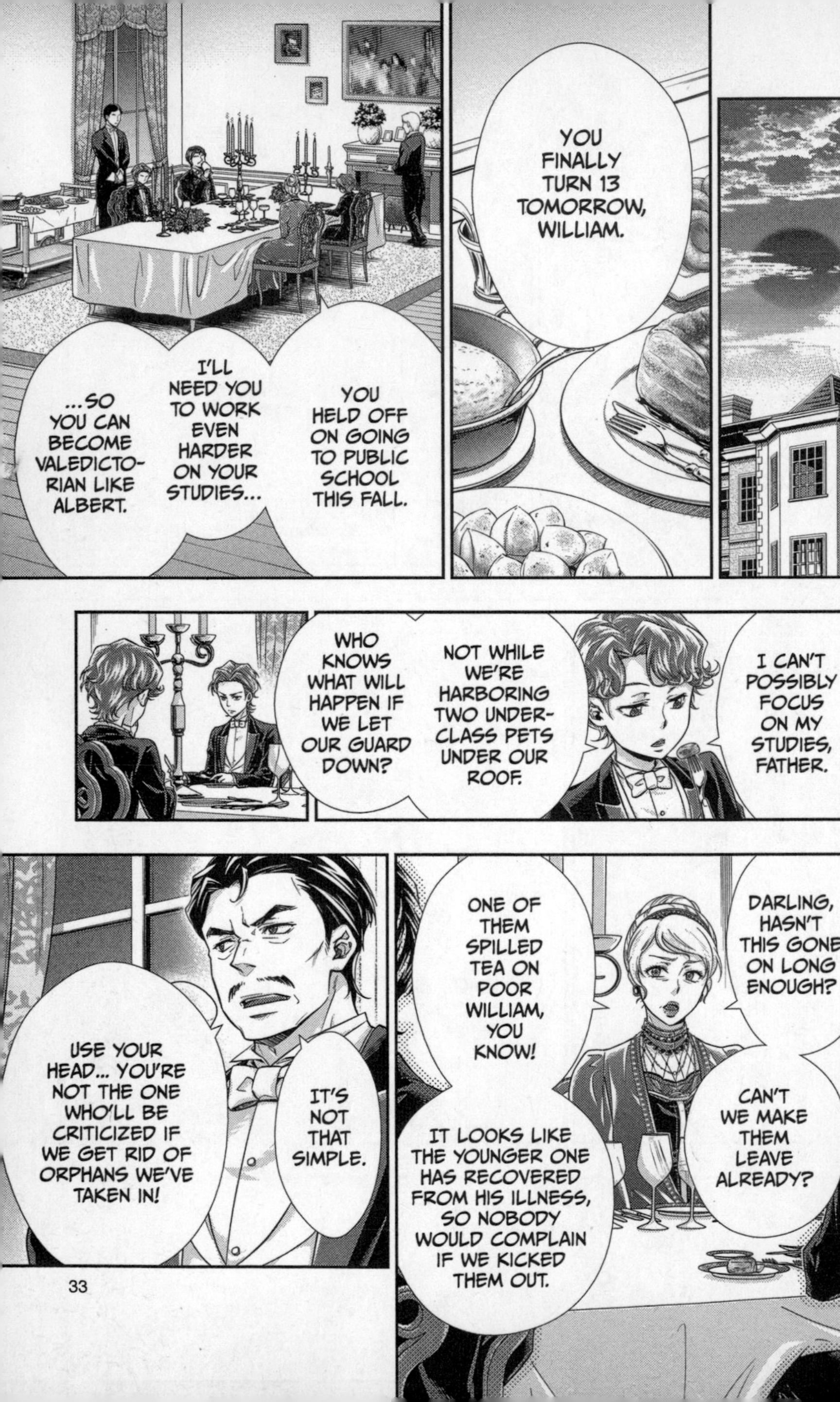
YOU FINALLY TURN 13 TOMORROW, WILLIAM.
YOU HELD OFF ON GOING TO PUBLIC SCHOOL THIS FALL.
I'LL NEED YOU TO WORK EVEN HARDER ON YOUR STUDIES...
...SO YOU CAN BECOME VALEDICTORIAN LIKE ALBERT.
I CAN'T POSSIBLY FOCUS ON MY STUDIES, FATHER.
NOT WHILE WE'RE HARBORING TWO UNDERCLASS PETS UNDER OUR ROOF.
WHO KNOWS WHAT WILL HAPPEN IF WE LET OUR GUARD DOWN?
DARLING, HASN'T THIS GONE ON LONG ENOUGH?
ONE OF THEM SPILLED TEA ON POOR WILLIAM, YOU KNOW!
CAN'T WE MAKE THEM LEAVE ALREADY?
IT LOOKS LIKE THE YOUNGER ONE HAS RECOVERED FROM HIS ILLNESS, SO NOBODY WOULD COMPLAIN IF WE KICKED THEM OUT.
IT'S NOT THAT SIMPLE.
USE YOUR HEAD... YOU'RE NOT THE ONE WHO'LL BE CRITICIZED IF WE GET RID OF ORPHANS WE'VE TAKEN IN!

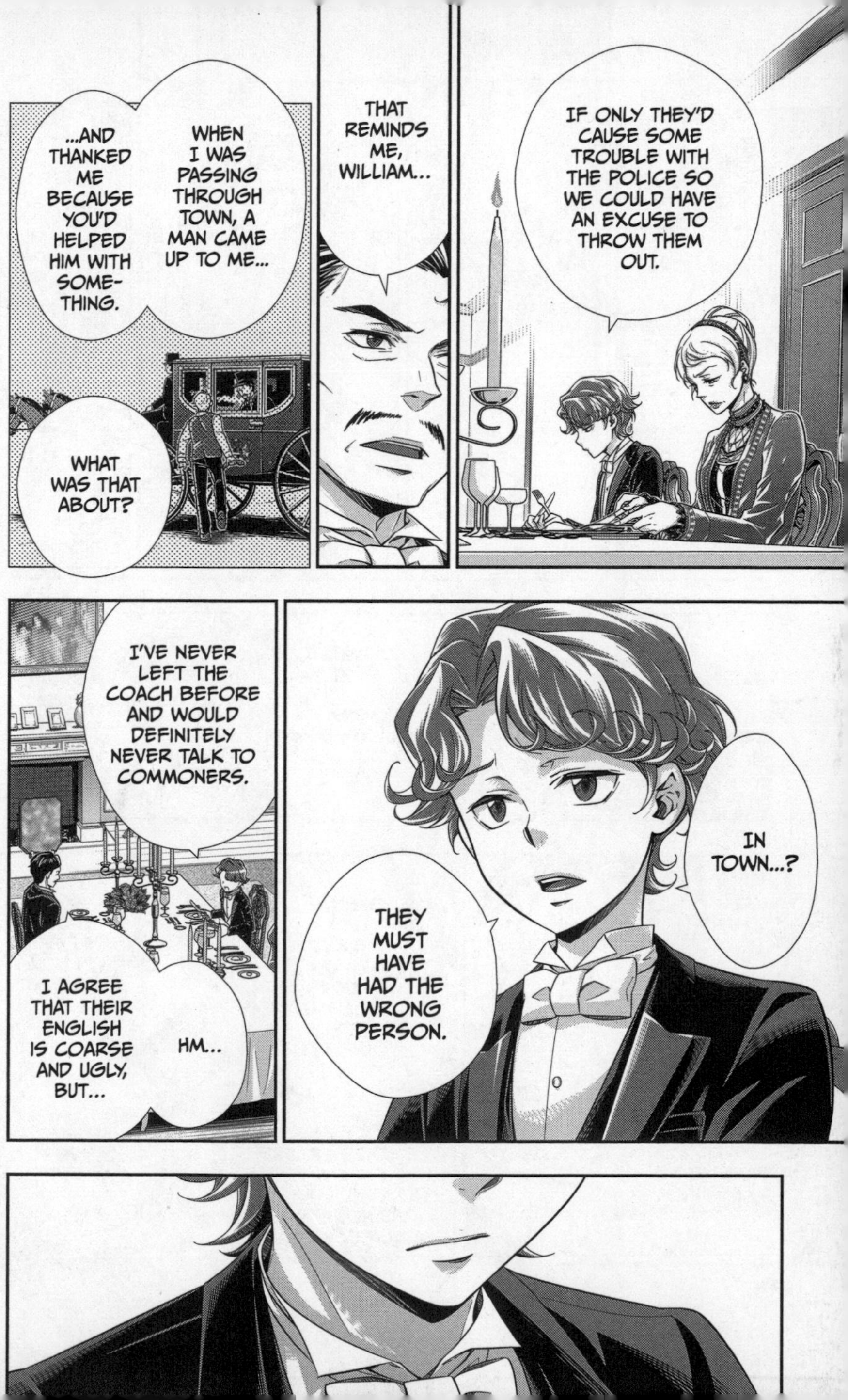
IF ONLY THEY'D CAUSE SOME TROUBLE WITH THE POLICE SO WE COULD HAVE AN EXCUSE TO THROW THEM OUT.
THAT REMINDS ME, WILLIAM...
WHEN I WAS PASSING THROUGH TOWN, A MAN CAME UP TO ME...
...AND THANKED ME BECAUSE YOU'D HELPED HIM WITH SOME-THING.
WHAT WAS THAT ABOUT?
IN TOWN...?
THEY MUST HAVE HAD THE WRONG PERSON.
I'VE NEVER LEFT THE COACH BEFORE AND WOULD DEFINITELY NEVER TALK TO COMMONERS.
HM...
I AGREE THAT THEIR ENGLISH IS COARSE AND UGLY, BUT...

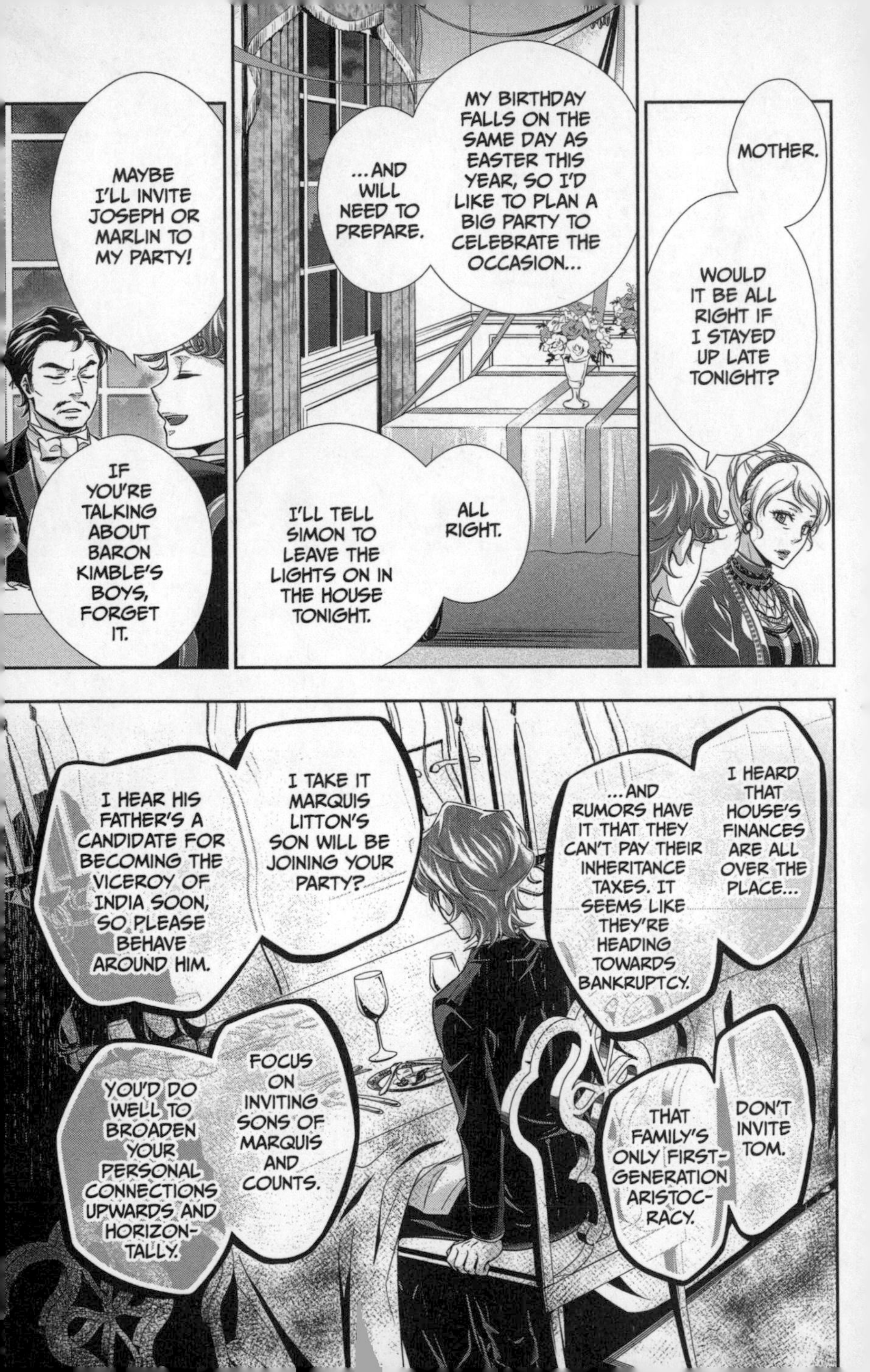
MOTHER.
WOULD IT BE ALL RIGHT IF I STAYED UP LATE TONIGHT?
MY BIRTHDAY FALLS ON THE SAME DAY AS EASTER THIS YEAR, SO I'D LIKE TO PLAN A BIG PARTY TO CELEBRATE THE OCCASION...
...AND WILL NEED TO PREPARE.
ALL RIGHT.
I'LL TELL SIMON TO LEAVE THE LIGHTS ON IN THE HOUSE TONIGHT.
MAYBE I'LL INVITE JOSEPH OR MARLIN TO MY PARTY!
IF YOU'RE TALKING ABOUT BARON KIMBLE'S BOYS, FORGET IT.
I HEARD THAT HOUSE'S FINANCES ARE ALL OVER THE PLACE...
...AND RUMORS HAVE IT THAT THEY CAN'T PAY THEIR INHERITANCE TAXES. IT SEEMS LIKE THEY'RE HEADING TOWARDS BANKRUPTCY.
I TAKE IT MARQUIS LITTON'S SON WILL BE JOINING YOUR PARTY?
I HEAR HIS FATHER'S A CANDIDATE FOR BECOMING THE VICEROY OF INDIA SOON, SO PLEASE BEHAVE AROUND HIM.
DON'T INVITE TOM.
THAT FAMILY'S ONLY FIRST-GENERATION ARISTOC-RACY.
FOCUS ON INVITING SONS OF MARQUIS AND COUNTS.
YOU'D DO WELL TO BROADEN YOUR PERSONAL CONNECTIONS UPWARDS AND HORIZON-TALLY.

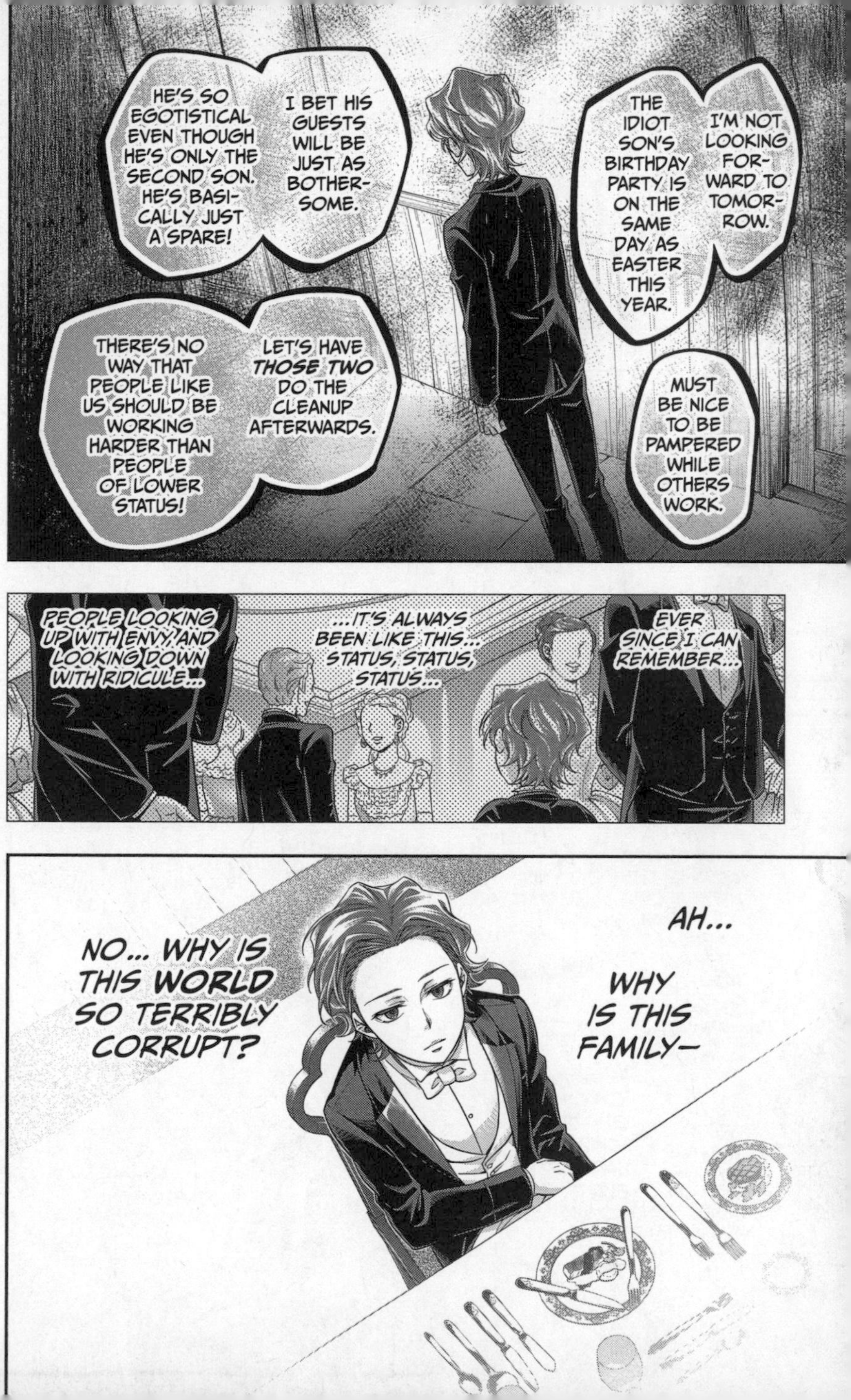
I'M NOT LOOKING FORWARD TO TOMORROW.
THE IDIOT SON'S BIRTHDAY PARTY IS ON THE SAME DAY AS EASTER THIS YEAR.
MUST BE NICE TO BE PAMPERED WHILE OTHERS WORK.
I BET HIS GUESTS WILL BE JUST AS BOTHERSOME.
HE'S SO EGOTISTICAL EVEN THOUGH HE'S ONLY THE SECOND SON. HE'S BASICALLY JUST A SPARE!
LET'S HAVE *THOSE TWO* DO THE CLEANUP AFTERWARDS.
THERE'S NO WAY THAT PEOPLE LIKE US SHOULD BE WORKING HARDER THAN PEOPLE OF LOWER STATUS!
EVER SINCE I CAN REMEMBER...
...IT'S ALWAYS BEEN LIKE THIS... STATUS, STATUS, STATUS...
PEOPLE LOOKING UP WITH ENVY, AND LOOKING DOWN WITH RIDICULE...
AH...
WHY IS THIS FAMILY—
NO... WHY IS THIS **WORLD** SO TERRIBLY CORRUPT?

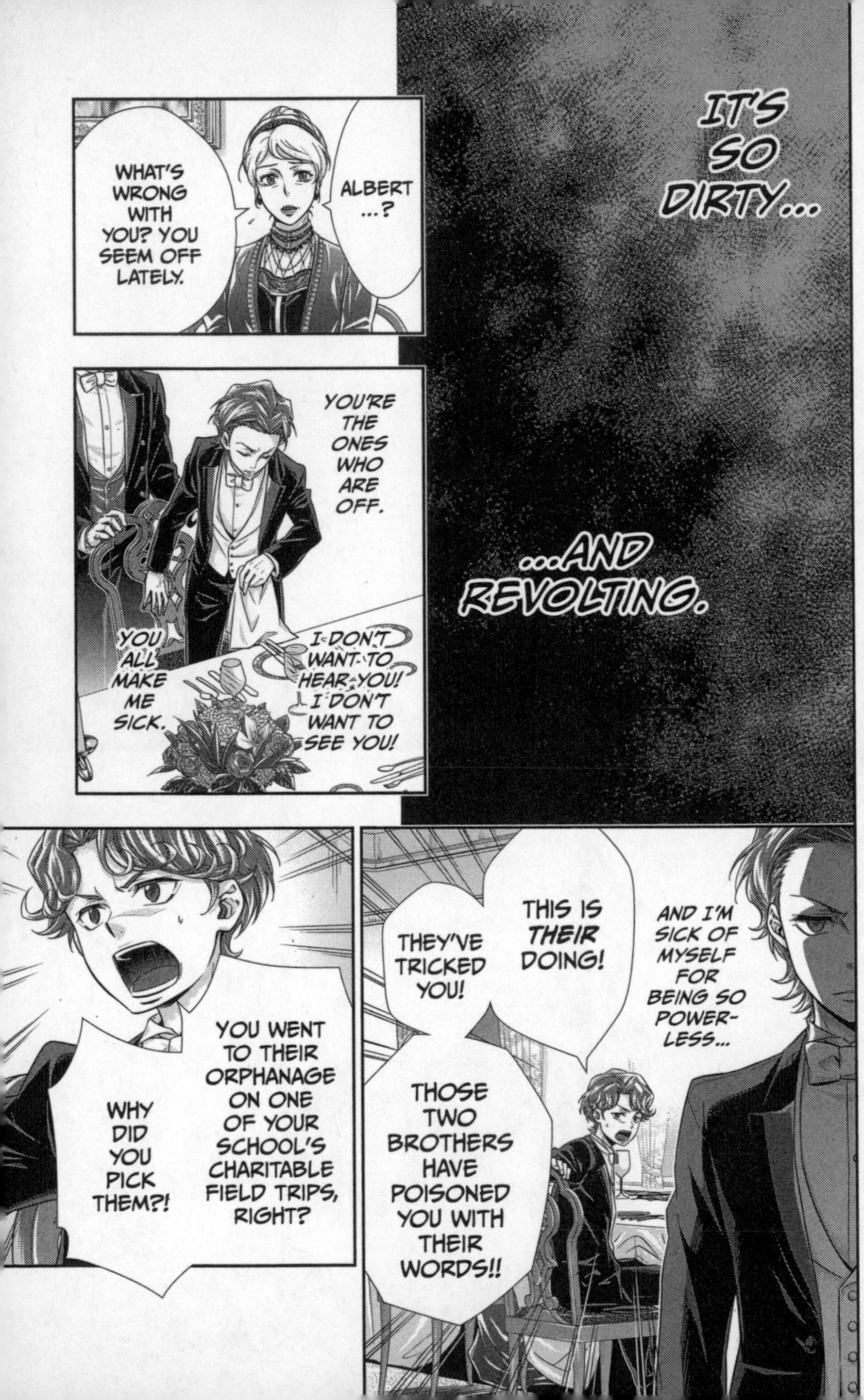
IT'S SO DIRTY...
...AND REVOLTING.
ALBERT ...?
WHAT'S WRONG WITH YOU? YOU SEEM OFF LATELY.
YOU'RE THE ONES WHO ARE OFF.
I DON'T WANT TO HEAR YOU! I DON'T WANT TO SEE YOU!
YOU ALL MAKE ME SICK.
AND I'M SICK OF MYSELF FOR BEING SO POWER-LESS...
THIS IS THEIR DOING!
THEY'VE TRICKED YOU!
THOSE TWO BROTHERS HAVE POISONED YOU WITH THEIR WORDS!!
YOU WENT TO THEIR ORPHANAGE ON ONE OF YOUR SCHOOL'S CHARITABLE FIELD TRIPS, RIGHT?
WHY DID YOU PICK THEM?!

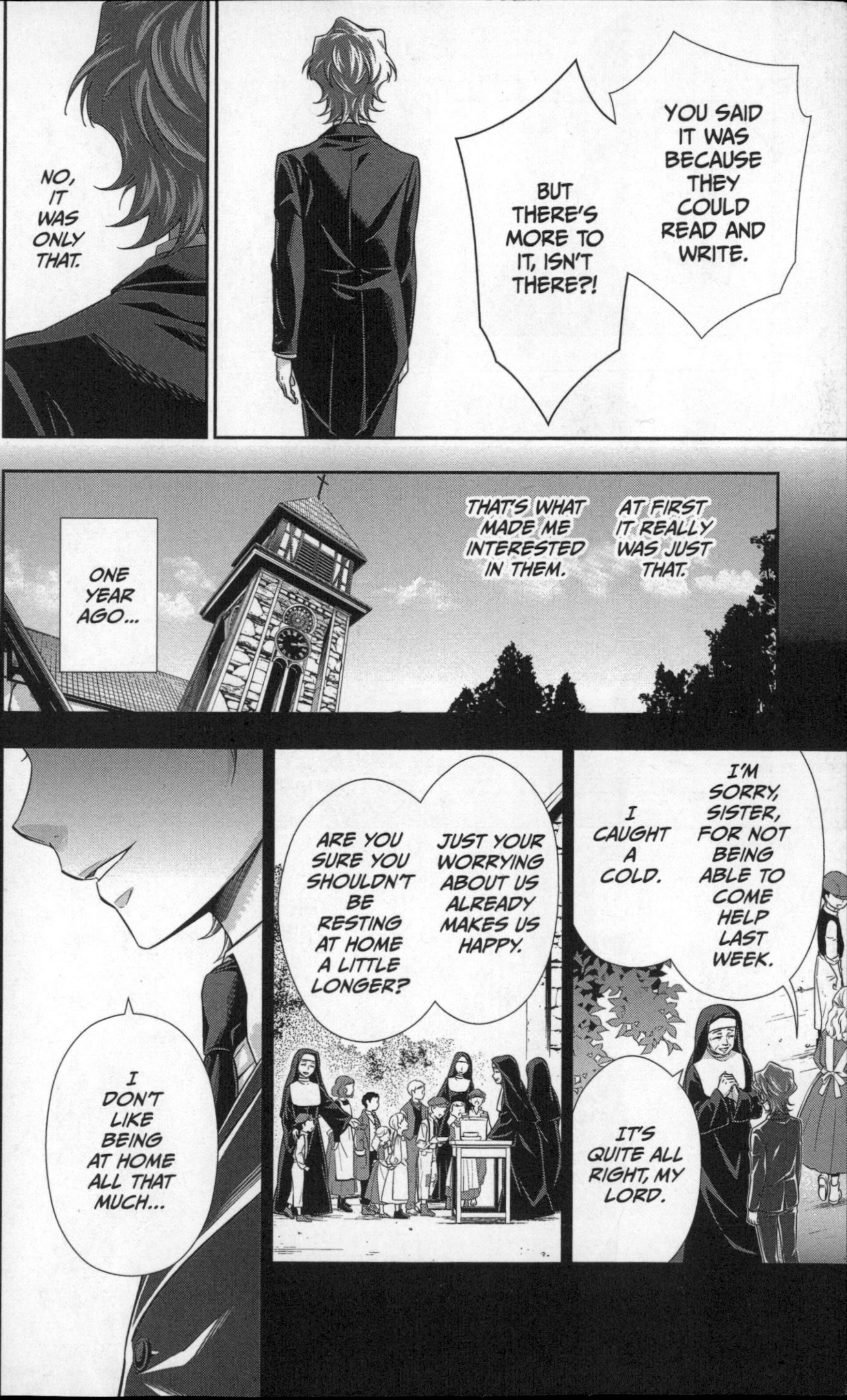

YOU SAID IT WAS BECAUSE THEY COULD READ AND WRITE.
BUT THERE'S MORE TO IT, ISN'T THERE?!
NO, IT WAS ONLY THAT.
AT FIRST IT REALLY WAS JUST THAT.
THAT'S WHAT MADE ME INTERESTED IN THEM.
ONE YEAR AGO...
I'M SORRY, SISTER, FOR NOT BEING ABLE TO COME HELP LAST WEEK.
I CAUGHT A COLD.
IT'S QUITE ALL RIGHT, MY LORD.
JUST YOUR WORRYING ABOUT US ALREADY MAKES US HAPPY.
ARE YOU SURE YOU SHOULDN'T BE RESTING AT HOME A LITTLE LONGER?
I DON'T LIKE BEING AT HOME ALL THAT MUCH...

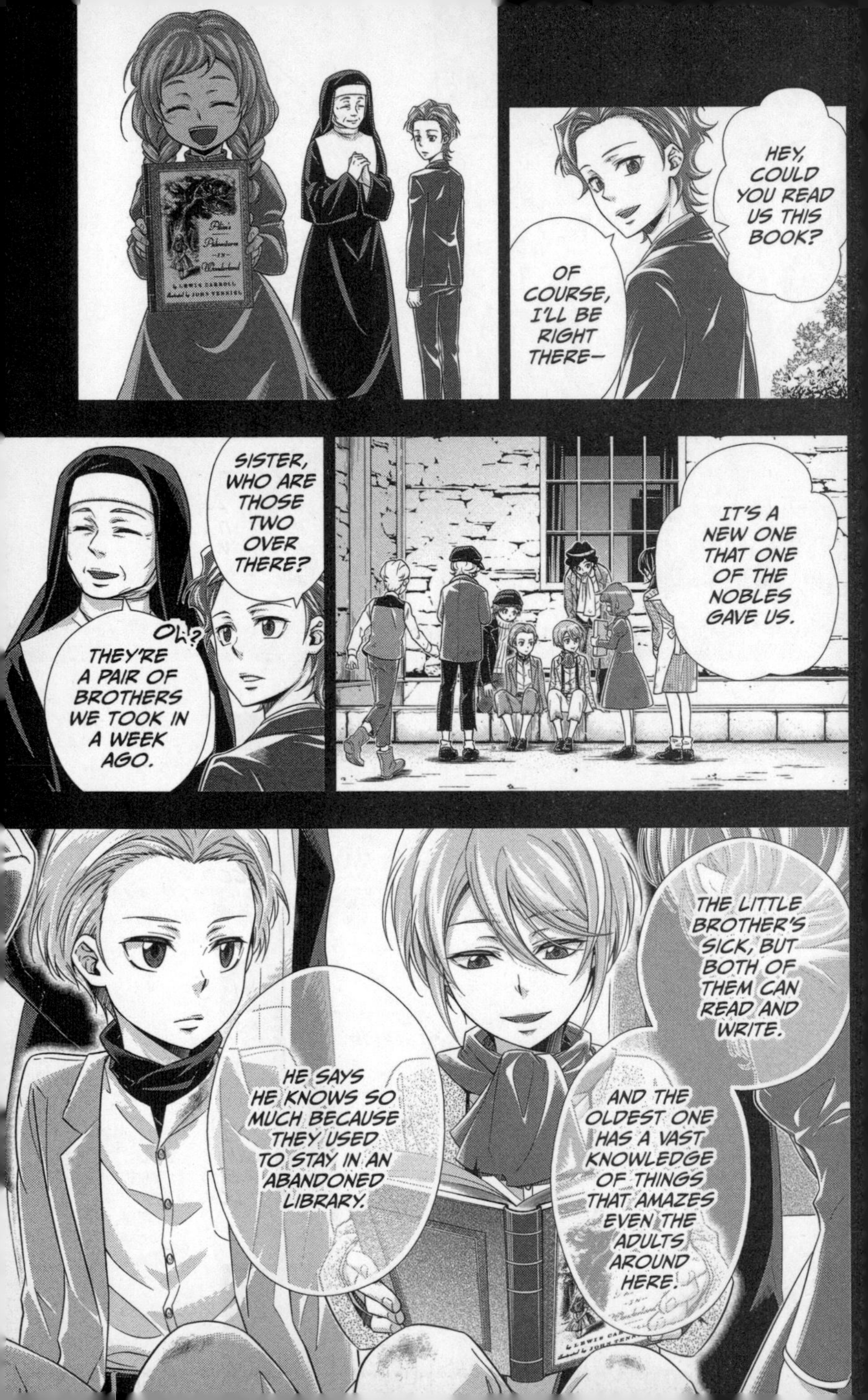
HEY, COULD YOU READ US THIS BOOK?
OF COURSE, I'LL BE RIGHT THERE—
IT'S A NEW ONE THAT ONE OF THE NOBLES GAVE US.
SISTER, WHO ARE THOSE TWO OVER THERE?
OH?
THEY'RE A PAIR OF BROTHERS WE TOOK IN A WEEK AGO.
THE LITTLE BROTHER'S SICK, BUT BOTH OF THEM CAN READ AND WRITE.
AND THE OLDEST ONE HAS A VAST KNOWLEDGE OF THINGS THAT AMAZES EVEN THE ADULTS AROUND HERE.
HE SAYS HE KNOWS SO MUCH BECAUSE THEY USED TO STAY IN AN ABANDONED LIBRARY.

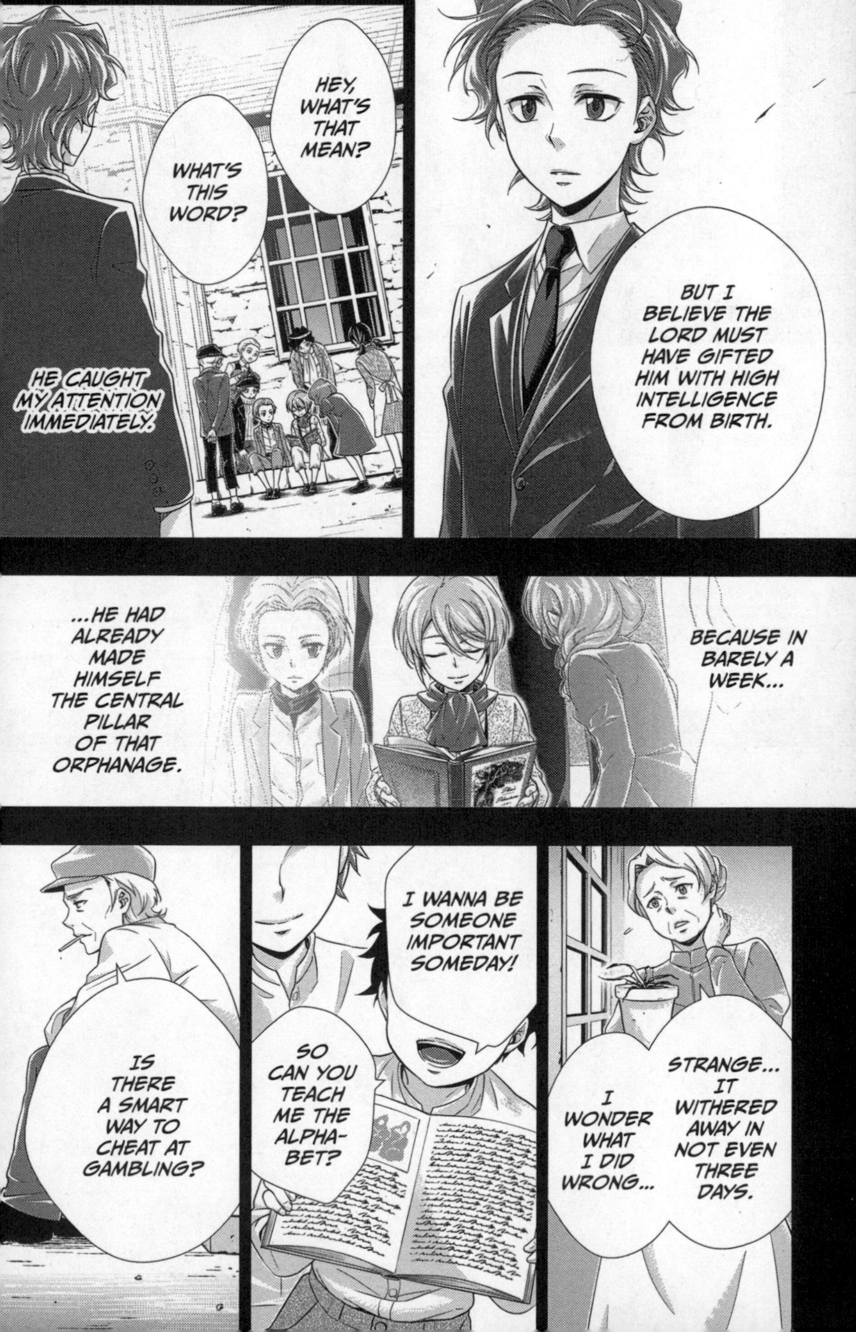
BUT I BELIEVE THE LORD MUST HAVE GIFTED HIM WITH HIGH INTELLIGENCE FROM BIRTH.
HEY, WHAT'S THAT MEAN?
WHAT'S THIS WORD?
HE CAUGHT MY ATTENTION IMMEDIATELY.
BECAUSE IN BARELY A WEEK...
...HE HAD ALREADY MADE HIMSELF THE CENTRAL PILLAR OF THAT ORPHANAGE.
STRANGE... IT WITHERED AWAY IN NOT EVEN THREE DAYS.
I WONDER WHAT I DID WRONG...
I WANNA BE SOMEONE IMPORTANT SOMEDAY!
SO CAN YOU TEACH ME THE ALPHA-BET?
IS THERE A SMART WAY TO CHEAT AT GAMBLING?

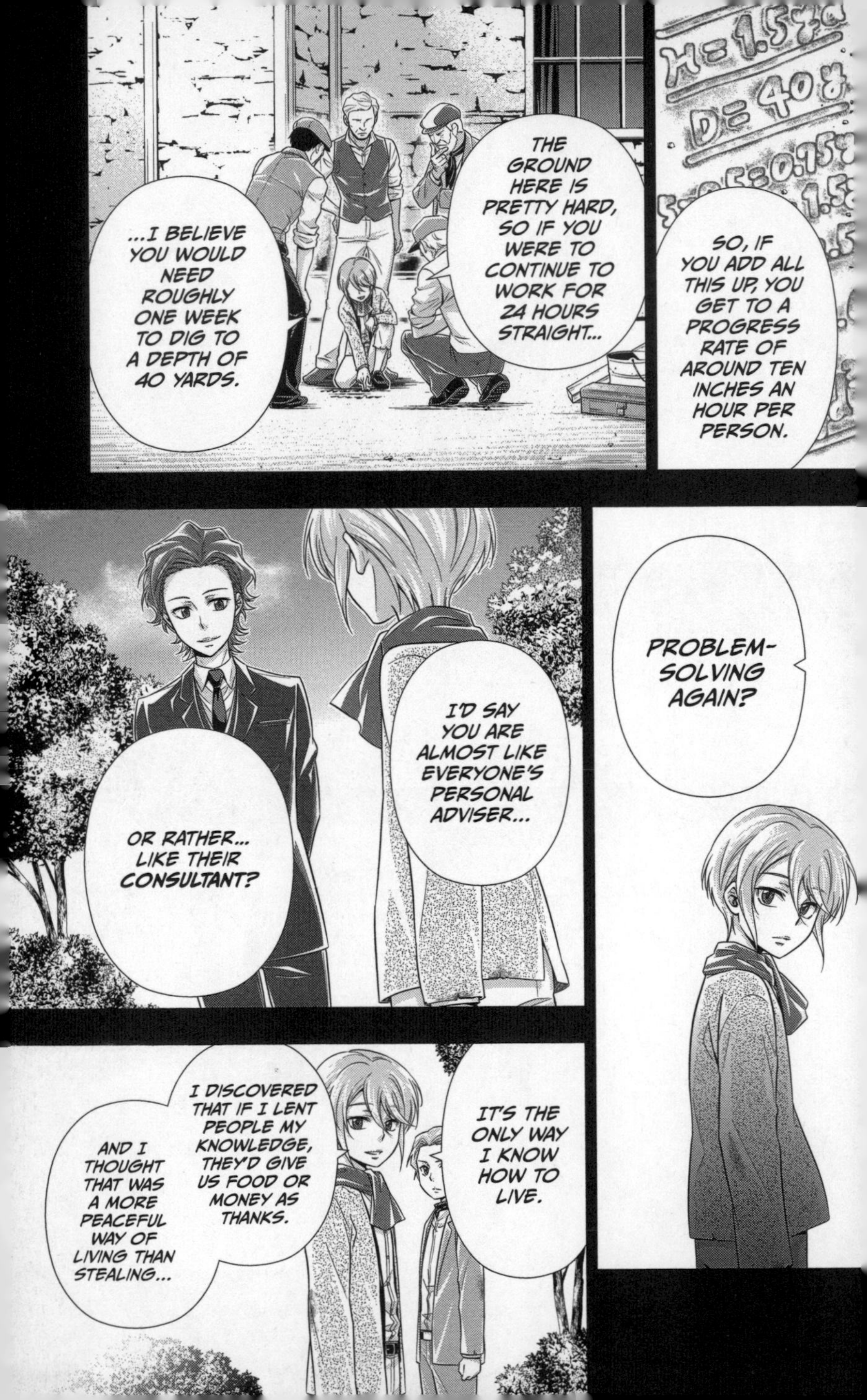
SO, IF YOU ADD ALL THIS UP, YOU GET TO A PROGRESS RATE OF AROUND TEN INCHES AN HOUR PER PERSON.
THE GROUND HERE IS PRETTY HARD, SO IF YOU WERE TO CONTINUE TO WORK FOR 24 HOURS STRAIGHT...
...I BELIEVE YOU WOULD NEED ROUGHLY ONE WEEK TO DIG TO A DEPTH OF 40 YARDS.
PROBLEM-SOLVING AGAIN?
I'D SAY YOU ARE ALMOST LIKE EVERYONE'S PERSONAL ADVISER...
OR RATHER... LIKE THEIR **CONSULTANT**?
IT'S THE ONLY WAY I KNOW HOW TO LIVE.
I DISCOVERED THAT IF I LENT PEOPLE MY KNOWLEDGE, THEY'D GIVE US FOOD OR MONEY AS THANKS.
AND I THOUGHT THAT WAS A MORE PEACEFUL WAY OF LIVING THAN STEALING...

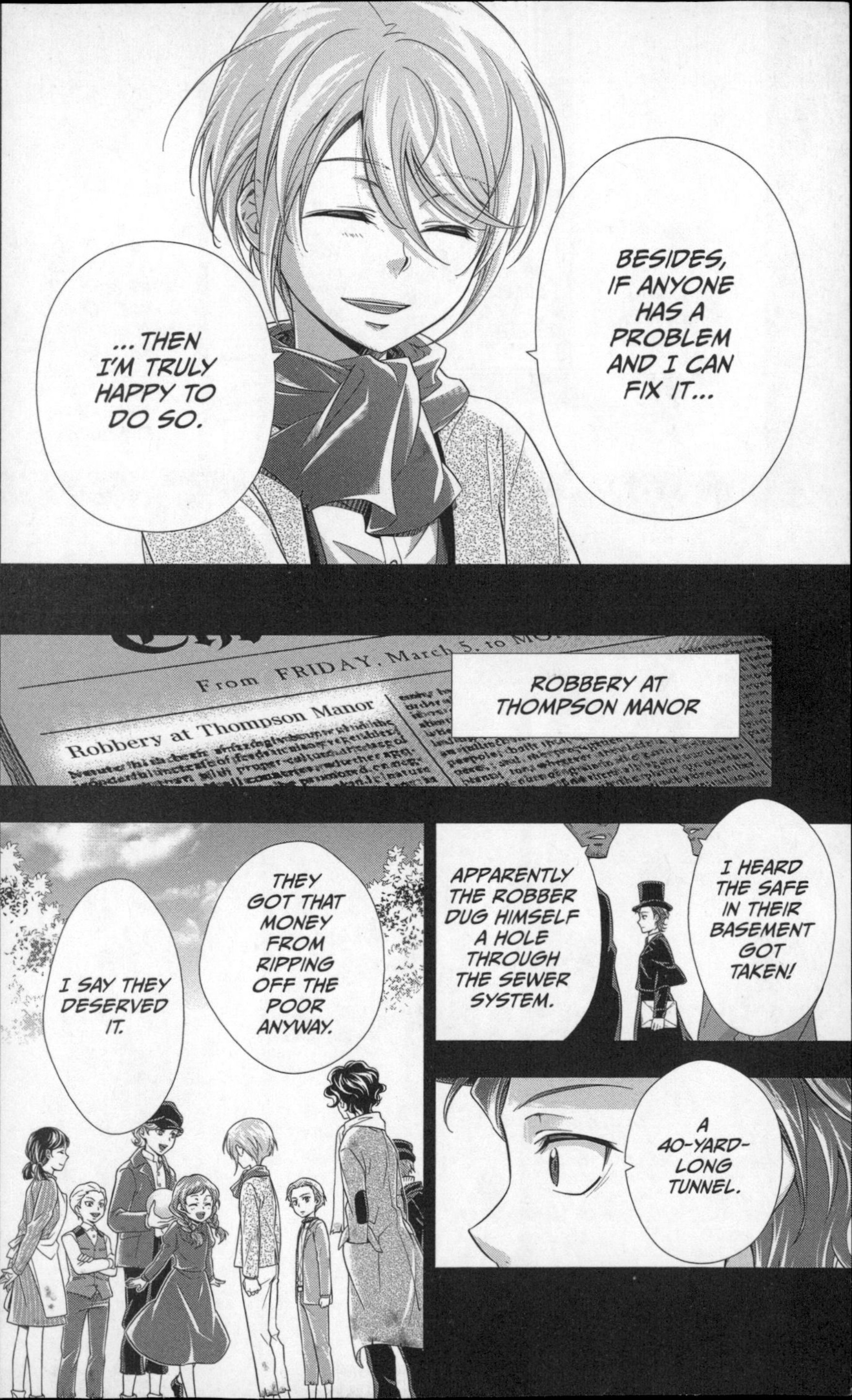
BESIDES, IF ANYONE HAS A PROBLEM AND I CAN FIX IT...
...THEN I'M TRULY HAPPY TO DO SO.
ROBBERY AT THOMPSON MANOR
From FRIDAY, March 5. to
Robbery at Thompson Manor
I HEARD THE SAFE IN THEIR BASEMENT GOT TAKEN!
APPARENTLY THE ROBBER DUG HIMSELF A HOLE THROUGH THE SEWER SYSTEM.
A 40-YARD-LONG TUNNEL.
THEY GOT THAT MONEY FROM RIPPING OFF THE POOR ANYWAY.
I SAY THEY DESERVED IT.

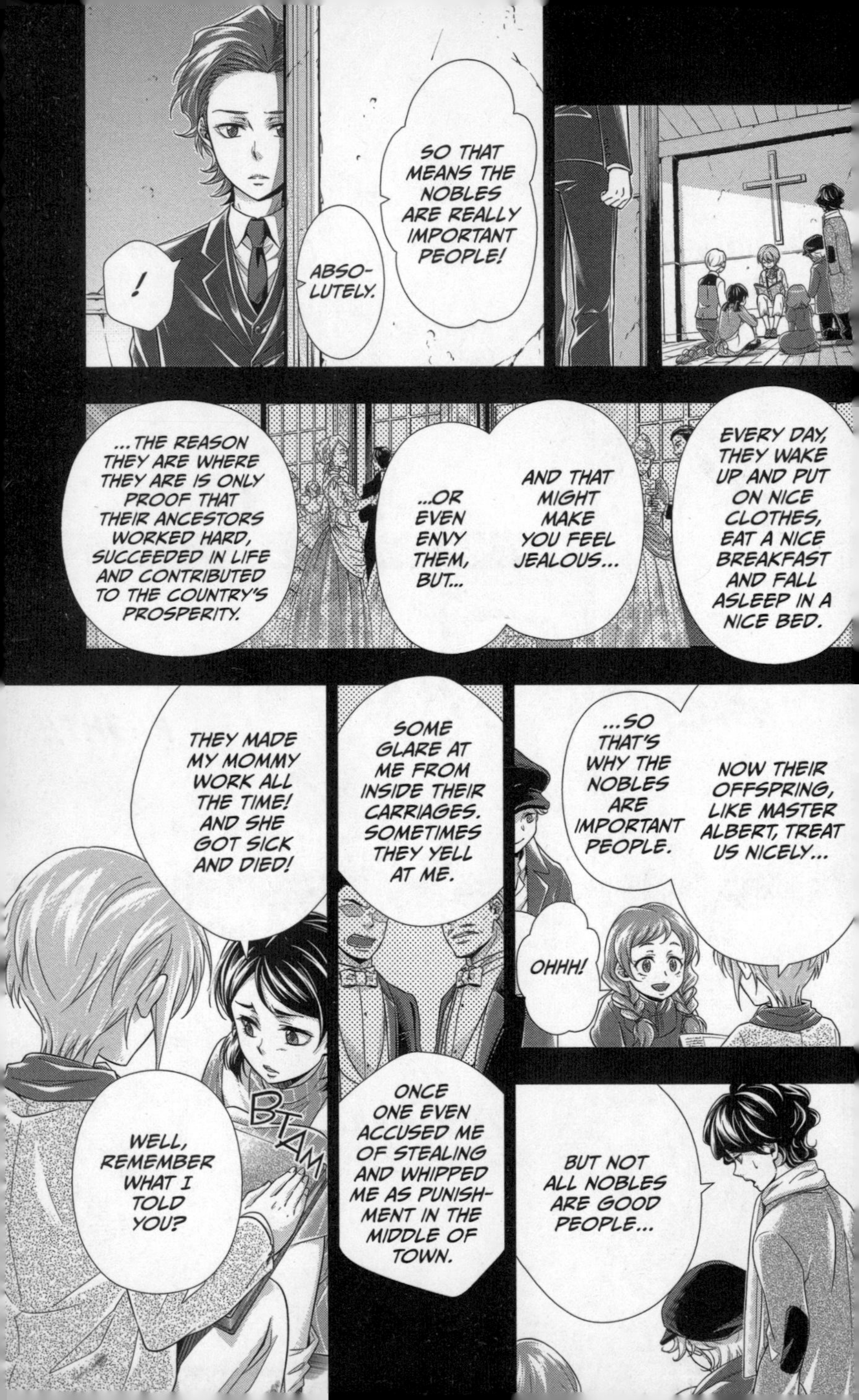
SO THAT MEANS THE NOBLES ARE REALLY IMPORTANT PEOPLE!
ABSO-LUTELY.
!
EVERY DAY, THEY WAKE UP AND PUT ON NICE CLOTHES, EAT A NICE BREAKFAST AND FALL ASLEEP IN A NICE BED.
AND THAT MIGHT MAKE YOU FEEL JEALOUS...
...OR EVEN ENVY THEM, BUT...
...THE REASON THEY ARE WHERE THEY ARE IS ONLY PROOF THAT THEIR ANCESTORS WORKED HARD, SUCCEEDED IN LIFE AND CONTRIBUTED TO THE COUNTRY'S PROSPERITY.
NOW THEIR OFFSPRING, LIKE MASTER ALBERT, TREAT US NICELY...
...SO THAT'S WHY THE NOBLES ARE IMPORTANT PEOPLE.
OHHH!
BUT NOT ALL NOBLES ARE GOOD PEOPLE...
SOME GLARE AT ME FROM INSIDE THEIR CARRIAGES. SOMETIMES THEY YELL AT ME.
ONCE ONE EVEN ACCUSED ME OF STEALING AND WHIPPED ME AS PUNISH-MENT IN THE MIDDLE OF TOWN.
THEY MADE MY MOMMY WORK ALL THE TIME! AND SHE GOT SICK AND DIED!
BLAM
WELL, REMEMBER WHAT I TOLD YOU?

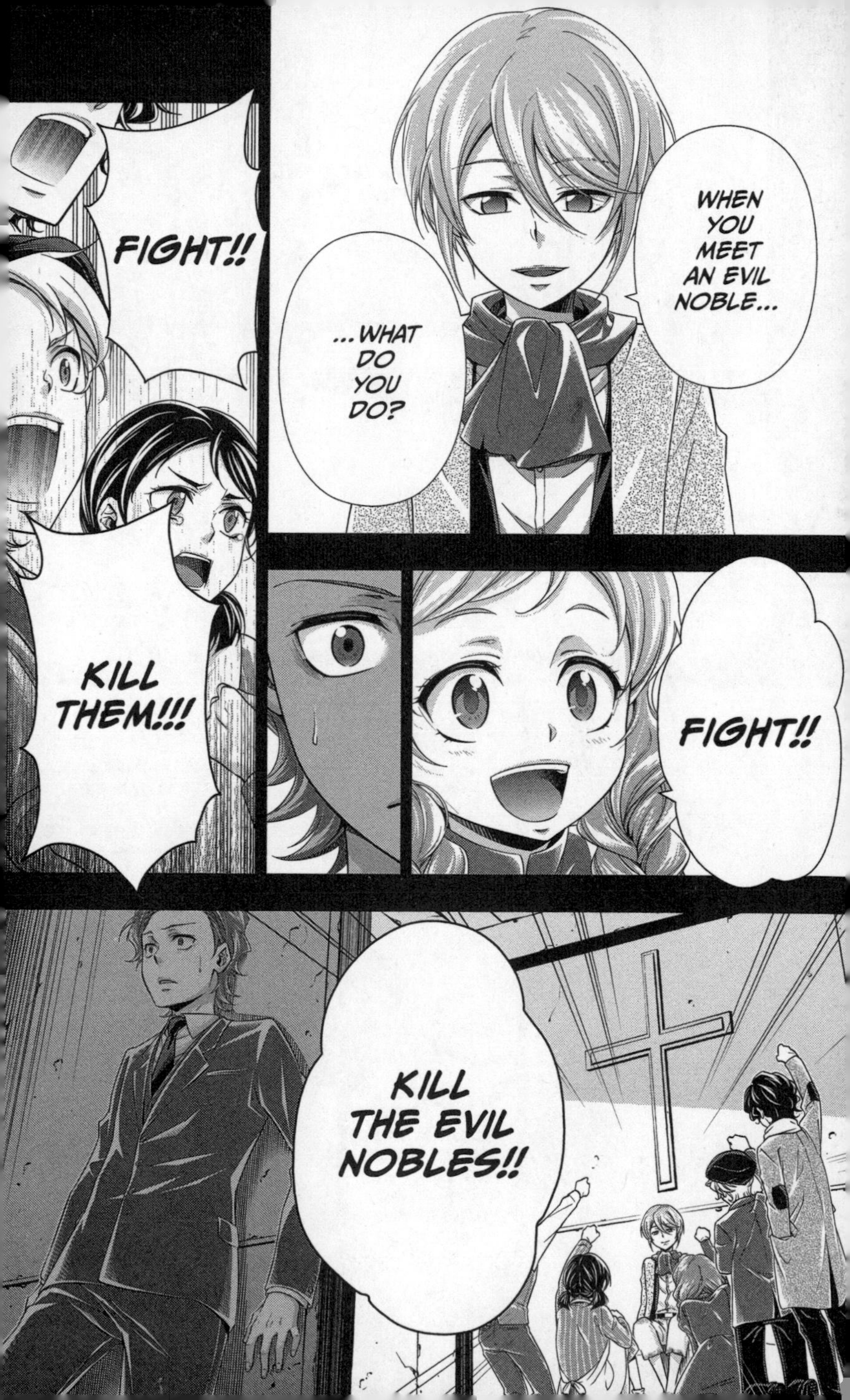
WHEN YOU MEET AN EVIL NOBLE...
...WHAT DO YOU DO?
FIGHT!!
FIGHT!!
KILL THEM!!!
KILL THE EVIL NOBLES!!

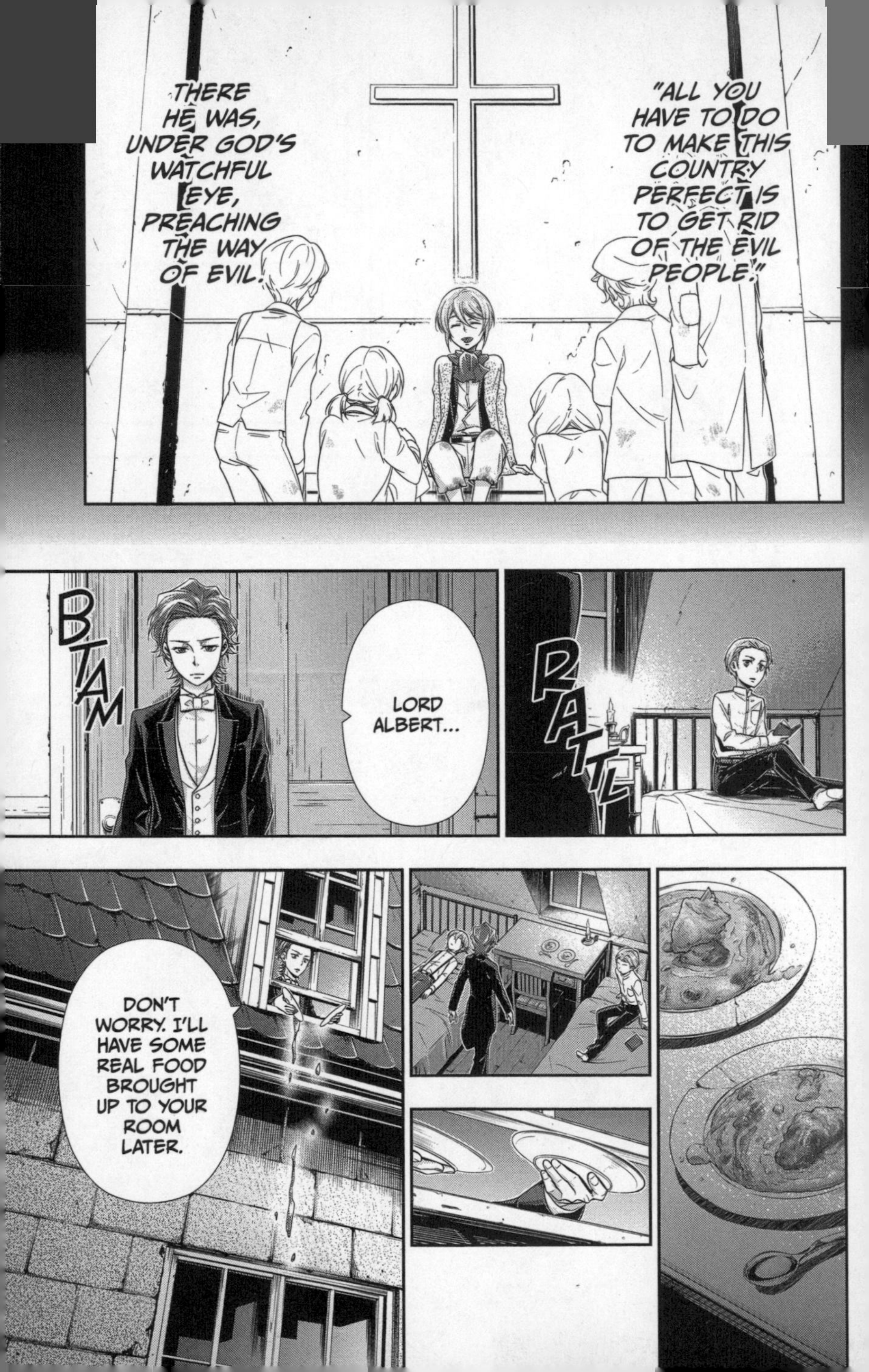
"ALL YOU HAVE TO DO TO MAKE THIS COUNTRY PERFECT IS TO GET RID OF THE EVIL PEOPLE."
THERE HE WAS, UNDER GOD'S WATCHFUL EYE, PREACHING THE WAY OF EVIL.
RATTL
LORD ALBERT...
BTAM
DON'T WORRY. I'LL HAVE SOME REAL FOOD BROUGHT UP TO YOUR ROOM LATER.

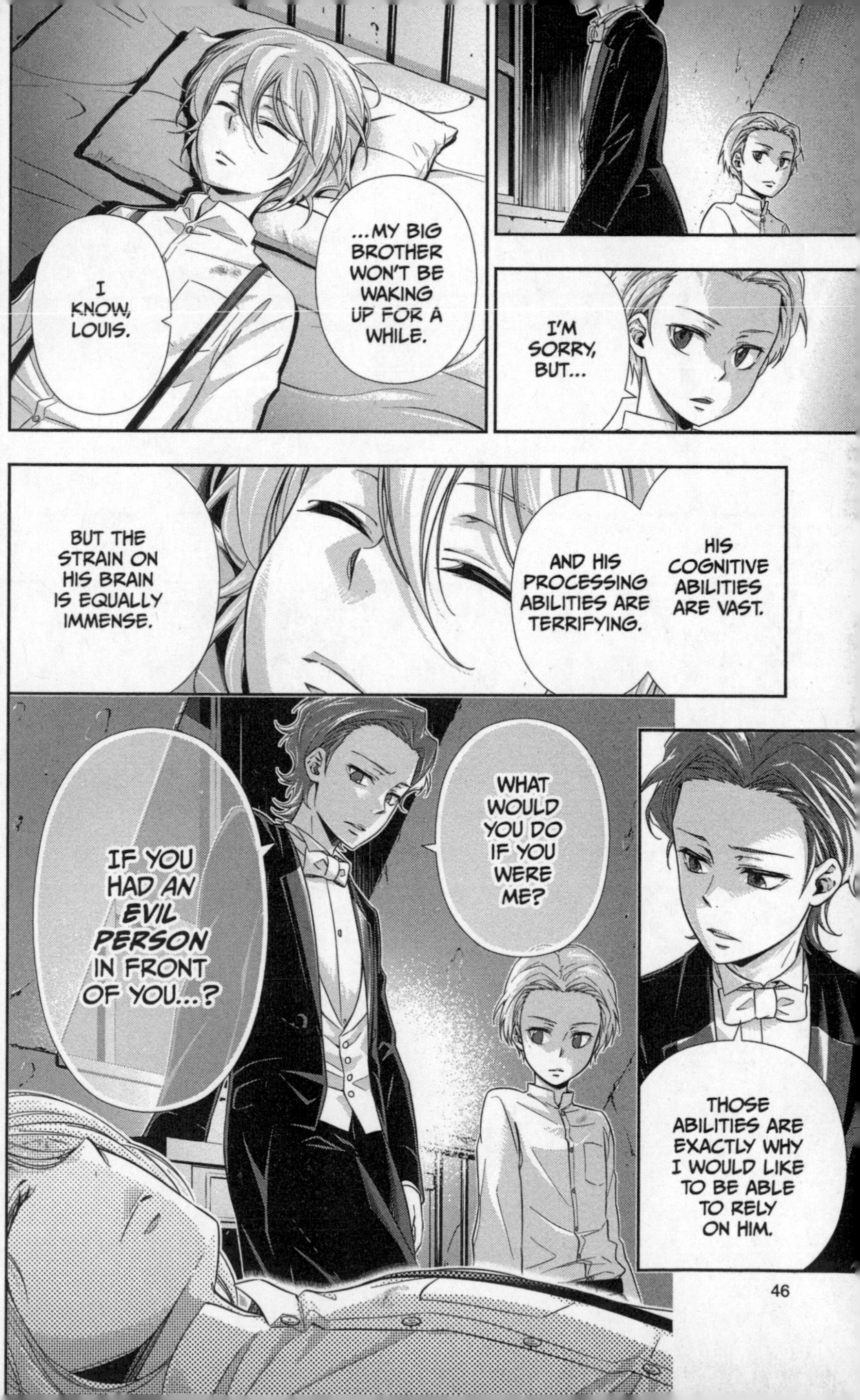
I'M SORRY, BUT...
...MY BIG BROTHER WON'T BE WAKING UP FOR A WHILE.
I KNOW, LOUIS.
HIS COGNITIVE ABILITIES ARE VAST.
AND HIS PROCESSING ABILITIES ARE TERRIFYING.
BUT THE STRAIN ON HIS BRAIN IS EQUALLY IMMENSE.
THOSE ABILITIES ARE EXACTLY WHY I WOULD LIKE TO BE ABLE TO RELY ON HIM.
WHAT WOULD YOU DO IF YOU WERE ME?
IF YOU HAD AN *EVIL PERSON* IN FRONT OF YOU...?

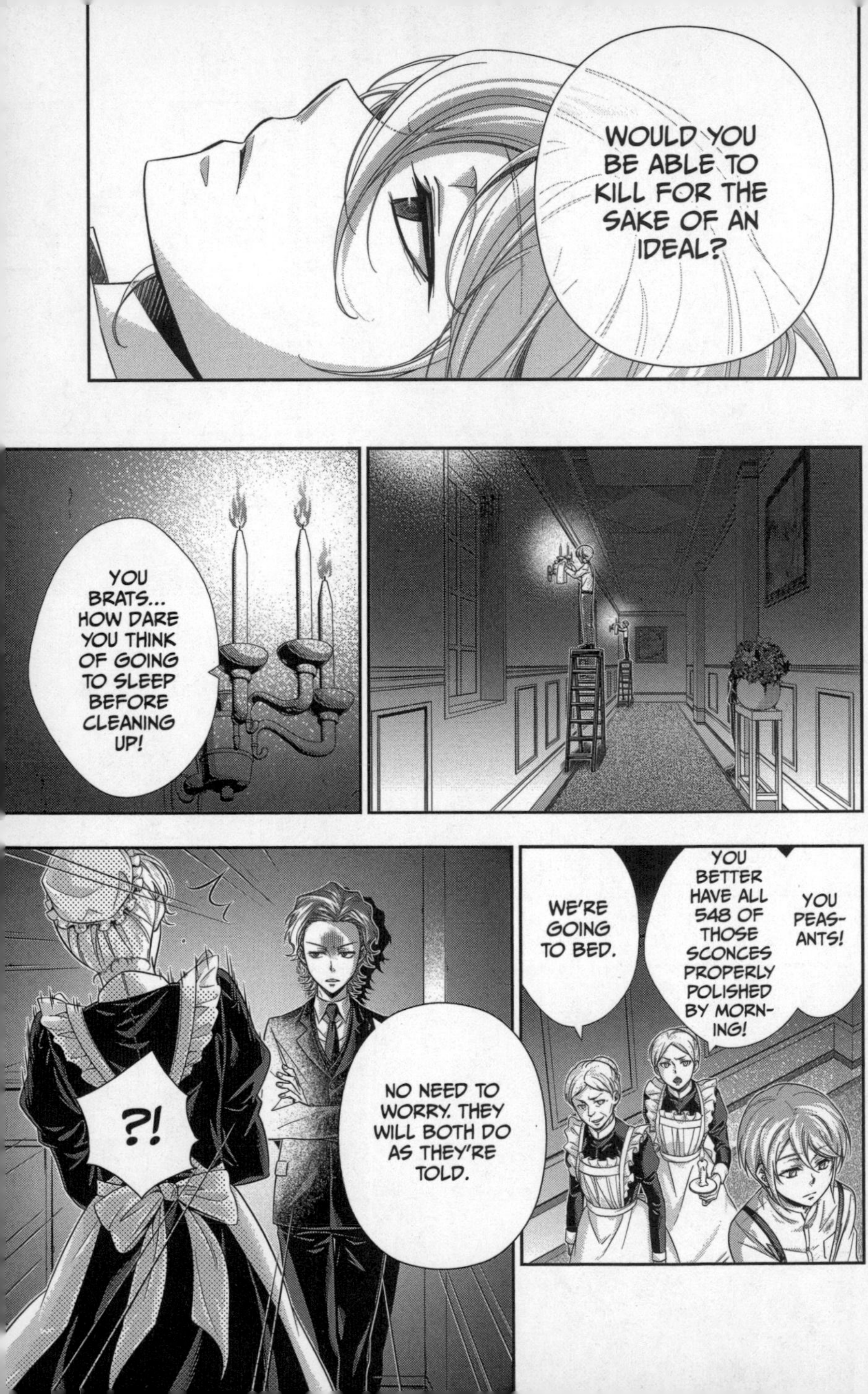
WOULD YOU BE ABLE TO KILL FOR THE SAKE OF AN IDEAL?
YOU BRATS... HOW DARE YOU THINK OF GOING TO SLEEP BEFORE CLEANING UP!
YOU PEAS-ANTS!
YOU BETTER HAVE ALL 548 OF THOSE SCONCES PROPERLY POLISHED BY MORN-ING!
WE'RE GOING TO BED.
NO NEED TO WORRY. THEY WILL BOTH DO AS THEY'RE TOLD.
?!

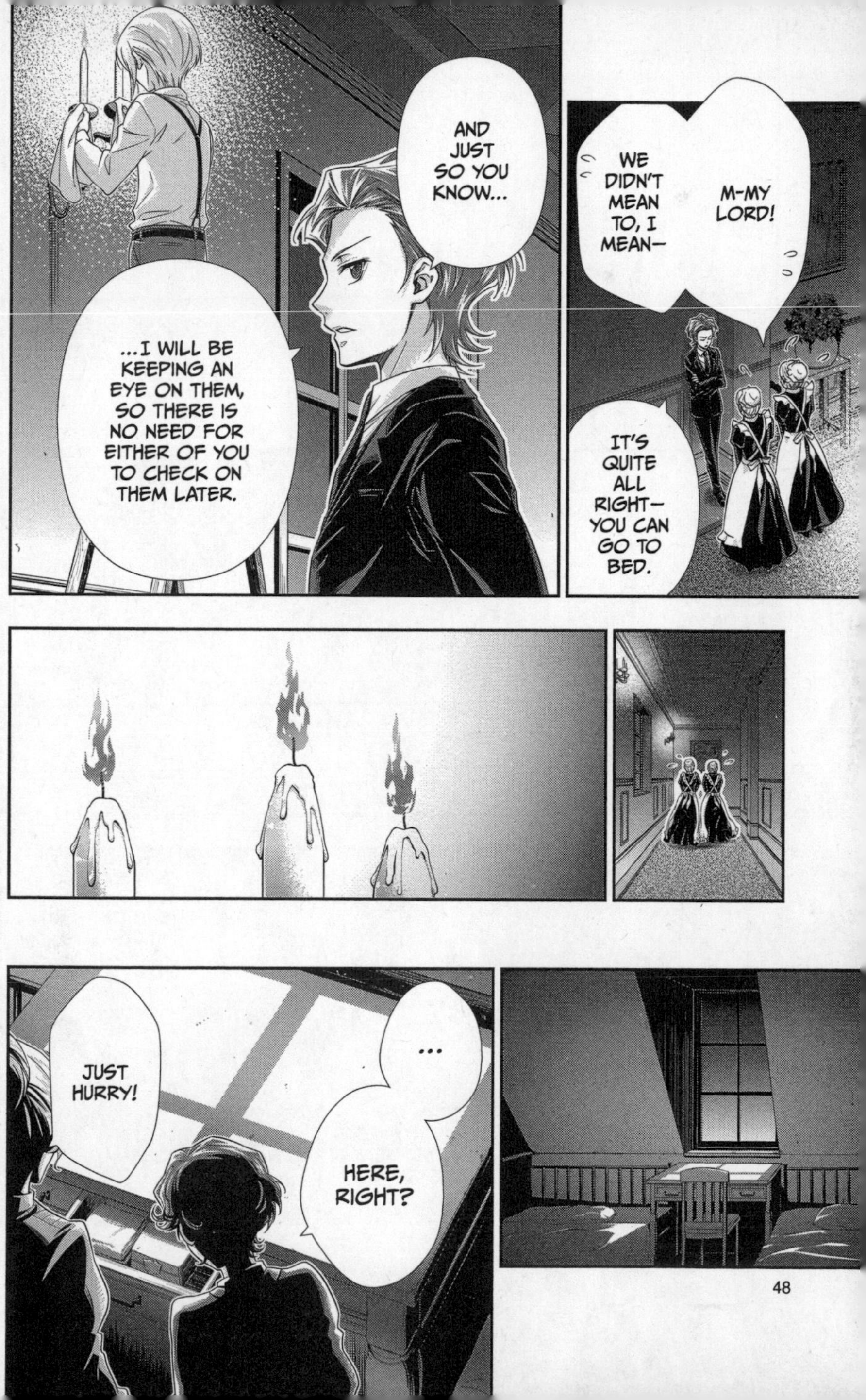
M-MY LORD!
WE DIDN'T MEAN TO, I MEAN—
IT'S QUITE ALL RIGHT— YOU CAN GO TO BED.
AND JUST SO YOU KNOW...
...I WILL BE KEEPING AN EYE ON THEM, SO THERE IS NO NEED FOR EITHER OF YOU TO CHECK ON THEM LATER.
...
HERE, RIGHT?
JUST HURRY!

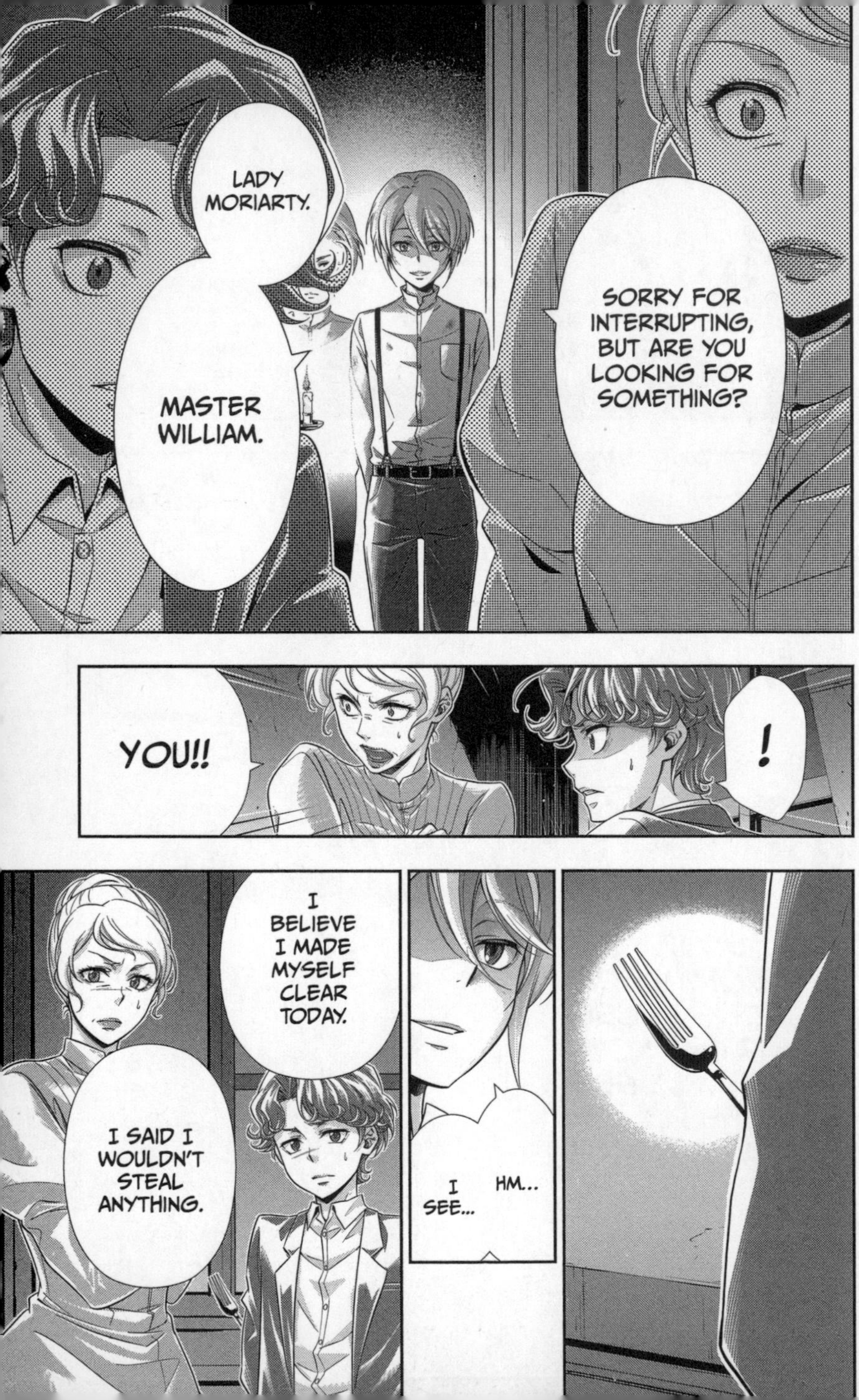
SORRY FOR INTERRUPTING, BUT ARE YOU LOOKING FOR SOMETHING?
LADY MORIARTY.
MASTER WILLIAM.
!
YOU!!
HM...
I SEE...
I BELIEVE I MADE MYSELF CLEAR TODAY.
I SAID I WOULDN'T STEAL ANYTHING.

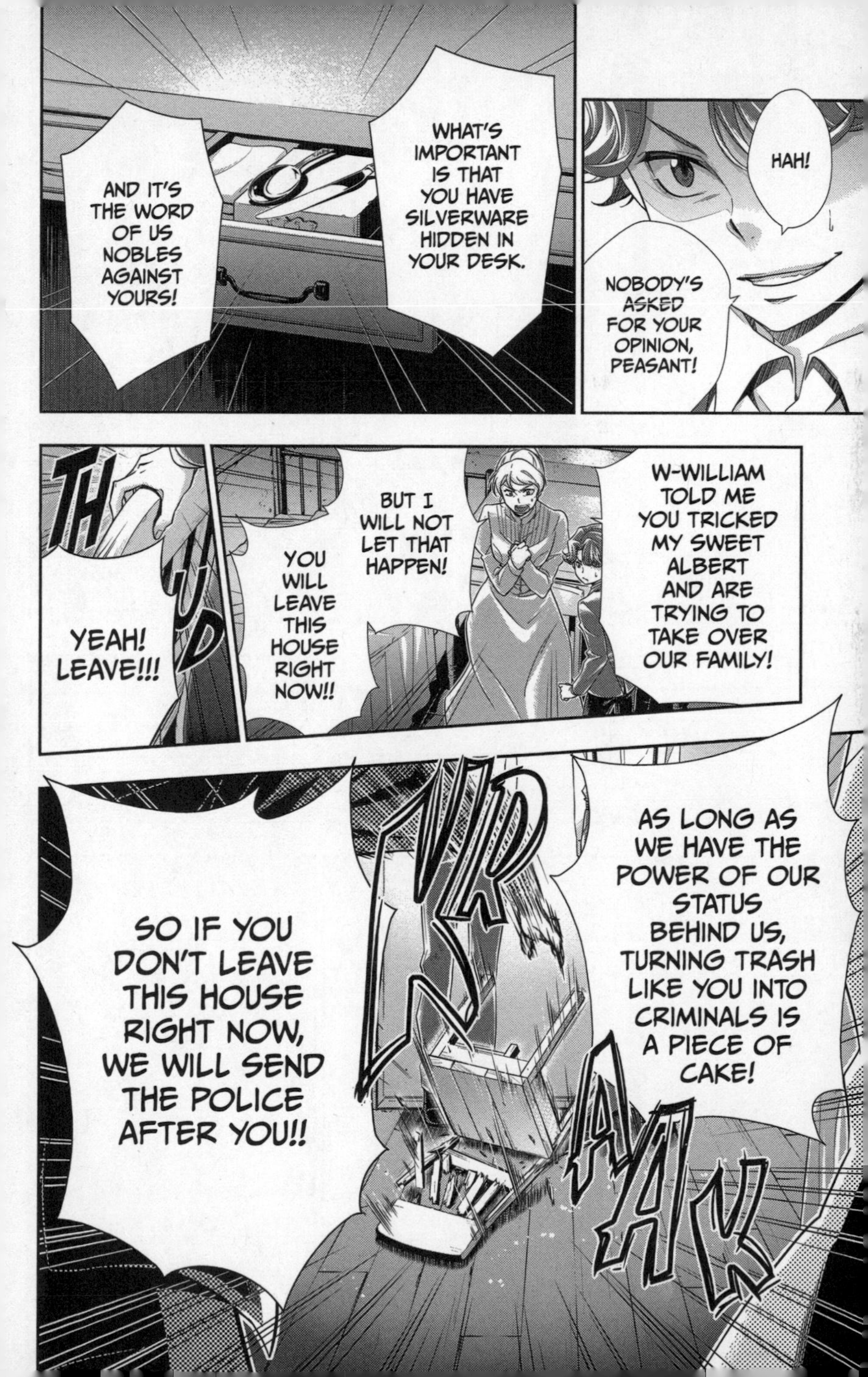
HAH!
NOBODY'S ASKED FOR YOUR OPINION, PEASANT!
WHAT'S IMPORTANT IS THAT YOU HAVE SILVERWARE HIDDEN IN YOUR DESK.
AND IT'S THE WORD OF US NOBLES AGAINST YOURS!
W-WILLIAM TOLD ME YOU TRICKED MY SWEET ALBERT AND ARE TRYING TO TAKE OVER OUR FAMILY!
BUT I WILL NOT LET THAT HAPPEN!
YOU WILL LEAVE THIS HOUSE RIGHT NOW!!
THUD
YEAH! LEAVE!!!
AS LONG AS WE HAVE THE POWER OF OUR STATUS BEHIND US, TURNING TRASH LIKE YOU INTO CRIMINALS IS A PIECE OF CAKE!
SLAM
SO IF YOU DON'T LEAVE THIS HOUSE RIGHT NOW, WE WILL SEND THE POLICE AFTER YOU!!

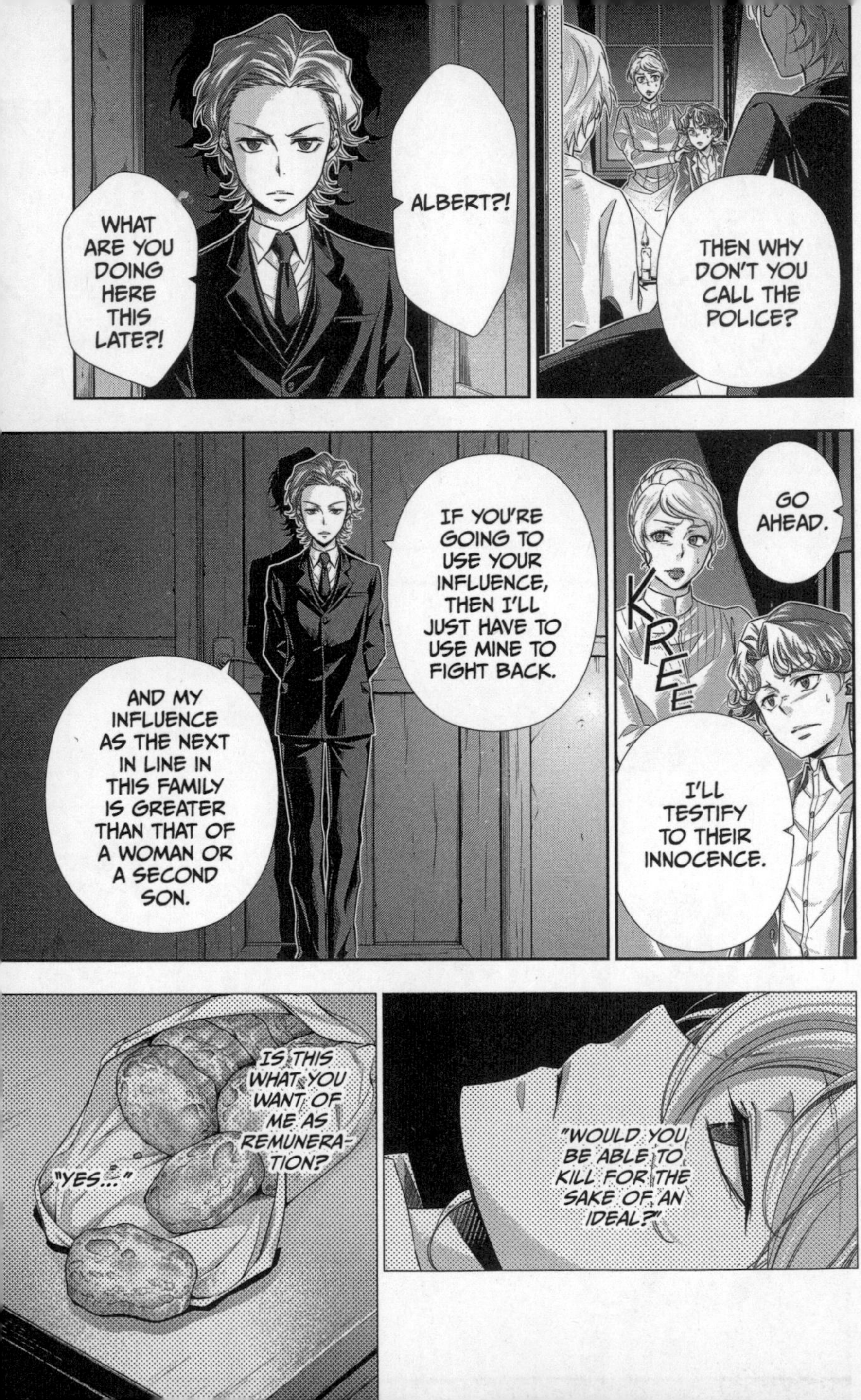
THEN WHY DON'T YOU CALL THE POLICE?
ALBERT?!
WHAT ARE YOU DOING HERE THIS LATE?!
GO AHEAD.
KREE
I'LL TESTIFY TO THEIR INNOCENCE.
IF YOU'RE GOING TO USE YOUR INFLUENCE, THEN I'LL JUST HAVE TO USE MINE TO FIGHT BACK.
AND MY INFLUENCE AS THE NEXT IN LINE IN THIS FAMILY IS GREATER THAN THAT OF A WOMAN OR A SECOND SON.
"WOULD YOU BE ABLE TO KILL FOR THE SAKE OF AN IDEAL?"
IS THIS WHAT YOU WANT OF ME AS REMUNERATION?
"YES..."

...THE INTELLIGENCE AND COURAGE TO OBTAIN MY IDEAL WORLD.

I WANT...

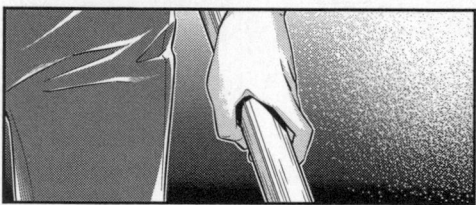

AS PER MASTER ALBERT'S REQUEST...

...I SHALL NOW BESTOW UPON YOU YOUR PUNISHMENT.

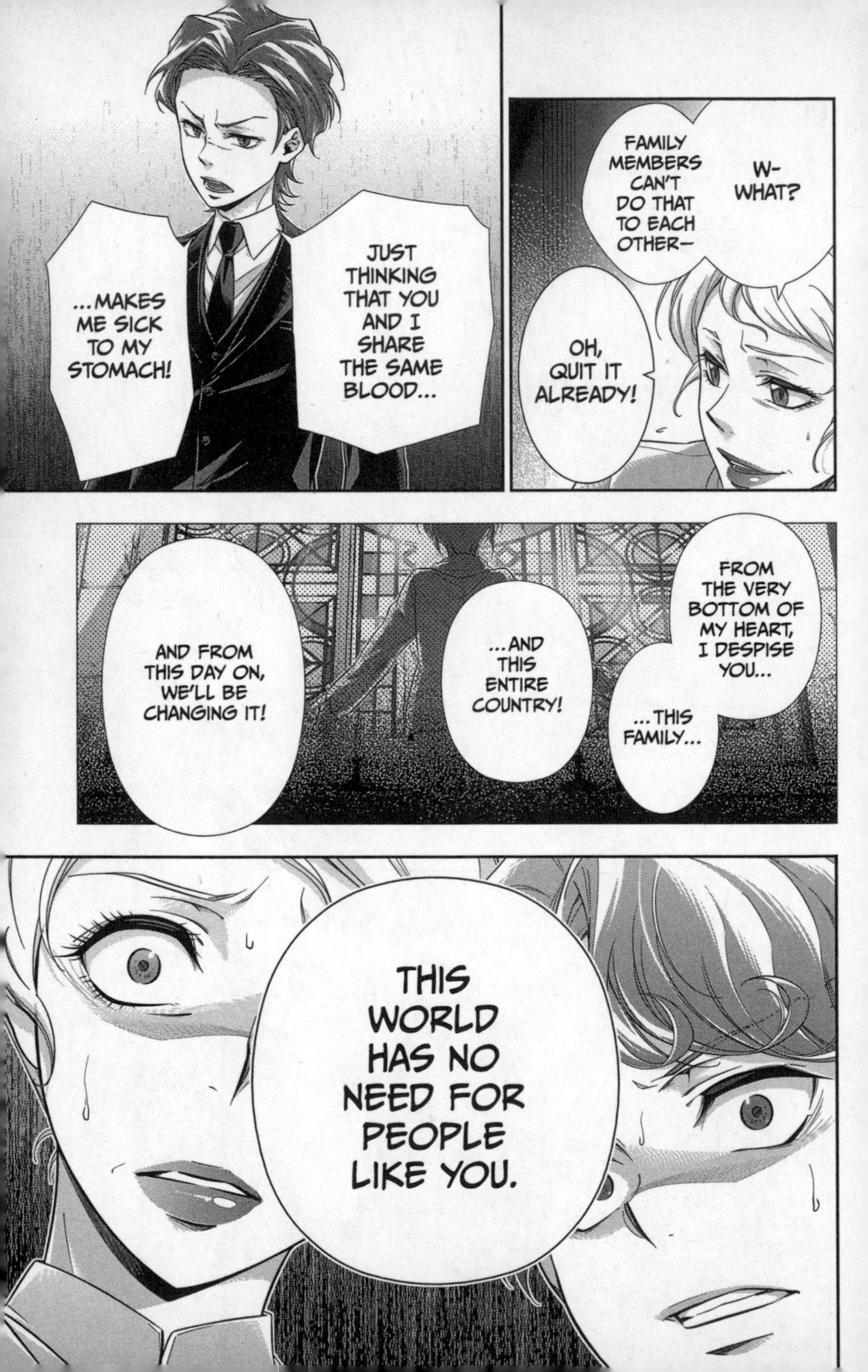
W-WHAT?
FAMILY MEMBERS CAN'T DO THAT TO EACH OTHER—
OH, QUIT IT ALREADY!
JUST THINKING THAT YOU AND I SHARE THE SAME BLOOD...
...MAKES ME SICK TO MY STOMACH!
FROM THE VERY BOTTOM OF MY HEART, I DESPISE YOU...
...THIS FAMILY...
...AND THIS ENTIRE COUNTRY!
AND FROM THIS DAY ON, WE'LL BE CHANGING IT!
THIS WORLD HAS NO NEED FOR PEOPLE LIKE YOU.

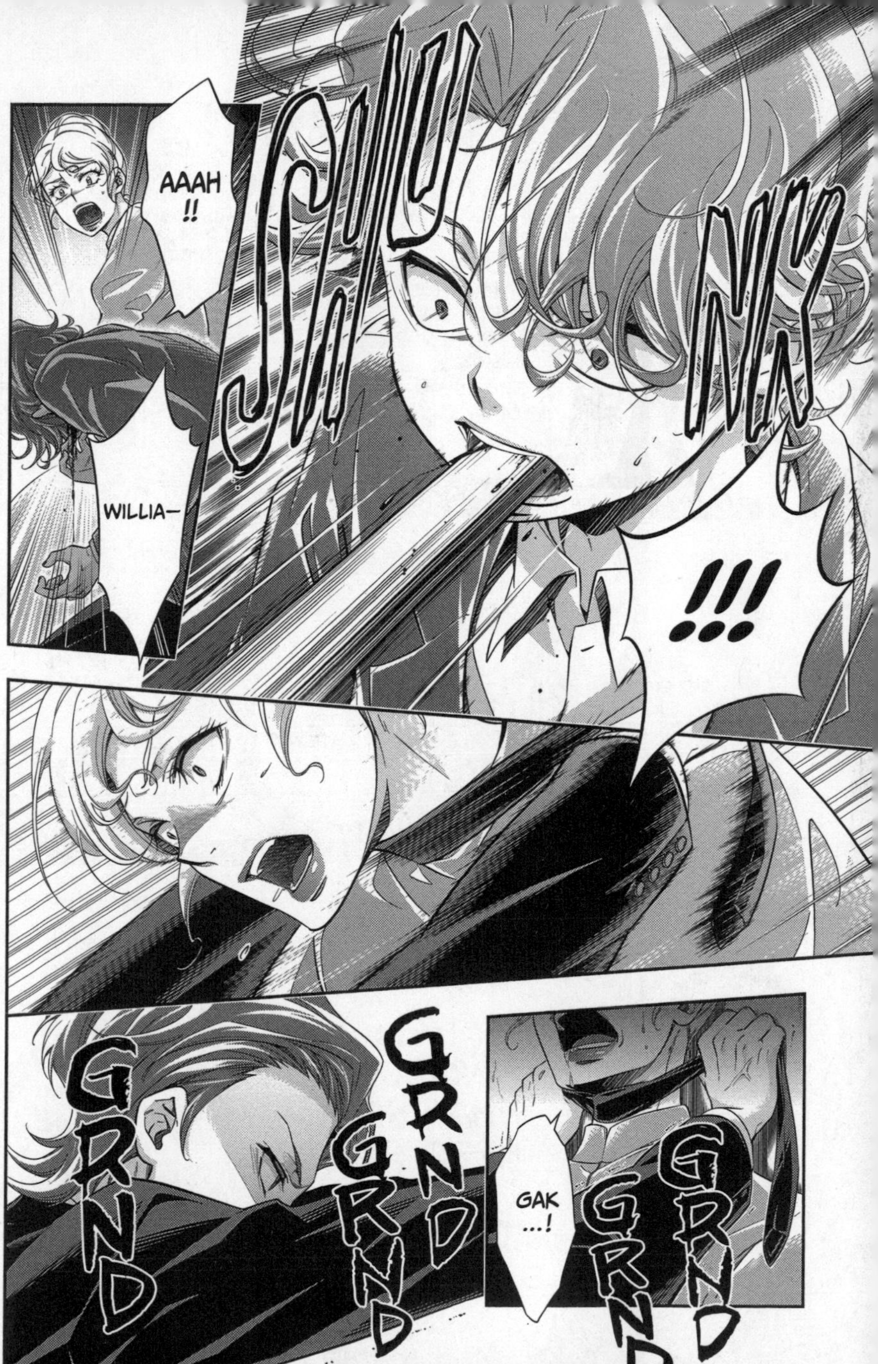
SCHUNK
!!!
AAAH !!
WILLIA—
GAK ...!
GRND
GRND
GRND
GRND
GRND

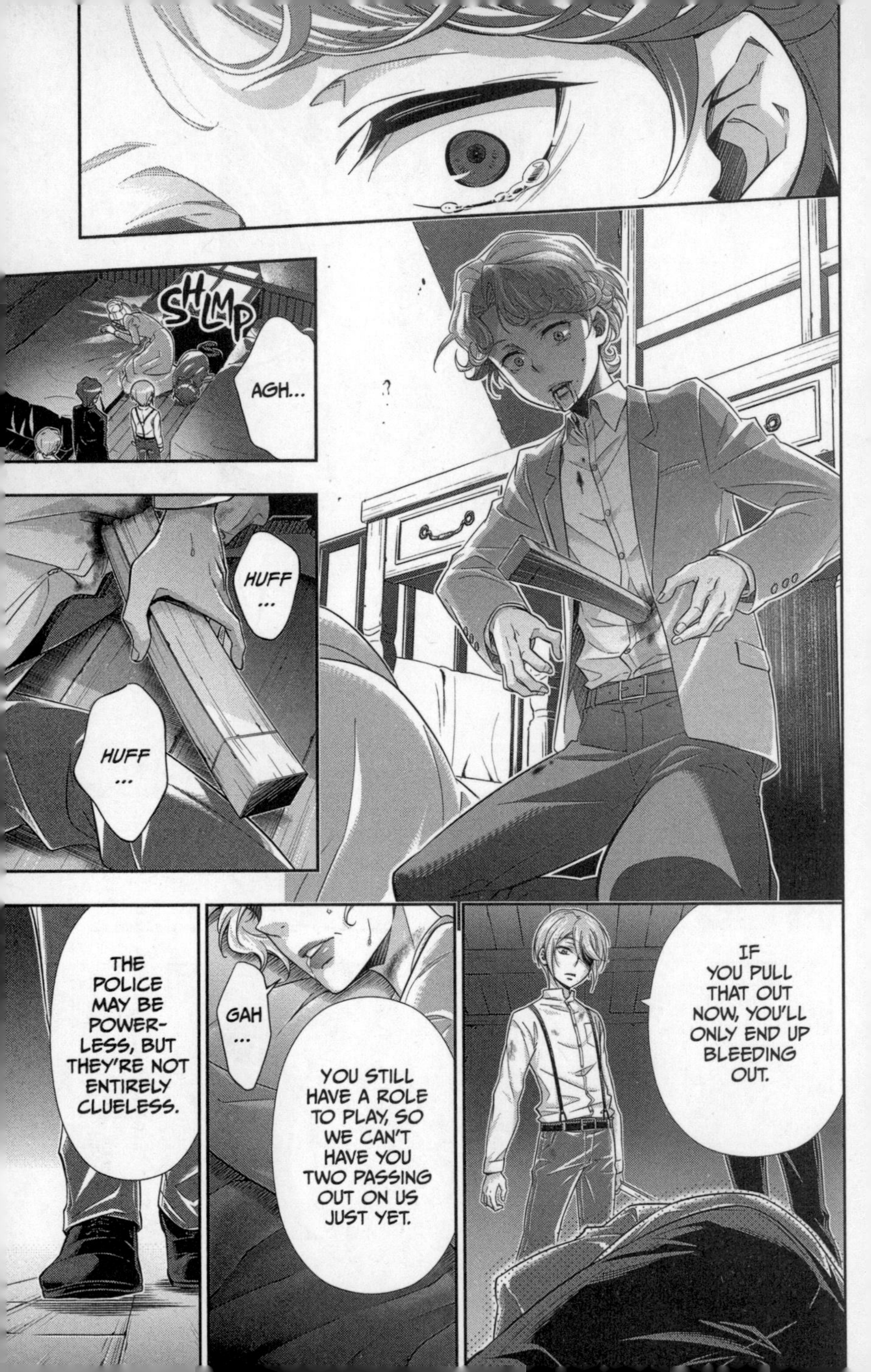
SHLMP
AGH...
HUFF ...
HUFF ...
IF YOU PULL THAT OUT NOW, YOU'LL ONLY END UP BLEEDING OUT.
GAH ...
YOU STILL HAVE A ROLE TO PLAY, SO WE CAN'T HAVE YOU TWO PASSING OUT ON US JUST YET.
THE POLICE MAY BE POWER-LESS, BUT THEY'RE NOT ENTIRELY CLUELESS.

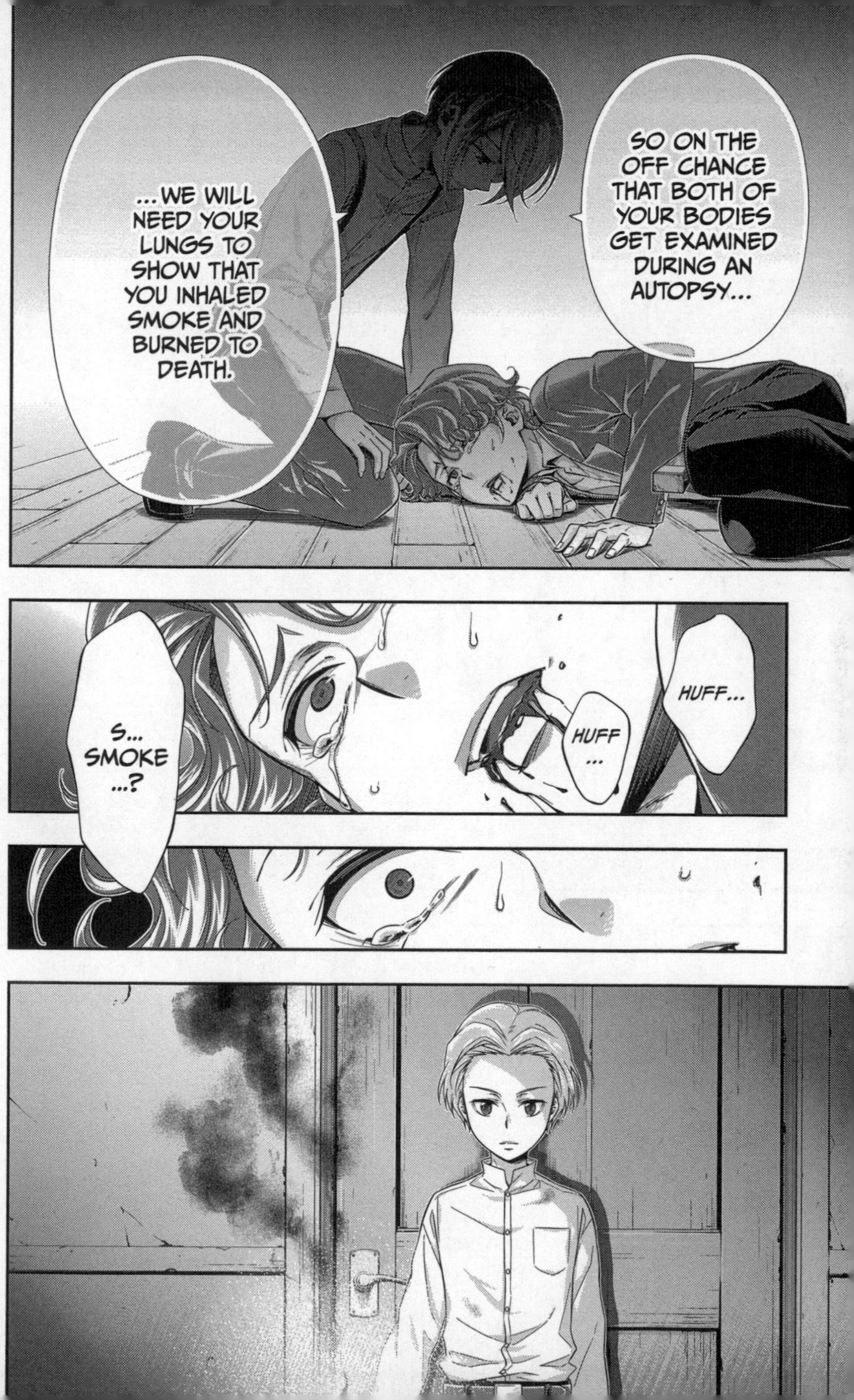
SO ON THE OFF CHANCE THAT BOTH OF YOUR BODIES GET EXAMINED DURING AN AUTOPSY...
...WE WILL NEED YOUR LUNGS TO SHOW THAT YOU INHALED SMOKE AND BURNED TO DEATH.
HUFF...
HUFF ...
S... SMOKE ...?

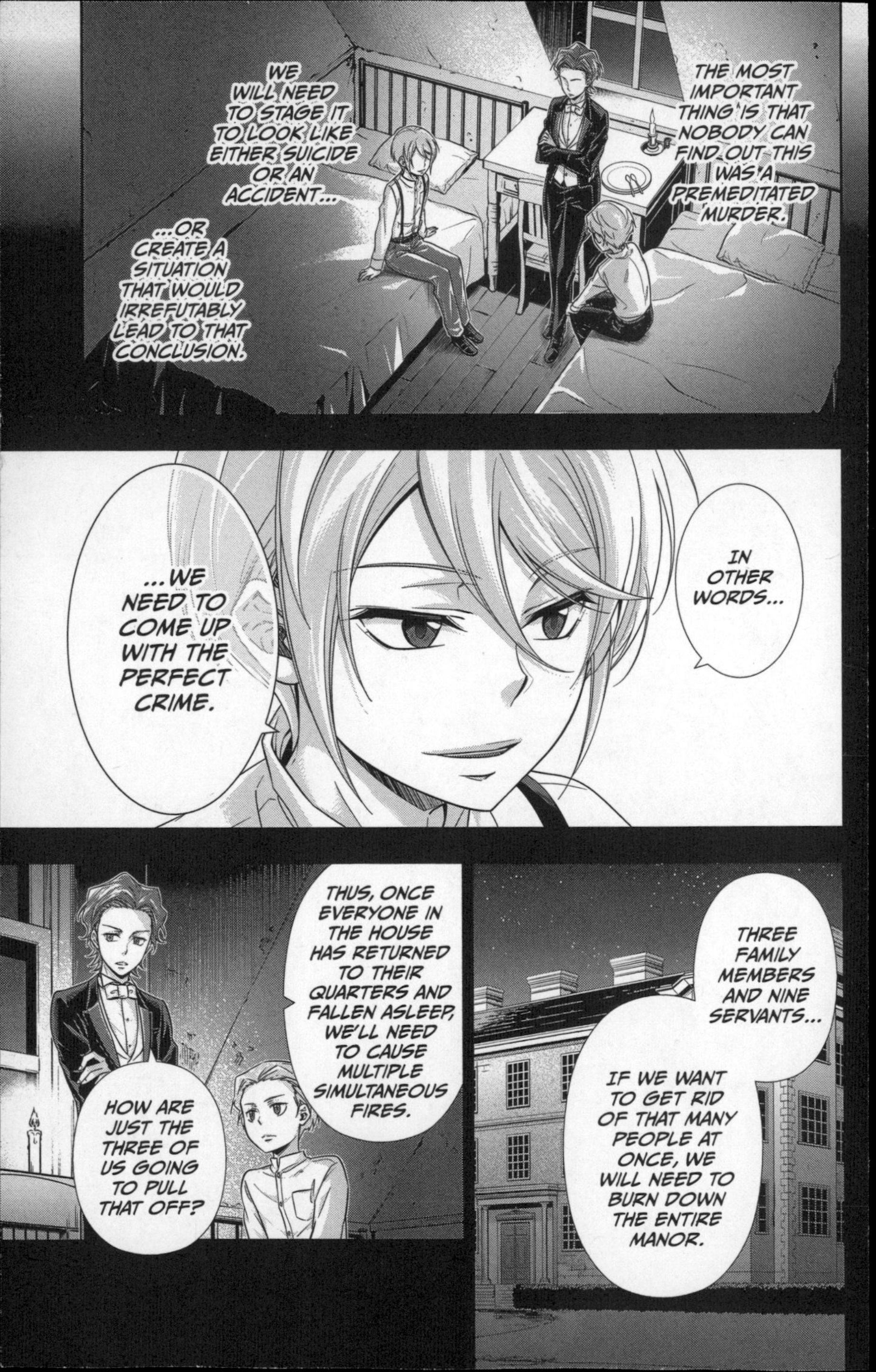
THE MOST IMPORTANT THING IS THAT NOBODY CAN FIND OUT THIS WAS A PREMEDITATED MURDER.
WE WILL NEED TO STAGE IT TO LOOK LIKE EITHER SUICIDE OR AN ACCIDENT...
...OR CREATE A SITUATION THAT WOULD IRREFUTABLY LEAD TO THAT CONCLUSION.
IN OTHER WORDS...
...WE NEED TO COME UP WITH THE PERFECT CRIME.
THREE FAMILY MEMBERS AND NINE SERVANTS...
IF WE WANT TO GET RID OF THAT MANY PEOPLE AT ONCE, WE WILL NEED TO BURN DOWN THE ENTIRE MANOR.
THUS, ONCE EVERYONE IN THE HOUSE HAS RETURNED TO THEIR QUARTERS AND FALLEN ASLEEP, WE'LL NEED TO CAUSE MULTIPLE SIMULTANEOUS FIRES.
HOW ARE JUST THE THREE OF US GOING TO PULL THAT OFF?

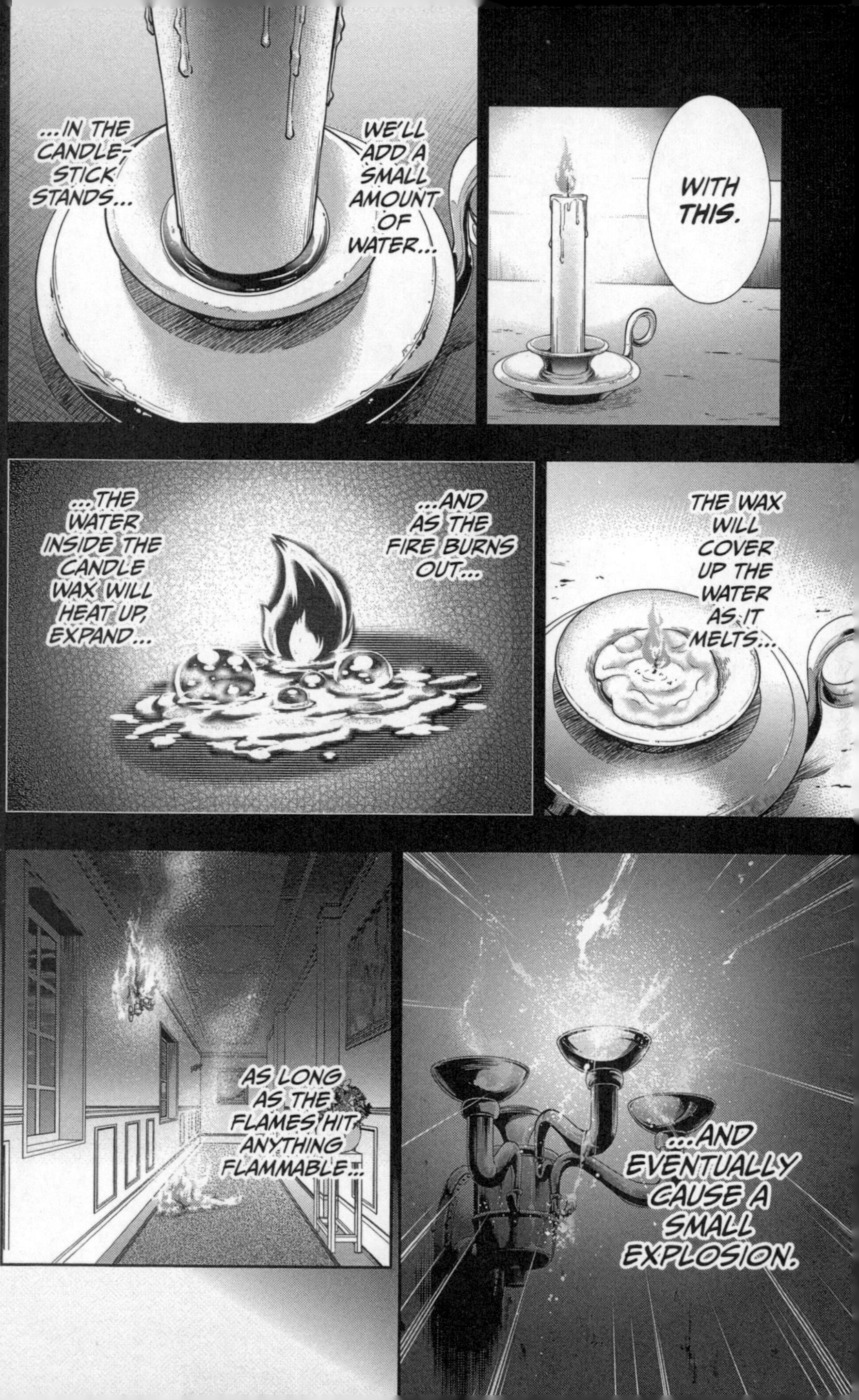
WITH THIS.
WE'LL ADD A SMALL AMOUNT OF WATER...
...IN THE CANDLE-STICK STANDS...
THE WAX WILL COVER UP THE WATER AS IT MELTS...
...AND AS THE FIRE BURNS OUT...
...THE WATER INSIDE THE CANDLE WAX WILL HEAT UP, EXPAND...
...AND EVENTUALLY CAUSE A SMALL EXPLOSION.
AS LONG AS THE FLAMES HIT ANYTHING FLAMMABLE...

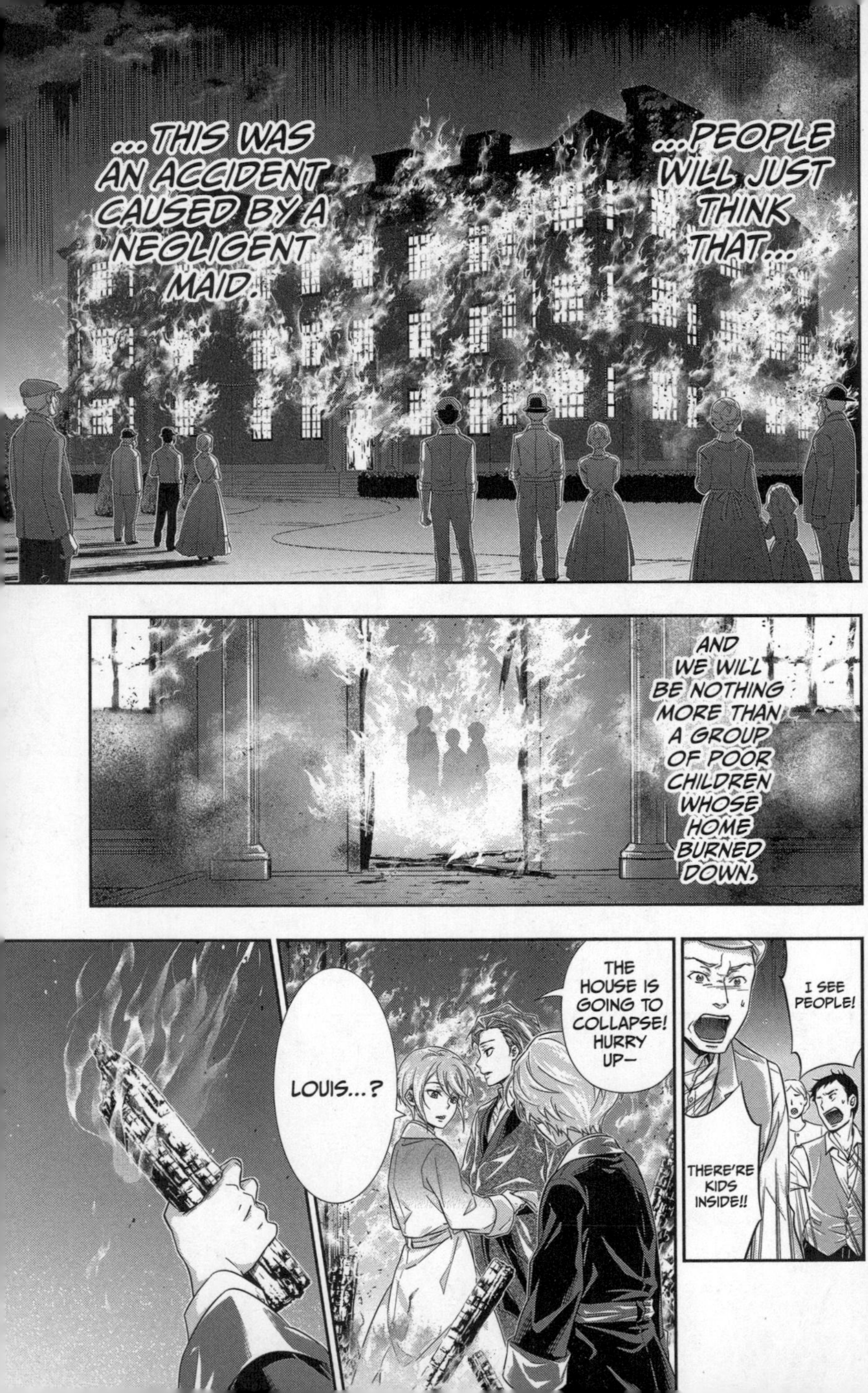
...PEOPLE WILL JUST THINK THAT...
...THIS WAS AN ACCIDENT CAUSED BY A NEGLIGENT MAID.
AND WE WILL BE NOTHING MORE THAN A GROUP OF POOR CHILDREN WHOSE HOME BURNED DOWN.
I SEE PEOPLE!
THERE'RE KIDS INSIDE!!
THE HOUSE IS GOING TO COLLAPSE! HURRY UP—
LOUIS...?

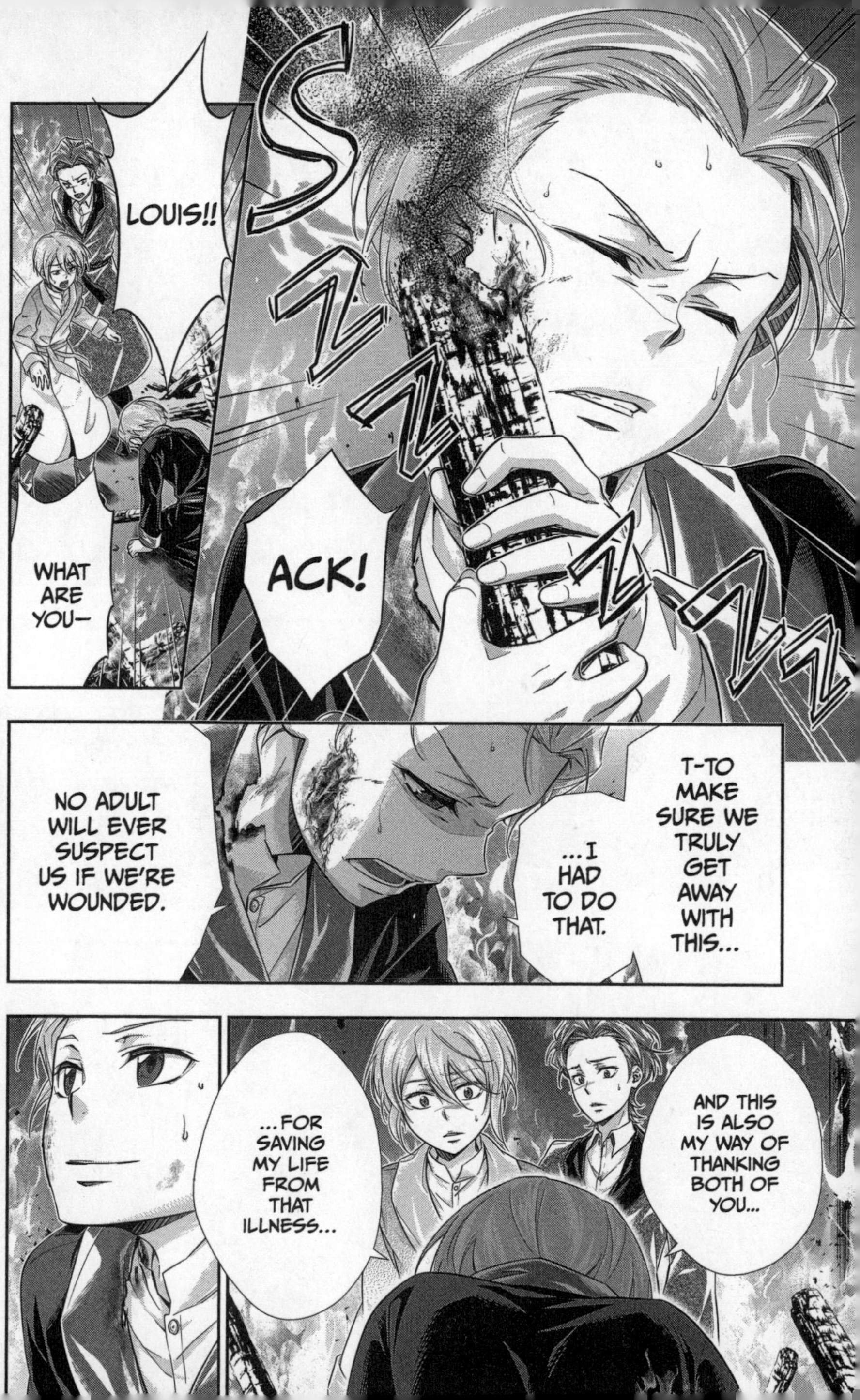
SZZZZZZ
ACK!
LOUIS!!
WHAT ARE YOU—
T-TO MAKE SURE WE TRULY GET AWAY WITH THIS...
...I HAD TO DO THAT.
NO ADULT WILL EVER SUSPECT US IF WE'RE WOUNDED.
AND THIS IS ALSO MY WAY OF THANKING BOTH OF YOU...
...FOR SAVING MY LIFE FROM THAT ILLNESS...

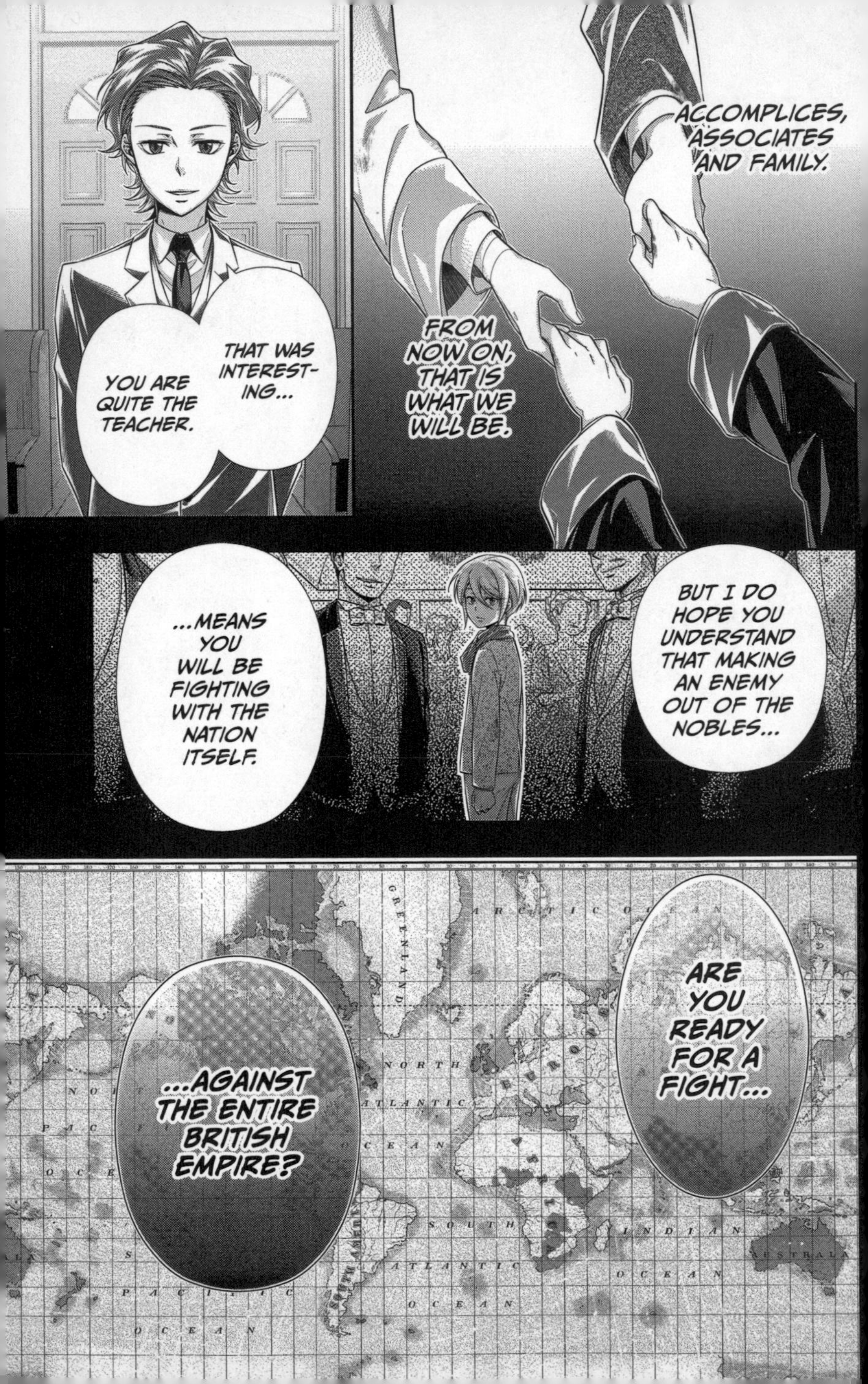
ACCOMPLICES, ASSOCIATES AND FAMILY.
FROM NOW ON, THAT IS WHAT WE WILL BE.
THAT WAS INTEREST-ING...
YOU ARE QUITE THE TEACHER.
BUT I DO HOPE YOU UNDERSTAND THAT MAKING AN ENEMY OUT OF THE NOBLES...
...MEANS YOU WILL BE FIGHTING WITH THE NATION ITSELF.
ARE YOU READY FOR A FIGHT...
...AGAINST THE ENTIRE BRITISH EMPIRE?

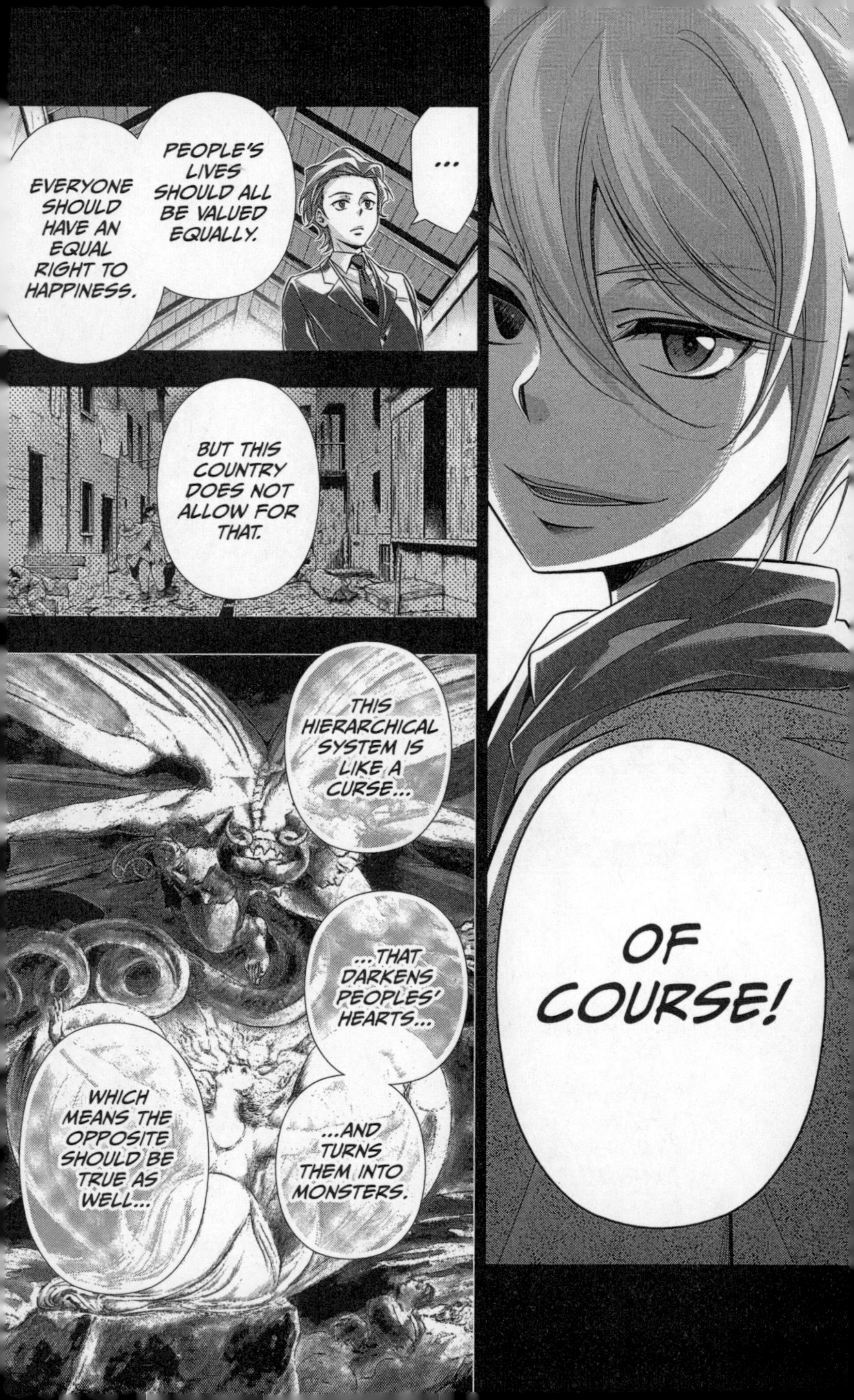
OF COURSE!
...
PEOPLE'S LIVES SHOULD ALL BE VALUED EQUALLY.
EVERYONE SHOULD HAVE AN EQUAL RIGHT TO HAPPINESS.
BUT THIS COUNTRY DOES NOT ALLOW FOR THAT.
THIS HIERARCHICAL SYSTEM IS LIKE A CURSE...
...THAT DARKENS PEOPLES' HEARTS...
...AND TURNS THEM INTO MONSTERS.
WHICH MEANS THE OPPOSITE SHOULD BE TRUE AS WELL...

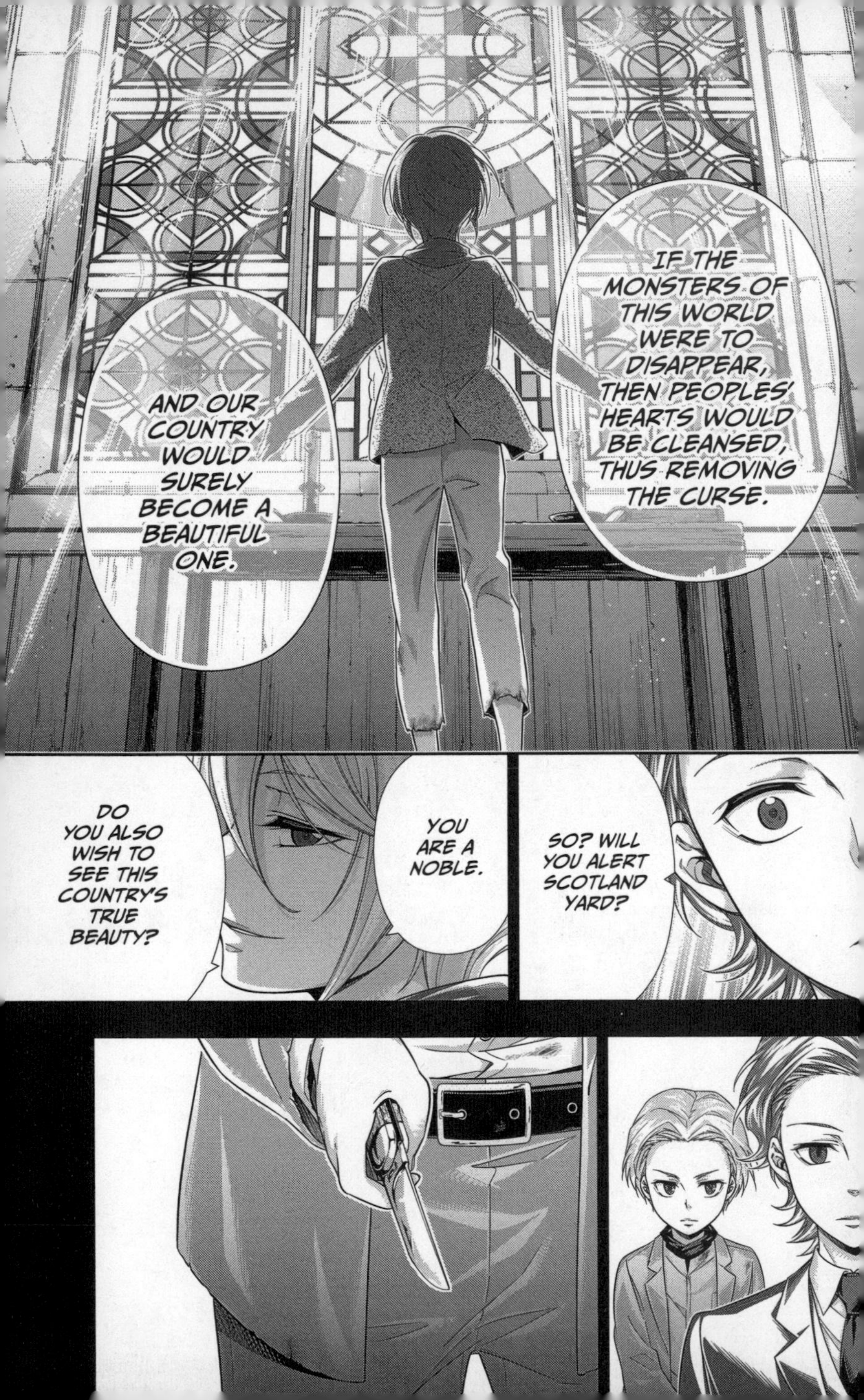
IF THE MONSTERS OF THIS WORLD WERE TO DISAPPEAR, THEN PEOPLES' HEARTS WOULD BE CLEANSED, THUS REMOVING THE CURSE.
AND OUR COUNTRY WOULD SURELY BECOME A BEAUTIFUL ONE.
SO? WILL YOU ALERT SCOTLAND YARD?
YOU ARE A NOBLE.
DO YOU ALSO WISH TO SEE THIS COUNTRY'S TRUE BEAUTY?

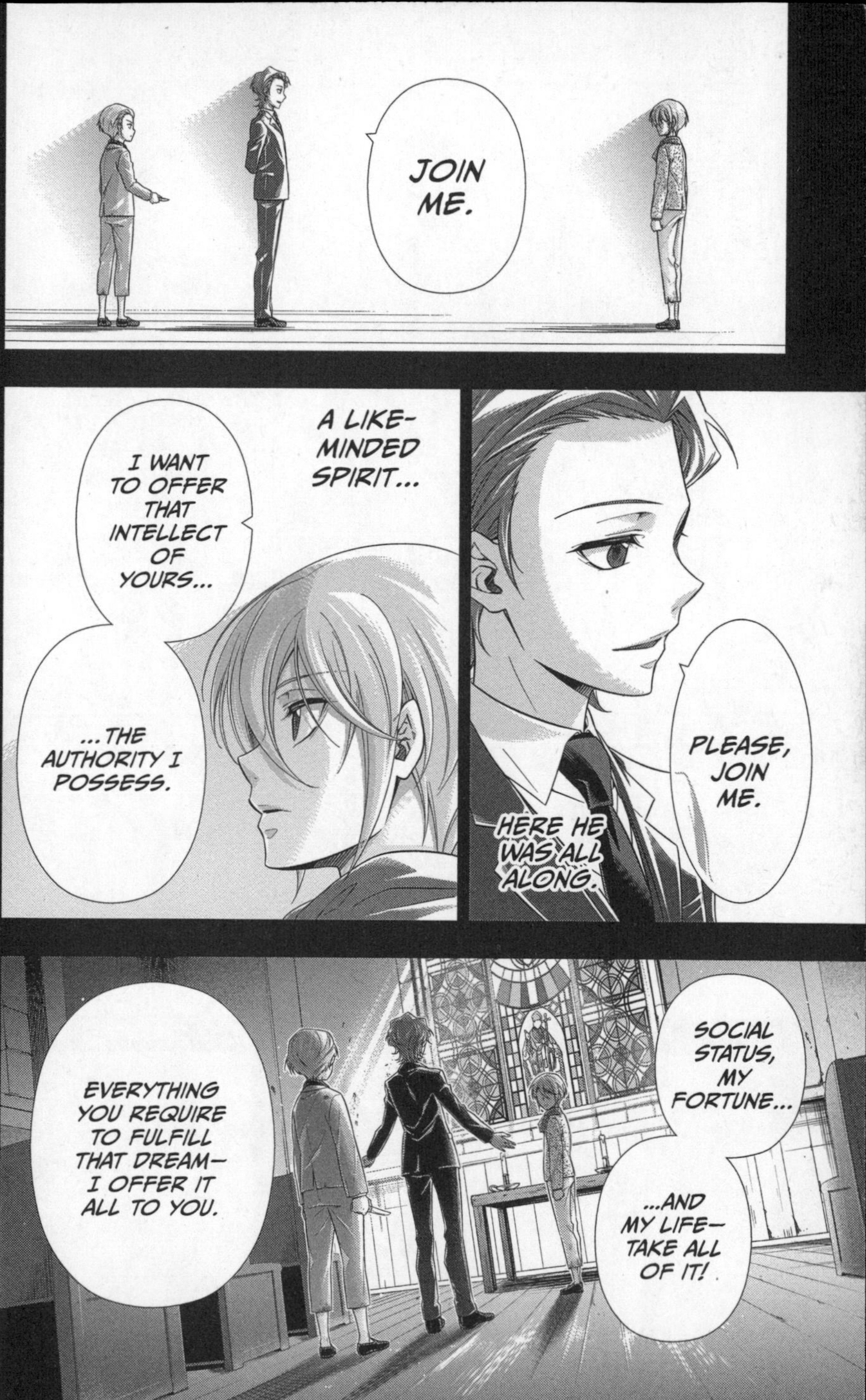
JOIN ME.
PLEASE, JOIN ME.
HERE HE WAS ALL ALONG.
A LIKE-MINDED SPIRIT...
I WANT TO OFFER THAT INTELLECT OF YOURS...
...THE AUTHORITY I POSSESS.
SOCIAL STATUS, MY FORTUNE...
...AND MY LIFE—TAKE ALL OF IT!
EVERYTHING YOU REQUIRE TO FULFILL THAT DREAM—I OFFER IT ALL TO YOU.

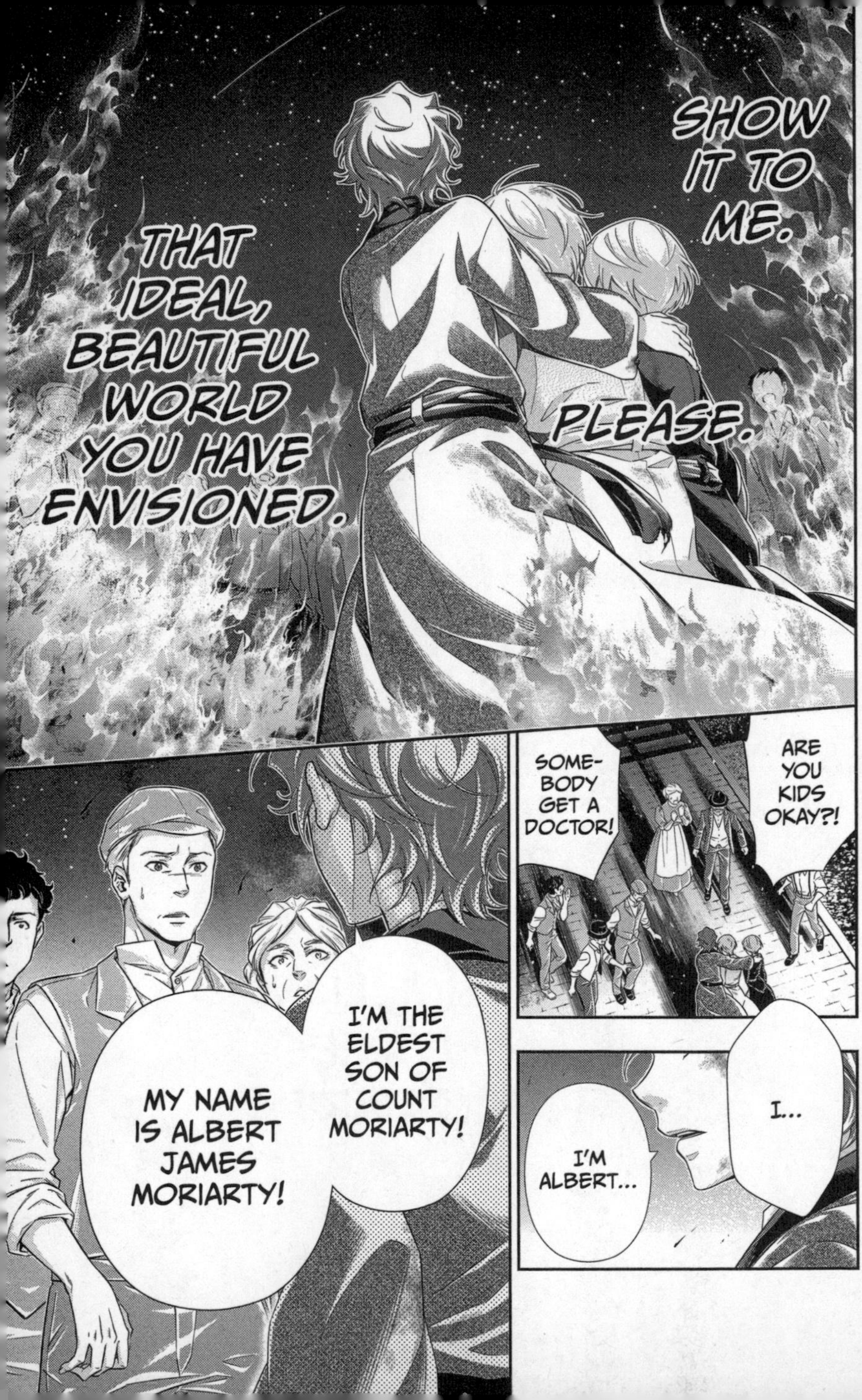
SHOW IT TO ME.
THAT IDEAL, BEAUTIFUL WORLD YOU HAVE ENVISIONED.
PLEASE.
ARE YOU KIDS OKAY?!
SOME-BODY GET A DOCTOR!
I...
I'M ALBERT...
MY NAME IS ALBERT JAMES MORIARTY!
I'M THE ELDEST SON OF COUNT MORIARTY!

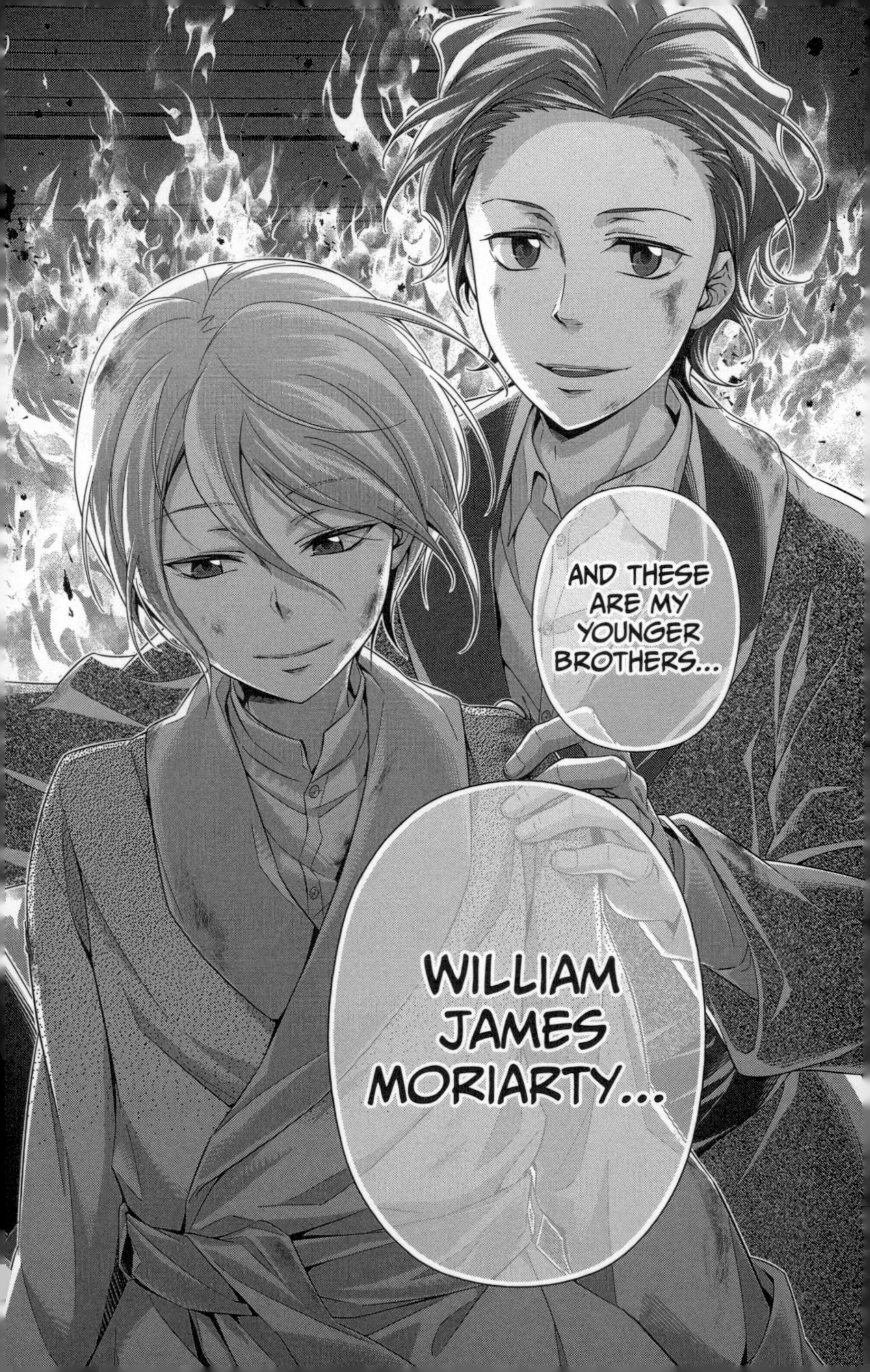
AND THESE ARE MY YOUNGER BROTHERS...
WILLIAM JAMES MORIARTY...

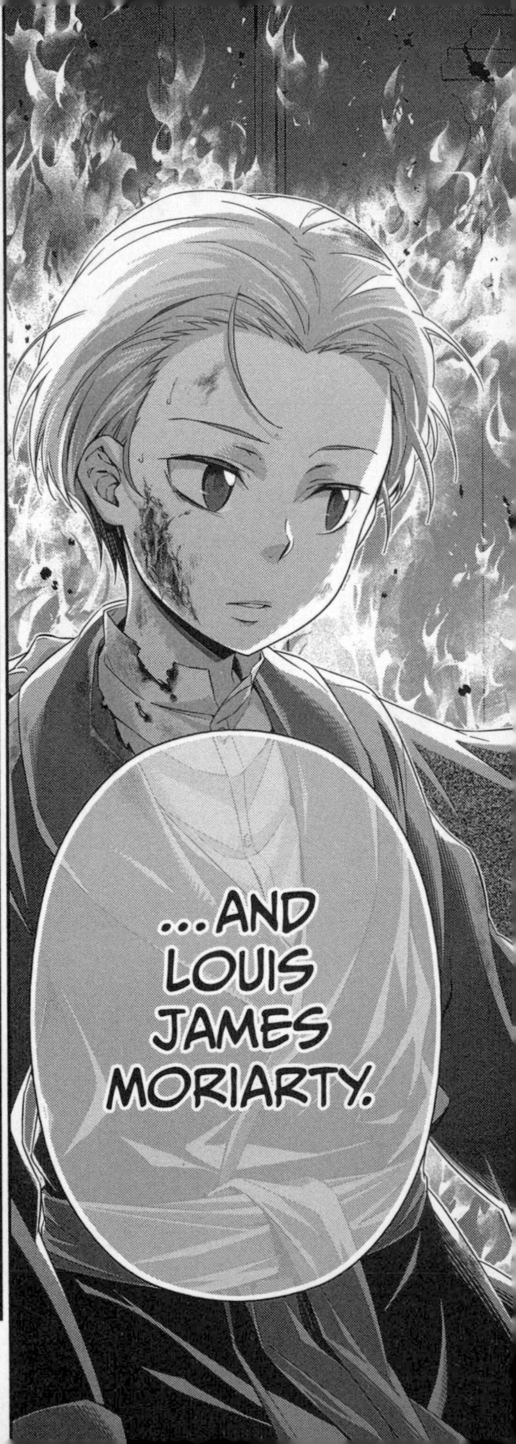
...AND LOUIS JAMES MORIARTY.

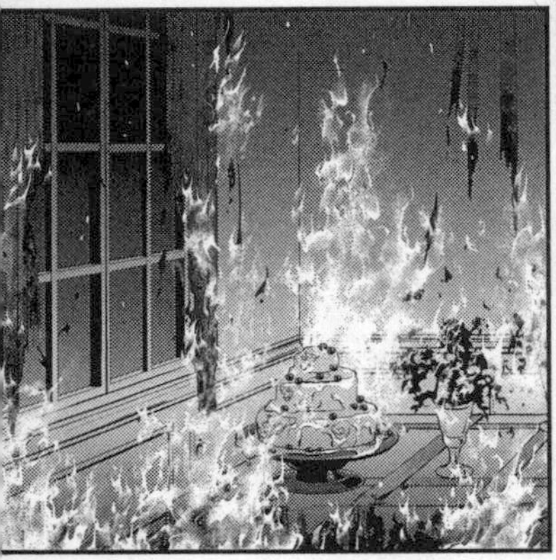

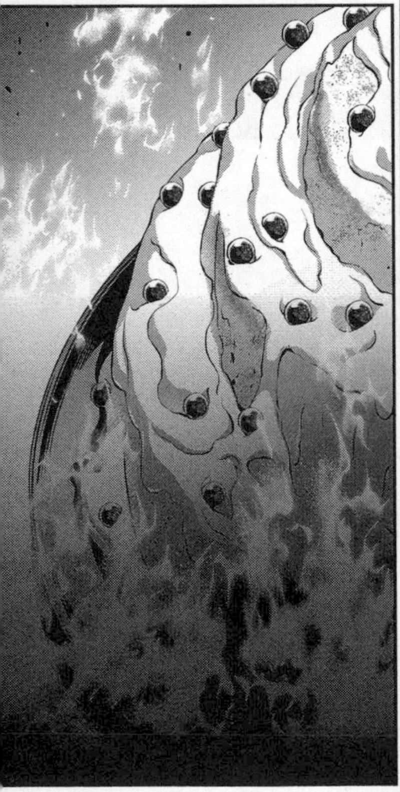

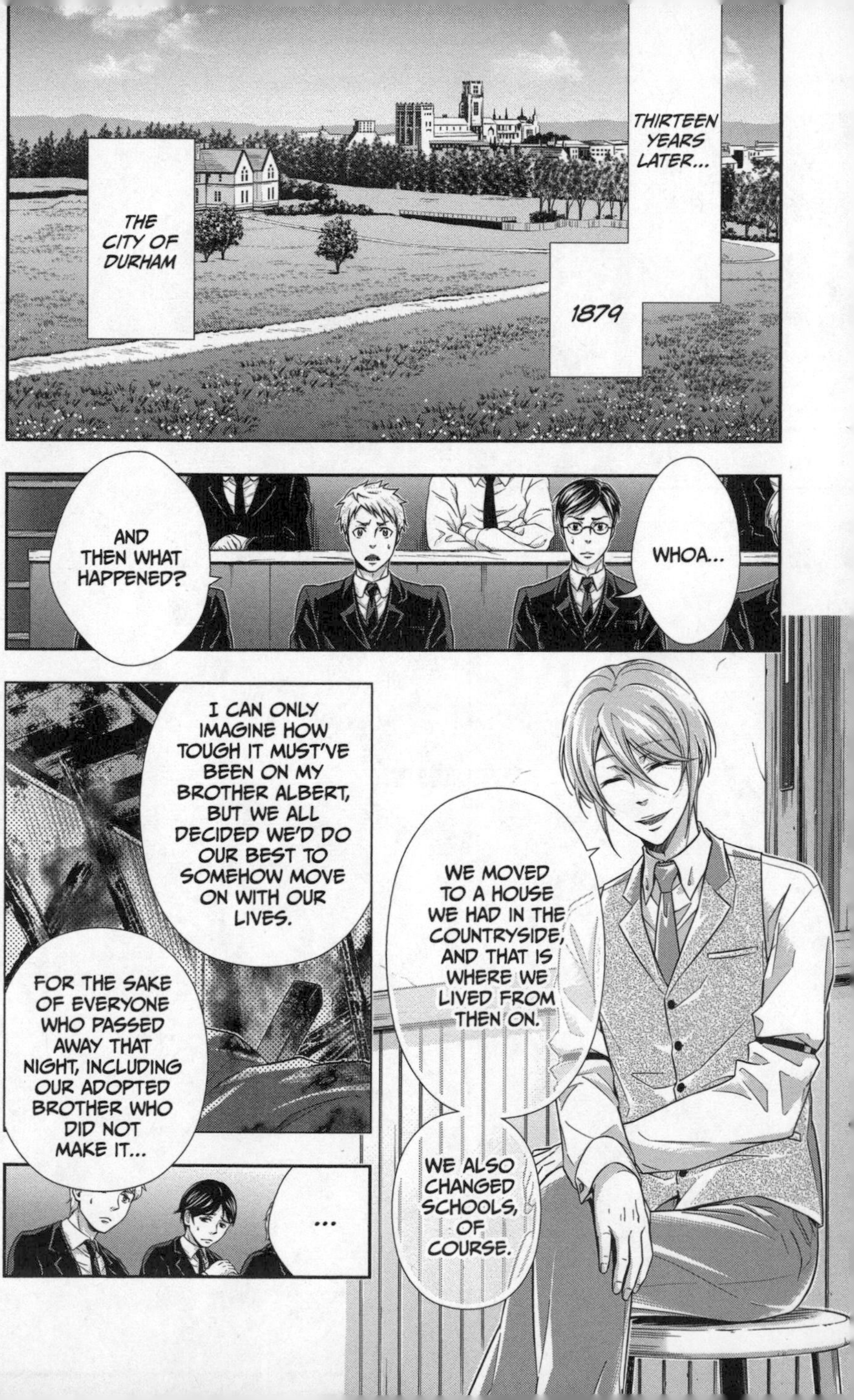
THIRTEEN YEARS LATER...
1879
THE CITY OF DURHAM
WHOA...
AND THEN WHAT HAPPENED?
WE MOVED TO A HOUSE WE HAD IN THE COUNTRYSIDE, AND THAT IS WHERE WE LIVED FROM THEN ON.
WE ALSO CHANGED SCHOOLS, OF COURSE.
I CAN ONLY IMAGINE HOW TOUGH IT MUST'VE BEEN ON MY BROTHER ALBERT, BUT WE ALL DECIDED WE'D DO OUR BEST TO SOMEHOW MOVE ON WITH OUR LIVES.
FOR THE SAKE OF EVERYONE WHO PASSED AWAY THAT NIGHT, INCLUDING OUR ADOPTED BROTHER WHO DID NOT MAKE IT...
...

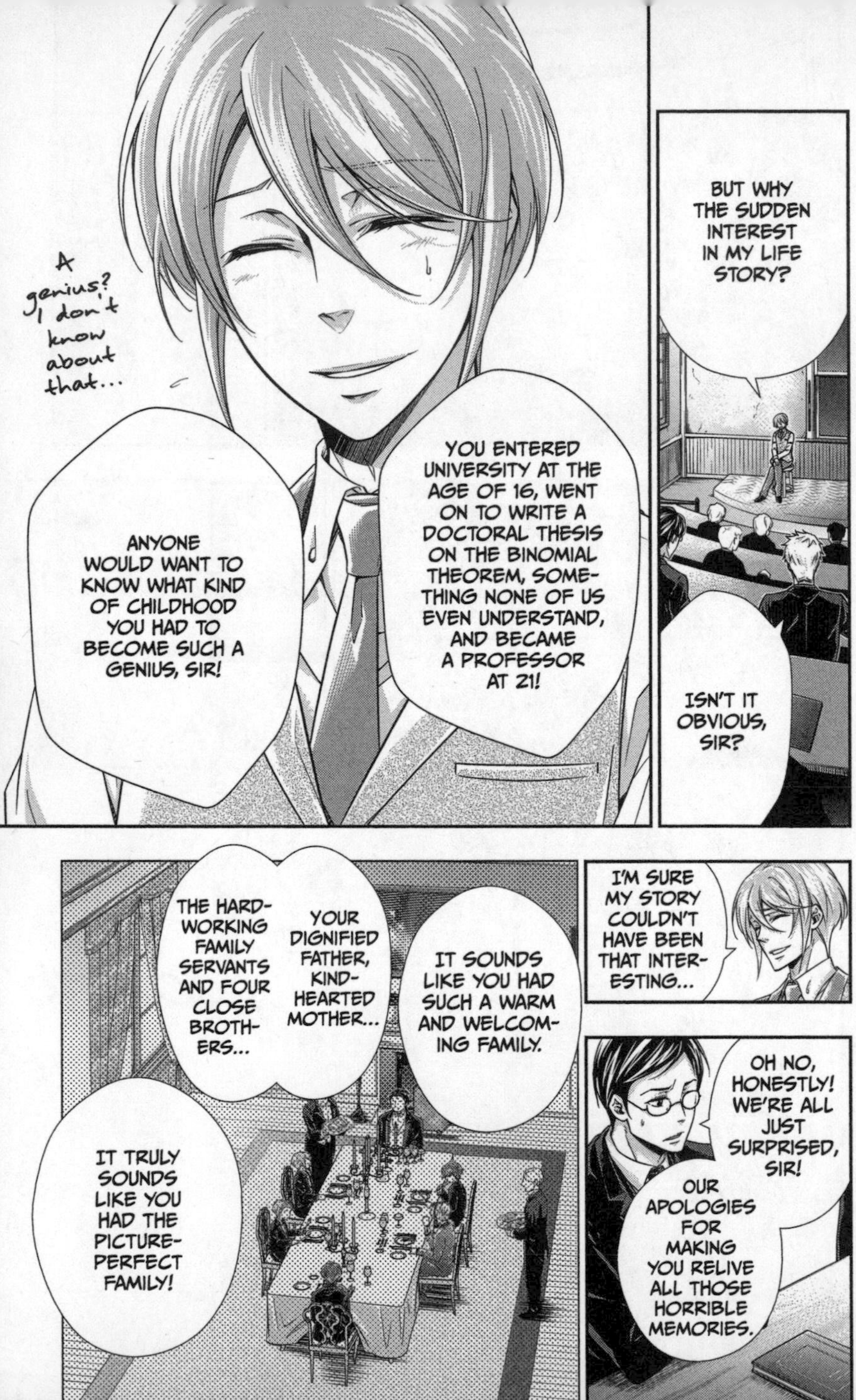
BUT WHY THE SUDDEN INTEREST IN MY LIFE STORY?
ISN'T IT OBVIOUS, SIR?
YOU ENTERED UNIVERSITY AT THE AGE OF 16, WENT ON TO WRITE A DOCTORAL THESIS ON THE BINOMIAL THEOREM, SOMETHING NONE OF US EVEN UNDERSTAND, AND BECAME A PROFESSOR AT 21!
ANYONE WOULD WANT TO KNOW WHAT KIND OF CHILDHOOD YOU HAD TO BECOME SUCH A GENIUS, SIR!
A genius? I don't know about that...
I'M SURE MY STORY COULDN'T HAVE BEEN THAT INTERESTING...
OH NO, HONESTLY! WE'RE ALL JUST SURPRISED, SIR!
OUR APOLOGIES FOR MAKING YOU RELIVE ALL THOSE HORRIBLE MEMORIES.
IT SOUNDS LIKE YOU HAD SUCH A WARM AND WELCOMING FAMILY.
YOUR DIGNIFIED FATHER, KIND-HEARTED MOTHER...
THE HARD-WORKING FAMILY SERVANTS AND FOUR CLOSE BROTHERS...
IT TRULY SOUNDS LIKE YOU HAD THE PICTURE-PERFECT FAMILY!

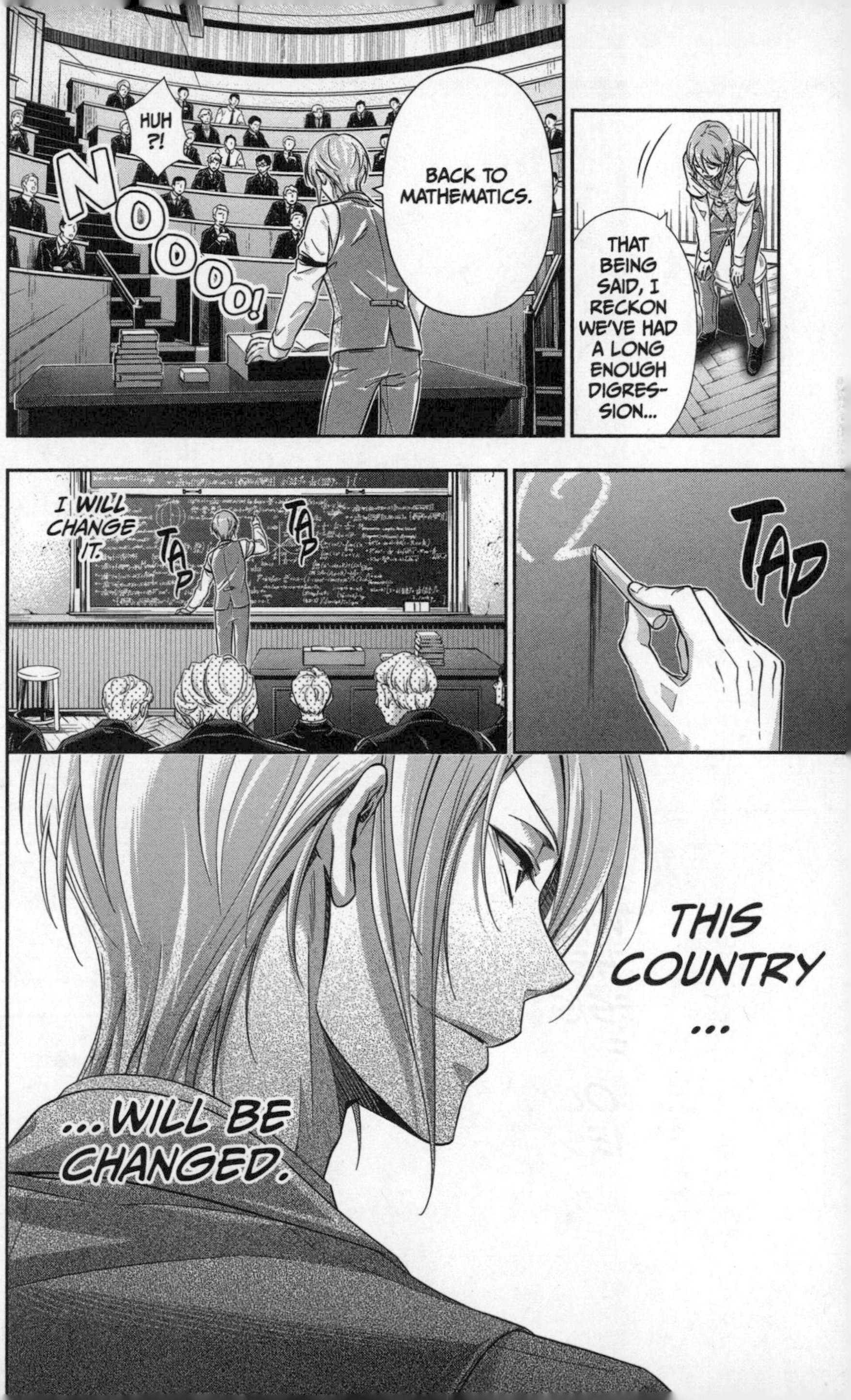
THAT BEING SAID, I RECKON WE'VE HAD A LONG ENOUGH DIGRES-SION...
BACK TO MATHEMATICS.
HUH ?!
NOOOO!
TAP
I WILL CHANGE IT.
TAP
TAP
THIS COUNTRY ...
...WILL BE CHANGED.

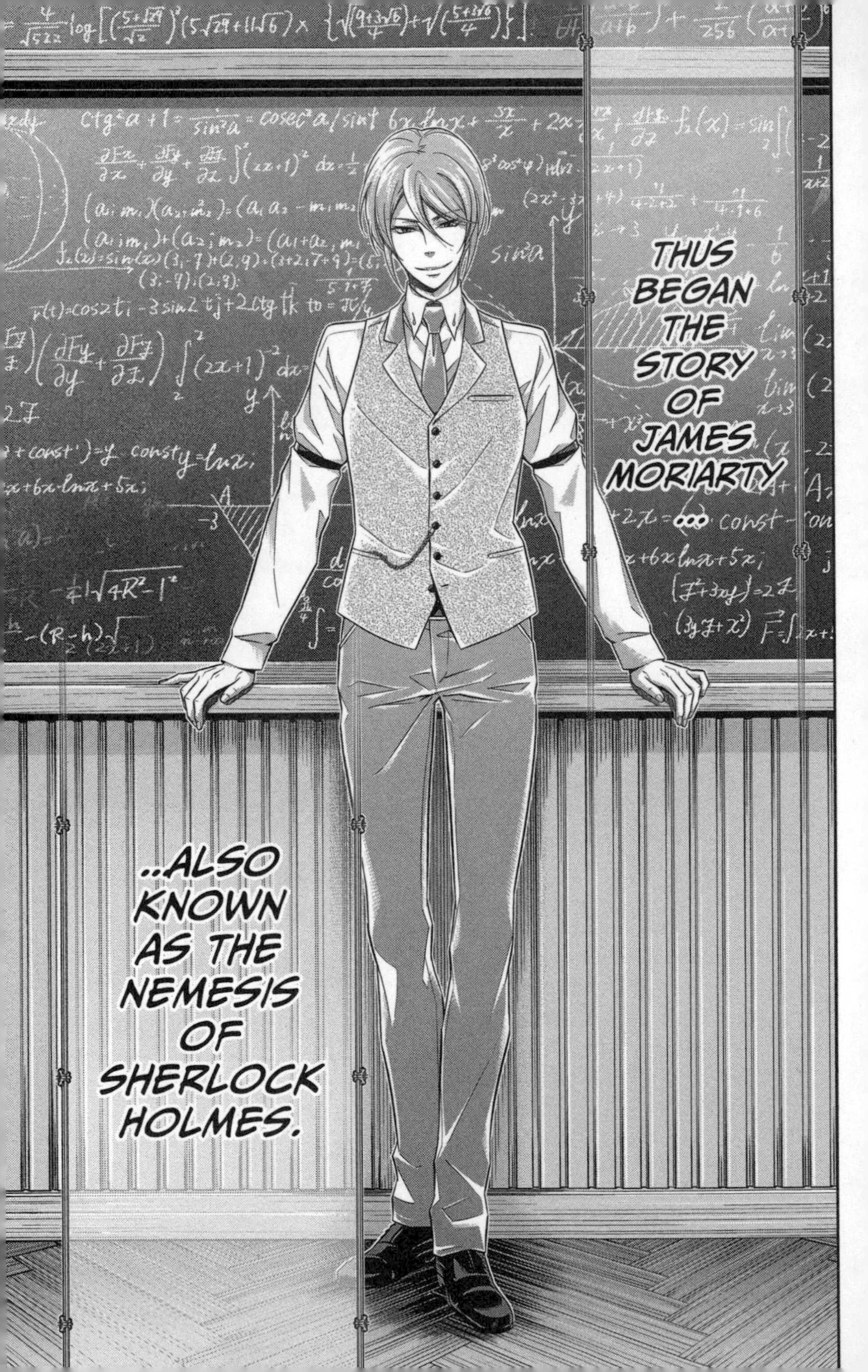
THUS BEGAN THE STORY OF JAMES MORIARTY...
..ALSO KNOWN AS THE NEMESIS OF SHERLOCK HOLMES.

What are you reading now, Brother?
This, Louis, is a book on housekeeping. It explains how to use candles and such...
You never know when something will come in handy.

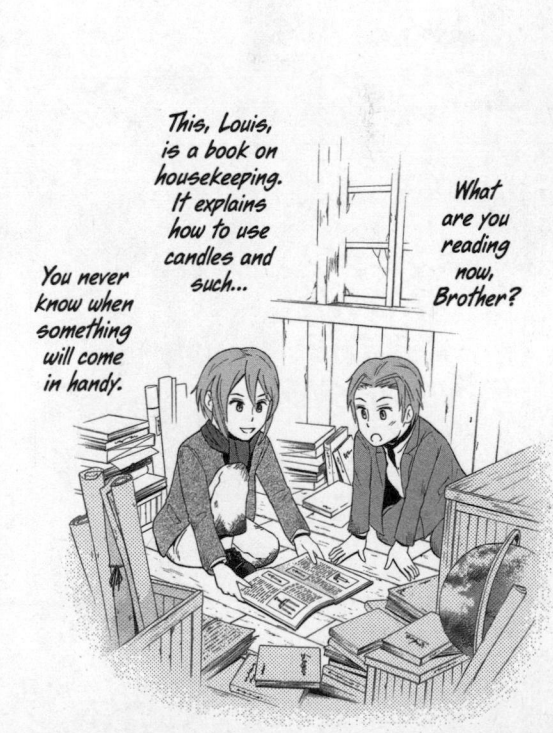

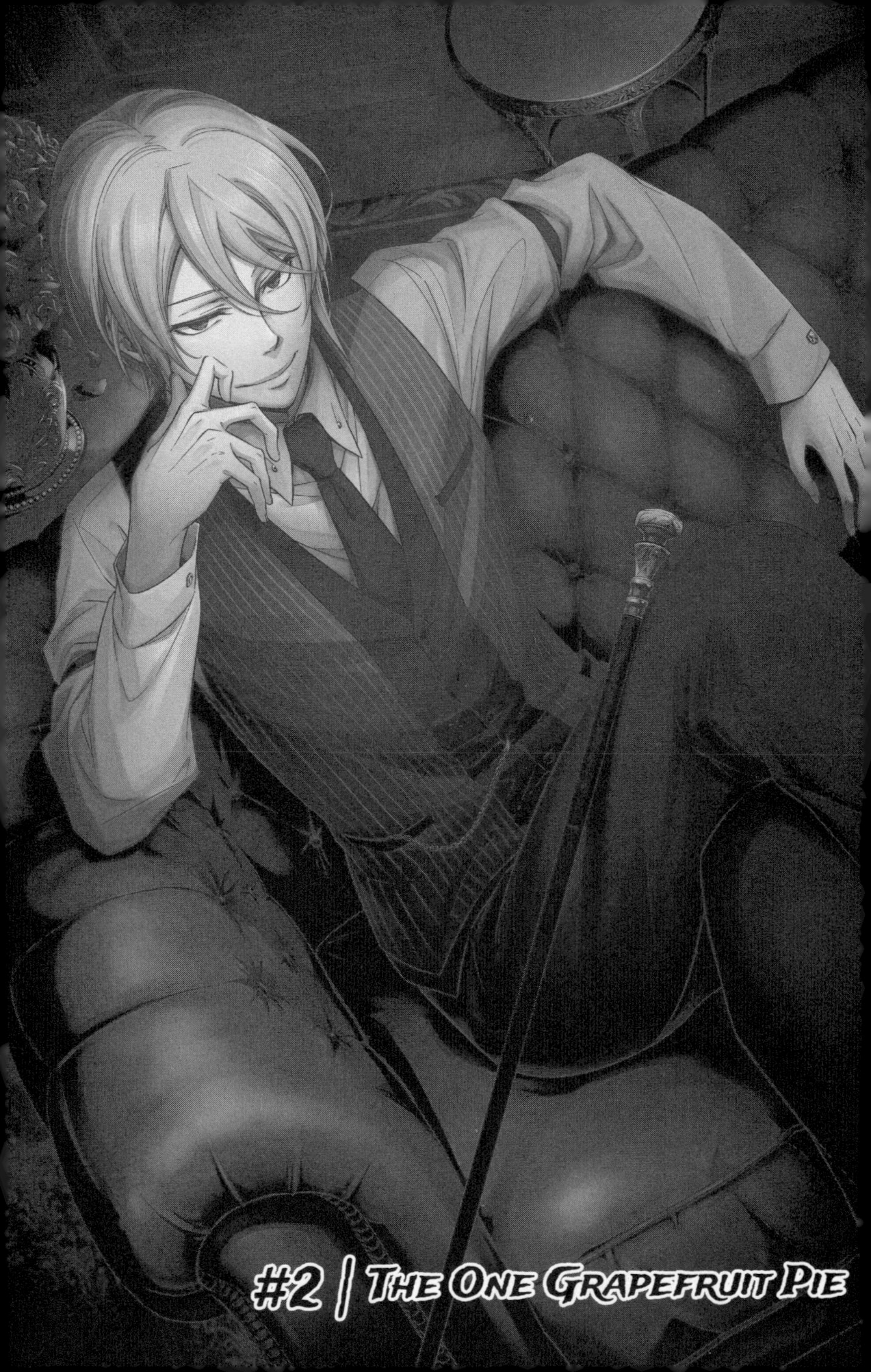

#2 | The One Grapefruit Pie

MORIARTY
THE PATRIOT

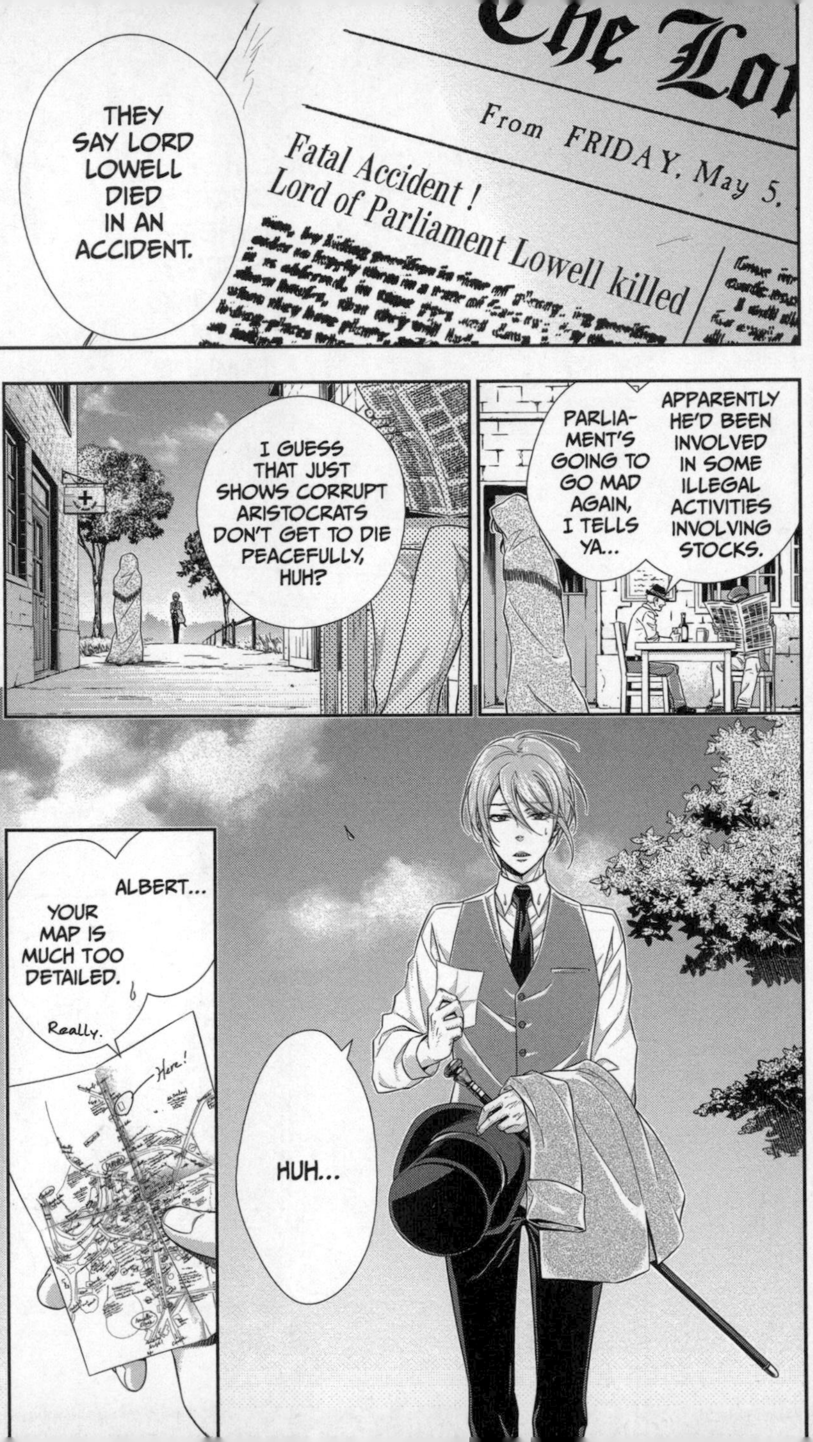
From FRIDAY, May 5,
Fatal Accident ! Lord of Parliament Lowell killed
THEY SAY LORD LOWELL DIED IN AN ACCIDENT.
APPARENTLY HE'D BEEN INVOLVED IN SOME ILLEGAL ACTIVITIES INVOLVING STOCKS.
PARLIA-MENT'S GOING TO GO MAD AGAIN, I TELLS YA...
I GUESS THAT JUST SHOWS CORRUPT ARISTOCRATS DON'T GET TO DIE PEACEFULLY, HUH?
HUH...
ALBERT... YOUR MAP IS MUCH TOO DETAILED.
Really.
Here!

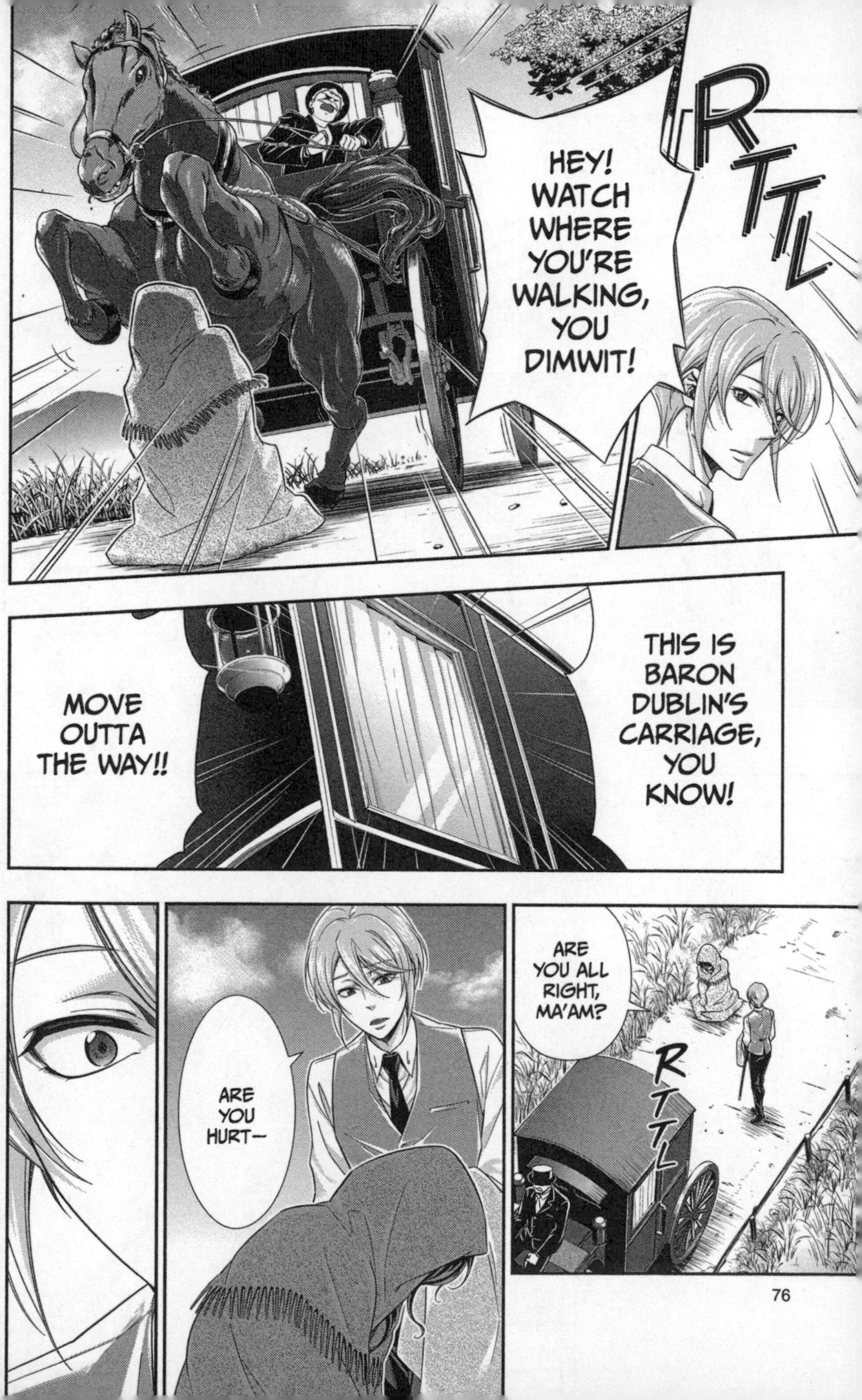
RTTL
HEY! WATCH WHERE YOU'RE WALKING, YOU DIMWIT!
THIS IS BARON DUBLIN'S CARRIAGE, YOU KNOW!
MOVE OUTTA THE WAY!!
ARE YOU ALL RIGHT, MA'AM?
RTTL
ARE YOU HURT—

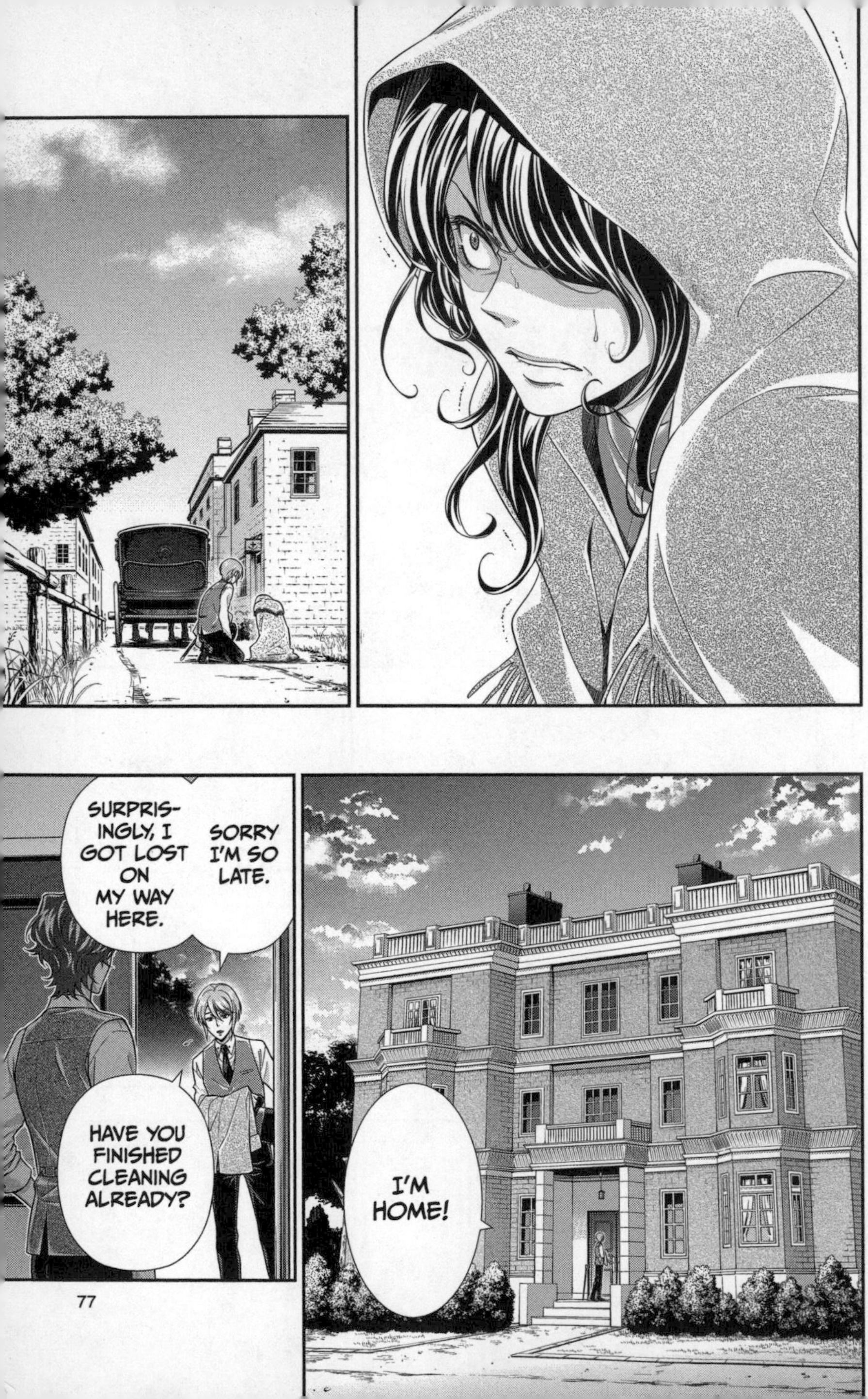
I'M HOME!
SORRY I'M SO LATE.
SURPRIS-INGLY, I GOT LOST ON MY WAY HERE.
HAVE YOU FINISHED CLEANING ALREADY?

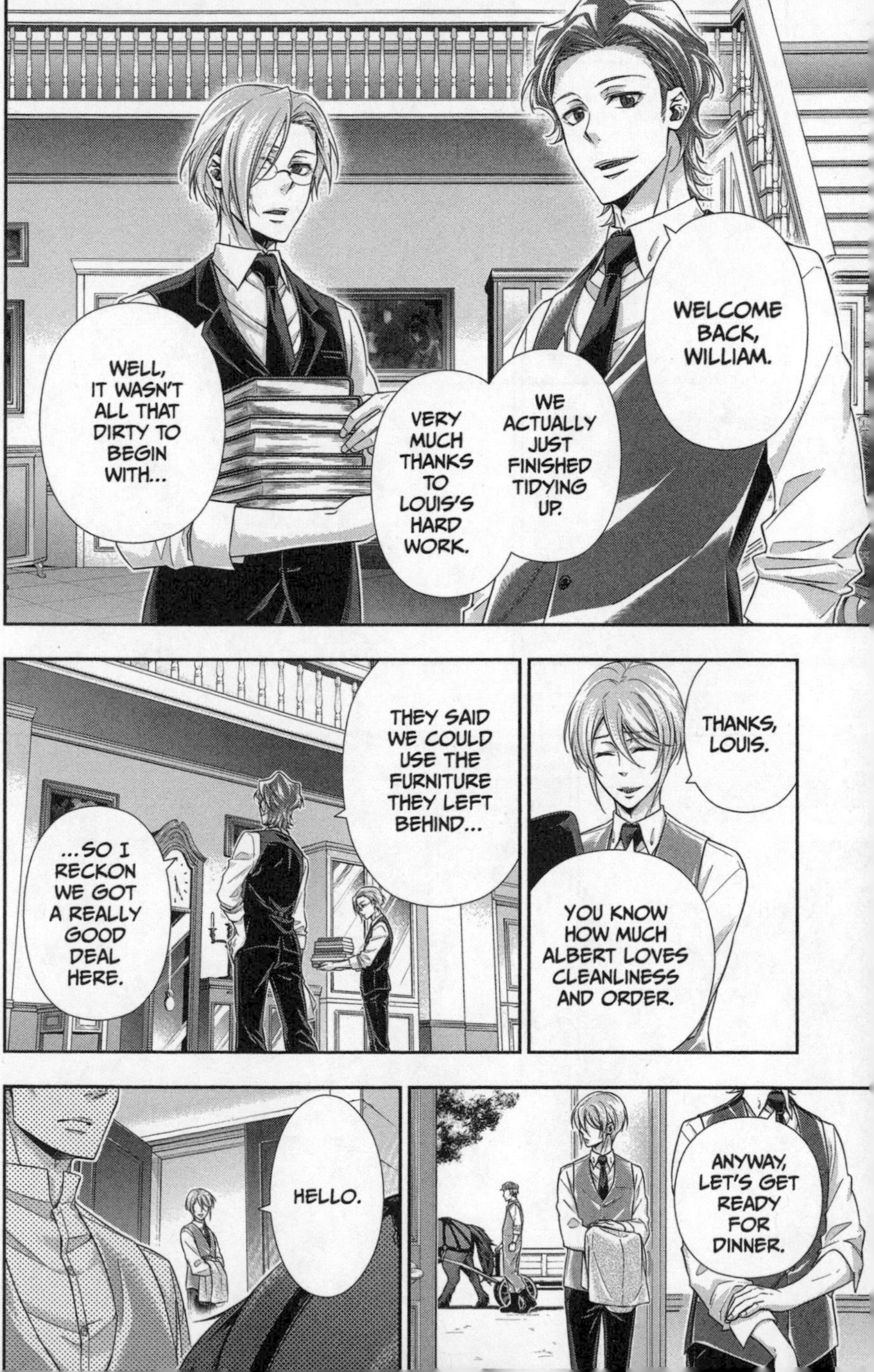
WELCOME BACK, WILLIAM.
WE ACTUALLY JUST FINISHED TIDYING UP.
VERY MUCH THANKS TO LOUIS'S HARD WORK.
WELL, IT WASN'T ALL THAT DIRTY TO BEGIN WITH...
THANKS, LOUIS.
YOU KNOW HOW MUCH ALBERT LOVES CLEANLINESS AND ORDER.
THEY SAID WE COULD USE THE FURNITURE THEY LEFT BEHIND...
...SO I RECKON WE GOT A REALLY GOOD DEAL HERE.
ANYWAY, LET'S GET READY FOR DINNER.
HELLO.

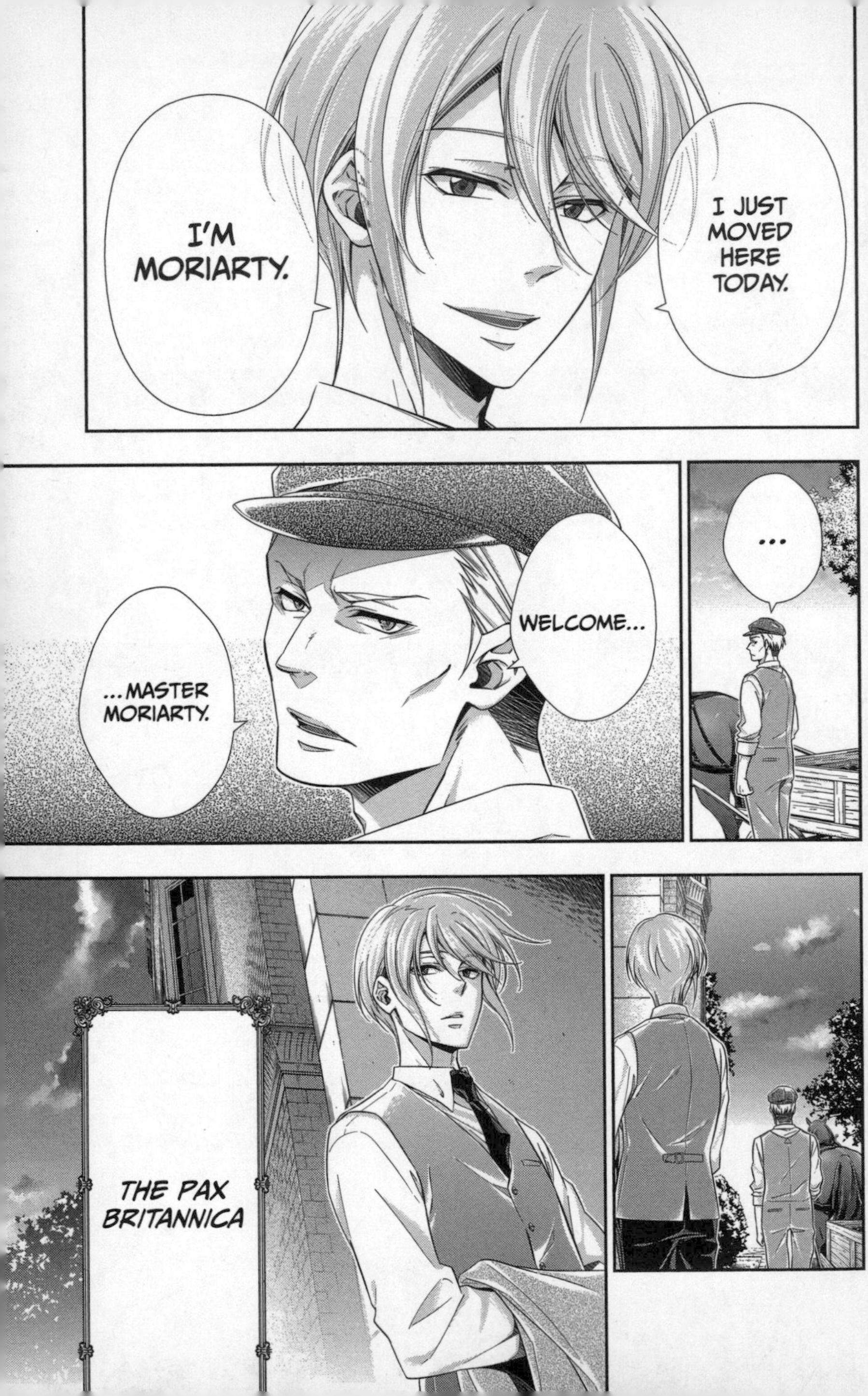
I JUST MOVED HERE TODAY.
I'M MORIARTY.
...
WELCOME...
...MASTER MORIARTY.
THE PAX BRITANNICA

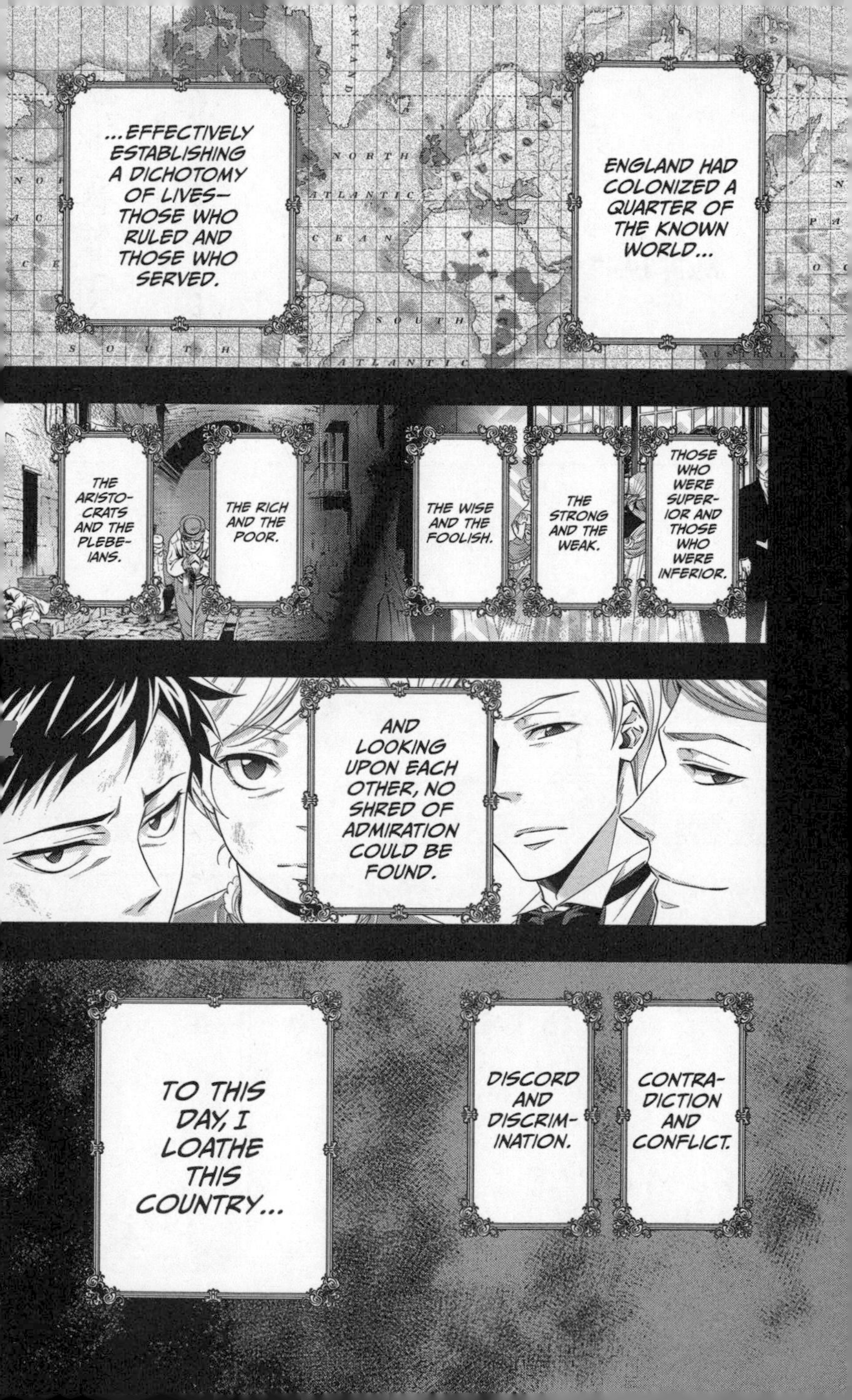
ENGLAND HAD COLONIZED A QUARTER OF THE KNOWN WORLD...
...EFFECTIVELY ESTABLISHING A DICHOTOMY OF LIVES—THOSE WHO RULED AND THOSE WHO SERVED.
THOSE WHO WERE SUPERIOR AND THOSE WHO WERE INFERIOR.
THE STRONG AND THE WEAK.
THE WISE AND THE FOOLISH.
THE RICH AND THE POOR.
THE ARISTOCRATS AND THE PLEBEIANS.
AND LOOKING UPON EACH OTHER, NO SHRED OF ADMIRATION COULD BE FOUND.
CONTRADICTION AND CONFLICT.
DISCORD AND DISCRIMINATION.
TO THIS DAY, I LOATHE THIS COUNTRY...

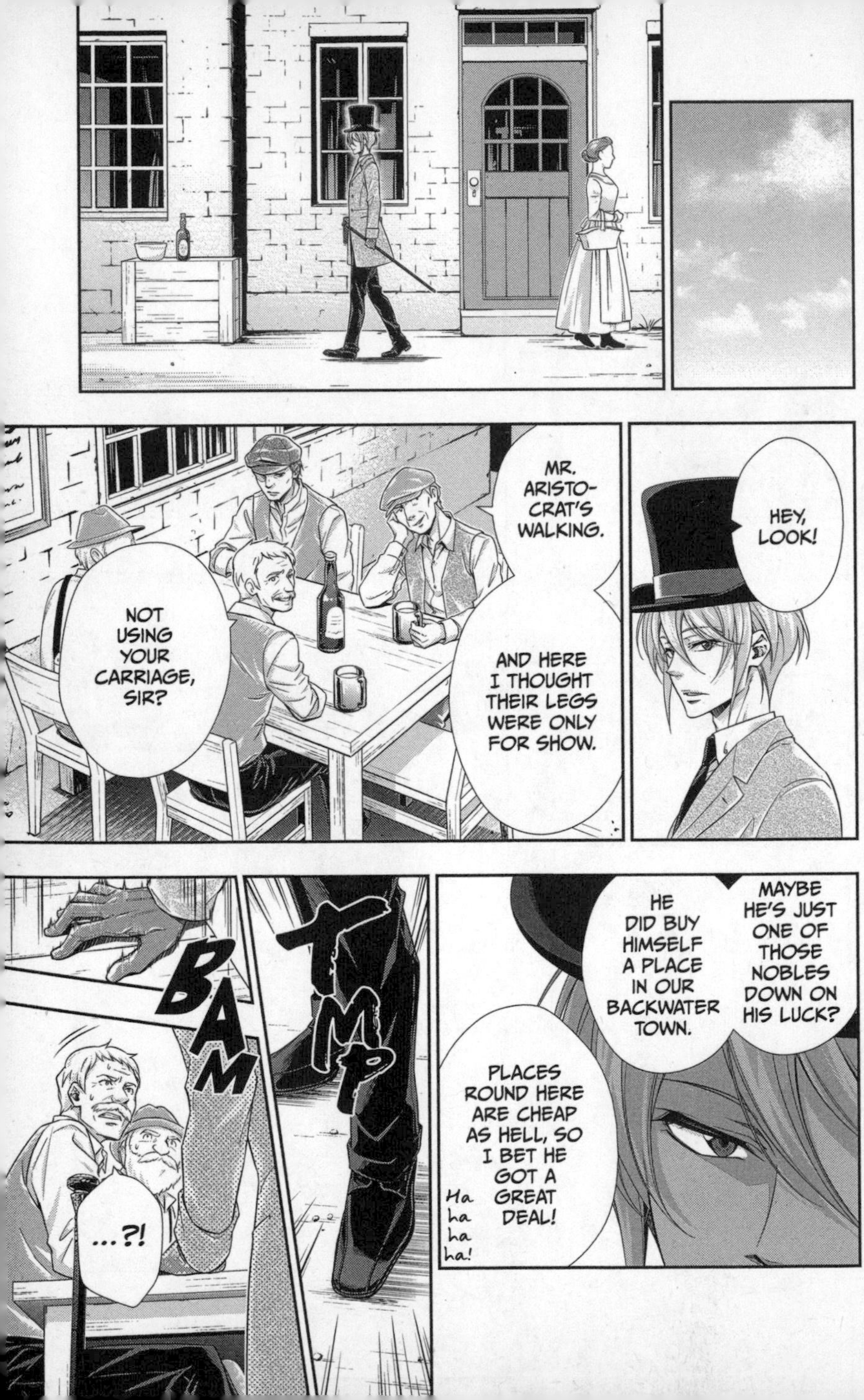
HEY, LOOK!
MR. ARISTO-CRAT'S WALKING.
AND HERE I THOUGHT THEIR LEGS WERE ONLY FOR SHOW.
NOT USING YOUR CARRIAGE, SIR?
MAYBE HE'S JUST ONE OF THOSE NOBLES DOWN ON HIS LUCK?
HE DID BUY HIMSELF A PLACE IN OUR BACKWATER TOWN.
PLACES ROUND HERE ARE CHEAP AS HELL, SO I BET HE GOT A GREAT DEAL!
Ha ha ha ha!
TMP
BAM
...?!

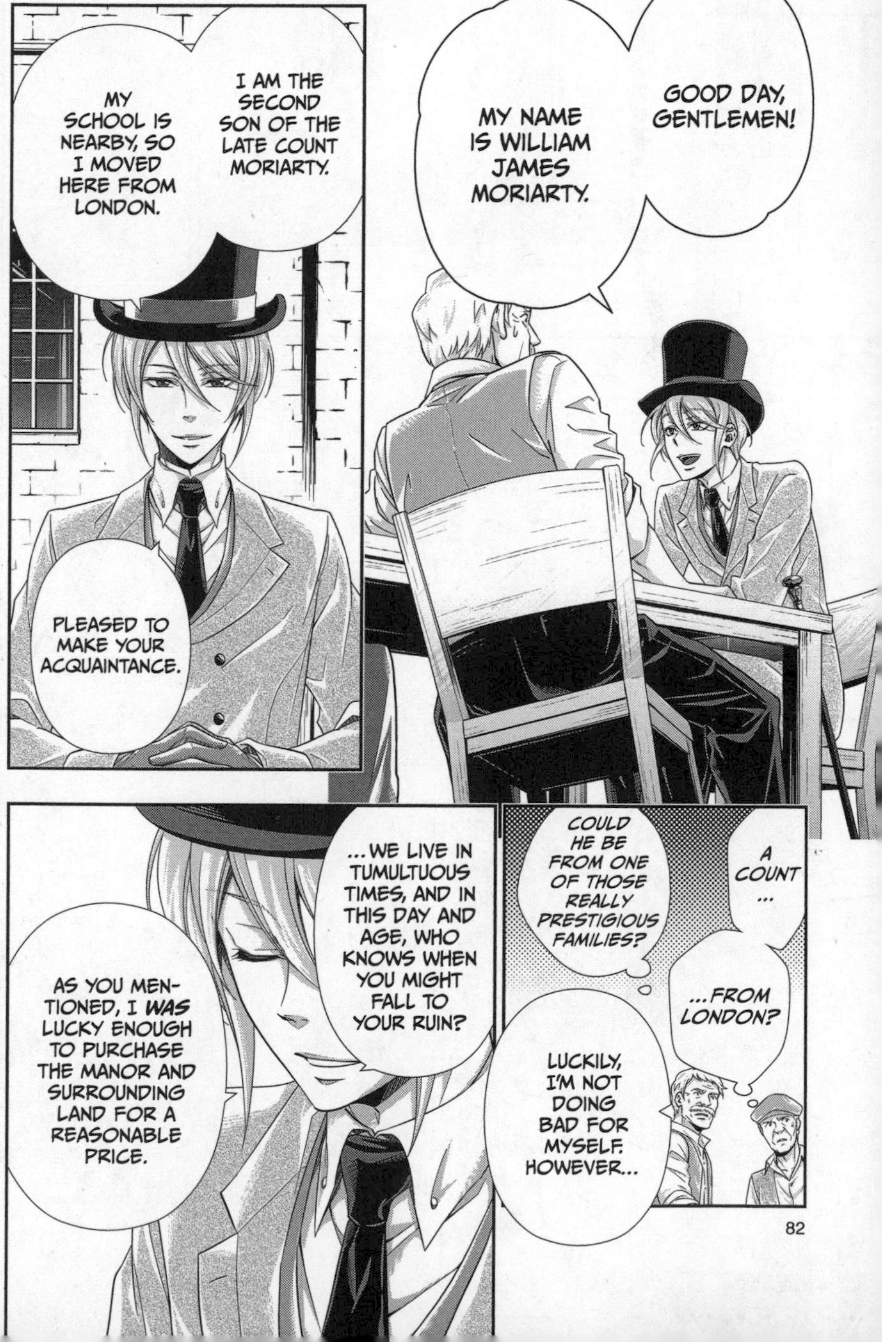
GOOD DAY, GENTLEMEN!
MY NAME IS WILLIAM JAMES MORIARTY.
I AM THE SECOND SON OF THE LATE COUNT MORIARTY.
MY SCHOOL IS NEARBY, SO I MOVED HERE FROM LONDON.
PLEASED TO MAKE YOUR ACQUAINTANCE.
A COUNT ...
COULD HE BE FROM ONE OF THOSE REALLY PRESTIGIOUS FAMILIES?
...FROM LONDON?
LUCKILY, I'M NOT DOING BAD FOR MYSELF. HOWEVER...
...WE LIVE IN TUMULTUOUS TIMES, AND IN THIS DAY AND AGE, WHO KNOWS WHEN YOU MIGHT FALL TO YOUR RUIN?
AS YOU MENTIONED, I *WAS* LUCKY ENOUGH TO PURCHASE THE MANOR AND SURROUNDING LAND FOR A REASONABLE PRICE.

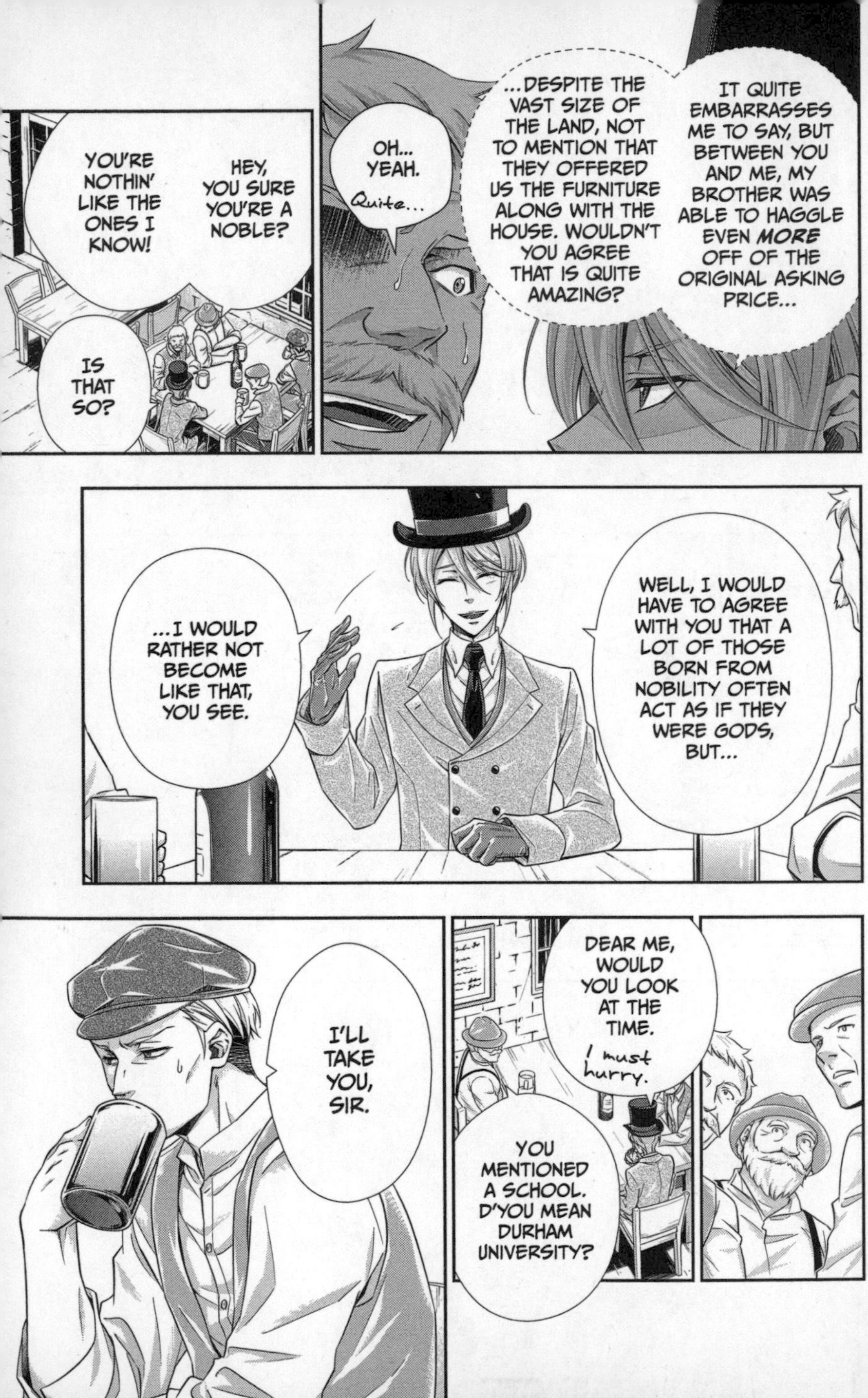
IT QUITE EMBARRASSES ME TO SAY, BUT BETWEEN YOU AND ME, MY BROTHER WAS ABLE TO HAGGLE EVEN *MORE* OFF OF THE ORIGINAL ASKING PRICE...
...DESPITE THE VAST SIZE OF THE LAND, NOT TO MENTION THAT THEY OFFERED US THE FURNITURE ALONG WITH THE HOUSE. WOULDN'T YOU AGREE THAT IS QUITE AMAZING?
OH... YEAH.
Quite...
HEY, YOU SURE YOU'RE A NOBLE?
YOU'RE NOTHIN' LIKE THE ONES I KNOW!
IS THAT SO?
WELL, I WOULD HAVE TO AGREE WITH YOU THAT A LOT OF THOSE BORN FROM NOBILITY OFTEN ACT AS IF THEY WERE GODS, BUT...
...I WOULD RATHER NOT BECOME LIKE THAT, YOU SEE.
DEAR ME, WOULD YOU LOOK AT THE TIME.
I must hurry.
YOU MENTIONED A SCHOOL. D'YOU MEAN DURHAM UNIVERSITY?
I'LL TAKE YOU, SIR.

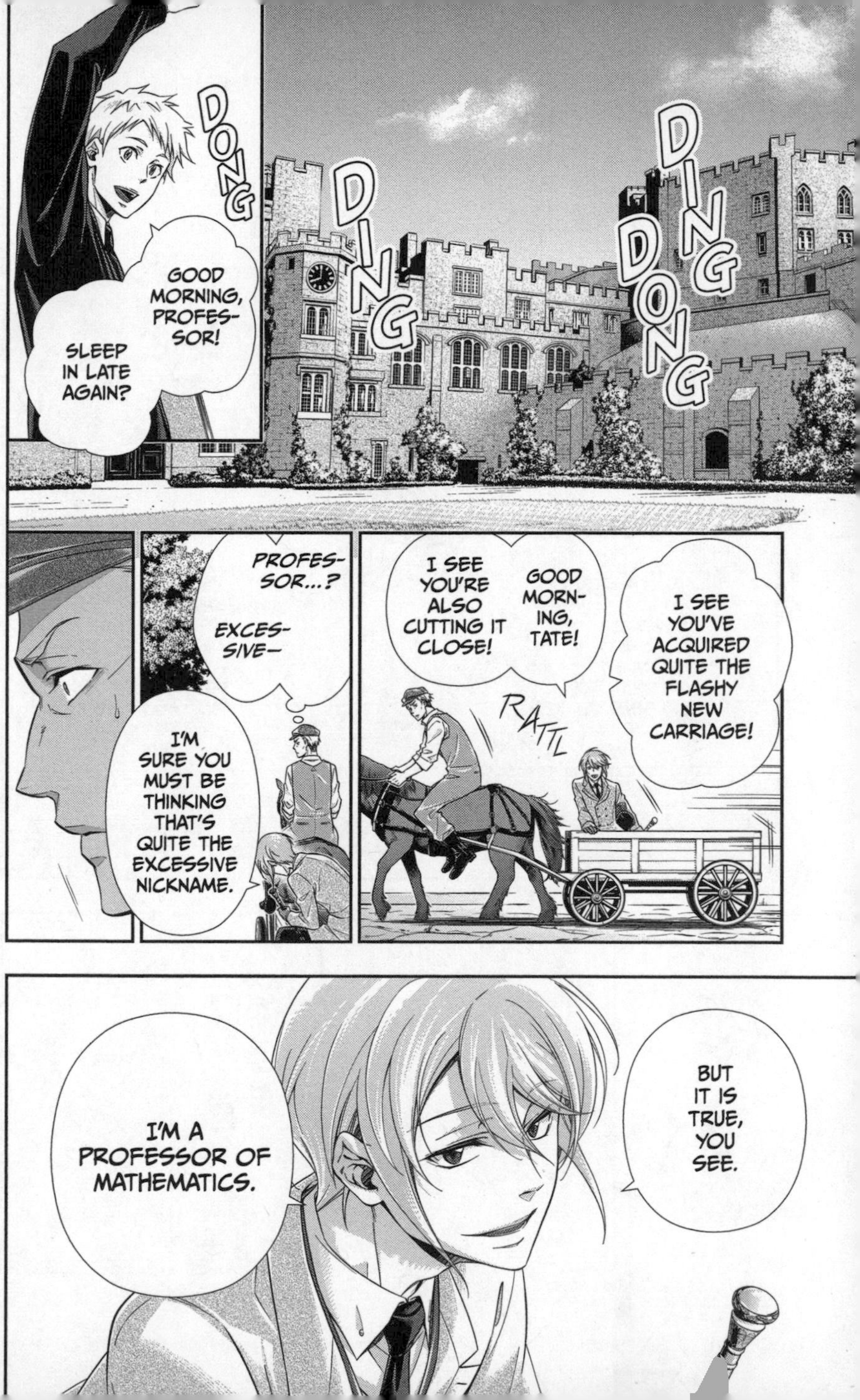
DING DONG
DING
DONG
GOOD MORNING, PROFESSOR!
SLEEP IN LATE AGAIN?
I SEE YOU'VE ACQUIRED QUITE THE FLASHY NEW CARRIAGE!
GOOD MORNING, TATE!
I SEE YOU'RE ALSO CUTTING IT CLOSE!
RATTL
PROFESSOR...?
EXCESSIVE—
I'M SURE YOU MUST BE THINKING THAT'S QUITE THE EXCESSIVE NICKNAME.
BUT IT IS TRUE, YOU SEE.
I'M A PROFESSOR OF MATHEMATICS.

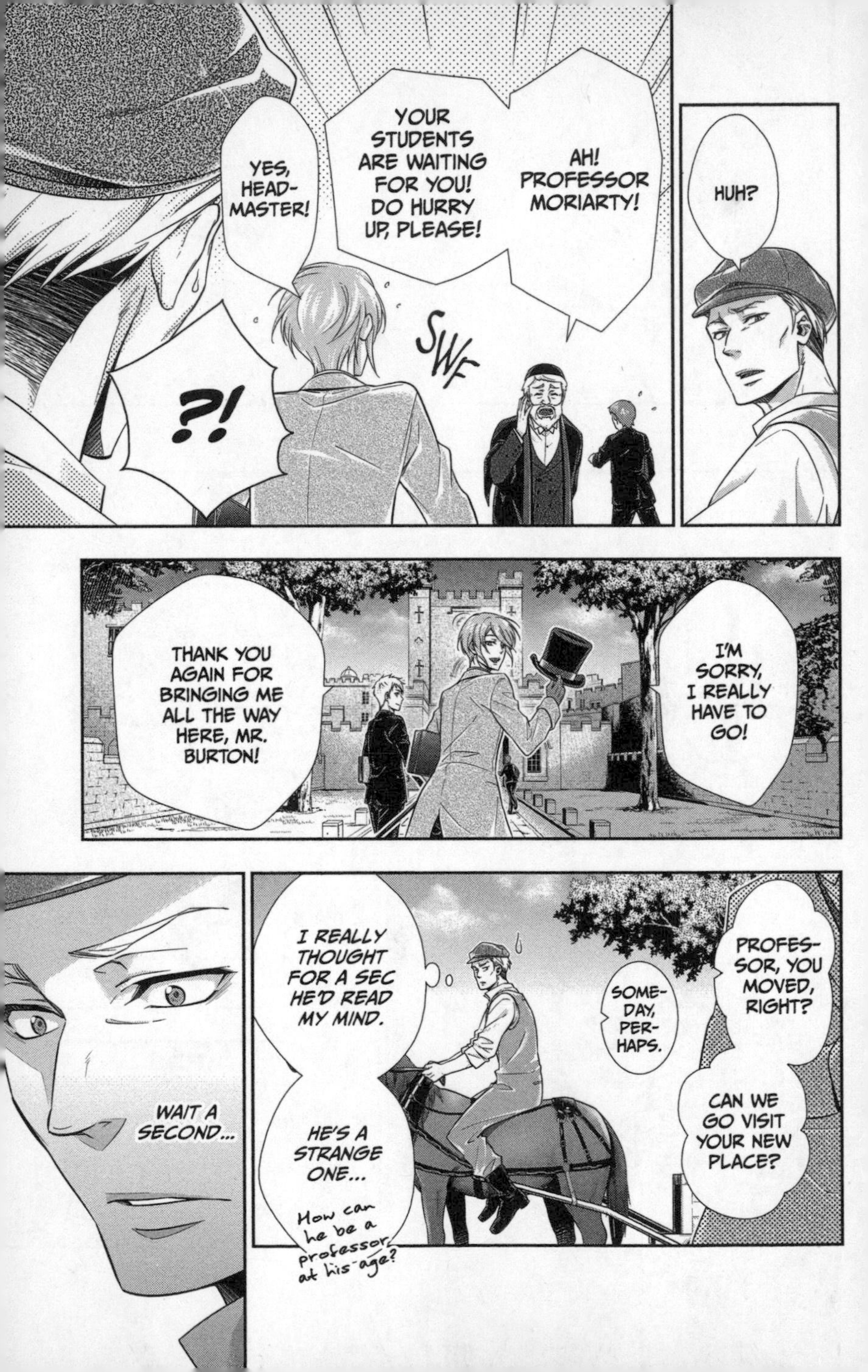
HUH?
AH! PROFESSOR MORIARTY!
YOUR STUDENTS ARE WAITING FOR YOU! DO HURRY UP, PLEASE!
SWF
YES, HEAD-MASTER!
?!
I'M SORRY, I REALLY HAVE TO GO!
THANK YOU AGAIN FOR BRINGING ME ALL THE WAY HERE, MR. BURTON!
PROFES-SOR, YOU MOVED, RIGHT?
CAN WE GO VISIT YOUR NEW PLACE?
SOME-DAY, PER-HAPS.
I REALLY THOUGHT FOR A SEC HE'D READ MY MIND.
HE'S A STRANGE ONE...
How can he be a professor at his age?
WAIT A SECOND...

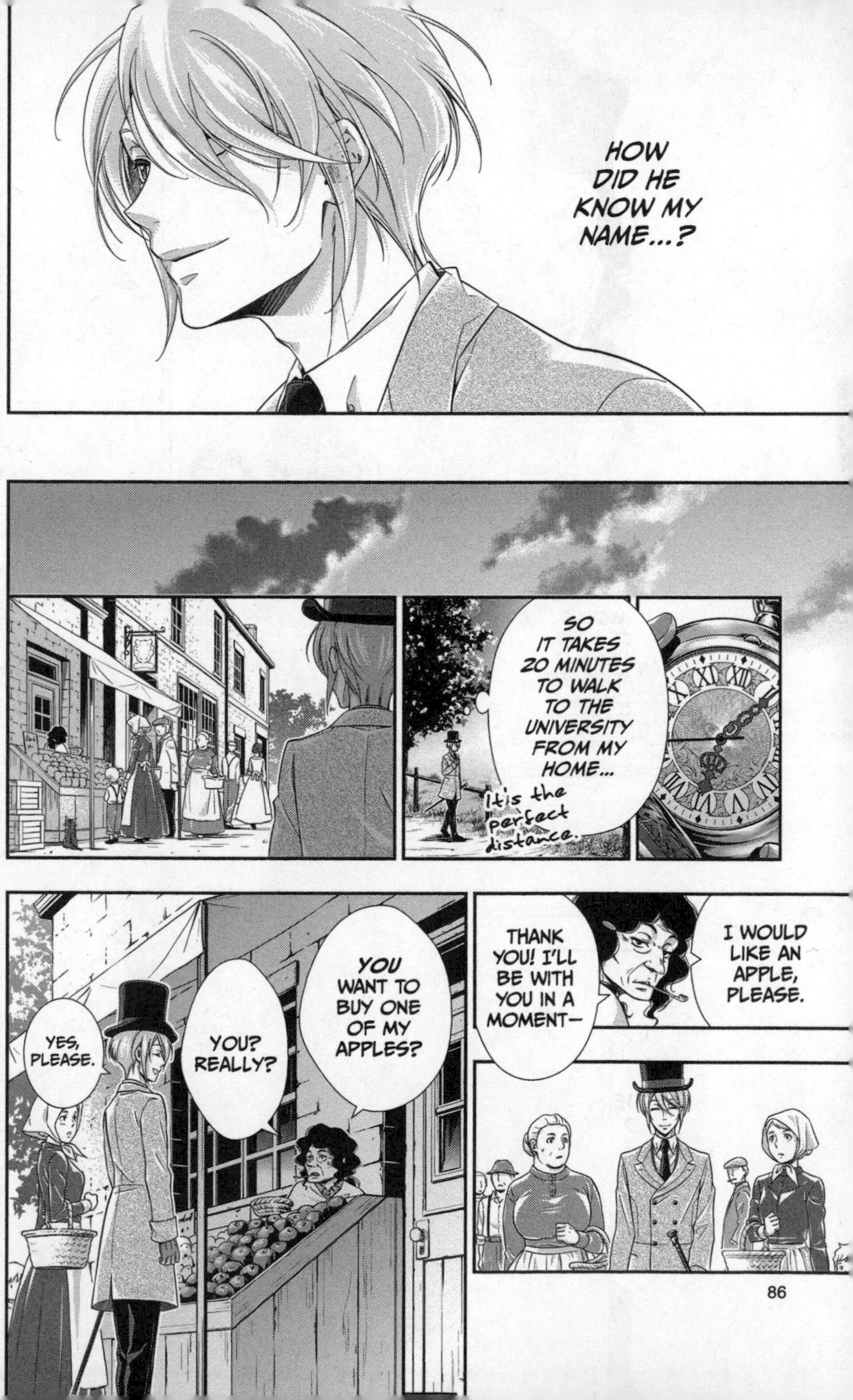
HOW DID HE KNOW MY NAME...?
SO IT TAKES 20 MINUTES TO WALK TO THE UNIVERSITY FROM MY HOME...
It's the perfect distance.
I WOULD LIKE AN APPLE, PLEASE.
THANK YOU! I'LL BE WITH YOU IN A MOMENT—
YOU WANT TO BUY ONE OF MY APPLES?
YOU? REALLY?
YES, PLEASE.

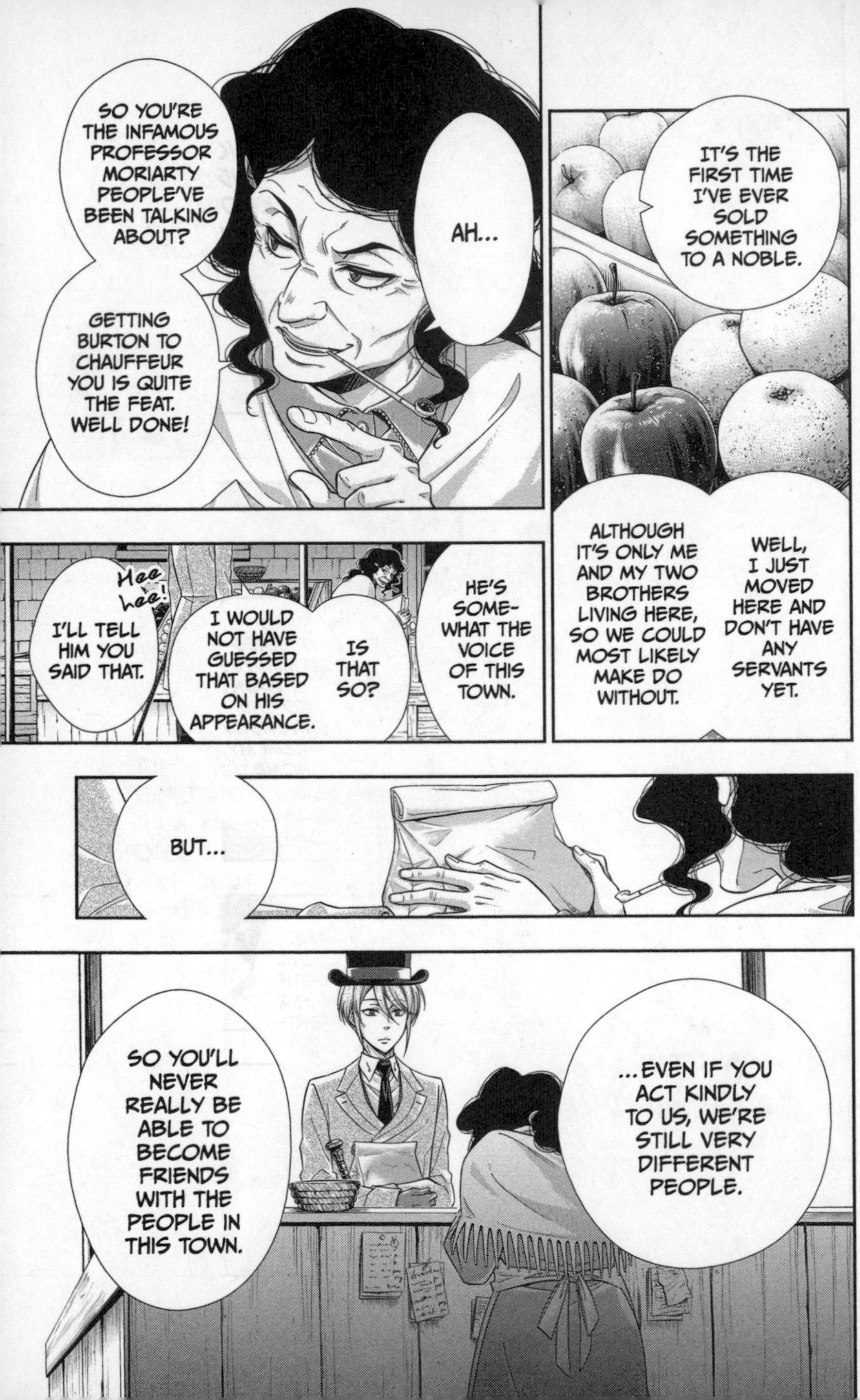
SO YOU'RE THE INFAMOUS PROFESSOR MORIARTY PEOPLE'VE BEEN TALKING ABOUT?
GETTING BURTON TO CHAUFFEUR YOU IS QUITE THE FEAT. WELL DONE!
AH...
IT'S THE FIRST TIME I'VE EVER SOLD SOMETHING TO A NOBLE.
WELL, I JUST MOVED HERE AND DON'T HAVE ANY SERVANTS YET.
ALTHOUGH IT'S ONLY ME AND MY TWO BROTHERS LIVING HERE, SO WE COULD MOST LIKELY MAKE DO WITHOUT.
HE'S SOME-WHAT THE VOICE OF THIS TOWN.
IS THAT SO?
I WOULD NOT HAVE GUESSED THAT BASED ON HIS APPEARANCE.
Hee hee!
I'LL TELL HIM YOU SAID THAT.
BUT...
...EVEN IF YOU ACT KINDLY TO US, WE'RE STILL VERY DIFFERENT PEOPLE.
SO YOU'LL NEVER REALLY BE ABLE TO BECOME FRIENDS WITH THE PEOPLE IN THIS TOWN.

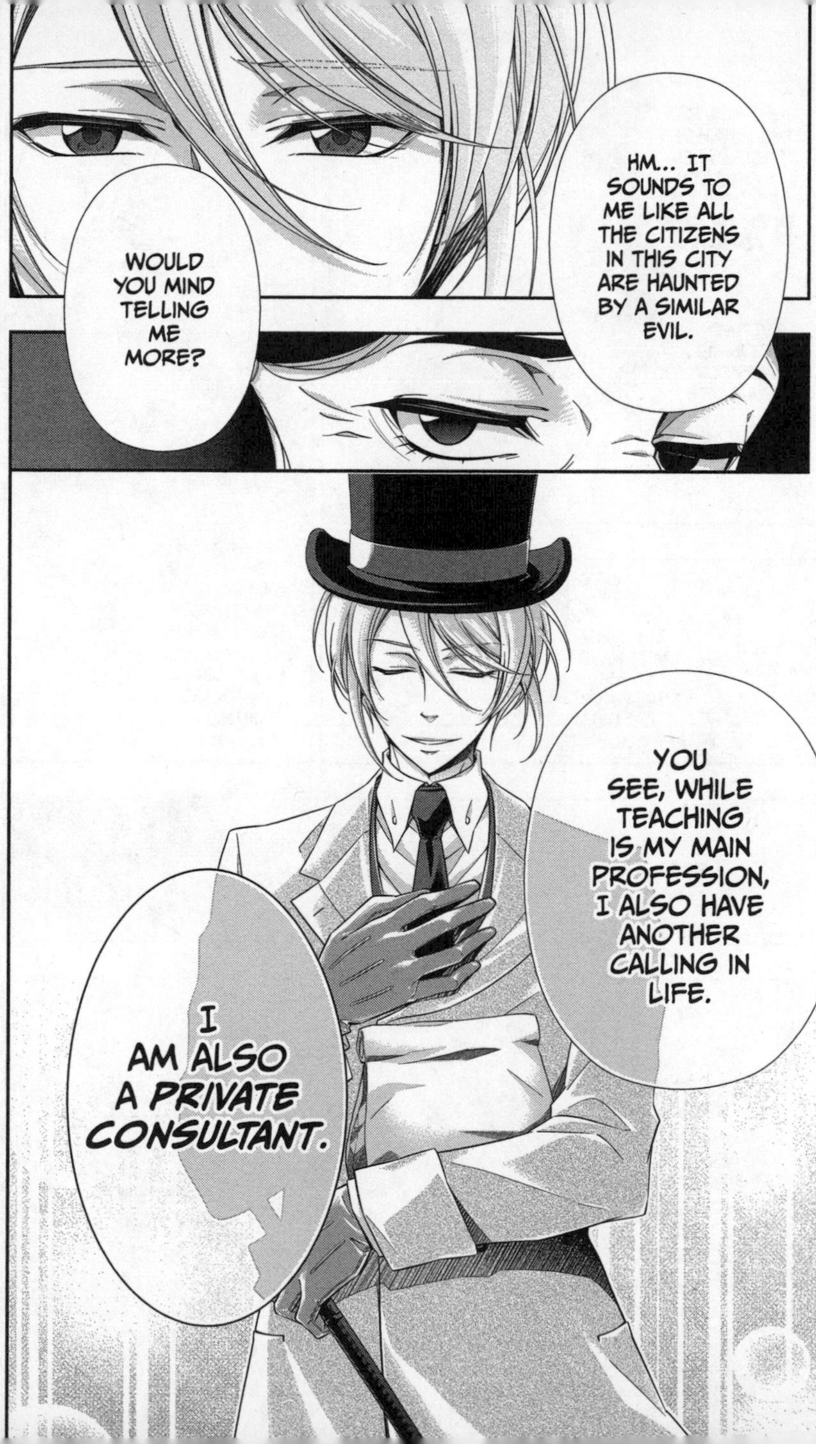
HM... IT SOUNDS TO ME LIKE ALL THE CITIZENS IN THIS CITY ARE HAUNTED BY A SIMILAR EVIL.
WOULD YOU MIND TELLING ME MORE?
YOU SEE, WHILE TEACHING IS MY MAIN PROFESSION, I ALSO HAVE ANOTHER CALLING IN LIFE.
I AM ALSO A *PRIVATE CONSULTANT*.

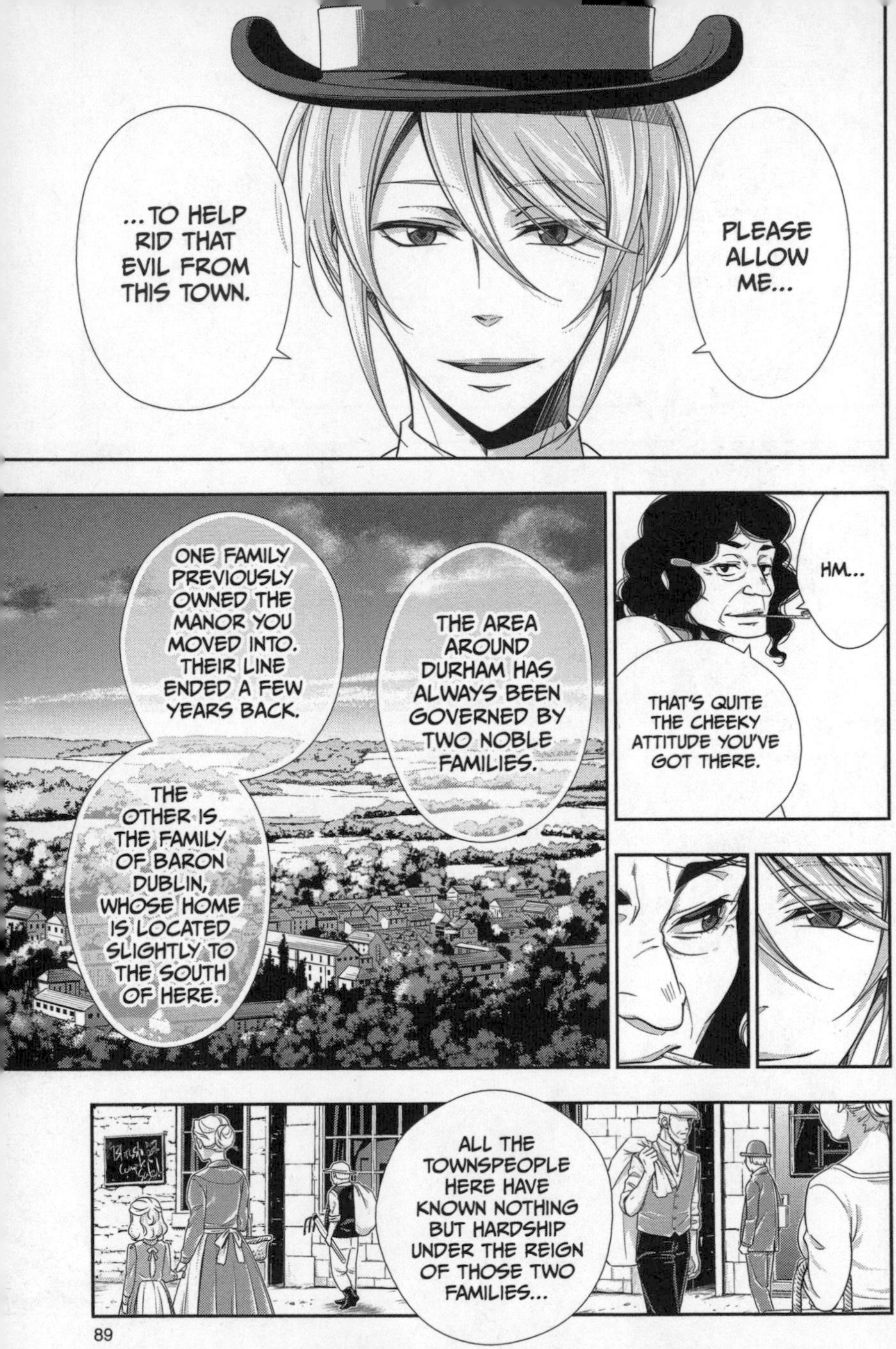
PLEASE ALLOW ME...
...TO HELP RID THAT EVIL FROM THIS TOWN.
HM...
THAT'S QUITE THE CHEEKY ATTITUDE YOU'VE GOT THERE.
THE AREA AROUND DURHAM HAS ALWAYS BEEN GOVERNED BY TWO NOBLE FAMILIES.
ONE FAMILY PREVIOUSLY OWNED THE MANOR YOU MOVED INTO. THEIR LINE ENDED A FEW YEARS BACK.
THE OTHER IS THE FAMILY OF BARON DUBLIN, WHOSE HOME IS LOCATED SLIGHTLY TO THE SOUTH OF HERE.
ALL THE TOWNSPEOPLE HERE HAVE KNOWN NOTHING BUT HARDSHIP UNDER THE REIGN OF THOSE TWO FAMILIES...

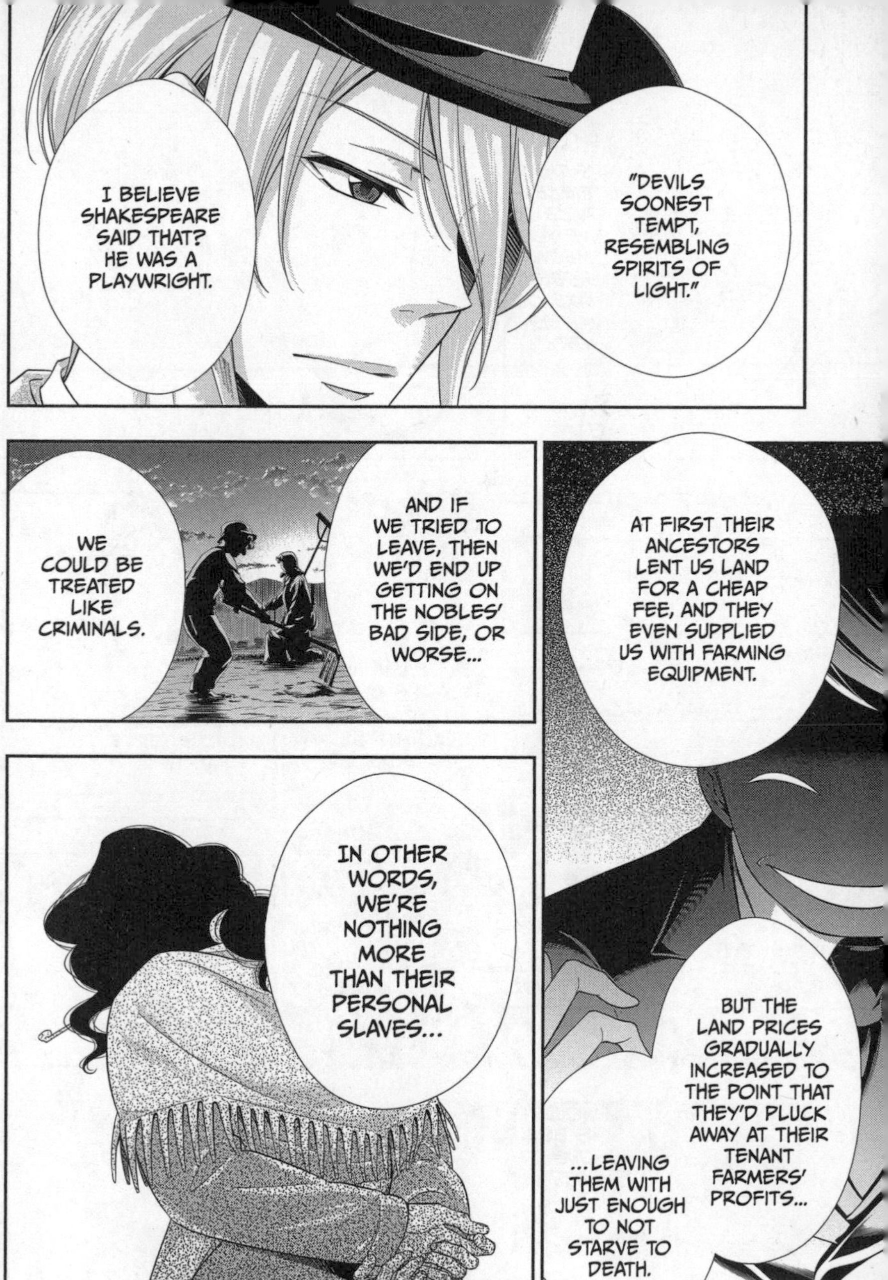
"DEVILS SOONEST TEMPT, RESEMBLING SPIRITS OF LIGHT."
I BELIEVE SHAKESPEARE SAID THAT? HE WAS A PLAYWRIGHT.
AT FIRST THEIR ANCESTORS LENT US LAND FOR A CHEAP FEE, AND THEY EVEN SUPPLIED US WITH FARMING EQUIPMENT.
BUT THE LAND PRICES GRADUALLY INCREASED TO THE POINT THAT THEY'D PLUCK AWAY AT THEIR TENANT FARMERS' PROFITS...
...LEAVING THEM WITH JUST ENOUGH TO NOT STARVE TO DEATH.
AND IF WE TRIED TO LEAVE, THEN WE'D END UP GETTING ON THE NOBLES' BAD SIDE, OR WORSE...
WE COULD BE TREATED LIKE CRIMINALS.
IN OTHER WORDS, WE'RE NOTHING MORE THAN THEIR PERSONAL SLAVES...

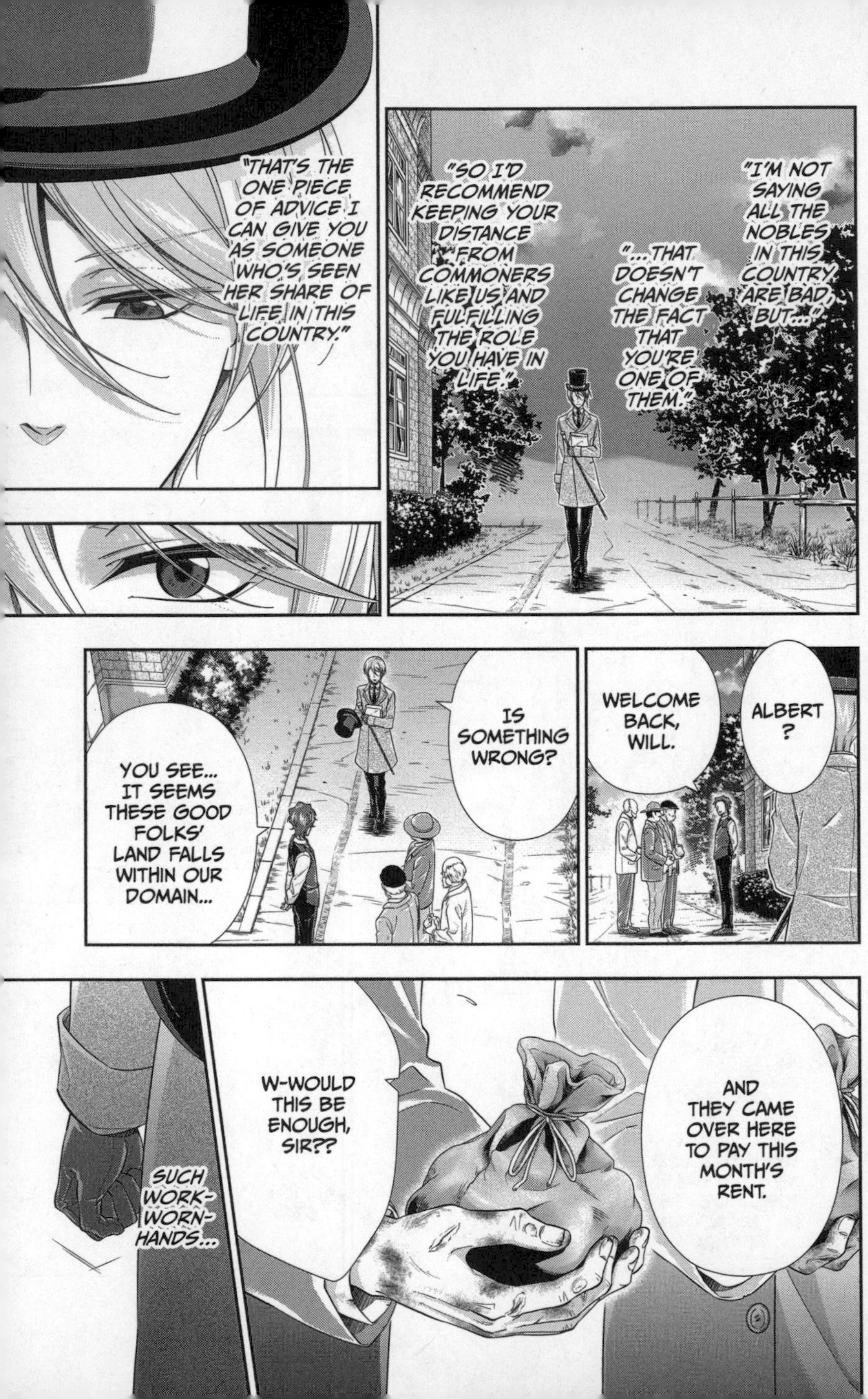
"I'M NOT SAYING ALL THE NOBLES IN THIS COUNTRY ARE BAD, BUT..."
"...THAT DOESN'T CHANGE THE FACT THAT YOU'RE ONE OF THEM."
"SO I'D RECOMMEND KEEPING YOUR DISTANCE FROM COMMONERS LIKE US AND FULFILLING THE ROLE YOU HAVE IN LIFE."
"THAT'S THE ONE PIECE OF ADVICE I CAN GIVE YOU AS SOMEONE WHO'S SEEN HER SHARE OF LIFE IN THIS COUNTRY."
ALBERT?
WELCOME BACK, WILL.
IS SOMETHING WRONG?
YOU SEE... IT SEEMS THESE GOOD FOLKS' LAND FALLS WITHIN OUR DOMAIN...
AND THEY CAME OVER HERE TO PAY THIS MONTH'S RENT.
W-WOULD THIS BE ENOUGH, SIR??
SUCH WORK-WORN-HANDS...

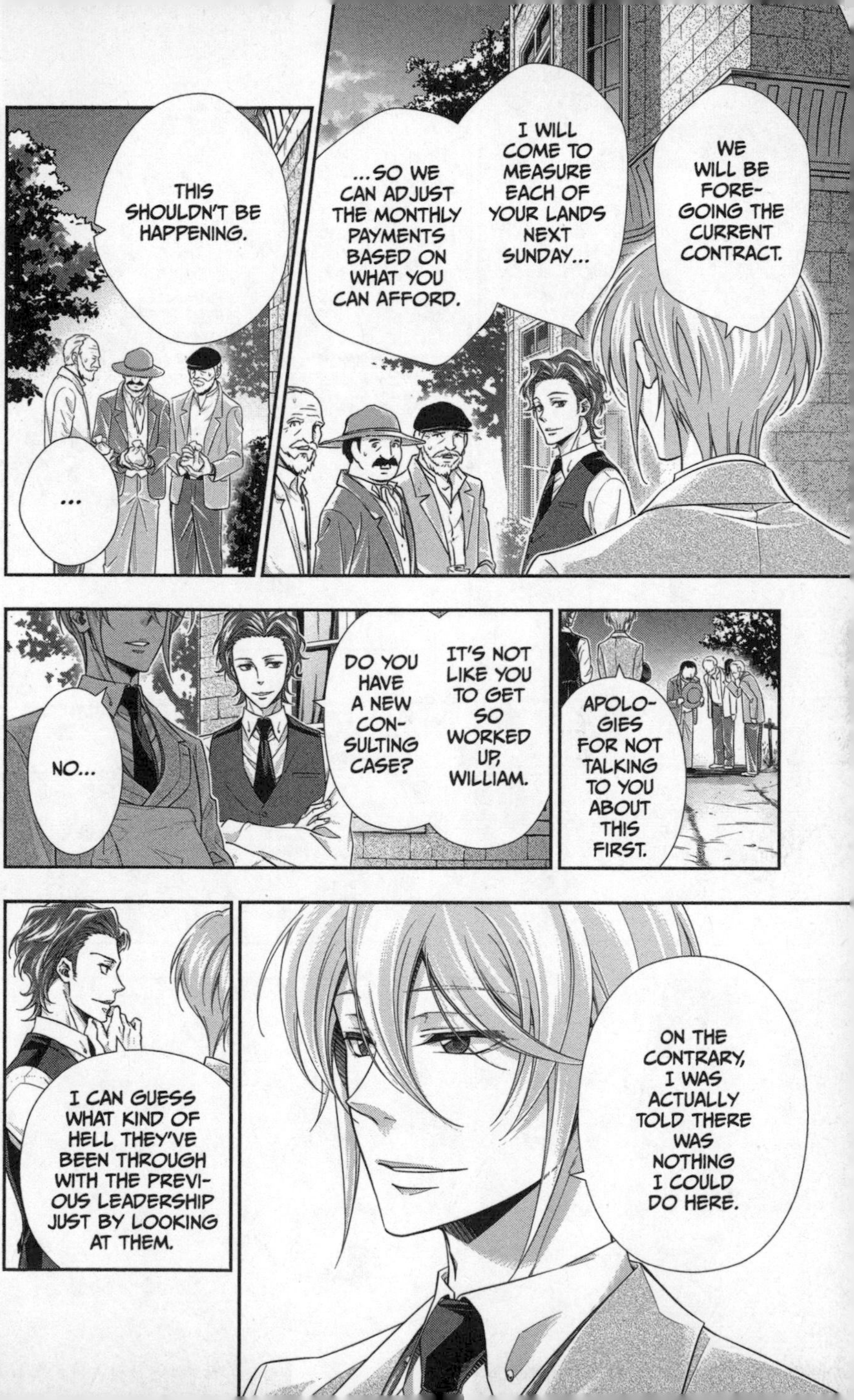
WE WILL BE FOREGOING THE CURRENT CONTRACT.
I WILL COME TO MEASURE EACH OF YOUR LANDS NEXT SUNDAY...
...SO WE CAN ADJUST THE MONTHLY PAYMENTS BASED ON WHAT YOU CAN AFFORD.
THIS SHOULDN'T BE HAPPENING.
...
APOLOGIES FOR NOT TALKING TO YOU ABOUT THIS FIRST.
IT'S NOT LIKE YOU TO GET SO WORKED UP, WILLIAM.
DO YOU HAVE A NEW CONSULTING CASE?
NO...
ON THE CONTRARY, I WAS ACTUALLY TOLD THERE WAS NOTHING I COULD DO HERE.
I CAN GUESS WHAT KIND OF HELL THEY'VE BEEN THROUGH WITH THE PREVIOUS LEADERSHIP JUST BY LOOKING AT THEM.

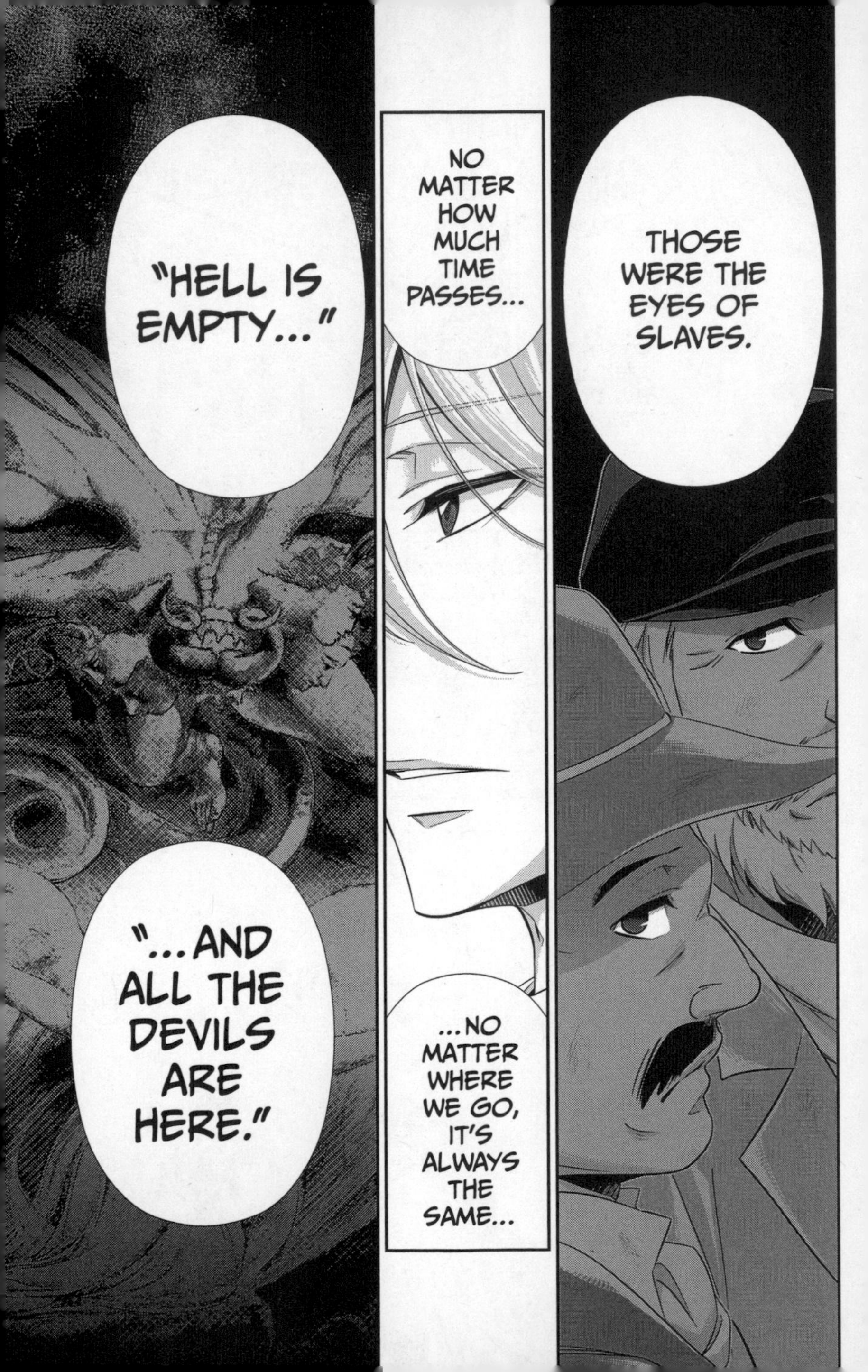
THOSE WERE THE EYES OF SLAVES.
NO MATTER HOW MUCH TIME PASSES...
...NO MATTER WHERE WE GO, IT'S ALWAYS THE SAME...
"HELL IS EMPTY..."
"...AND ALL THE DEVILS ARE HERE."

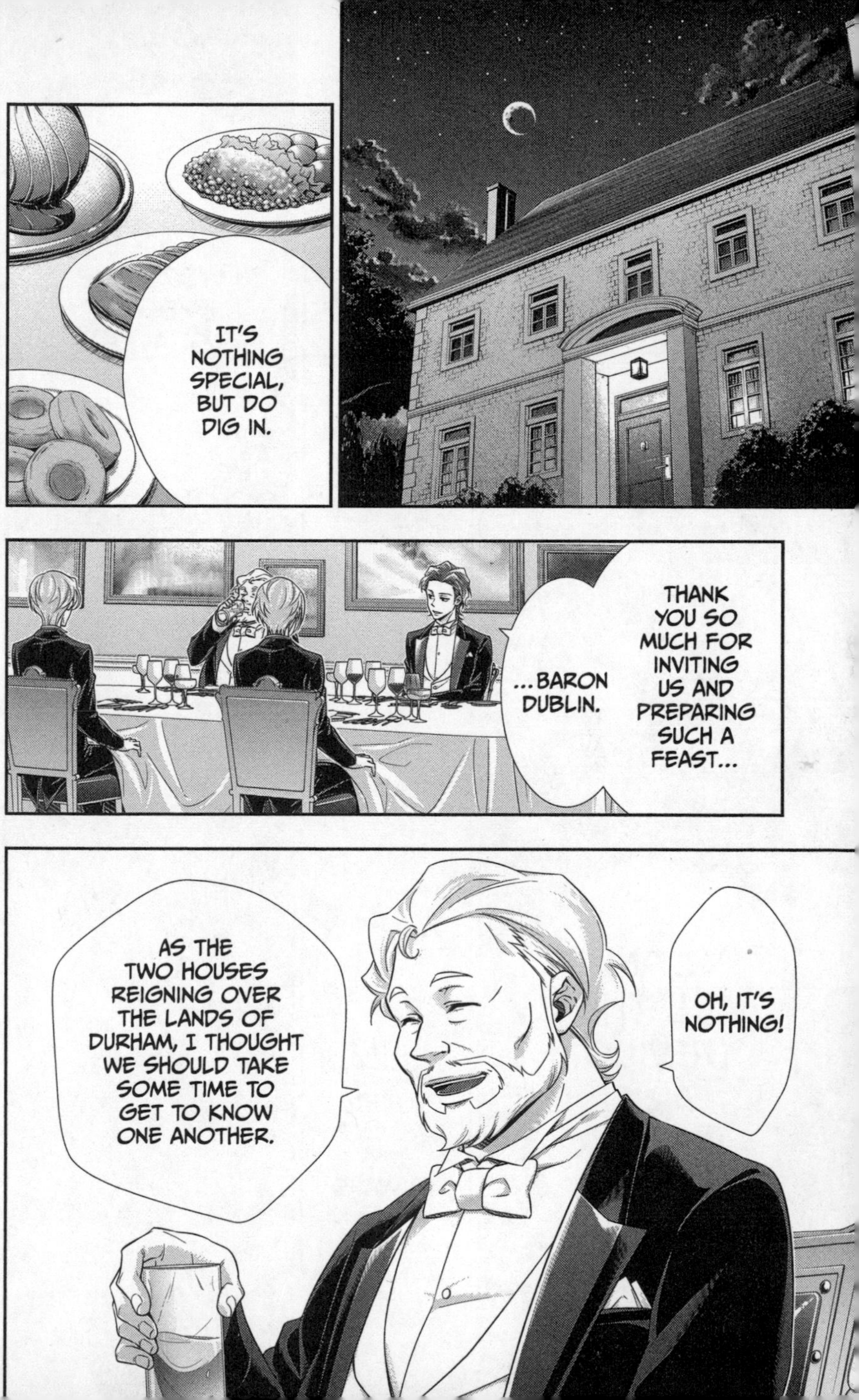
IT'S NOTHING SPECIAL, BUT DO DIG IN.
THANK YOU SO MUCH FOR INVITING US AND PREPARING SUCH A FEAST...
...BARON DUBLIN.
OH, IT'S NOTHING!
AS THE TWO HOUSES REIGNING OVER THE LANDS OF DURHAM, I THOUGHT WE SHOULD TAKE SOME TIME TO GET TO KNOW ONE ANOTHER.

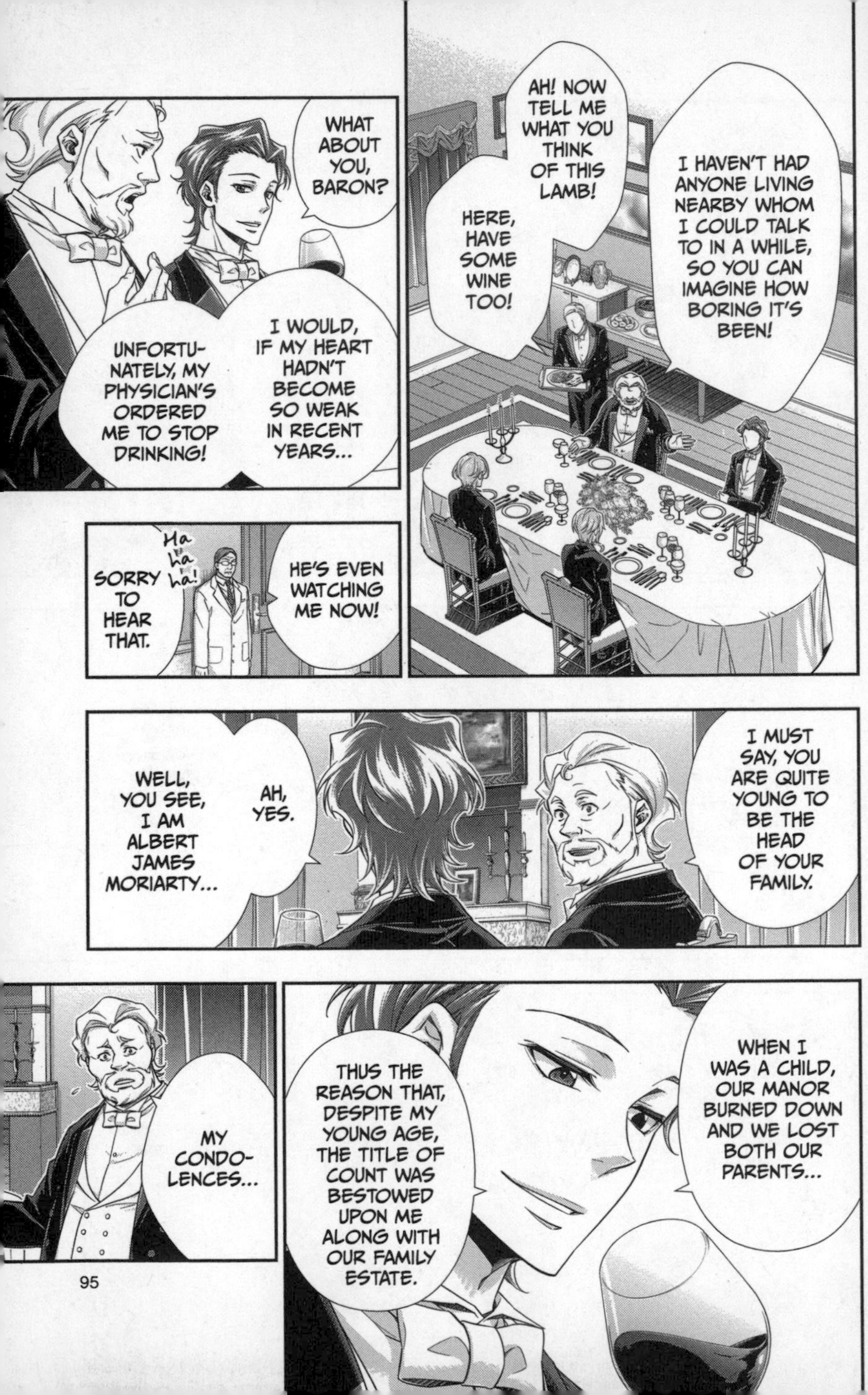
I HAVEN'T HAD ANYONE LIVING NEARBY WHOM I COULD TALK TO IN A WHILE, SO YOU CAN IMAGINE HOW BORING IT'S BEEN!
AH! NOW TELL ME WHAT YOU THINK OF THIS LAMB!
HERE, HAVE SOME WINE TOO!
WHAT ABOUT YOU, BARON?
I WOULD, IF MY HEART HADN'T BECOME SO WEAK IN RECENT YEARS...
UNFORTU-NATELY, MY PHYSICIAN'S ORDERED ME TO STOP DRINKING!
HE'S EVEN WATCHING ME NOW!
Ha ha ha!
SORRY TO HEAR THAT.
I MUST SAY, YOU ARE QUITE YOUNG TO BE THE HEAD OF YOUR FAMILY.
AH, YES.
WELL, YOU SEE, I AM ALBERT JAMES MORIARTY...
WHEN I WAS A CHILD, OUR MANOR BURNED DOWN AND WE LOST BOTH OUR PARENTS...
THUS THE REASON THAT, DESPITE MY YOUNG AGE, THE TITLE OF COUNT WAS BESTOWED UPON ME ALONG WITH OUR FAMILY ESTATE.
MY CONDO-LENCES...

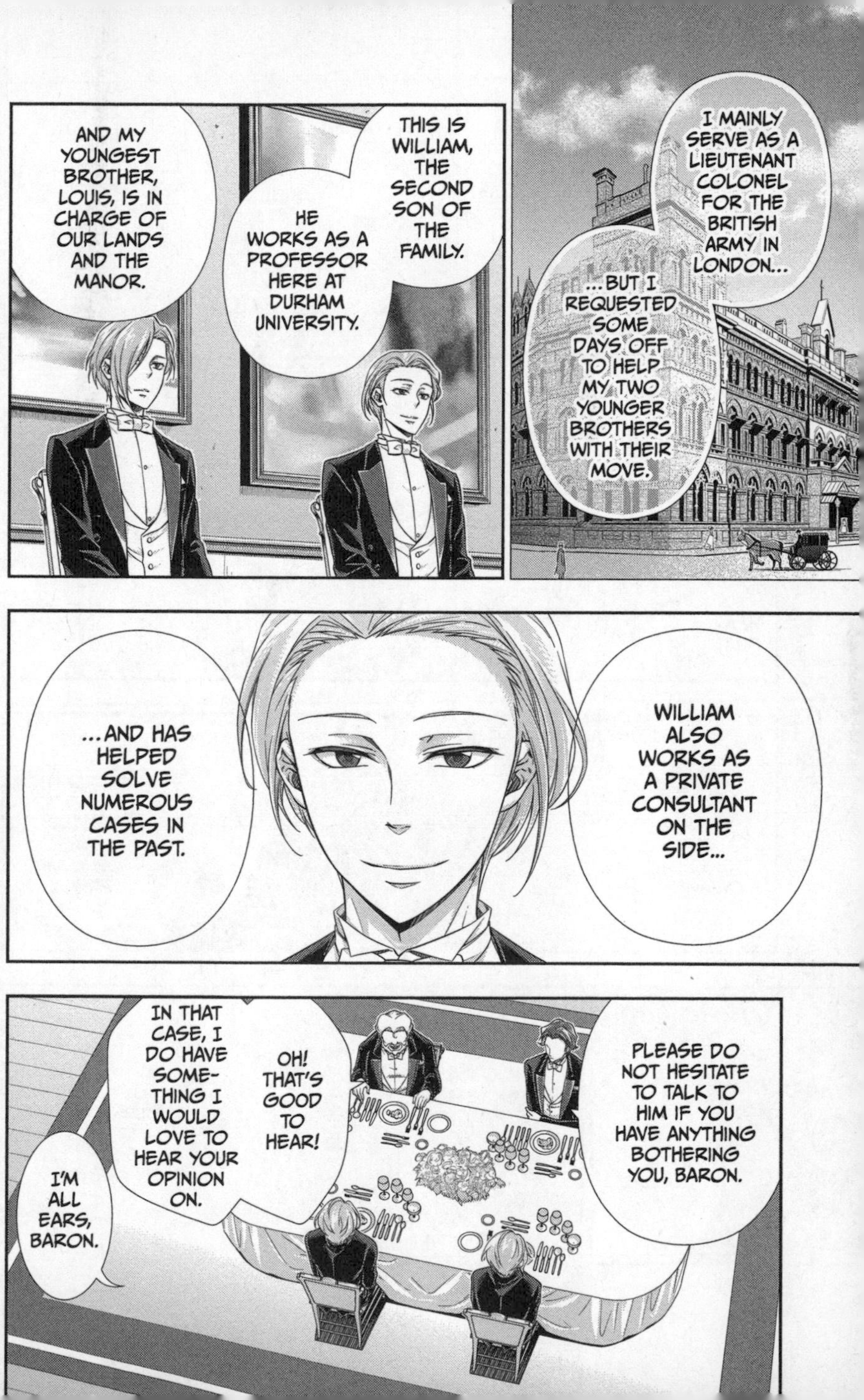
I MAINLY SERVE AS A LIEUTENANT COLONEL FOR THE BRITISH ARMY IN LONDON...
...BUT I REQUESTED SOME DAYS OFF TO HELP MY TWO YOUNGER BROTHERS WITH THEIR MOVE.
THIS IS WILLIAM, THE SECOND SON OF THE FAMILY.
HE WORKS AS A PROFESSOR HERE AT DURHAM UNIVERSITY.
AND MY YOUNGEST BROTHER, LOUIS, IS IN CHARGE OF OUR LANDS AND THE MANOR.
WILLIAM ALSO WORKS AS A PRIVATE CONSULTANT ON THE SIDE...
...AND HAS HELPED SOLVE NUMEROUS CASES IN THE PAST.
PLEASE DO NOT HESITATE TO TALK TO HIM IF YOU HAVE ANYTHING BOTHERING YOU, BARON.
OH! THAT'S GOOD TO HEAR!
IN THAT CASE, I DO HAVE SOME-THING I WOULD LOVE TO HEAR YOUR OPINION ON.
I'M ALL EARS, BARON.

AND I ALSO HAVE NO OTHER LIVING RELATIVES!

YES!

SO NOW YOU LACK AN HEIR?

...15 YEARS AGO, I LOST MY WIFE.

WELL, I WOULDN'T CALL IT A WORRY EXACTLY, BUT...

AND I DON'T HAVE ANY CHILDREN.

SO I WAS WONDERING IF YOU COULD LOOK INTO THE RELATIVES OF MY LATE WIFE? I HAVEN'T HAD CONTACT WITH THEM IN A WHILE.

IF YOU ARE LOOKING TO FIND YOUR WIFE'S RELATIVES, THEN I BELIEVE ASKING A PRIVATE INVESTIGATOR WOULD BE A MUCH QUICKER AND MORE SURE-FIRE SOLUTION.

I'M SORRY...

WHILE ON THE SUBJECT OF LAND, BARON...

I'LL BE SURE TO TRY OUT THE METHOD YOU SUG-GESTED.

OH, NON-SENSE! I HADN'T THOUGHT OF THAT!

I'M SORRY I CAN'T BE OF MORE ASSIS-TANCE TO YOU.

A PRIVATE INVESTI-GATOR?

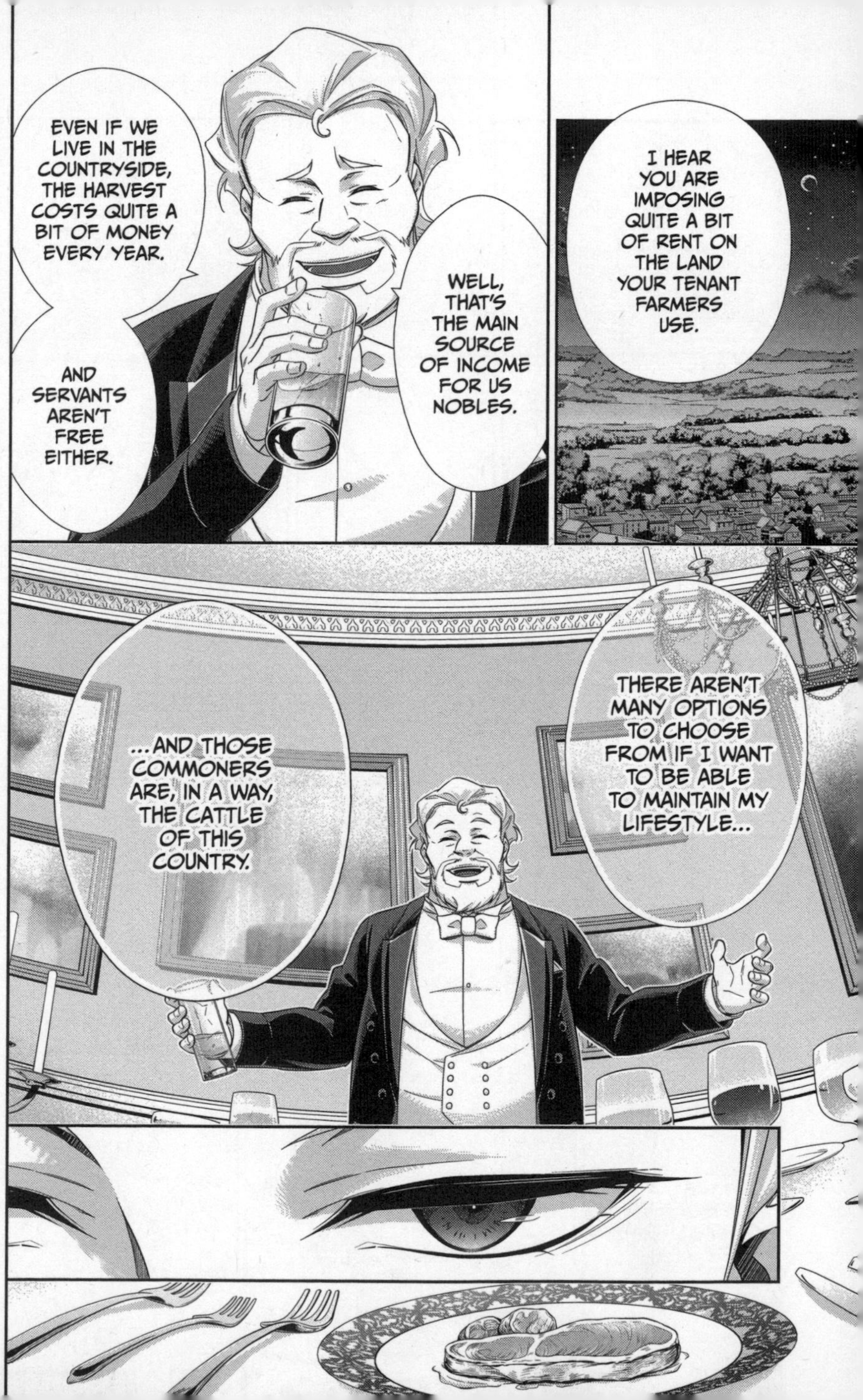
I HEAR YOU ARE IMPOSING QUITE A BIT OF RENT ON THE LAND YOUR TENANT FARMERS USE.
WELL, THAT'S THE MAIN SOURCE OF INCOME FOR US NOBLES.
EVEN IF WE LIVE IN THE COUNTRYSIDE, THE HARVEST COSTS QUITE A BIT OF MONEY EVERY YEAR.
AND SERVANTS AREN'T FREE EITHER.
THERE AREN'T MANY OPTIONS TO CHOOSE FROM IF I WANT TO BE ABLE TO MAINTAIN MY LIFESTYLE...
...AND THOSE COMMONERS ARE, IN A WAY, THE CATTLE OF THIS COUNTRY.

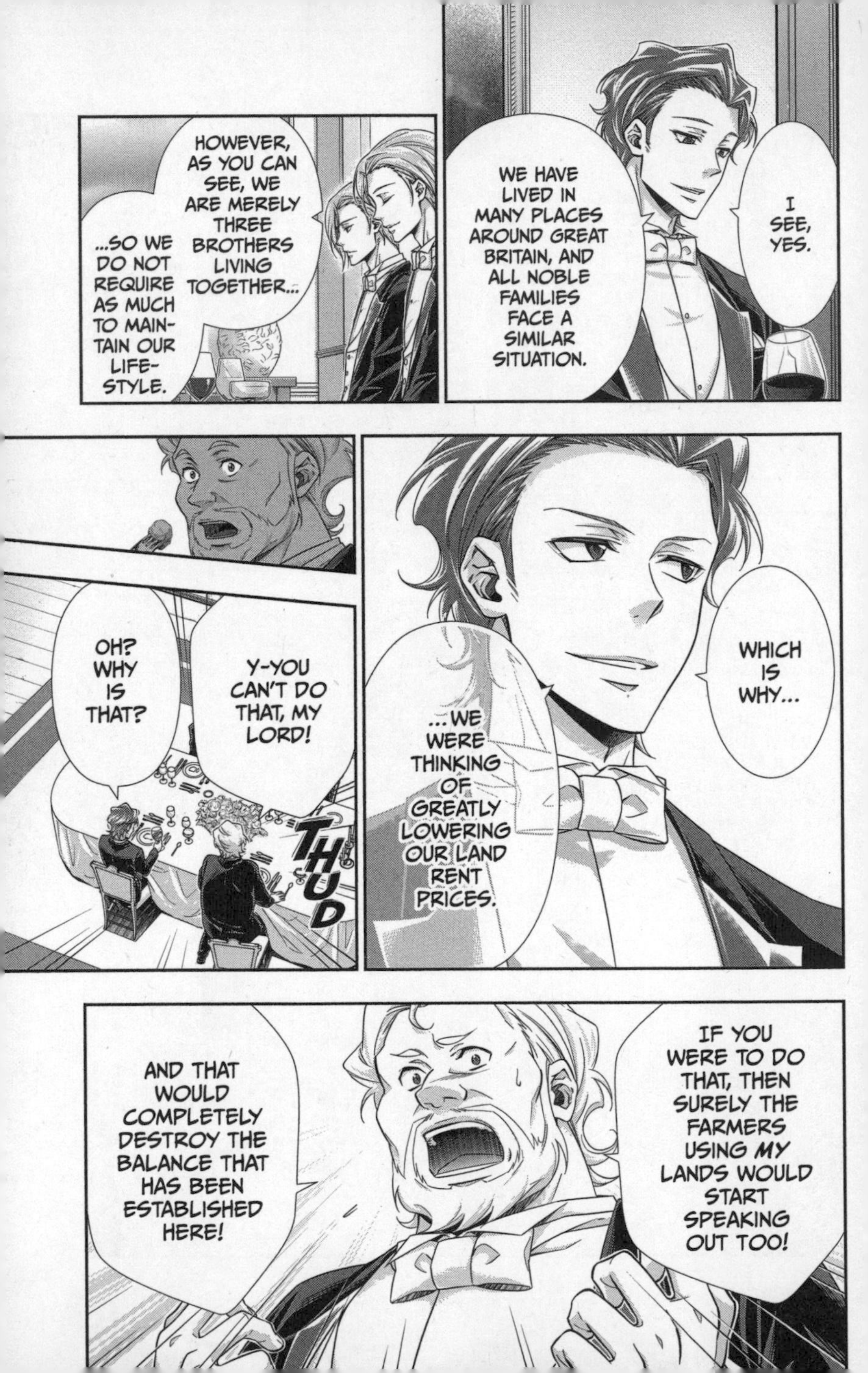
I SEE, YES.
WE HAVE LIVED IN MANY PLACES AROUND GREAT BRITAIN, AND ALL NOBLE FAMILIES FACE A SIMILAR SITUATION.
HOWEVER, AS YOU CAN SEE, WE ARE MERELY THREE BROTHERS LIVING TOGETHER...
...SO WE DO NOT REQUIRE AS MUCH TO MAIN-TAIN OUR LIFE-STYLE.
WHICH IS WHY...
...WE WERE THINKING OF GREATLY LOWERING OUR LAND RENT PRICES.
Y-YOU CAN'T DO THAT, MY LORD!
THUD
OH? WHY IS THAT?
IF YOU WERE TO DO THAT, THEN SURELY THE FARMERS USING MY LANDS WOULD START SPEAKING OUT TOO!
AND THAT WOULD COMPLETELY DESTROY THE BALANCE THAT HAS BEEN ESTABLISHED HERE!

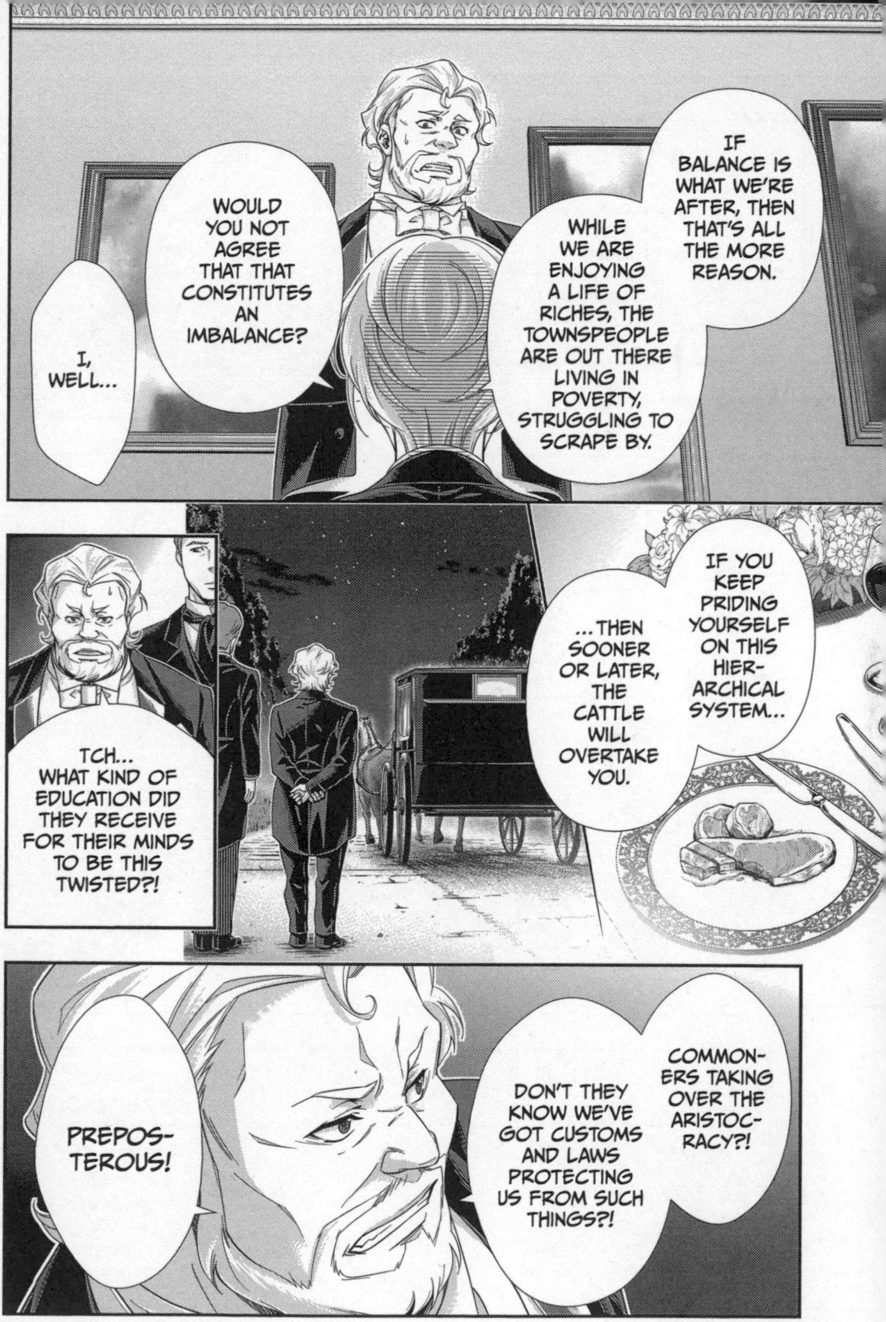
IF BALANCE IS WHAT WE'RE AFTER, THEN THAT'S ALL THE MORE REASON.
WHILE WE ARE ENJOYING A LIFE OF RICHES, THE TOWNSPEOPLE ARE OUT THERE LIVING IN POVERTY, STRUGGLING TO SCRAPE BY.
WOULD YOU NOT AGREE THAT THAT CONSTITUTES AN IMBALANCE?
I, WELL...
IF YOU KEEP PRIDING YOURSELF ON THIS HIER-ARCHICAL SYSTEM...
...THEN SOONER OR LATER, THE CATTLE WILL OVERTAKE YOU.
TCH... WHAT KIND OF EDUCATION DID THEY RECEIVE FOR THEIR MINDS TO BE THIS TWISTED?!
COMMON-ERS TAKING OVER THE ARISTOC-RACY?!
DON'T THEY KNOW WE'VE GOT CUSTOMS AND LAWS PROTECTING US FROM SUCH THINGS?!
PREPOS-TEROUS!

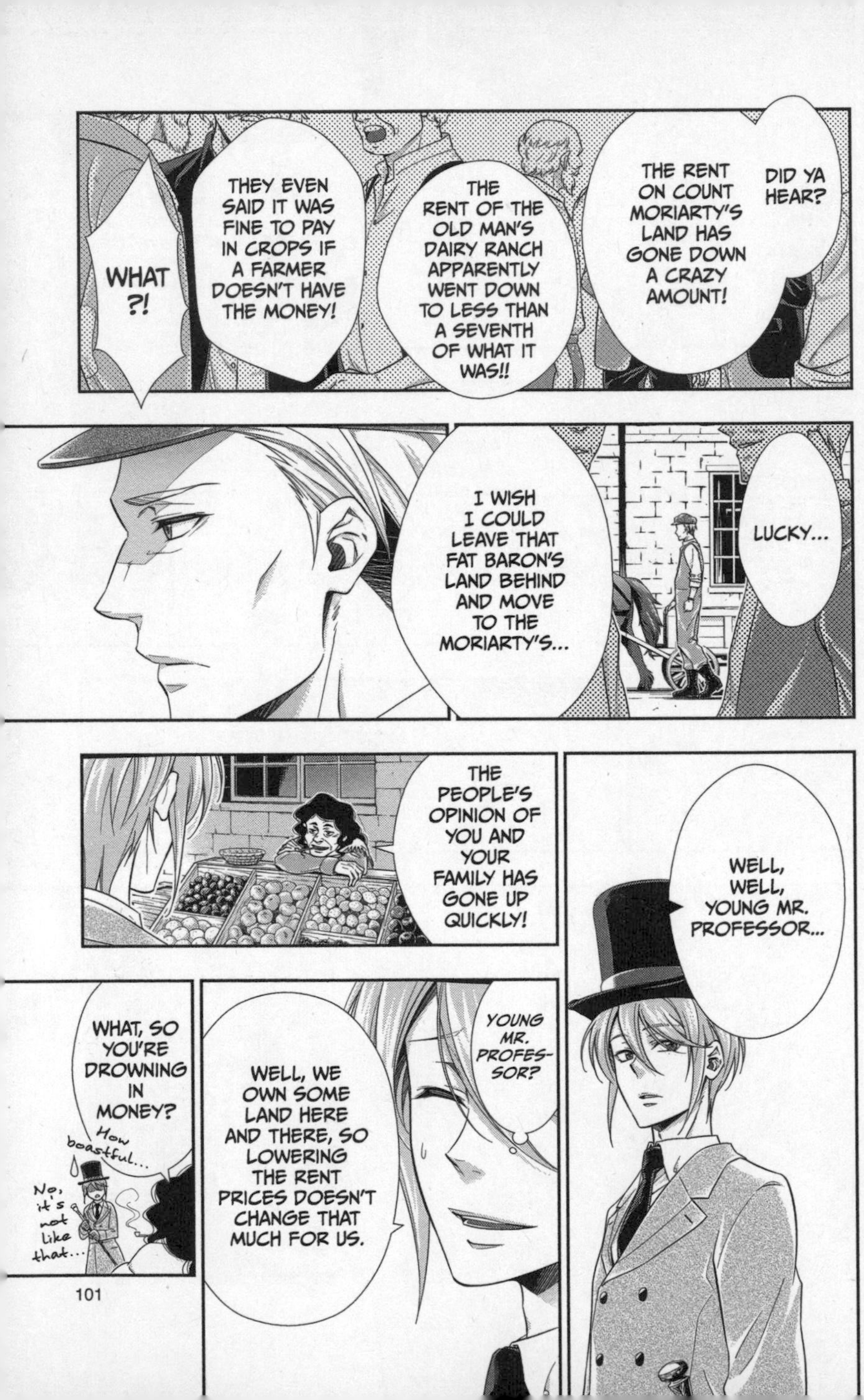
DID YA HEAR?
THE RENT ON COUNT MORIARTY'S LAND HAS GONE DOWN A CRAZY AMOUNT!
THE RENT OF THE OLD MAN'S DAIRY RANCH APPARENTLY WENT DOWN TO LESS THAN A SEVENTH OF WHAT IT WAS!!
THEY EVEN SAID IT WAS FINE TO PAY IN CROPS IF A FARMER DOESN'T HAVE THE MONEY!
WHAT ?!
LUCKY...
I WISH I COULD LEAVE THAT FAT BARON'S LAND BEHIND AND MOVE TO THE MORIARTY'S...
WELL, WELL, YOUNG MR. PROFESSOR...
THE PEOPLE'S OPINION OF YOU AND YOUR FAMILY HAS GONE UP QUICKLY!
YOUNG MR. PROFES-SOR?
WELL, WE OWN SOME LAND HERE AND THERE, SO LOWERING THE RENT PRICES DOESN'T CHANGE THAT MUCH FOR US.
WHAT, SO YOU'RE DROWNING IN MONEY?
How boastful...
No, it's not like that...

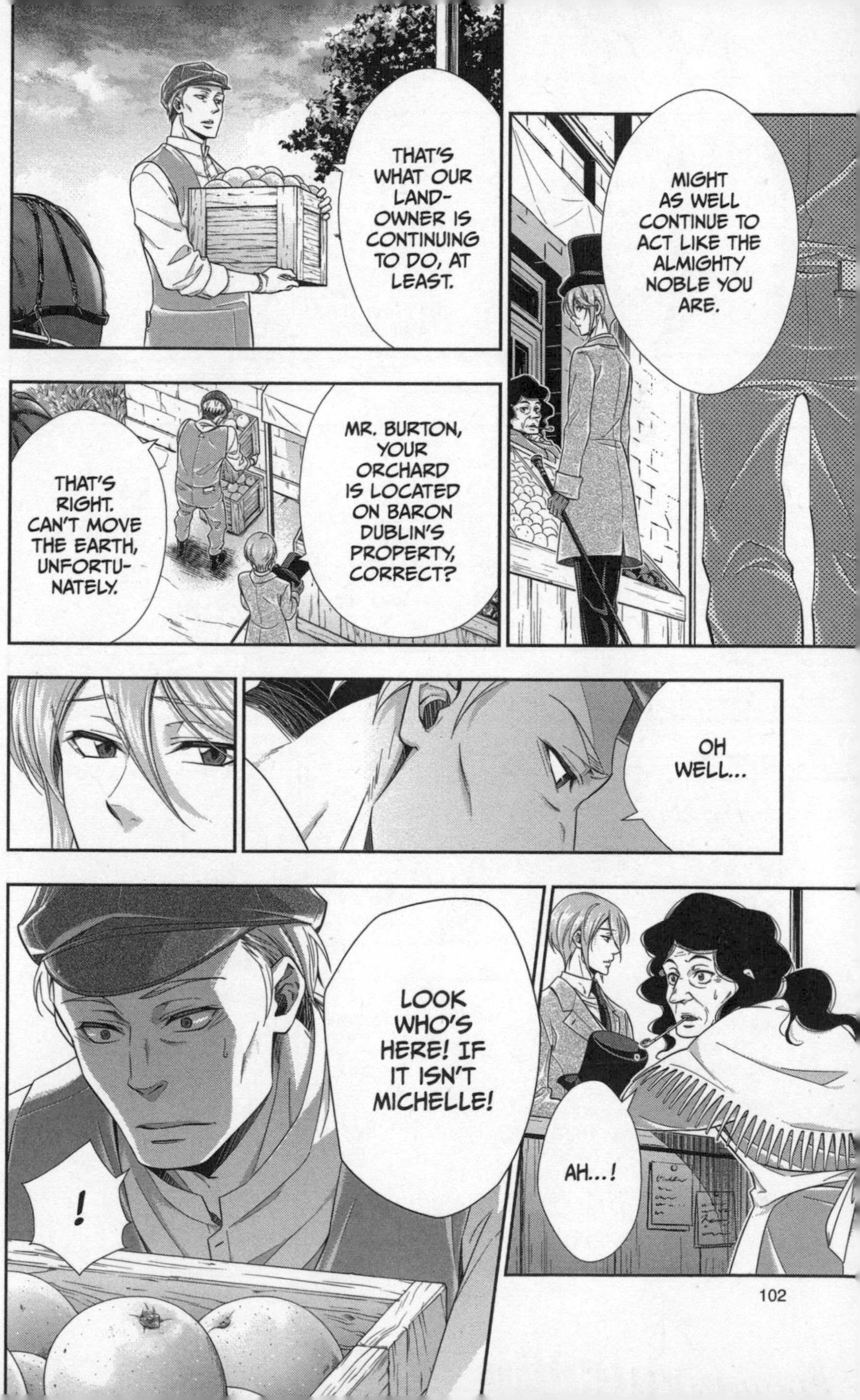
MIGHT AS WELL CONTINUE TO ACT LIKE THE ALMIGHTY NOBLE YOU ARE.
THAT'S WHAT OUR LAND-OWNER IS CONTINUING TO DO, AT LEAST.
MR. BURTON, YOUR ORCHARD IS LOCATED ON BARON DUBLIN'S PROPERTY, CORRECT?
THAT'S RIGHT. CAN'T MOVE THE EARTH, UNFORTU-NATELY.
OH WELL...
AH...!
LOOK WHO'S HERE! IF IT ISN'T MICHELLE!
!

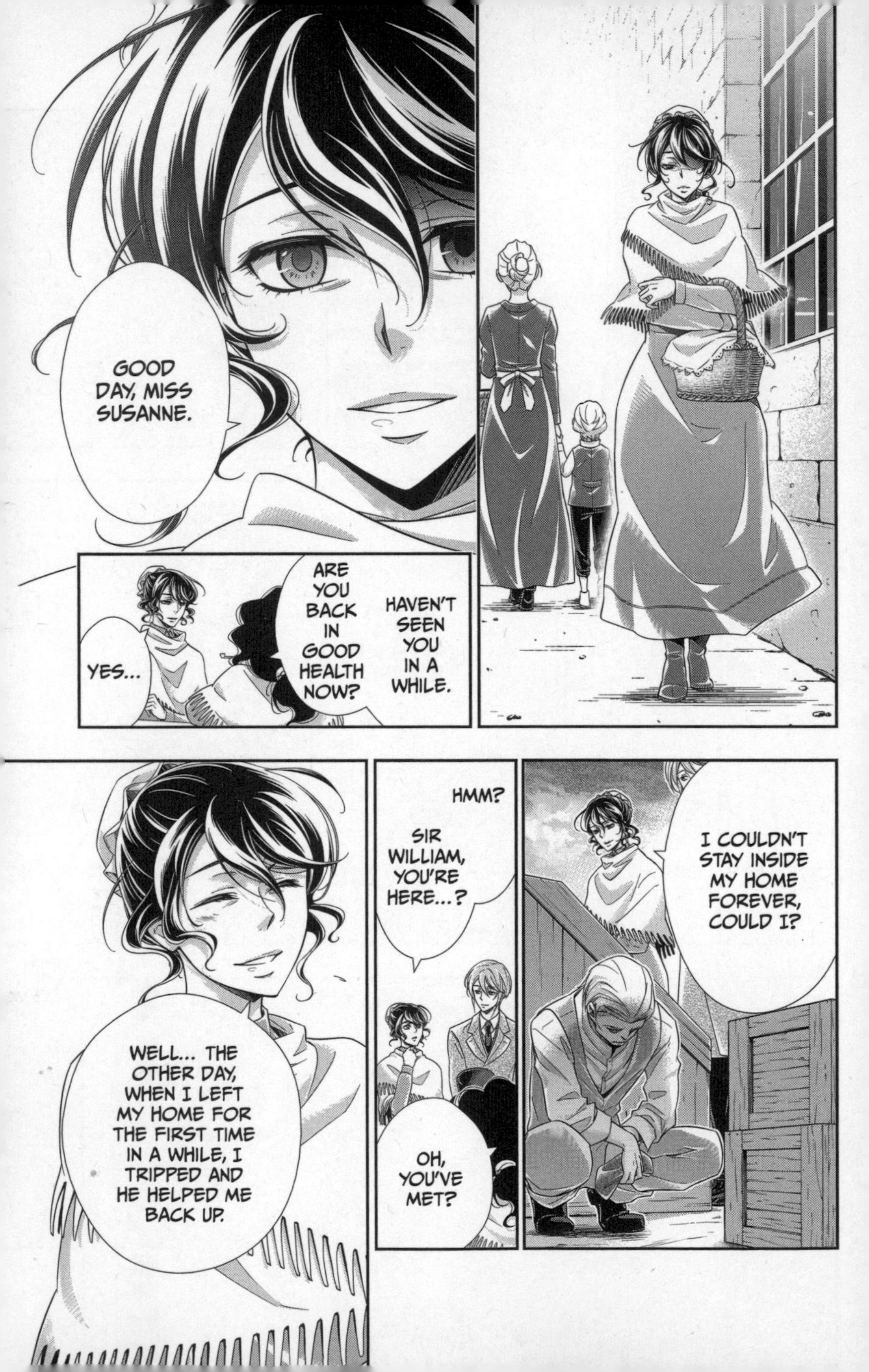
GOOD DAY, MISS SUSANNE.
HAVEN'T SEEN YOU IN A WHILE.
ARE YOU BACK IN GOOD HEALTH NOW?
YES...
I COULDN'T STAY INSIDE MY HOME FOREVER, COULD I?
HMM?
SIR WILLIAM, YOU'RE HERE...?
OH, YOU'VE MET?
WELL... THE OTHER DAY, WHEN I LEFT MY HOME FOR THE FIRST TIME IN A WHILE, I TRIPPED AND HE HELPED ME BACK UP.

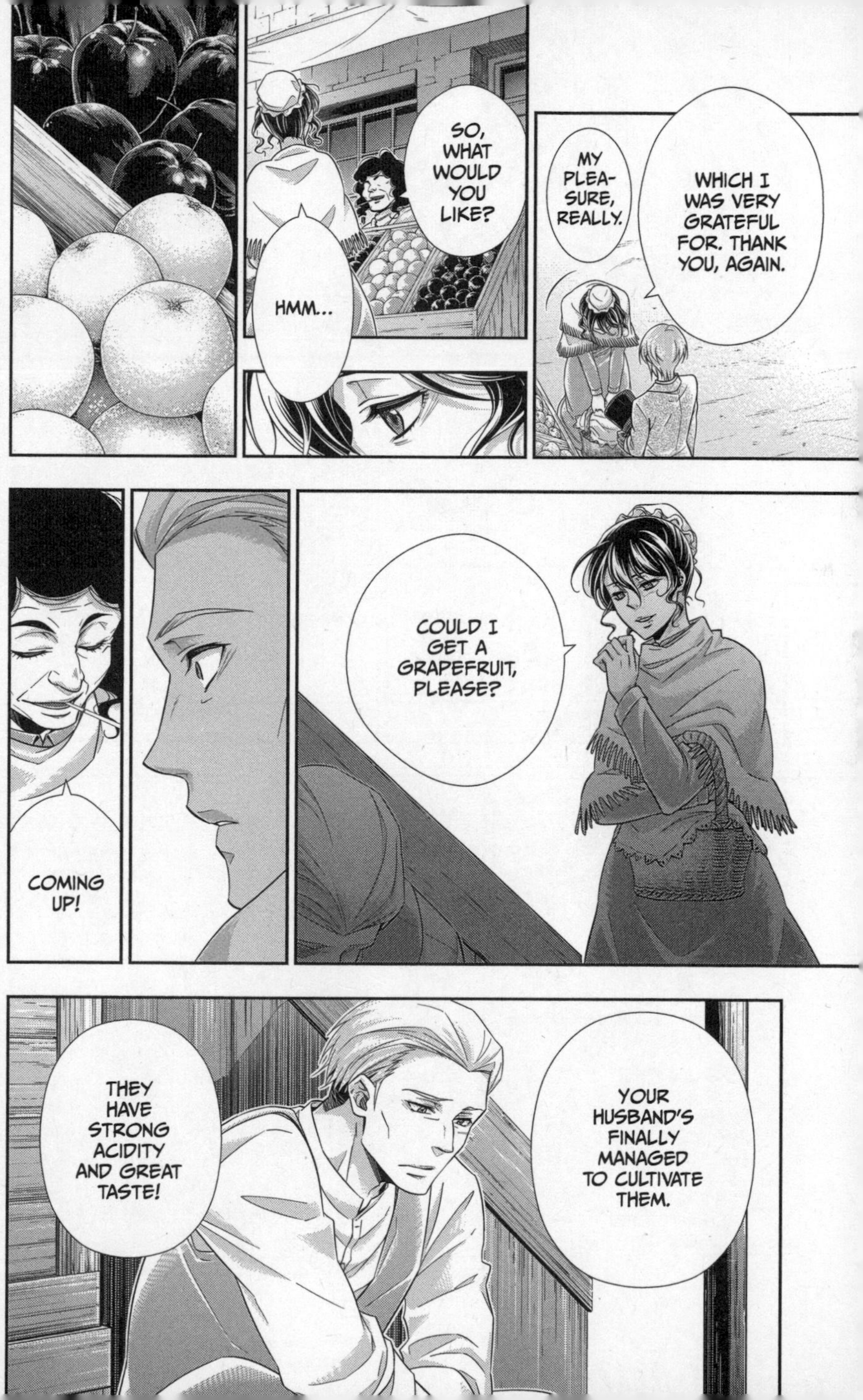
WHICH I WAS VERY GRATEFUL FOR. THANK YOU, AGAIN.
MY PLEA-SURE, REALLY.
SO, WHAT WOULD YOU LIKE?
HMM...
COULD I GET A GRAPEFRUIT, PLEASE?
COMING UP!
YOUR HUSBAND'S FINALLY MANAGED TO CULTIVATE THEM.
THEY HAVE STRONG ACIDITY AND GREAT TASTE!

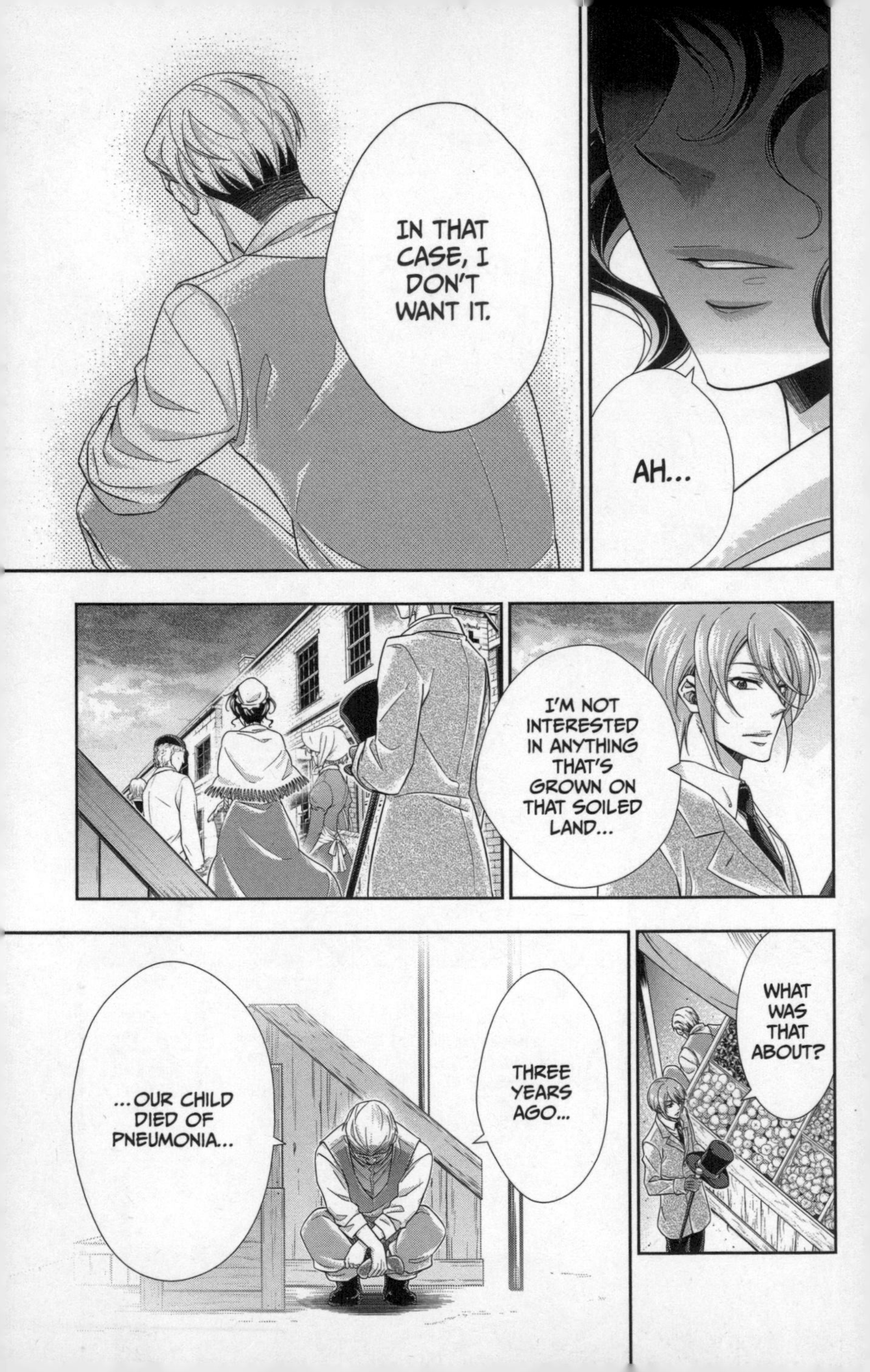
AH...
IN THAT CASE, I DON'T WANT IT.
I'M NOT INTERESTED IN ANYTHING THAT'S GROWN ON THAT SOILED LAND...
WHAT WAS THAT ABOUT?
THREE YEARS AGO...
...OUR CHILD DIED OF PNEUMONIA...

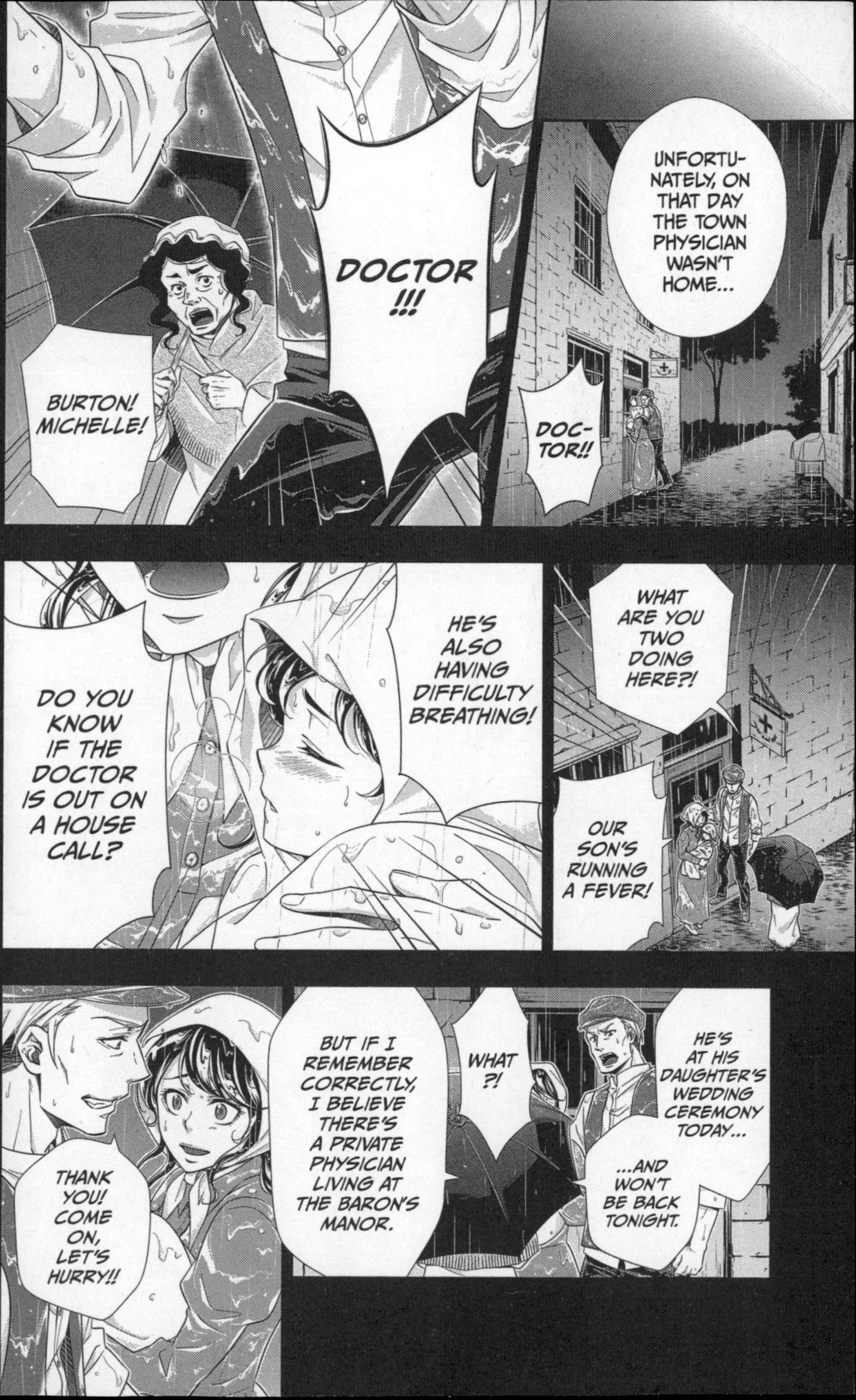
UNFORTUNATELY, ON THAT DAY THE TOWN PHYSICIAN WASN'T HOME...
DOCTOR!!
DOCTOR !!!
BURTON! MICHELLE!
WHAT ARE YOU TWO DOING HERE?!
OUR SON'S RUNNING A FEVER!
HE'S ALSO HAVING DIFFICULTY BREATHING!
DO YOU KNOW IF THE DOCTOR IS OUT ON A HOUSE CALL?
HE'S AT HIS DAUGHTER'S WEDDING CEREMONY TODAY...
...AND WON'T BE BACK TONIGHT.
WHAT ?!
BUT IF I REMEMBER CORRECTLY, I BELIEVE THERE'S A PRIVATE PHYSICIAN LIVING AT THE BARON'S MANOR.
THANK YOU! COME ON, LET'S HURRY!!

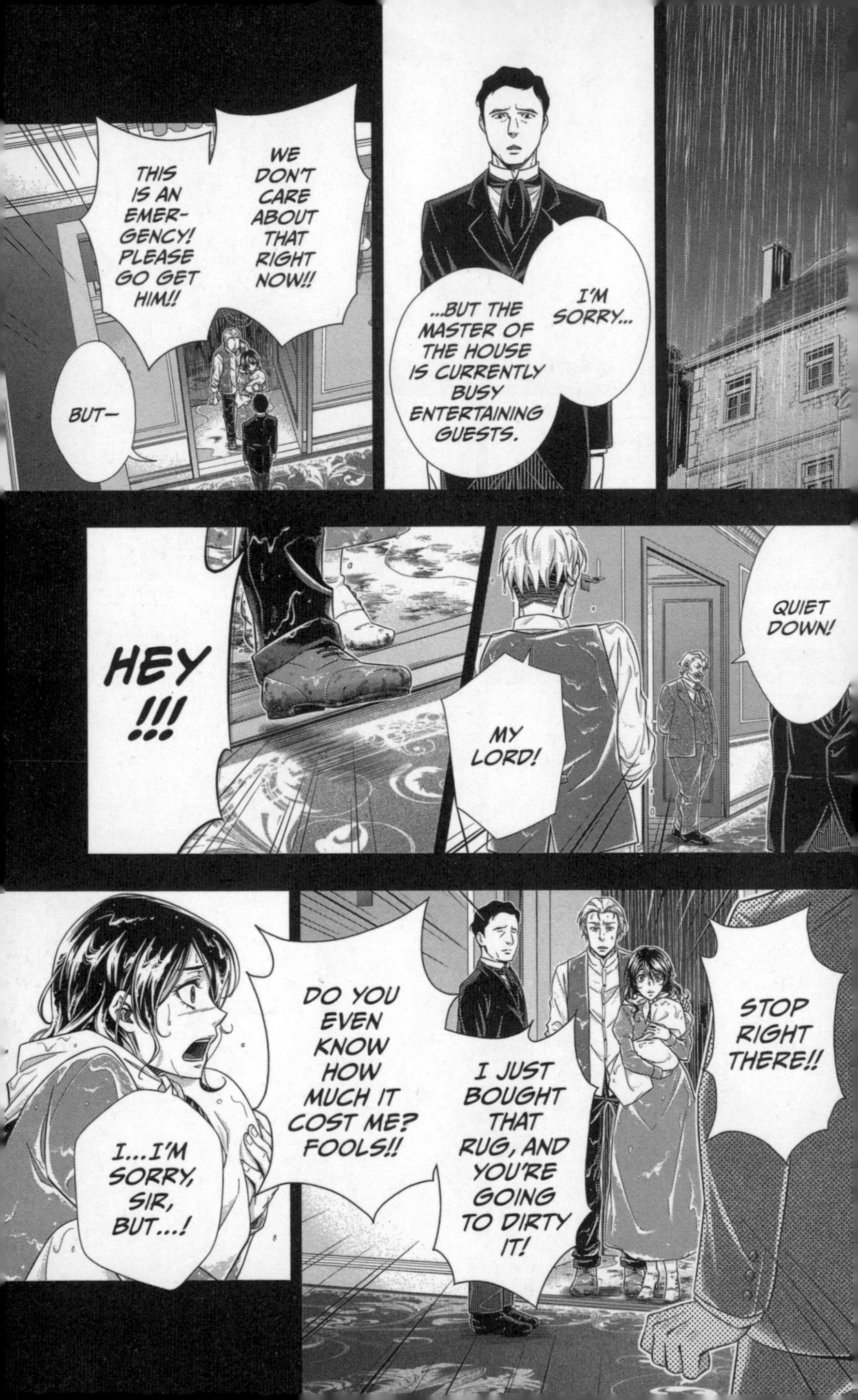
I'M SORRY...
...BUT THE MASTER OF THE HOUSE IS CURRENTLY BUSY ENTERTAINING GUESTS.
WE DON'T CARE ABOUT THAT RIGHT NOW!!
THIS IS AN EMER-GENCY! PLEASE GO GET HIM!!
BUT—
QUIET DOWN!
MY LORD!
HEY!!!
STOP RIGHT THERE!!
I JUST BOUGHT THAT RUG, AND YOU'RE GOING TO DIRTY IT!
DO YOU EVEN KNOW HOW MUCH IT COST ME? FOOLS!!
I...I'M SORRY, SIR, BUT...!

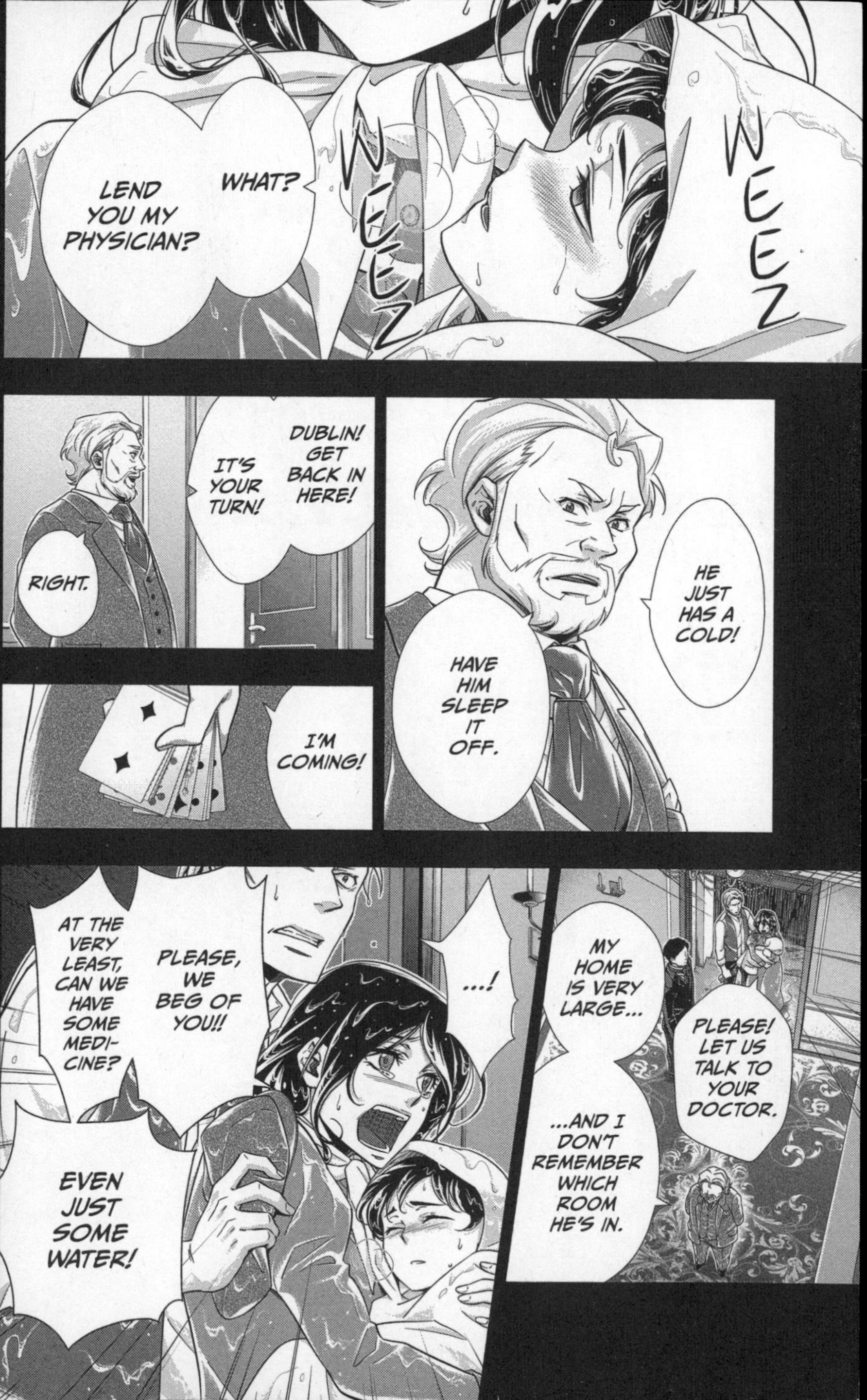
WEEZ
WEEZ
WHAT?
LEND YOU MY PHYSICIAN?
HE JUST HAS A COLD!
HAVE HIM SLEEP IT OFF.
DUBLIN! GET BACK IN HERE!
IT'S YOUR TURN!
RIGHT.
I'M COMING!
PLEASE! LET US TALK TO YOUR DOCTOR.
MY HOME IS VERY LARGE...
...AND I DON'T REMEMBER WHICH ROOM HE'S IN.
...!
PLEASE, WE BEG OF YOU!!
AT THE VERY LEAST, CAN WE HAVE SOME MEDI-CINE?
EVEN JUST SOME WATER!

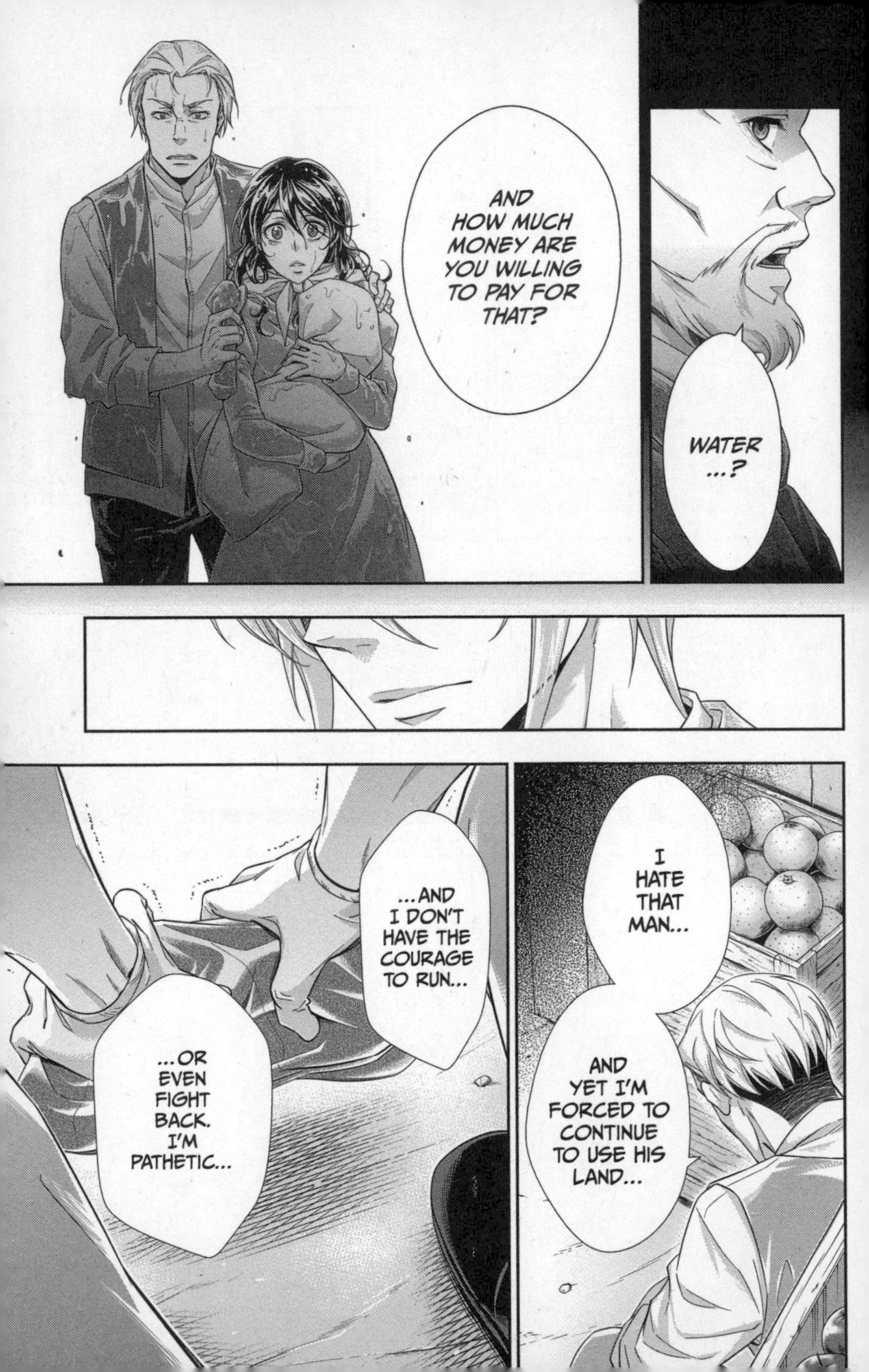
WATER ...?
AND HOW MUCH MONEY ARE YOU WILLING TO PAY FOR THAT?
I HATE THAT MAN...
AND YET I'M FORCED TO CONTINUE TO USE HIS LAND...
...AND I DON'T HAVE THE COURAGE TO RUN...
...OR EVEN FIGHT BACK. I'M PATHETIC...

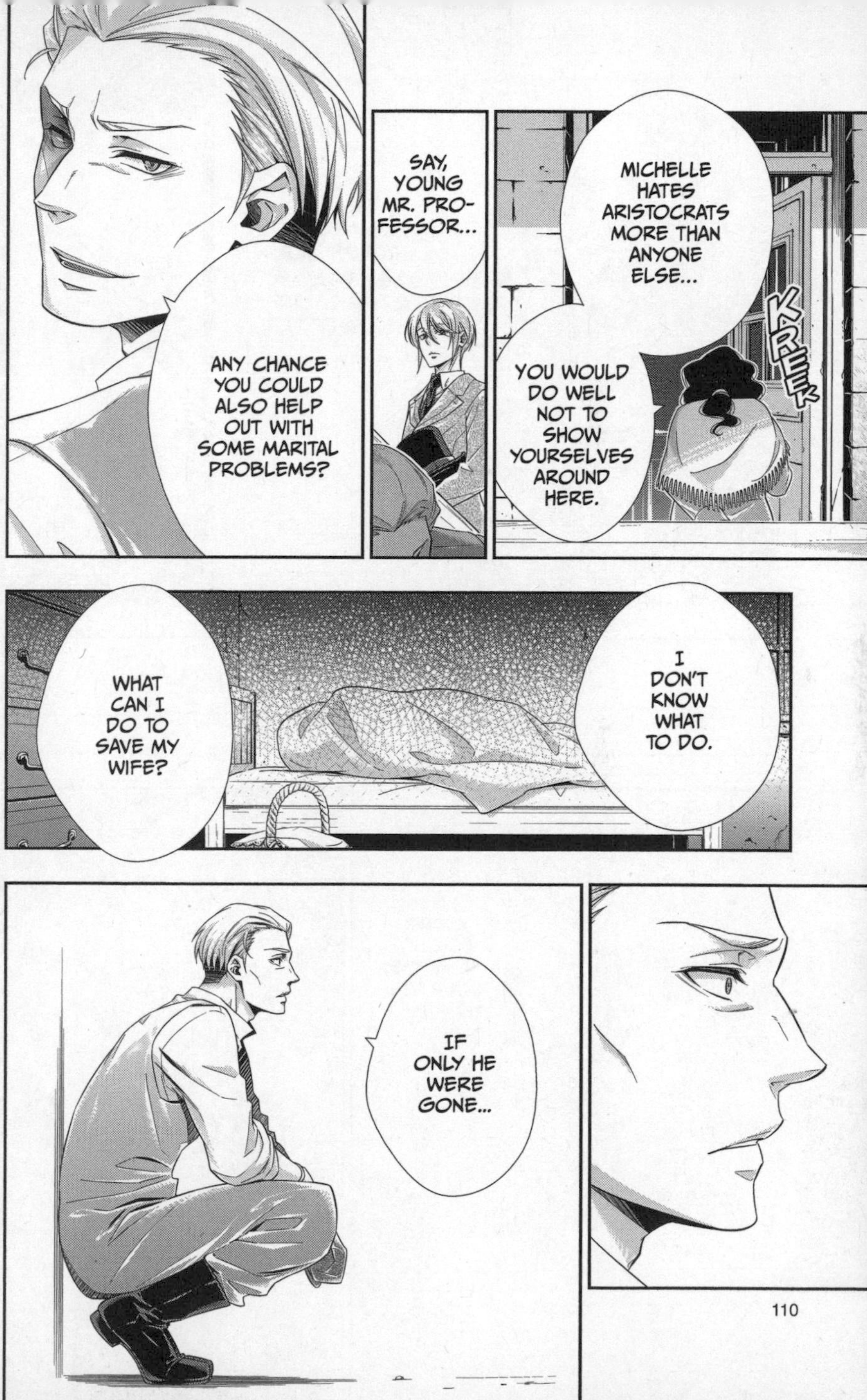
MICHELLE HATES ARISTOCRATS MORE THAN ANYONE ELSE...
YOU WOULD DO WELL NOT TO SHOW YOURSELVES AROUND HERE.
KREEK
SAY, YOUNG MR. PRO-FESSOR...
ANY CHANCE YOU COULD ALSO HELP OUT WITH SOME MARITAL PROBLEMS?
I DON'T KNOW WHAT TO DO.
WHAT CAN I DO TO SAVE MY WIFE?
IF ONLY HE WERE GONE...

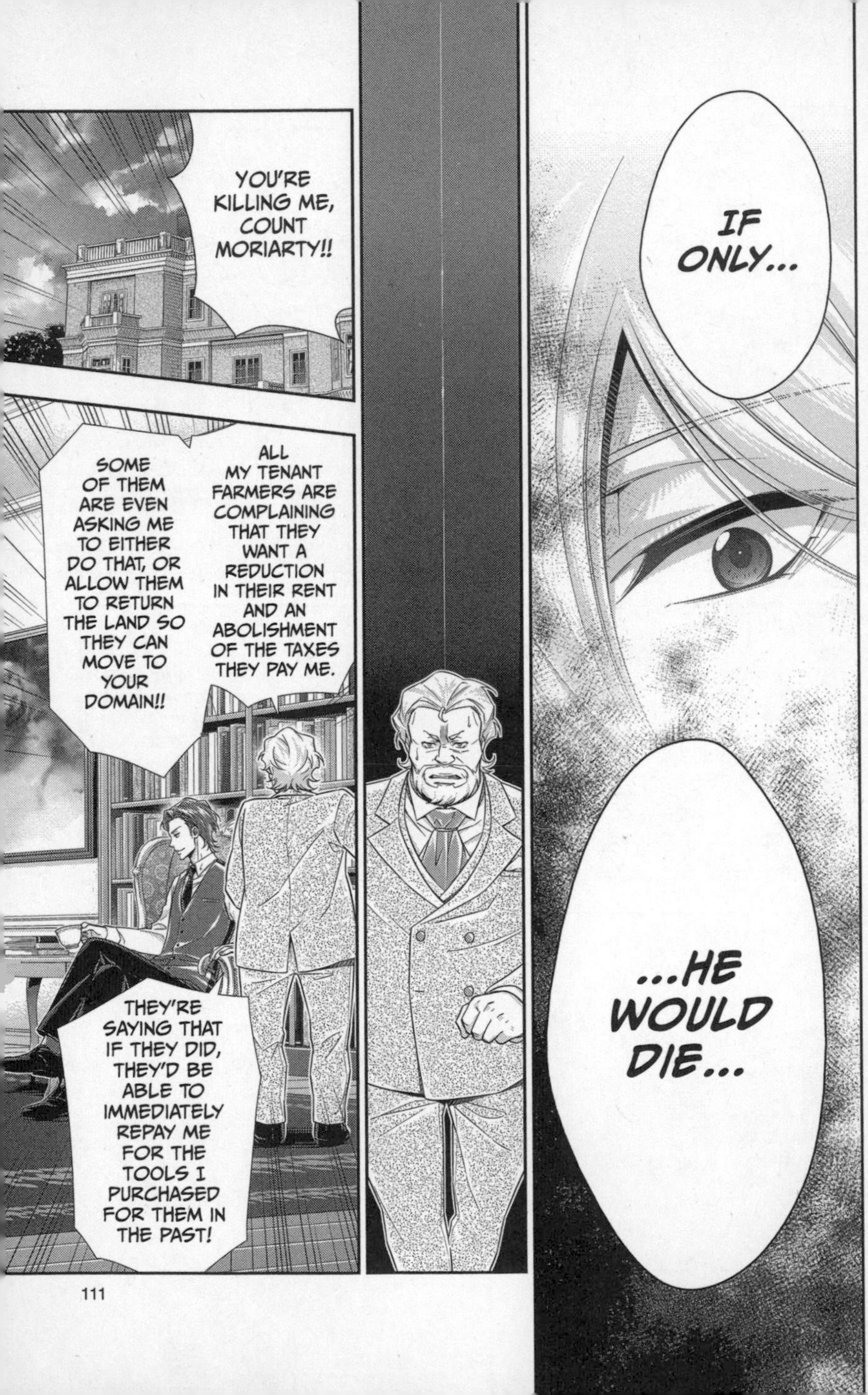

IF ONLY...
...HE WOULD DIE...
YOU'RE KILLING ME, COUNT MORIARTY!!
ALL MY TENANT FARMERS ARE COMPLAINING THAT THEY WANT A REDUCTION IN THEIR RENT AND AN ABOLISHMENT OF THE TAXES THEY PAY ME.
SOME OF THEM ARE EVEN ASKING ME TO EITHER DO THAT, OR ALLOW THEM TO RETURN THE LAND SO THEY CAN MOVE TO YOUR DOMAIN!!
THEY'RE SAYING THAT IF THEY DID, THEY'D BE ABLE TO IMMEDIATELY REPAY ME FOR THE TOOLS I PURCHASED FOR THEM IN THE PAST!

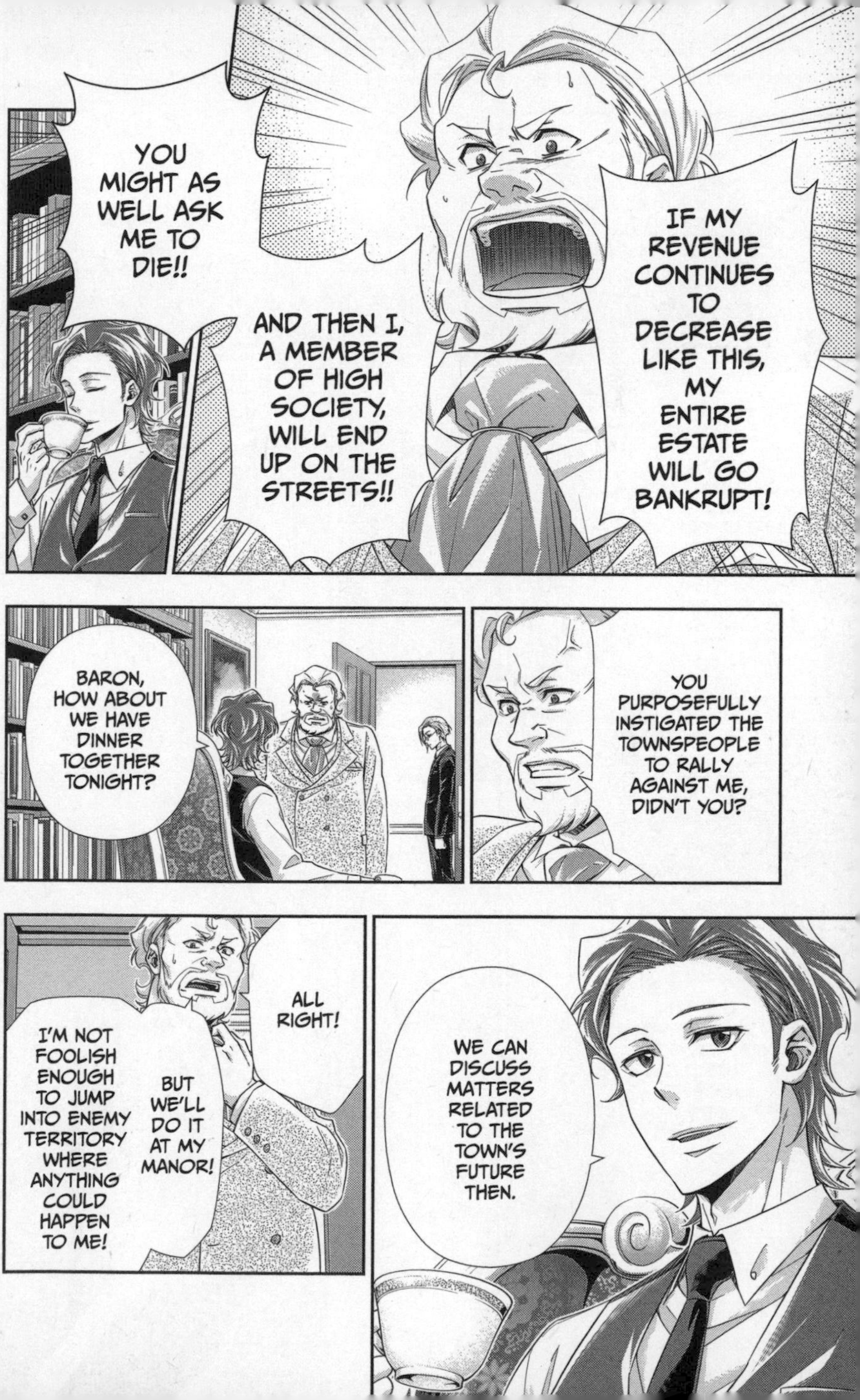
IF MY REVENUE CONTINUES TO DECREASE LIKE THIS, MY ENTIRE ESTATE WILL GO BANKRUPT!
AND THEN I, A MEMBER OF HIGH SOCIETY, WILL END UP ON THE STREETS!!
YOU MIGHT AS WELL ASK ME TO DIE!!
YOU PURPOSEFULLY INSTIGATED THE TOWNSPEOPLE TO RALLY AGAINST ME, DIDN'T YOU?
BARON, HOW ABOUT WE HAVE DINNER TOGETHER TONIGHT?
WE CAN DISCUSS MATTERS RELATED TO THE TOWN'S FUTURE THEN.
ALL RIGHT!
BUT WE'LL DO IT AT MY MANOR!
I'M NOT FOOLISH ENOUGH TO JUMP INTO ENEMY TERRITORY WHERE ANYTHING COULD HAPPEN TO ME!

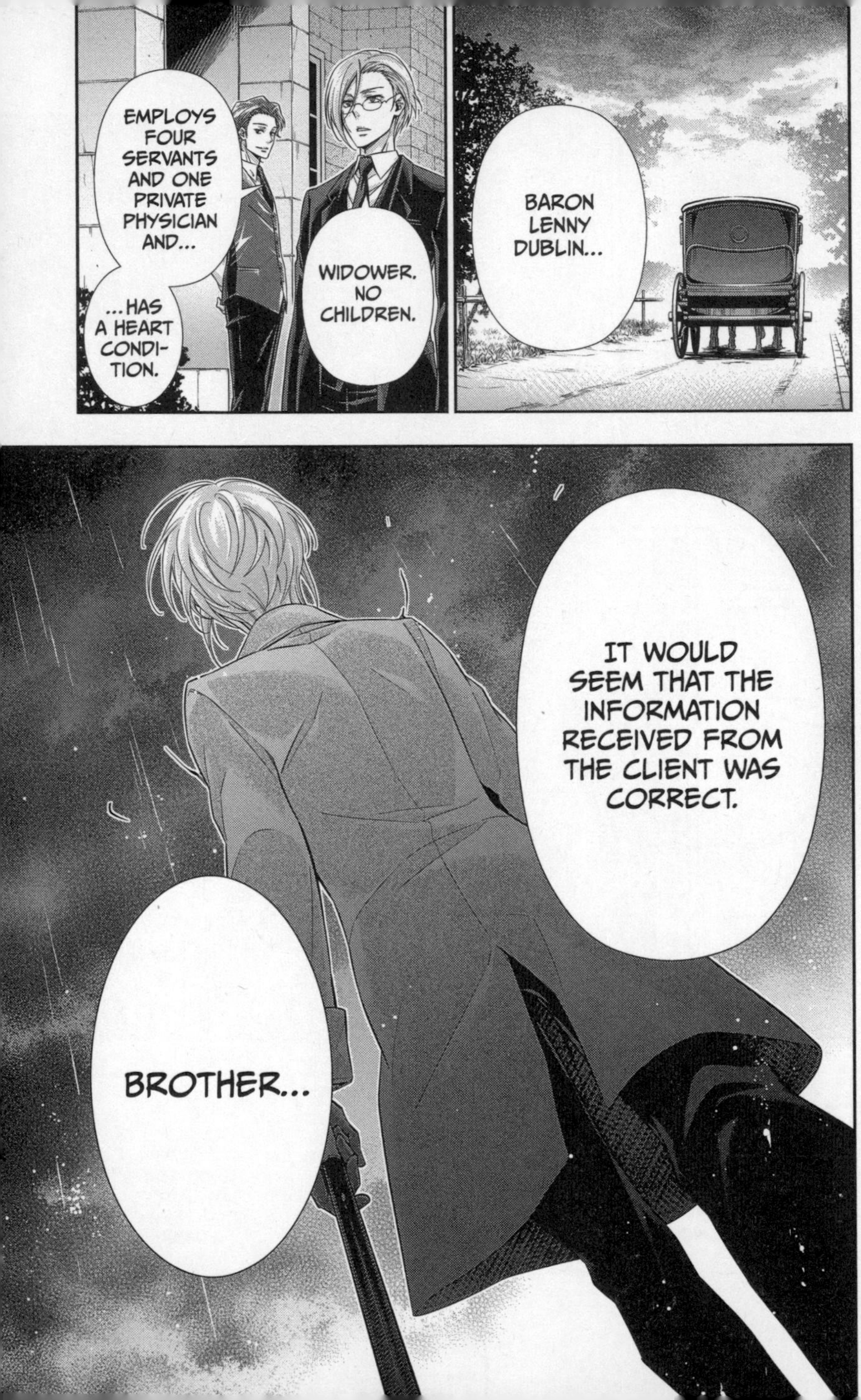
BARON LENNY DUBLIN...
WIDOWER. NO CHILDREN.
EMPLOYS FOUR SERVANTS AND ONE PRIVATE PHYSICIAN AND...
...HAS A HEART CONDI-TION.
IT WOULD SEEM THAT THE INFORMATION RECEIVED FROM THE CLIENT WAS CORRECT.
BROTHER...

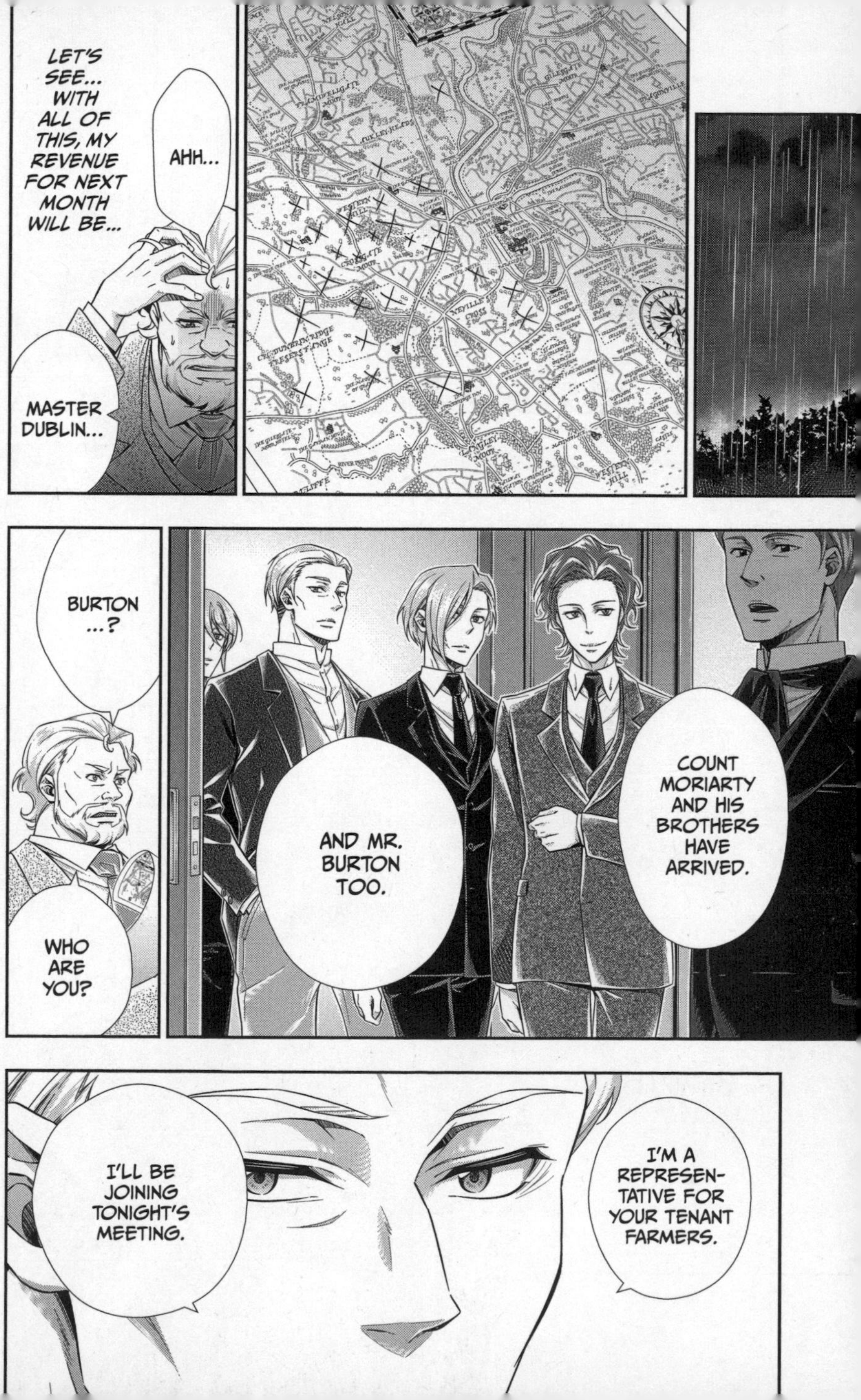
LET'S SEE... WITH ALL OF THIS, MY REVENUE FOR NEXT MONTH WILL BE...
AHH...
MASTER DUBLIN...
COUNT MORIARTY AND HIS BROTHERS HAVE ARRIVED.
AND MR. BURTON TOO.
BURTON ...?
WHO ARE YOU?
I'M A REPRESEN-TATIVE FOR YOUR TENANT FARMERS.
I'LL BE JOINING TONIGHT'S MEETING.

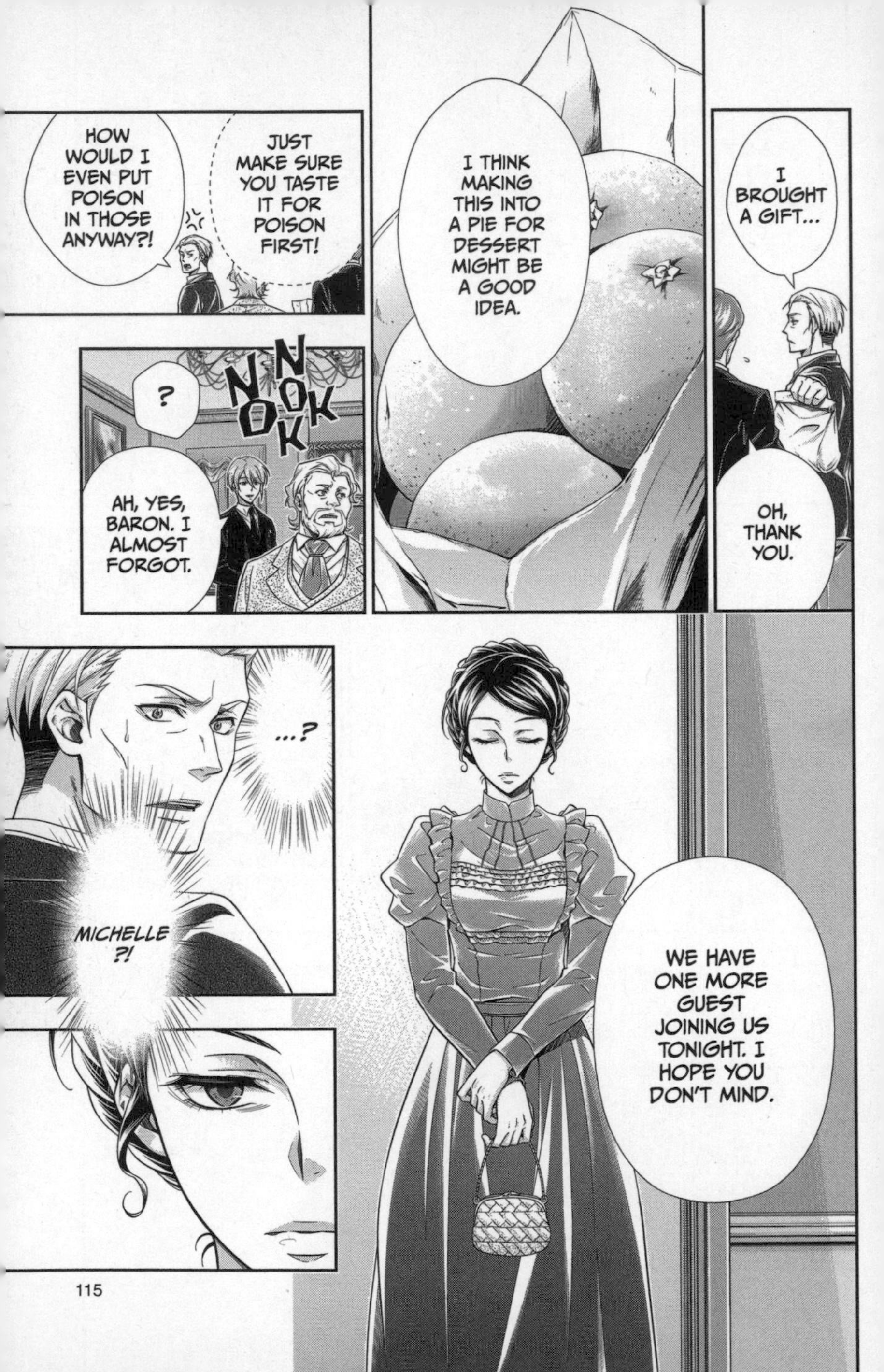
I BROUGHT A GIFT...
OH, THANK YOU.
I THINK MAKING THIS INTO A PIE FOR DESSERT MIGHT BE A GOOD IDEA.
JUST MAKE SURE YOU TASTE IT FOR POISON FIRST!
HOW WOULD I EVEN PUT POISON IN THOSE ANYWAY?!
NOK NOK
?
AH, YES, BARON. I ALMOST FORGOT.
WE HAVE ONE MORE GUEST JOINING US TONIGHT. I HOPE YOU DON'T MIND.
...?
MICHELLE ?!

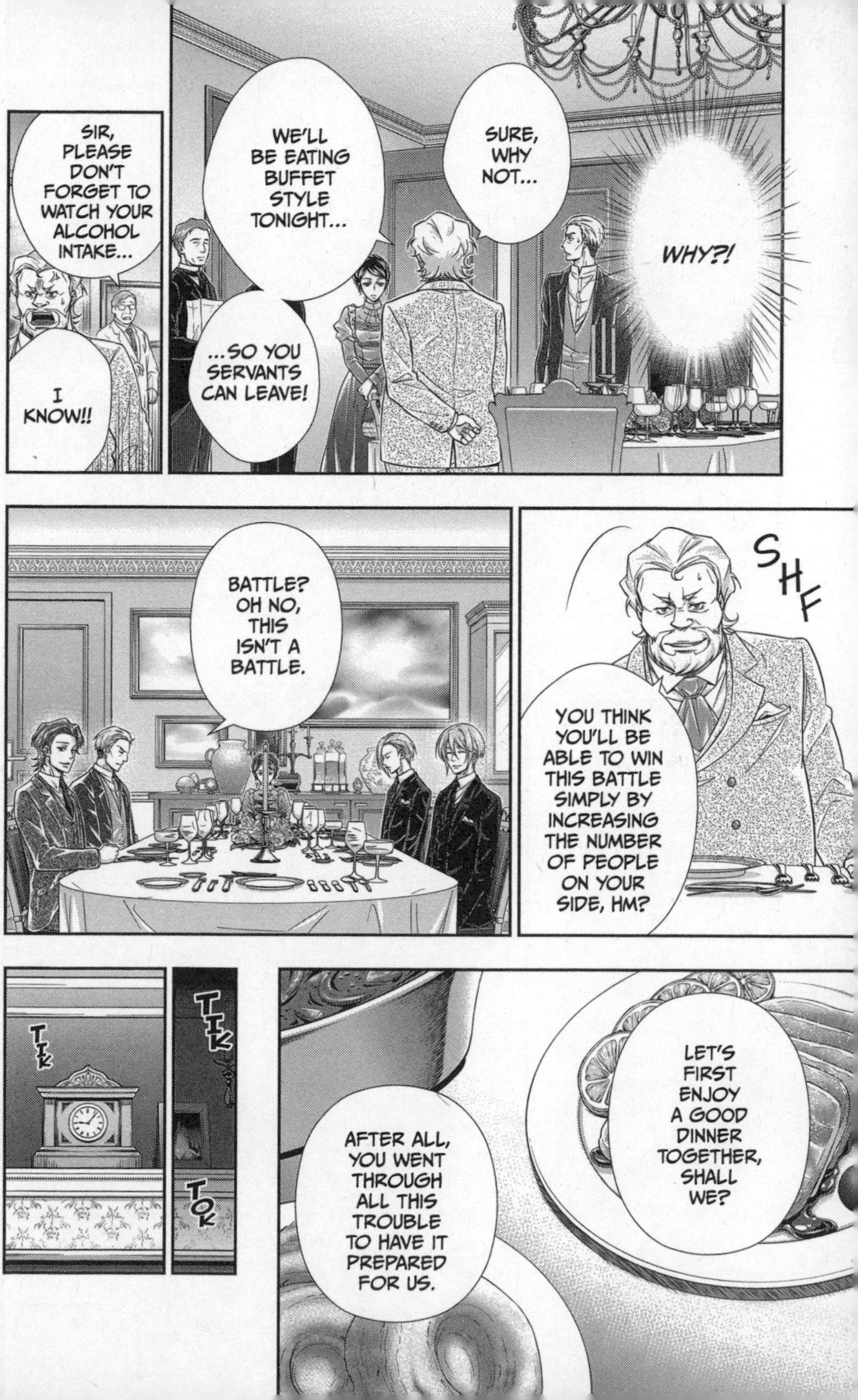
WE'LL BE EATING BUFFET STYLE TONIGHT...
...SO YOU SERVANTS CAN LEAVE!
SURE, WHY NOT...
WHY?!
SIR, PLEASE DON'T FORGET TO WATCH YOUR ALCOHOL INTAKE...
I KNOW!!
SHF
YOU THINK YOU'LL BE ABLE TO WIN THIS BATTLE SIMPLY BY INCREASING THE NUMBER OF PEOPLE ON YOUR SIDE, HM?
BATTLE? OH NO, THIS ISN'T A BATTLE.
LET'S FIRST ENJOY A GOOD DINNER TOGETHER, SHALL WE?
AFTER ALL, YOU WENT THROUGH ALL THIS TROUBLE TO HAVE IT PREPARED FOR US.
TIK
TOK
TIK

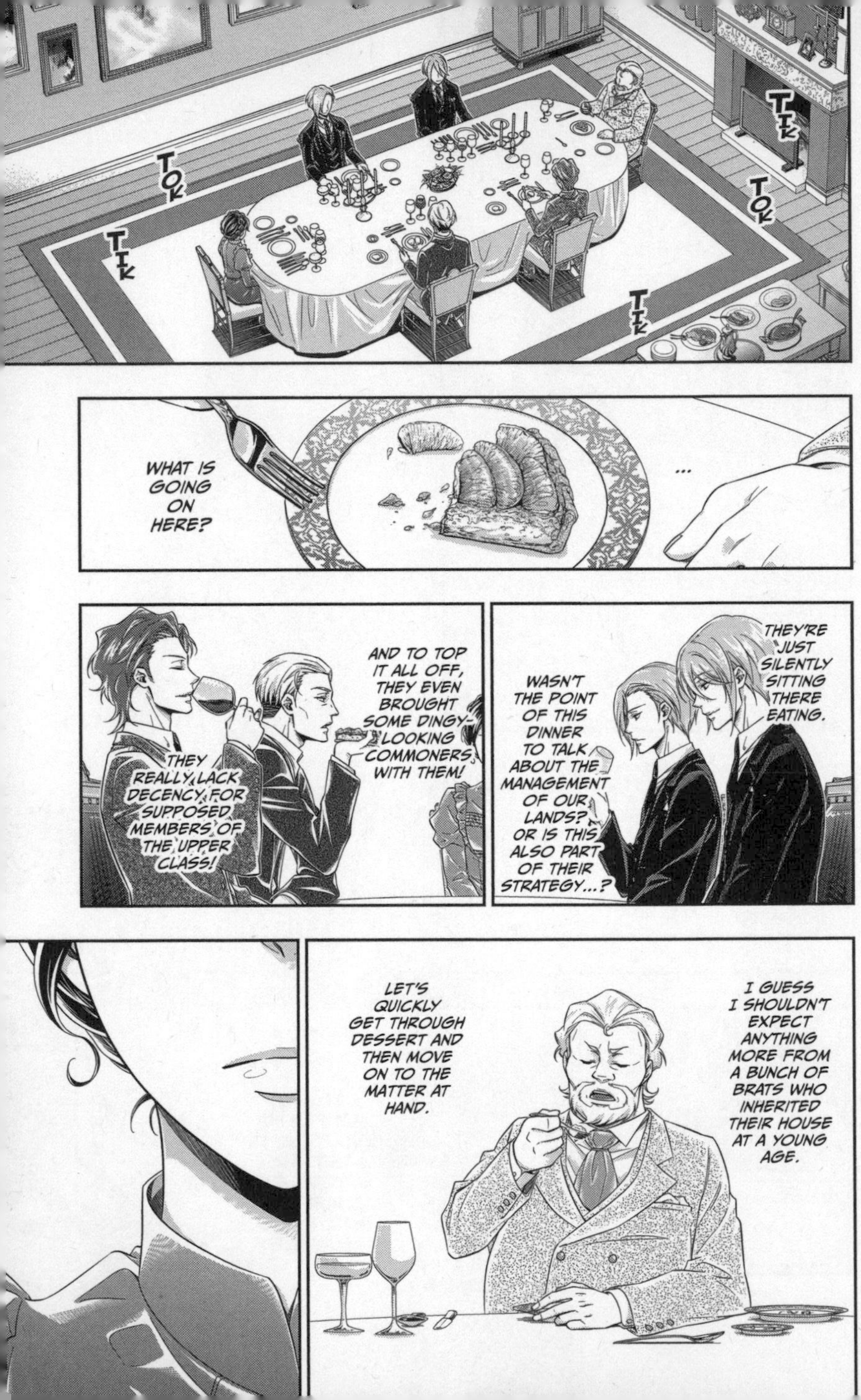
TIK
TOK
TIK
TOK
TIK
...
WHAT IS GOING ON HERE?
THEY'RE JUST SILENTLY SITTING THERE EATING.
WASN'T THE POINT OF THIS DINNER TO TALK ABOUT THE MANAGEMENT OF OUR LANDS? OR IS THIS ALSO PART OF THEIR STRATEGY...?
AND TO TOP IT ALL OFF, THEY EVEN BROUGHT SOME DINGY-LOOKING COMMONERS WITH THEM!
THEY REALLY LACK DECENCY FOR SUPPOSED MEMBERS OF THE UPPER CLASS!
I GUESS I SHOULDN'T EXPECT ANYTHING MORE FROM A BUNCH OF BRATS WHO INHERITED THEIR HOUSE AT A YOUNG AGE.
LET'S QUICKLY GET THROUGH DESSERT AND THEN MOVE ON TO THE MATTER AT HAND.

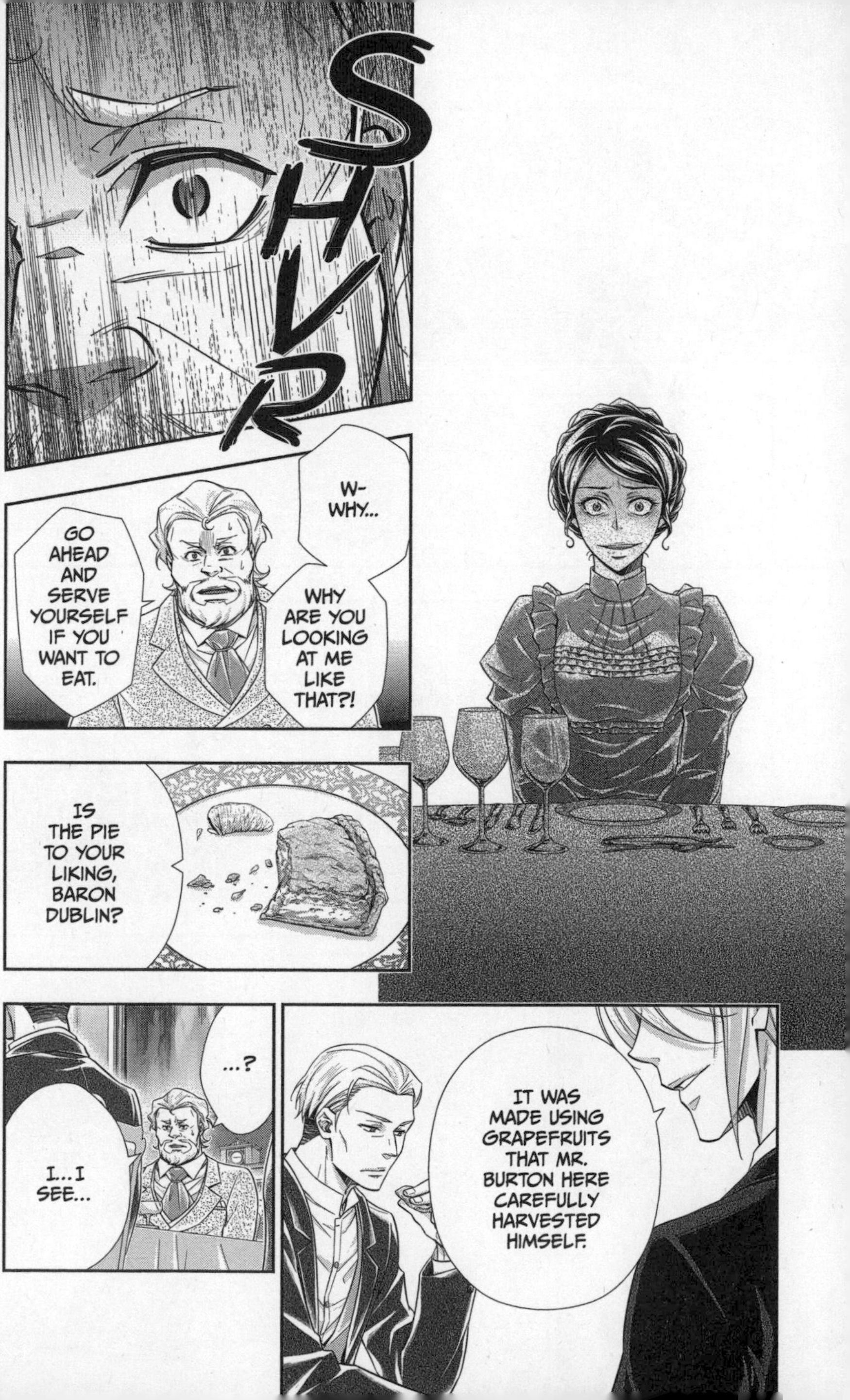
SHLR
W-WHY...
WHY ARE YOU LOOKING AT ME LIKE THAT?!
GO AHEAD AND SERVE YOURSELF IF YOU WANT TO EAT.
IS THE PIE TO YOUR LIKING, BARON DUBLIN?
IT WAS MADE USING GRAPEFRUITS THAT MR. BURTON HERE CAREFULLY HARVESTED HIMSELF.
...?
I...I SEE...

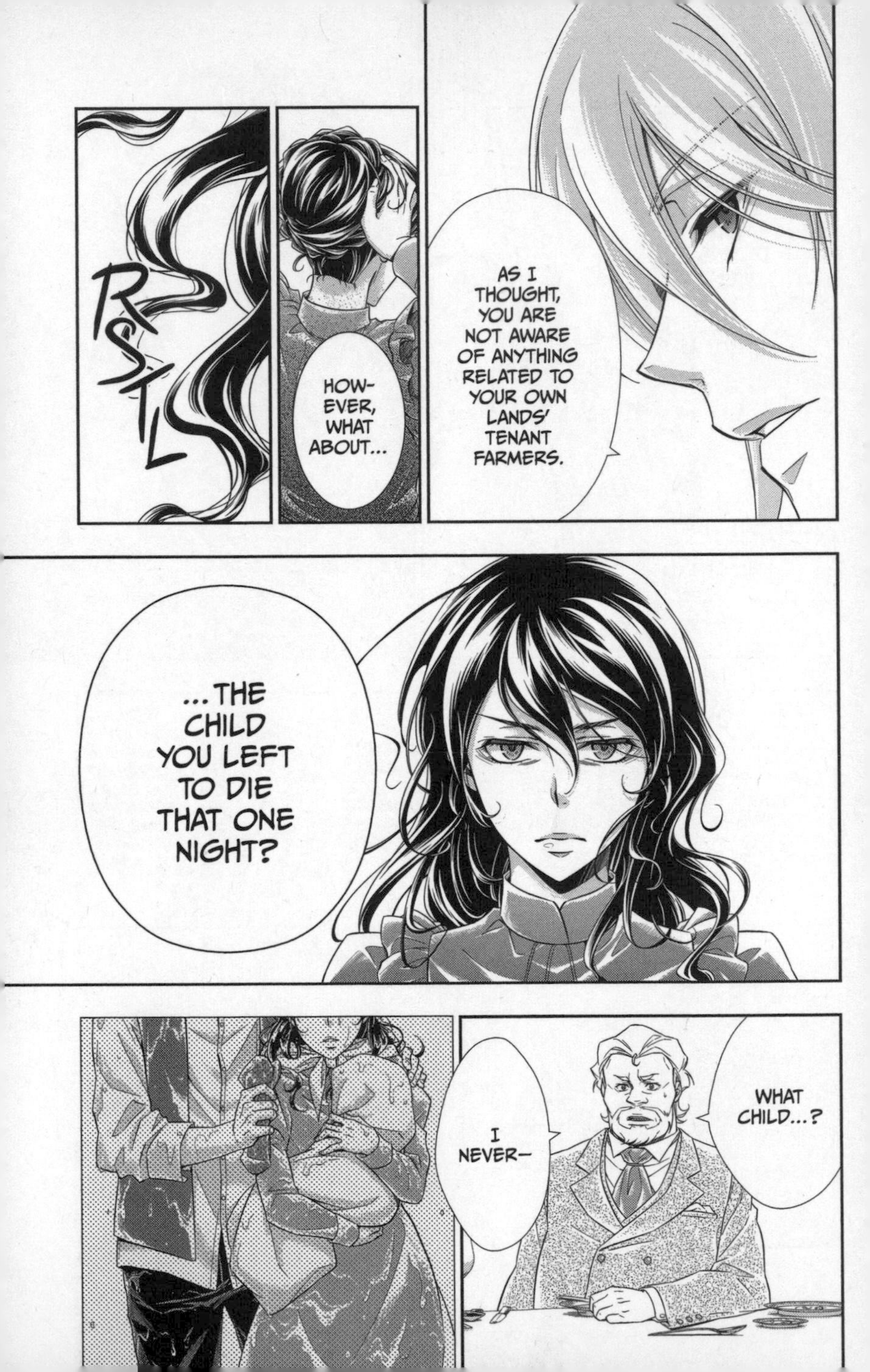
AS I THOUGHT, YOU ARE NOT AWARE OF ANYTHING RELATED TO YOUR OWN LANDS' TENANT FARMERS.
HOW-EVER, WHAT ABOUT...
RSTL
...THE CHILD YOU LEFT TO DIE THAT ONE NIGHT?
WHAT CHILD...?
I NEVER—

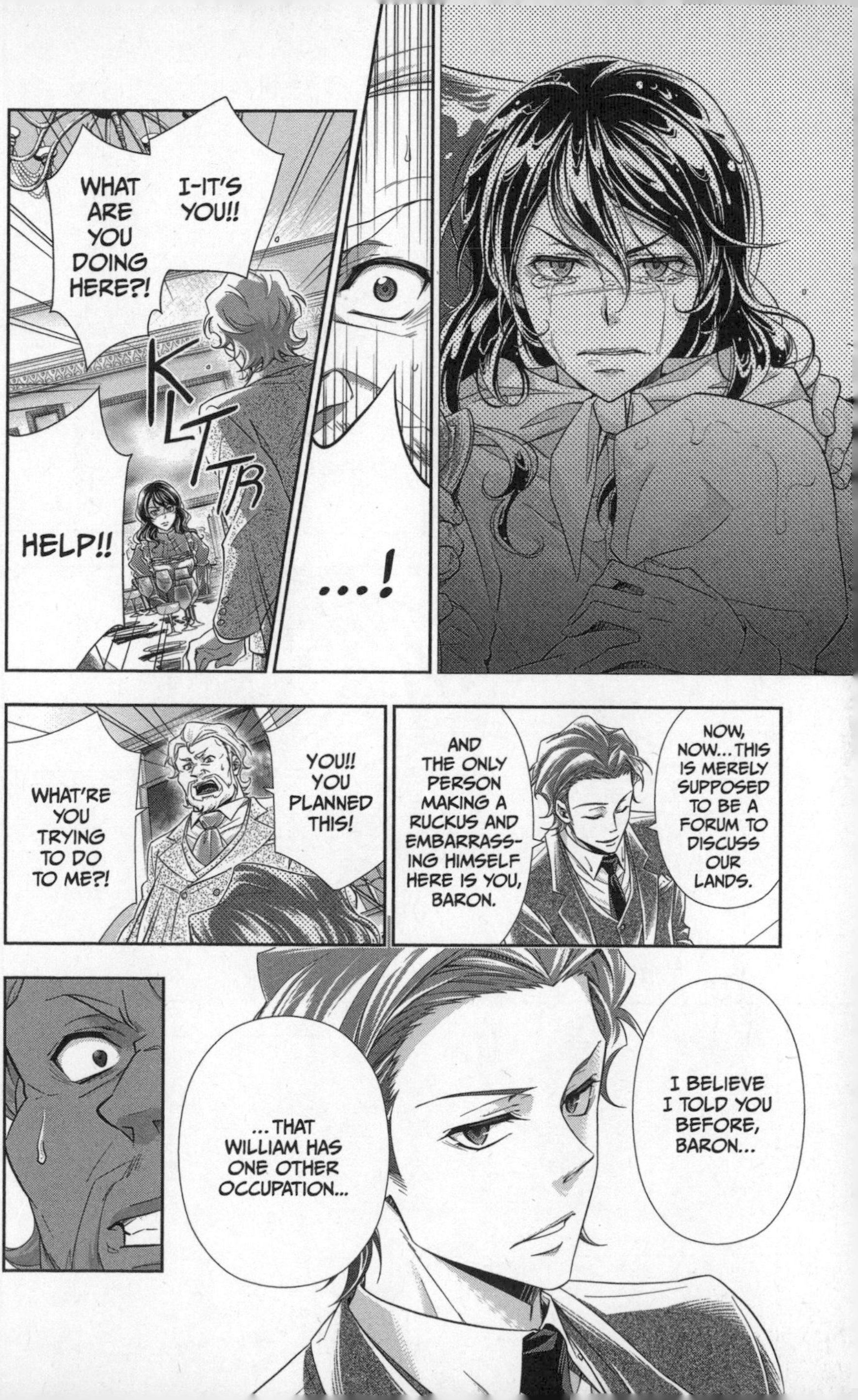
...!
I-IT'S YOU!!
WHAT ARE YOU DOING HERE?!
KLTTR
HELP!!
NOW, NOW...THIS IS MERELY SUPPOSED TO BE A FORUM TO DISCUSS OUR LANDS.
AND THE ONLY PERSON MAKING A RUCKUS AND EMBARRASSING HIMSELF HERE IS YOU, BARON.
YOU!! YOU PLANNED THIS!
WHAT'RE YOU TRYING TO DO TO ME?!
I BELIEVE I TOLD YOU BEFORE, BARON...
...THAT WILLIAM HAS ONE OTHER OCCUPATION...

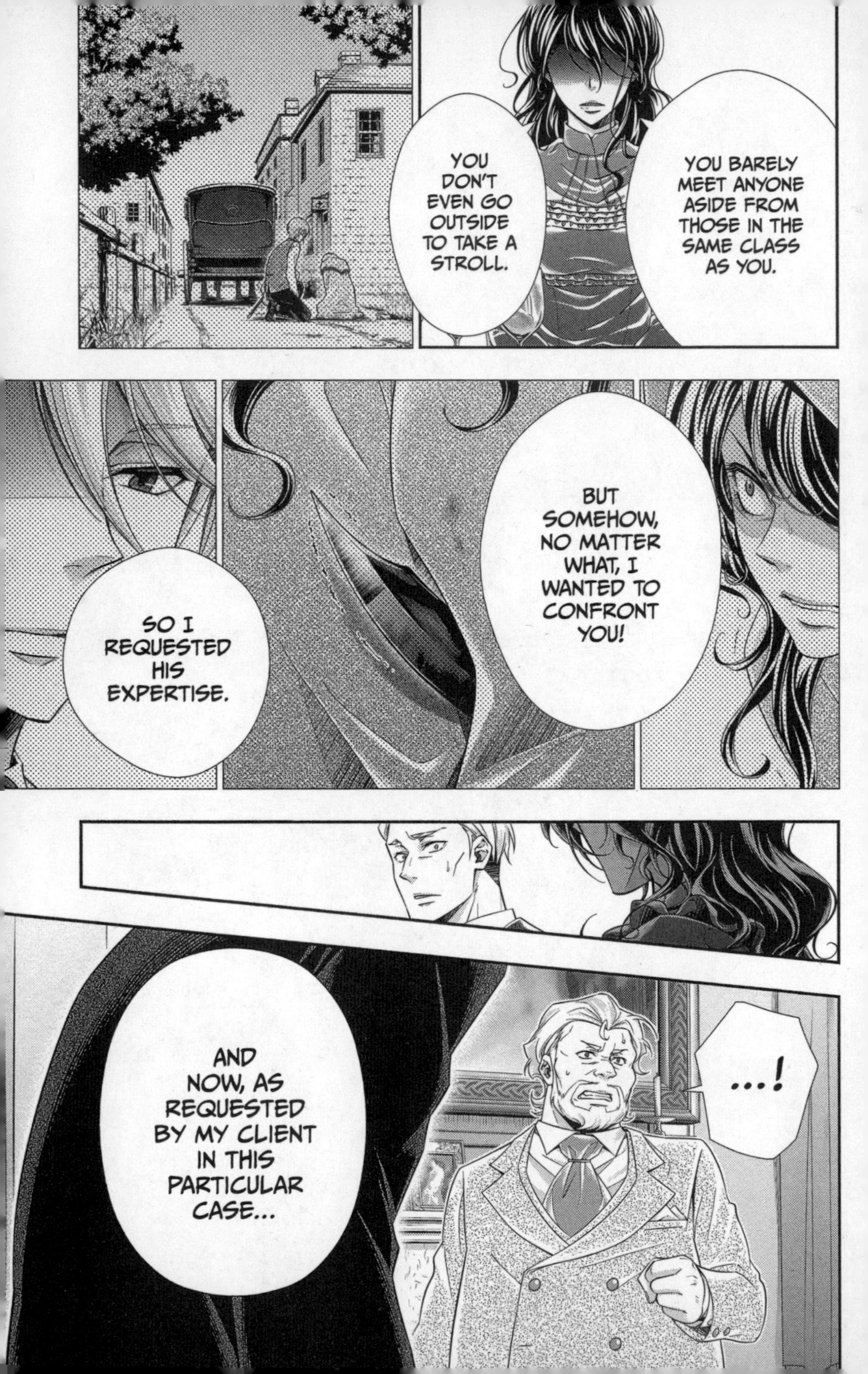
YOU BARELY MEET ANYONE ASIDE FROM THOSE IN THE SAME CLASS AS YOU.
YOU DON'T EVEN GO OUTSIDE TO TAKE A STROLL.
BUT SOMEHOW, NO MATTER WHAT, I WANTED TO CONFRONT YOU!
SO I REQUESTED HIS EXPERTISE.
...!
AND NOW, AS REQUESTED BY MY CLIENT IN THIS PARTICULAR CASE...

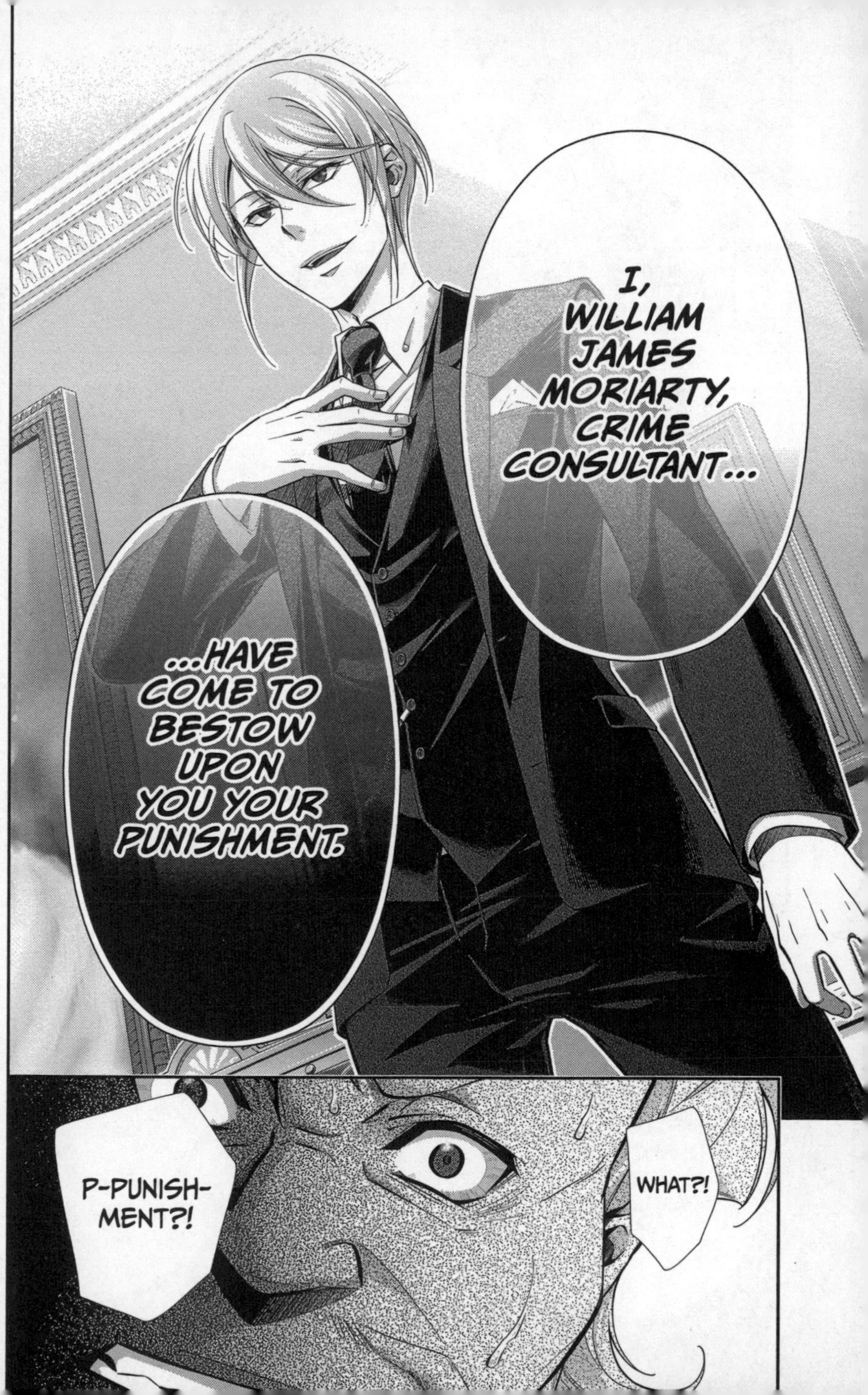
I, WILLIAM JAMES MORIARTY, CRIME CONSULTANT...
...HAVE COME TO BESTOW UPON YOU YOUR PUNISHMENT.
WHAT?!
P-PUNISHMENT?!

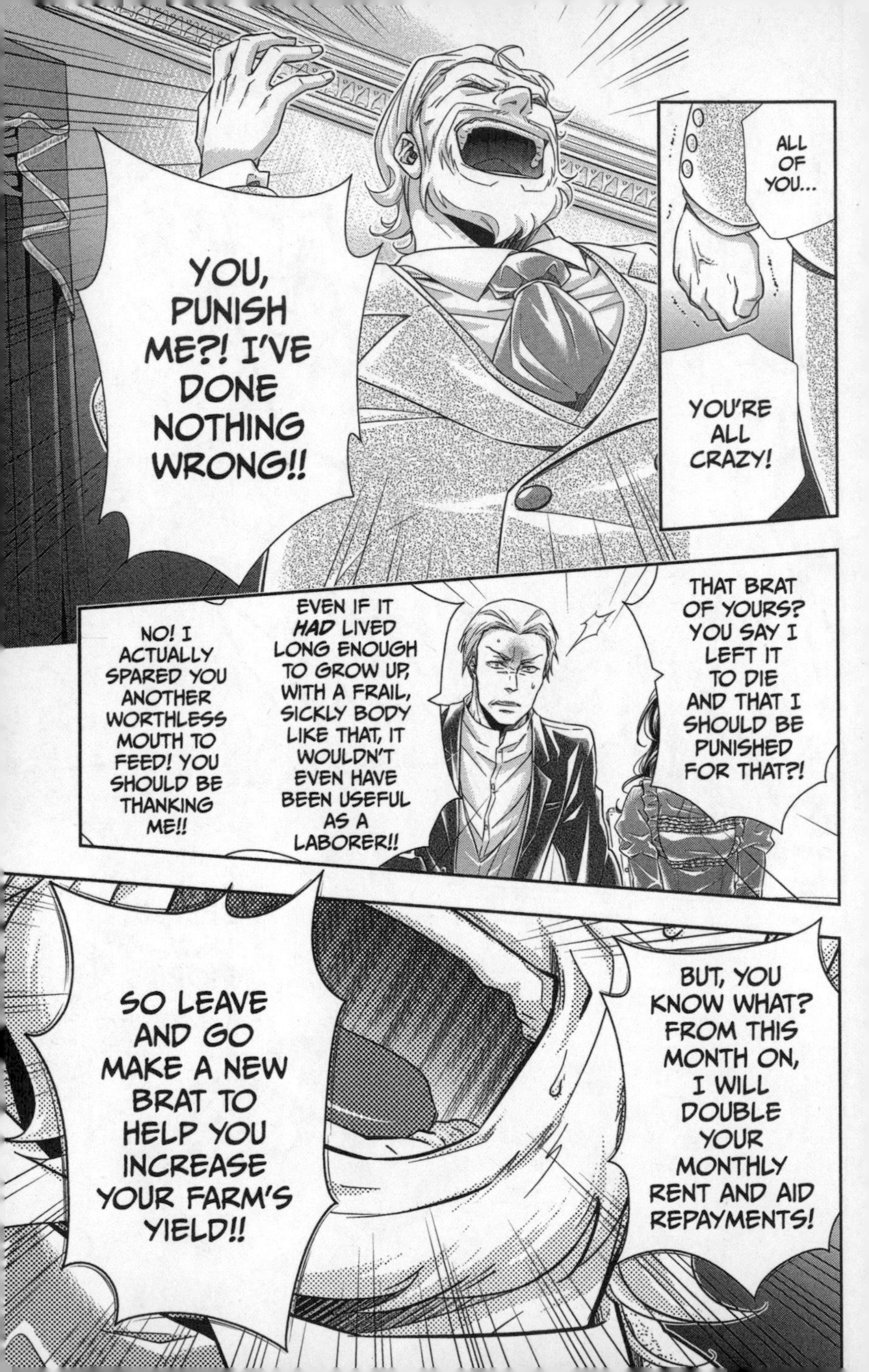
ALL OF YOU...
YOU'RE ALL CRAZY!
YOU, PUNISH ME?! I'VE DONE NOTHING WRONG!!
THAT BRAT OF YOURS? YOU SAY I LEFT IT TO DIE AND THAT I SHOULD BE PUNISHED FOR THAT?!
EVEN IF IT *HAD* LIVED LONG ENOUGH TO GROW UP, WITH A FRAIL, SICKLY BODY LIKE THAT, IT WOULDN'T EVEN HAVE BEEN USEFUL AS A LABORER!!
NO! I ACTUALLY SPARED YOU ANOTHER WORTHLESS MOUTH TO FEED! YOU SHOULD BE THANKING ME!!
BUT, YOU KNOW WHAT? FROM THIS MONTH ON, I WILL DOUBLE YOUR MONTHLY RENT AND AID REPAYMENTS!
SO LEAVE AND GO MAKE A NEW BRAT TO HELP YOU INCREASE YOUR FARM'S YIELD!!

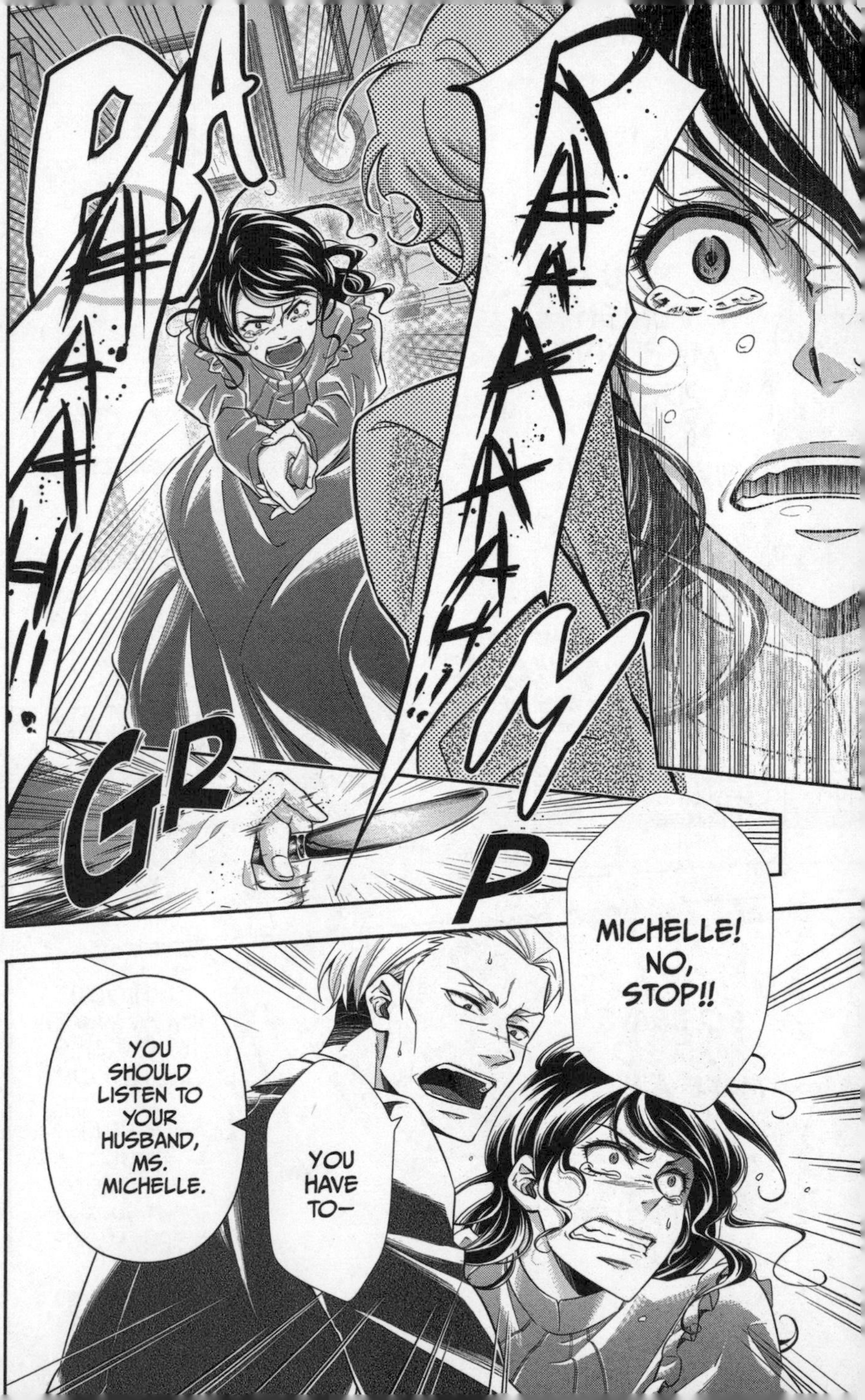
MICHELLE! NO, STOP!!
YOU HAVE TO—
YOU SHOULD LISTEN TO YOUR HUSBAND, MS. MICHELLE.

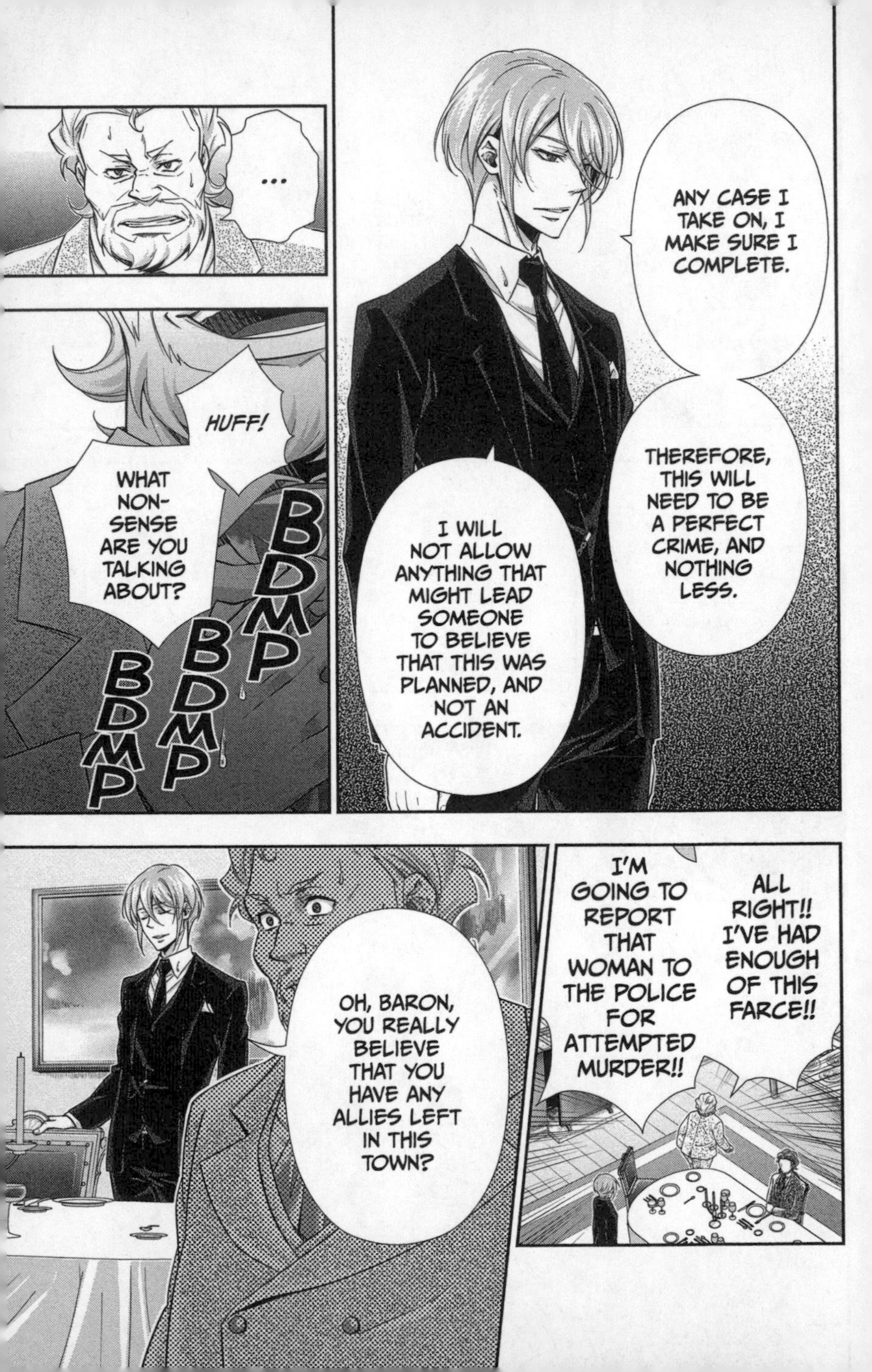
ANY CASE I TAKE ON, I MAKE SURE I COMPLETE.
THEREFORE, THIS WILL NEED TO BE A PERFECT CRIME, AND NOTHING LESS.
I WILL NOT ALLOW ANYTHING THAT MIGHT LEAD SOMEONE TO BELIEVE THAT THIS WAS PLANNED, AND NOT AN ACCIDENT.
...
HUFF!
WHAT NON-SENSE ARE YOU TALKING ABOUT?
BDMP
BDMP
BDMP
ALL RIGHT!! I'VE HAD ENOUGH OF THIS FARCE!!
I'M GOING TO REPORT THAT WOMAN TO THE POLICE FOR ATTEMPTED MURDER!!
OH, BARON, YOU REALLY BELIEVE THAT YOU HAVE ANY ALLIES LEFT IN THIS TOWN?

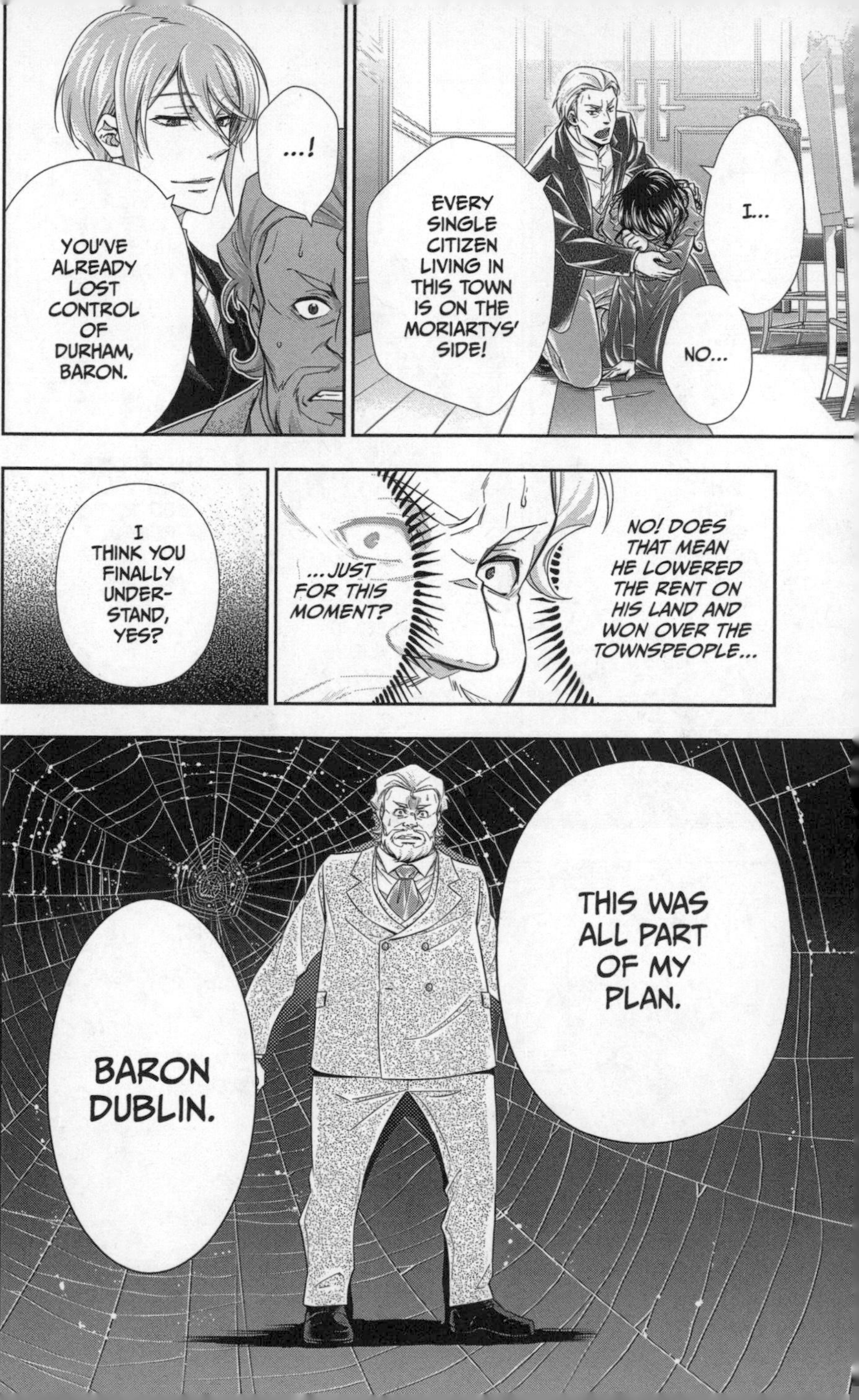
I...
NO...
EVERY SINGLE CITIZEN LIVING IN THIS TOWN IS ON THE MORIARTYS' SIDE!
...!
YOU'VE ALREADY LOST CONTROL OF DURHAM, BARON.
NO! DOES THAT MEAN HE LOWERED THE RENT ON HIS LAND AND WON OVER THE TOWNSPEOPLE...
...JUST FOR THIS MOMENT?
I THINK YOU FINALLY UNDER-STAND, YES?
THIS WAS ALL PART OF MY PLAN.
BARON DUBLIN.

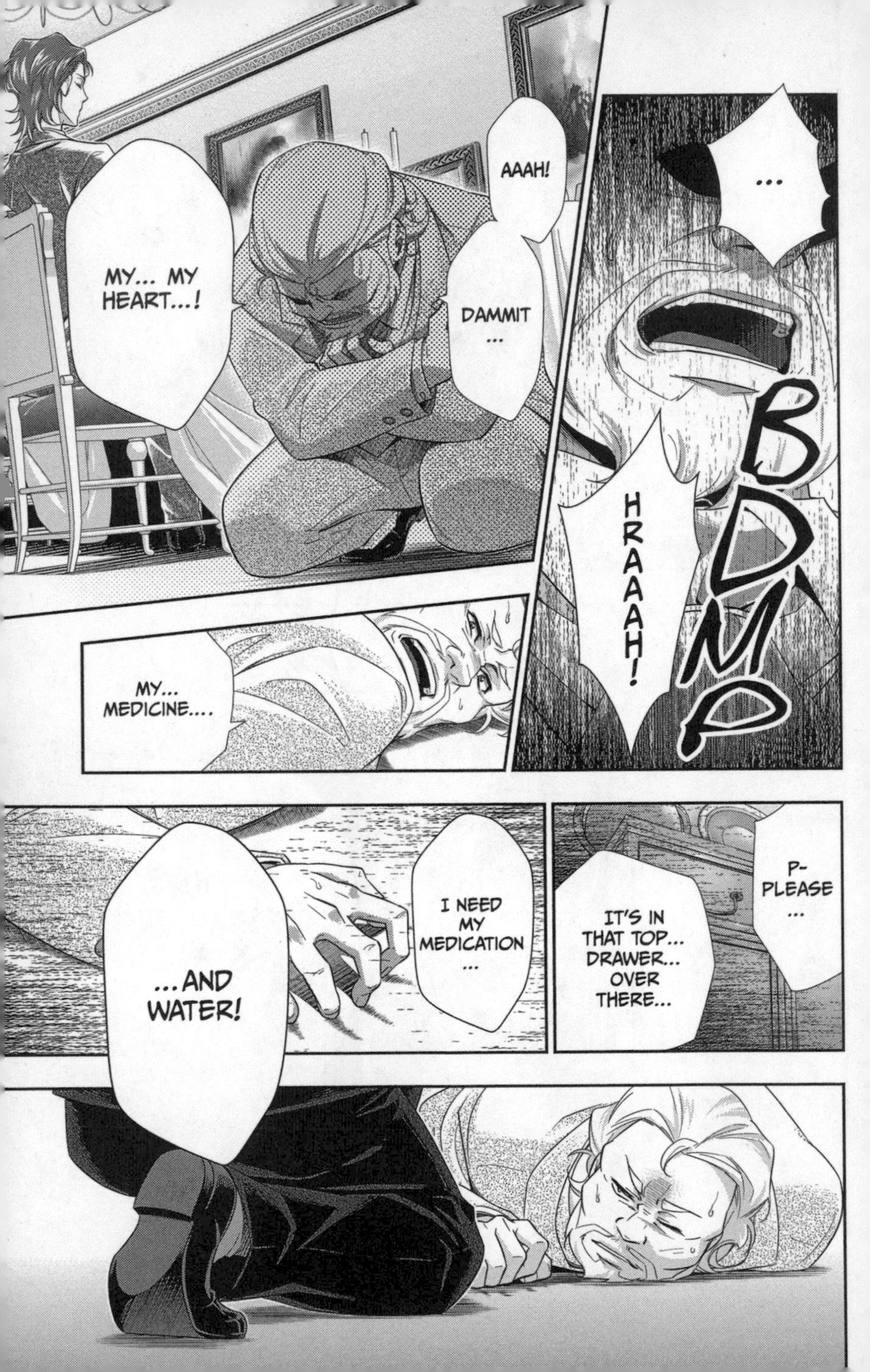
...
HRAAAAH!
BDMP
AAAH!
DAMMIT ...
MY... MY HEART...!
MY... MEDICINE....
P- PLEASE ...
IT'S IN THAT TOP... DRAWER... OVER THERE...
I NEED MY MEDICATION ...
...AND WATER!

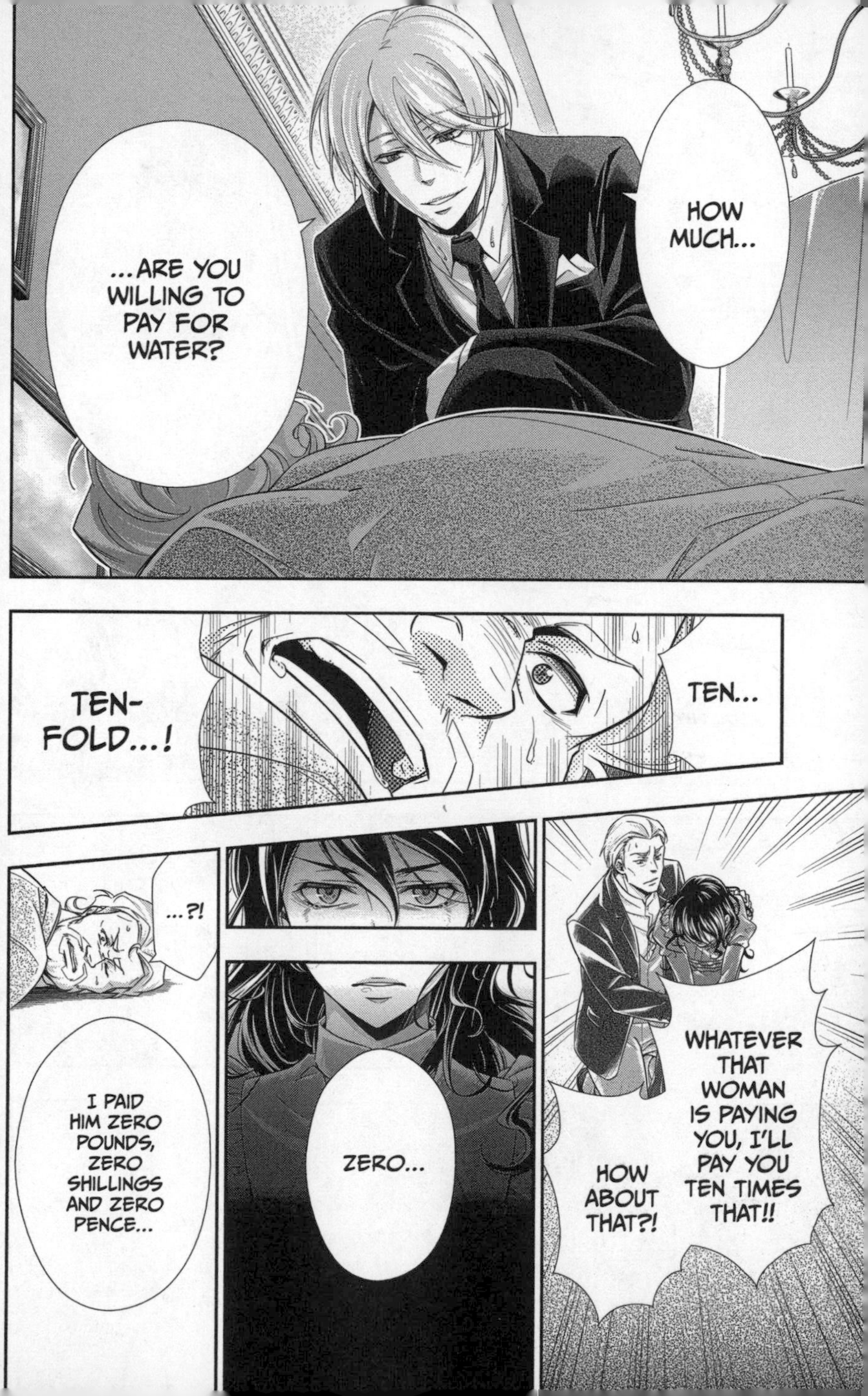
HOW MUCH...
...ARE YOU WILLING TO PAY FOR WATER?
TEN...
TEN-FOLD...!
WHATEVER THAT WOMAN IS PAYING YOU, I'LL PAY YOU TEN TIMES THAT!!
HOW ABOUT THAT?!
ZERO...
...?!
I PAID HIM ZERO POUNDS, ZERO SHILLINGS AND ZERO PENCE...

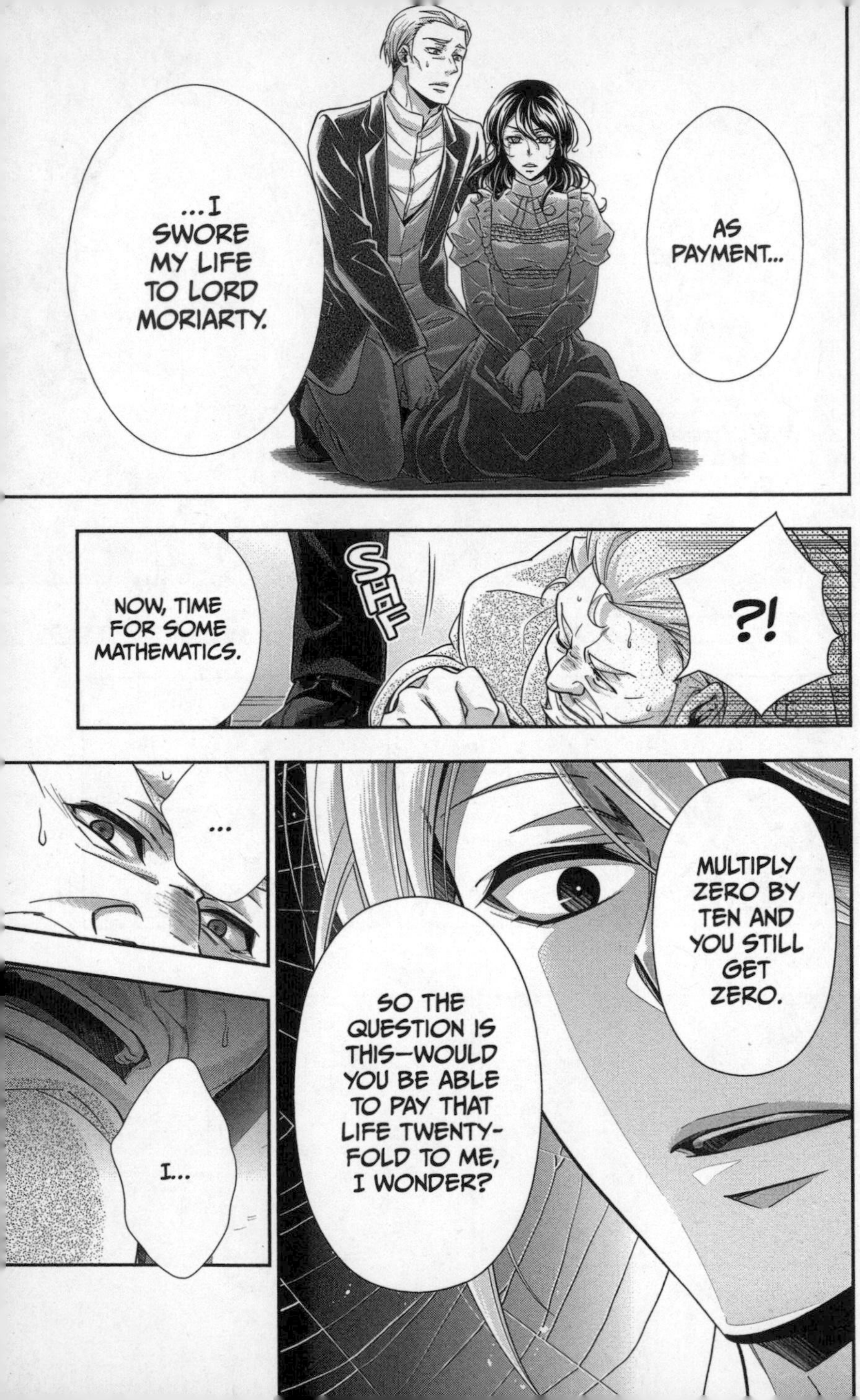
AS PAYMENT...
...I SWORE MY LIFE TO LORD MORIARTY.
?!
NOW, TIME FOR SOME MATHEMATICS.
MULTIPLY ZERO BY TEN AND YOU STILL GET ZERO.
SO THE QUESTION IS THIS—WOULD YOU BE ABLE TO PAY THAT LIFE TWENTY-FOLD TO ME, I WONDER?
...
I...

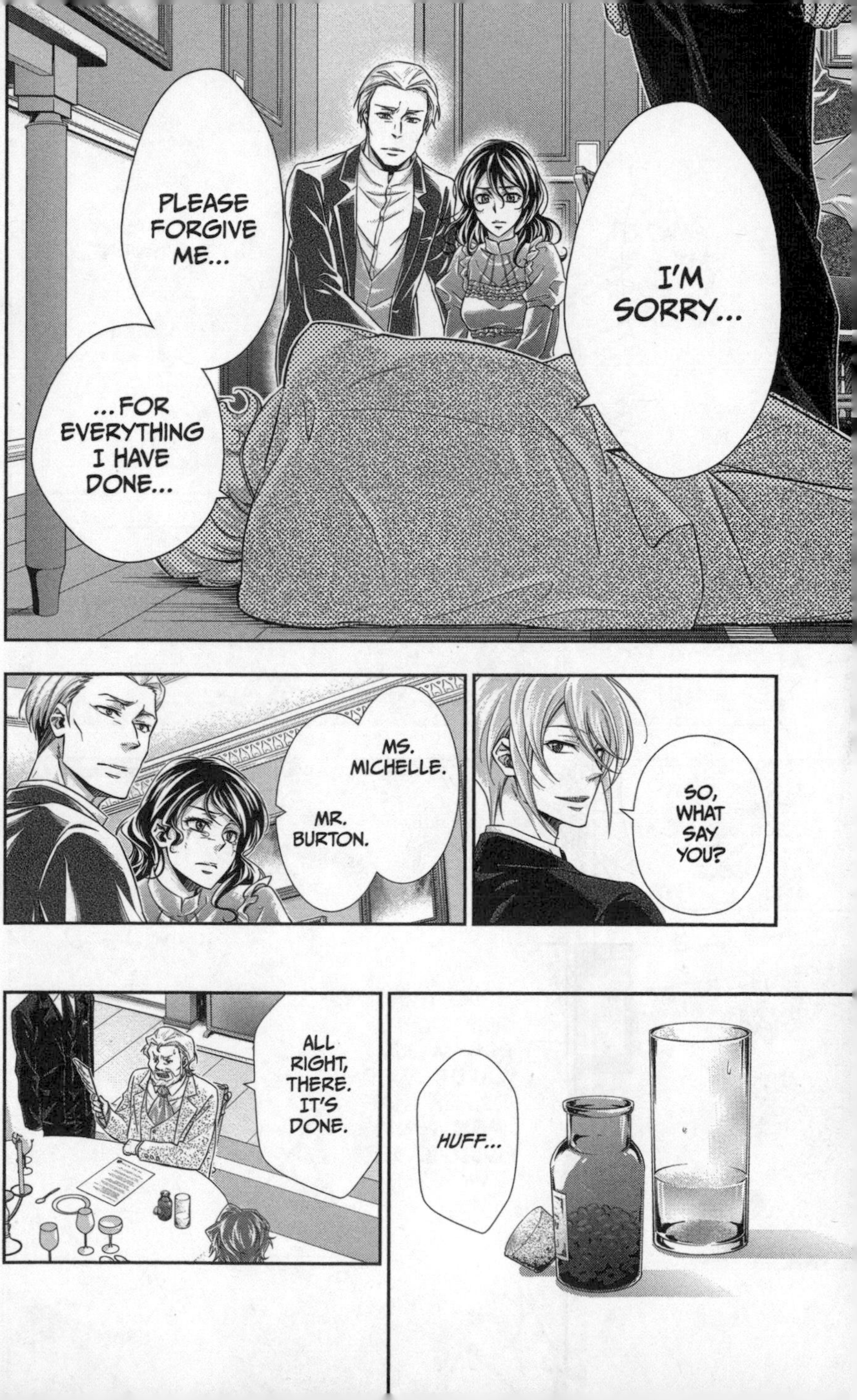
I'M SORRY...
PLEASE FORGIVE ME...
...FOR EVERYTHING I HAVE DONE...
SO, WHAT SAY YOU?
MS. MICHELLE.
MR. BURTON.
HUFF...
ALL RIGHT, THERE. IT'S DONE.

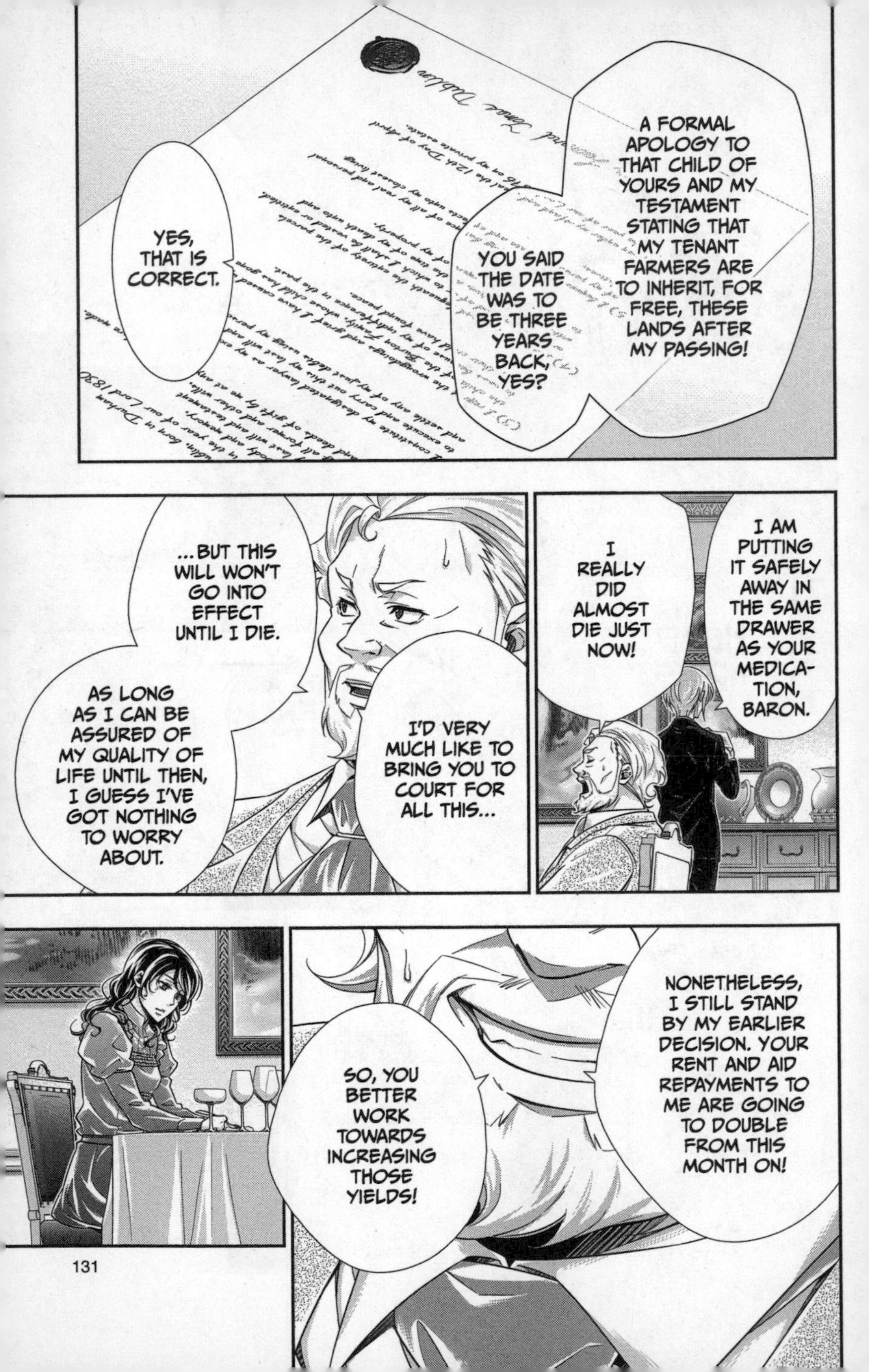
A FORMAL APOLOGY TO THAT CHILD OF YOURS AND MY TESTAMENT STATING THAT MY TENANT FARMERS ARE TO INHERIT, FOR FREE, THESE LANDS AFTER MY PASSING!
YOU SAID THE DATE WAS TO BE THREE YEARS BACK, YES?
YES, THAT IS CORRECT.
I AM PUTTING IT SAFELY AWAY IN THE SAME DRAWER AS YOUR MEDICATION, BARON.
I REALLY DID ALMOST DIE JUST NOW!
I'D VERY MUCH LIKE TO BRING YOU TO COURT FOR ALL THIS...
...BUT THIS WILL WON'T GO INTO EFFECT UNTIL I DIE.
AS LONG AS I CAN BE ASSURED OF MY QUALITY OF LIFE UNTIL THEN, I GUESS I'VE GOT NOTHING TO WORRY ABOUT.
NONETHELESS, I STILL STAND BY MY EARLIER DECISION. YOUR RENT AND AID REPAYMENTS TO ME ARE GOING TO DOUBLE FROM THIS MONTH ON!
SO, YOU BETTER WORK TOWARDS INCREASING THOSE YIELDS!

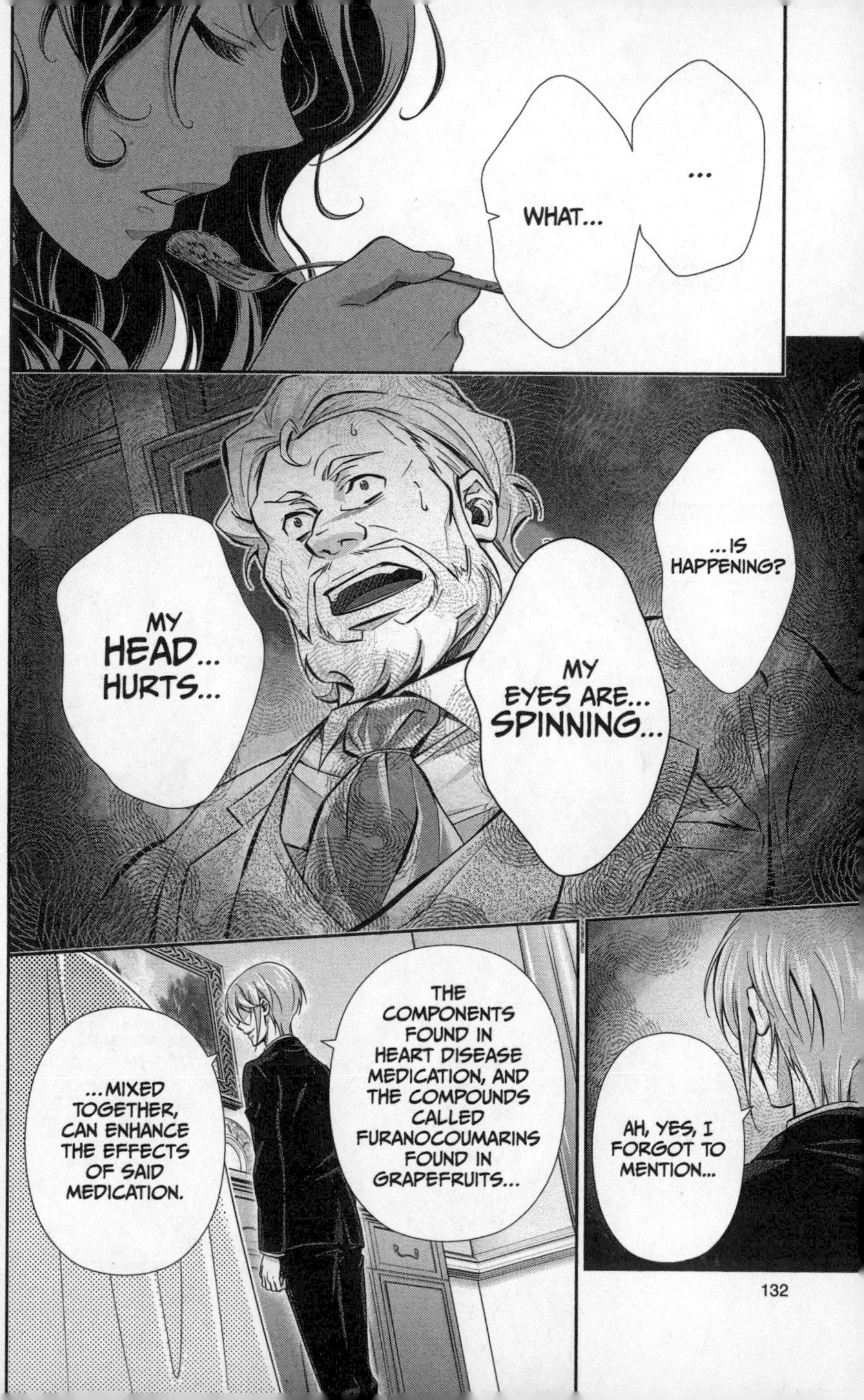
...
WHAT...
...IS HAPPENING?
MY EYES ARE... SPINNING...
MY HEAD... HURTS...
AH, YES, I FORGOT TO MENTION...
THE COMPONENTS FOUND IN HEART DISEASE MEDICATION, AND THE COMPOUNDS CALLED FURANOCOUMARINS FOUND IN GRAPEFRUITS...
...MIXED TOGETHER, CAN ENHANCE THE EFFECTS OF SAID MEDICATION.

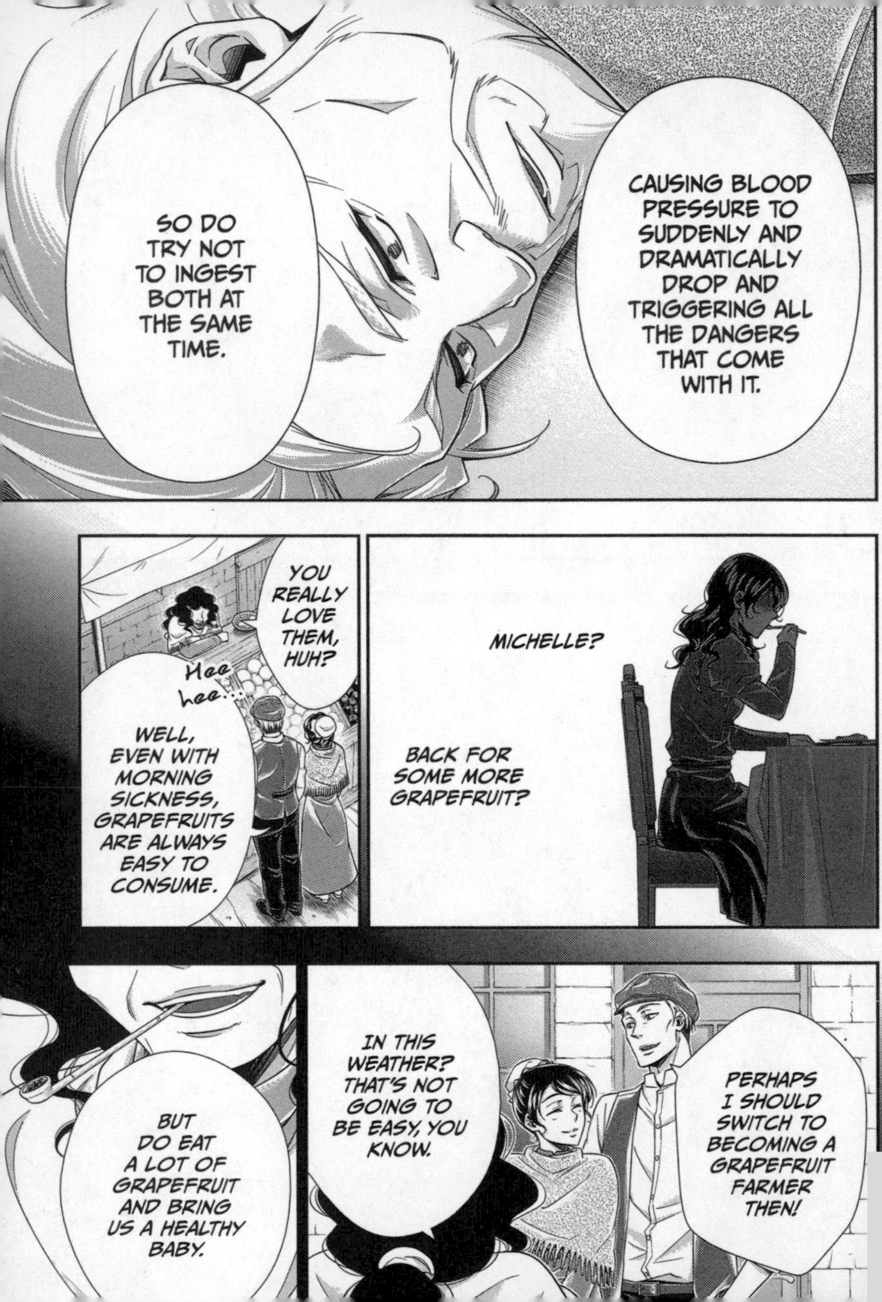
CAUSING BLOOD PRESSURE TO SUDDENLY AND DRAMATICALLY DROP AND TRIGGERING ALL THE DANGERS THAT COME WITH IT.
SO DO TRY NOT TO INGEST BOTH AT THE SAME TIME.
MICHELLE?
BACK FOR SOME MORE GRAPEFRUIT?
YOU REALLY LOVE THEM, HUH?
Hee hee...
WELL, EVEN WITH MORNING SICKNESS, GRAPEFRUITS ARE ALWAYS EASY TO CONSUME.
PERHAPS I SHOULD SWITCH TO BECOMING A GRAPEFRUIT FARMER THEN!
IN THIS WEATHER? THAT'S NOT GOING TO BE EASY, YOU KNOW.
BUT DO EAT A LOT OF GRAPEFRUIT AND BRING US A HEALTHY BABY.

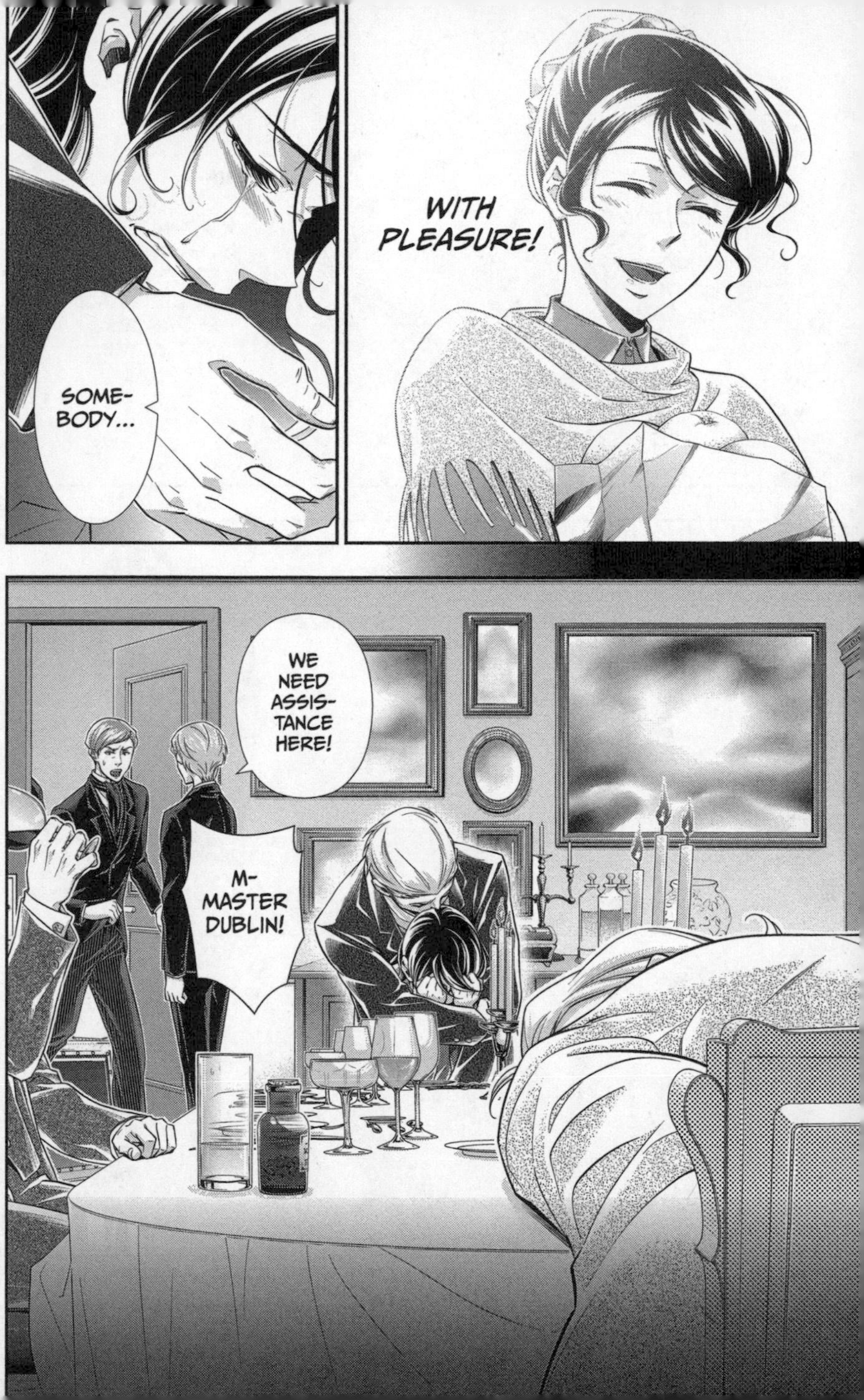
WITH PLEASURE!
SOME-BODY...
WE NEED ASSIS-TANCE HERE!
M-MASTER DUBLIN!

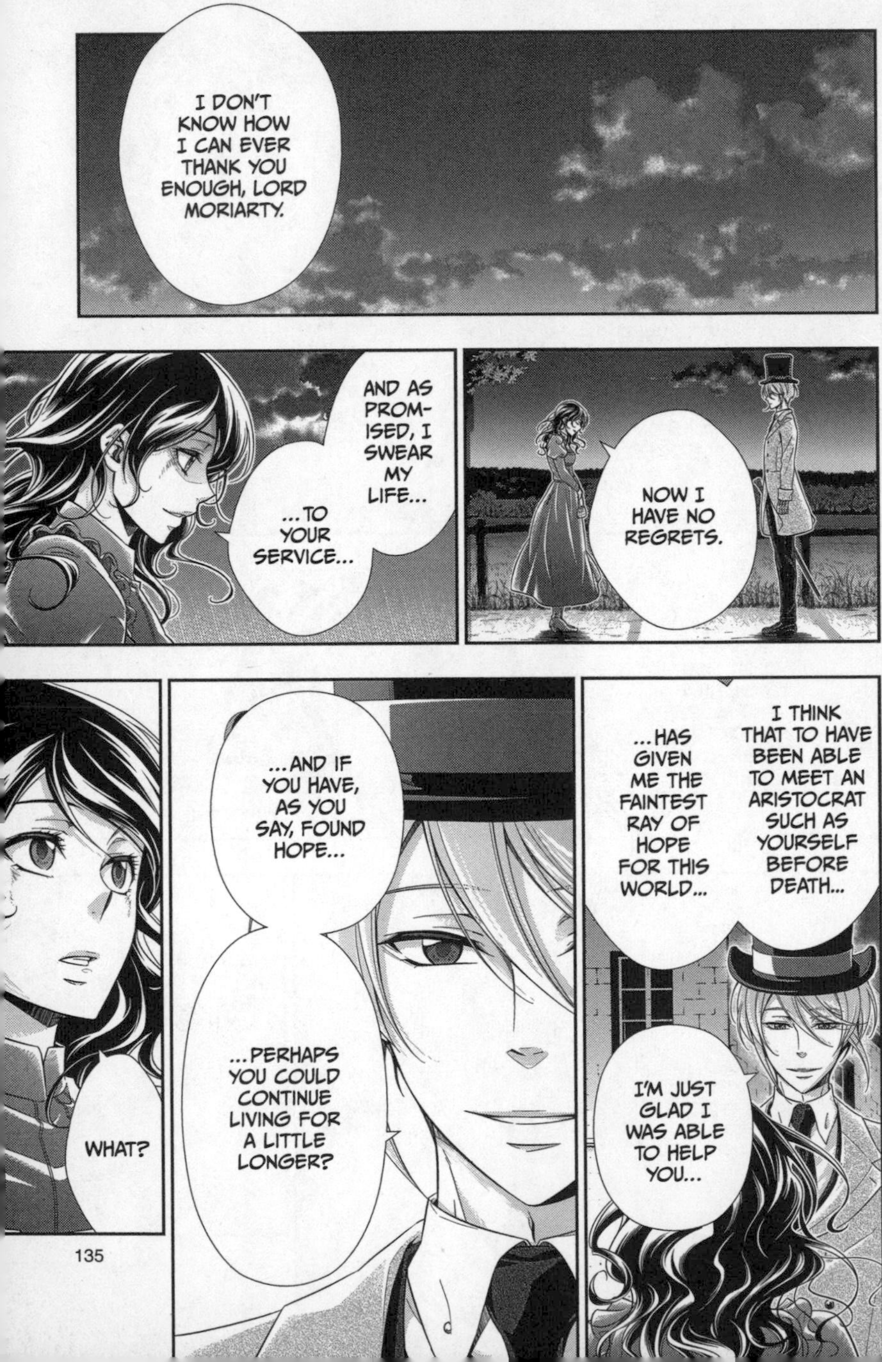
I DON'T KNOW HOW I CAN EVER THANK YOU ENOUGH, LORD MORIARTY.
NOW I HAVE NO REGRETS.
AND AS PROMISED, I SWEAR MY LIFE...
...TO YOUR SERVICE...
I THINK THAT TO HAVE BEEN ABLE TO MEET AN ARISTOCRAT SUCH AS YOURSELF BEFORE DEATH...
...HAS GIVEN ME THE FAINTEST RAY OF HOPE FOR THIS WORLD...
I'M JUST GLAD I WAS ABLE TO HELP YOU...
...AND IF YOU HAVE, AS YOU SAY, FOUND HOPE...
...PERHAPS YOU COULD CONTINUE LIVING FOR A LITTLE LONGER?
WHAT?

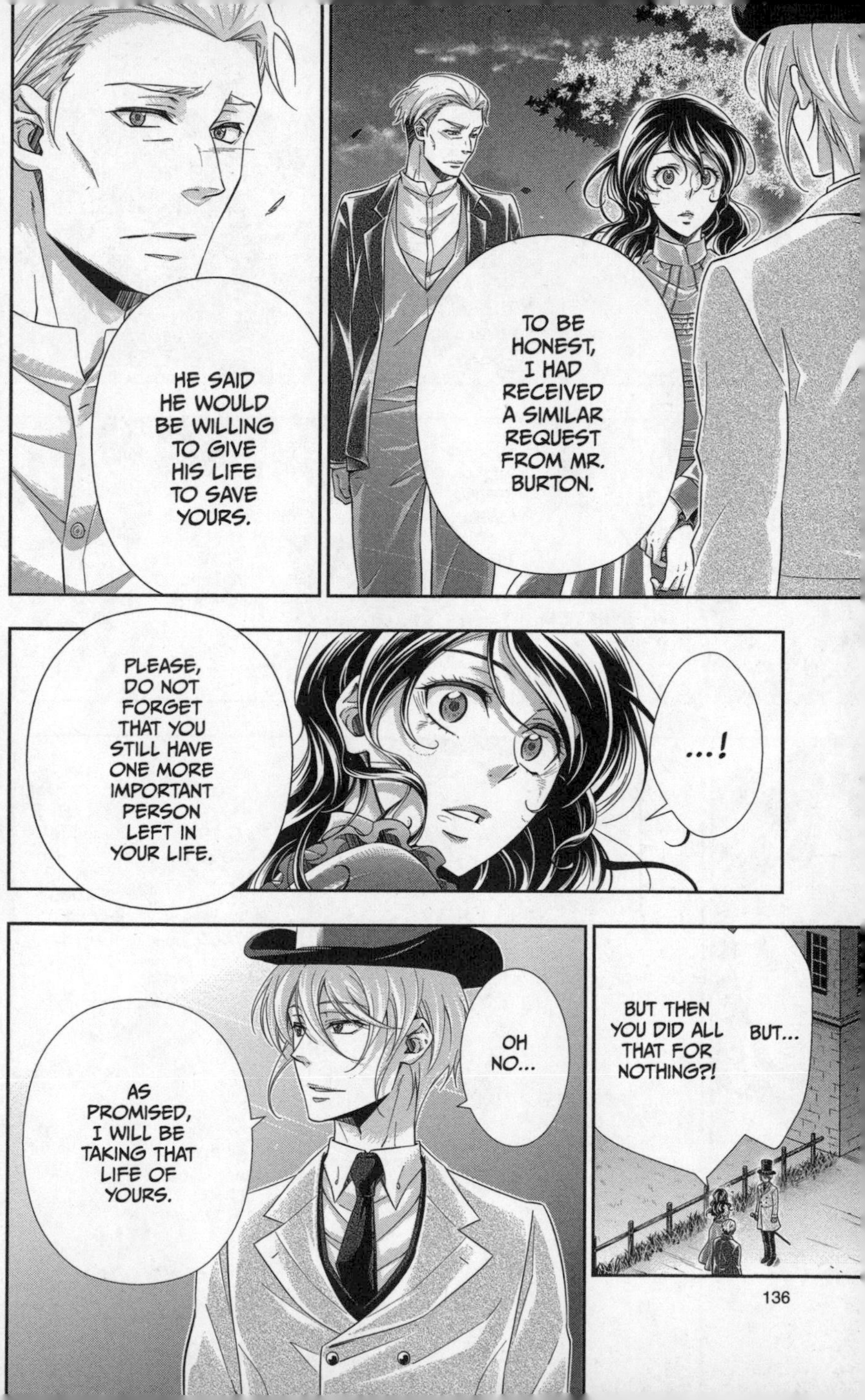
TO BE HONEST, I HAD RECEIVED A SIMILAR REQUEST FROM MR. BURTON.
HE SAID HE WOULD BE WILLING TO GIVE HIS LIFE TO SAVE YOURS.
...!
PLEASE, DO NOT FORGET THAT YOU STILL HAVE ONE MORE IMPORTANT PERSON LEFT IN YOUR LIFE.
BUT...
BUT THEN YOU DID ALL THAT FOR NOTHING?!
OH NO...
AS PROMISED, I WILL BE TAKING THAT LIFE OF YOURS.

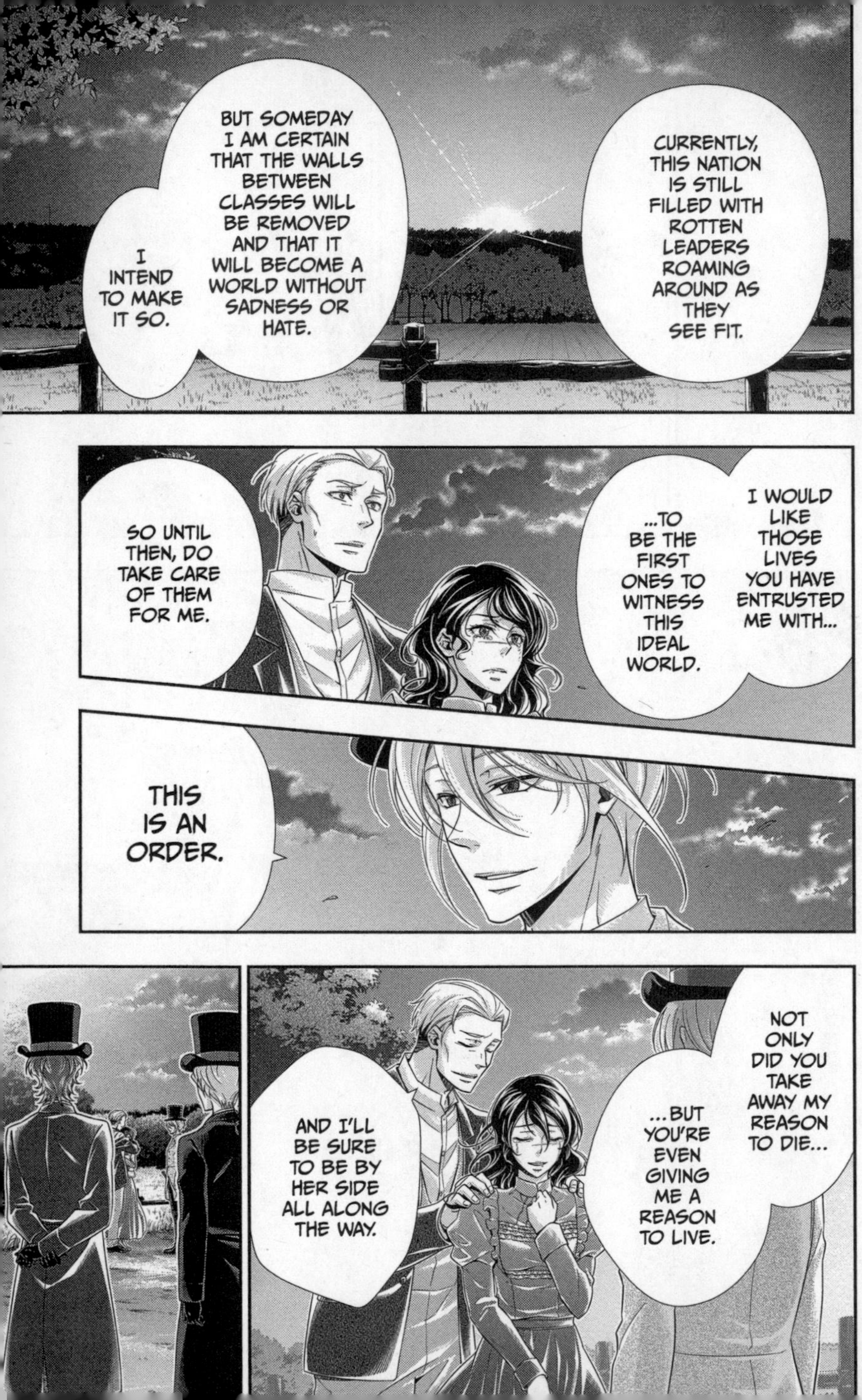
CURRENTLY, THIS NATION IS STILL FILLED WITH ROTTEN LEADERS ROAMING AROUND AS THEY SEE FIT.
BUT SOMEDAY I AM CERTAIN THAT THE WALLS BETWEEN CLASSES WILL BE REMOVED AND THAT IT WILL BECOME A WORLD WITHOUT SADNESS OR HATE.
I INTEND TO MAKE IT SO.
I WOULD LIKE THOSE LIVES YOU HAVE ENTRUSTED ME WITH...
...TO BE THE FIRST ONES TO WITNESS THIS IDEAL WORLD.
SO UNTIL THEN, DO TAKE CARE OF THEM FOR ME.
THIS IS AN ORDER.
NOT ONLY DID YOU TAKE AWAY MY REASON TO DIE...
...BUT YOU'RE EVEN GIVING ME A REASON TO LIVE.
AND I'LL BE SURE TO BE BY HER SIDE ALL ALONG THE WAY.

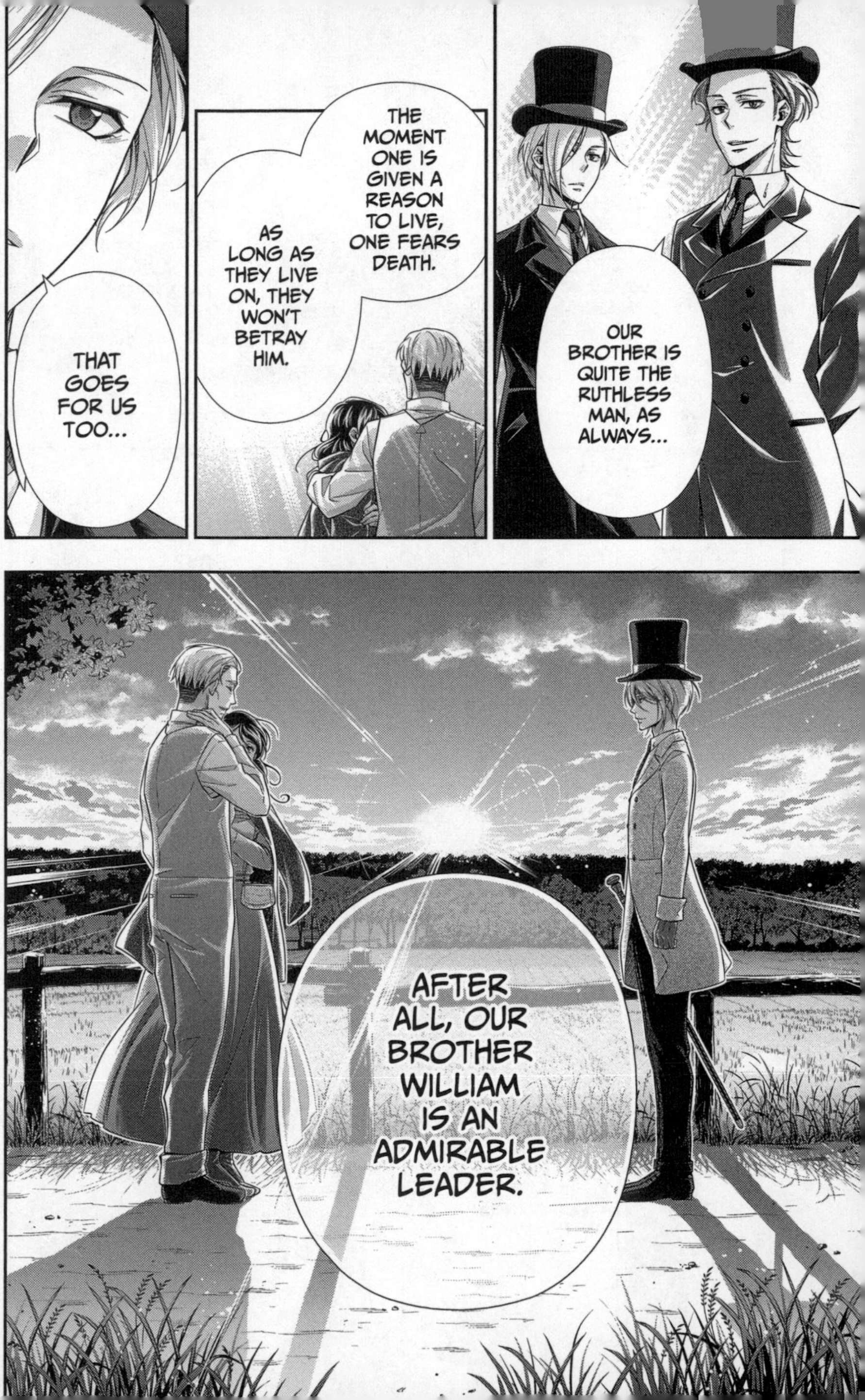
OUR BROTHER IS QUITE THE RUTHLESS MAN, AS ALWAYS...
THE MOMENT ONE IS GIVEN A REASON TO LIVE, ONE FEARS DEATH.
AS LONG AS THEY LIVE ON, THEY WON'T BETRAY HIM.
THAT GOES FOR US TOO...
AFTER ALL, OUR BROTHER WILLIAM IS AN ADMIRABLE LEADER.

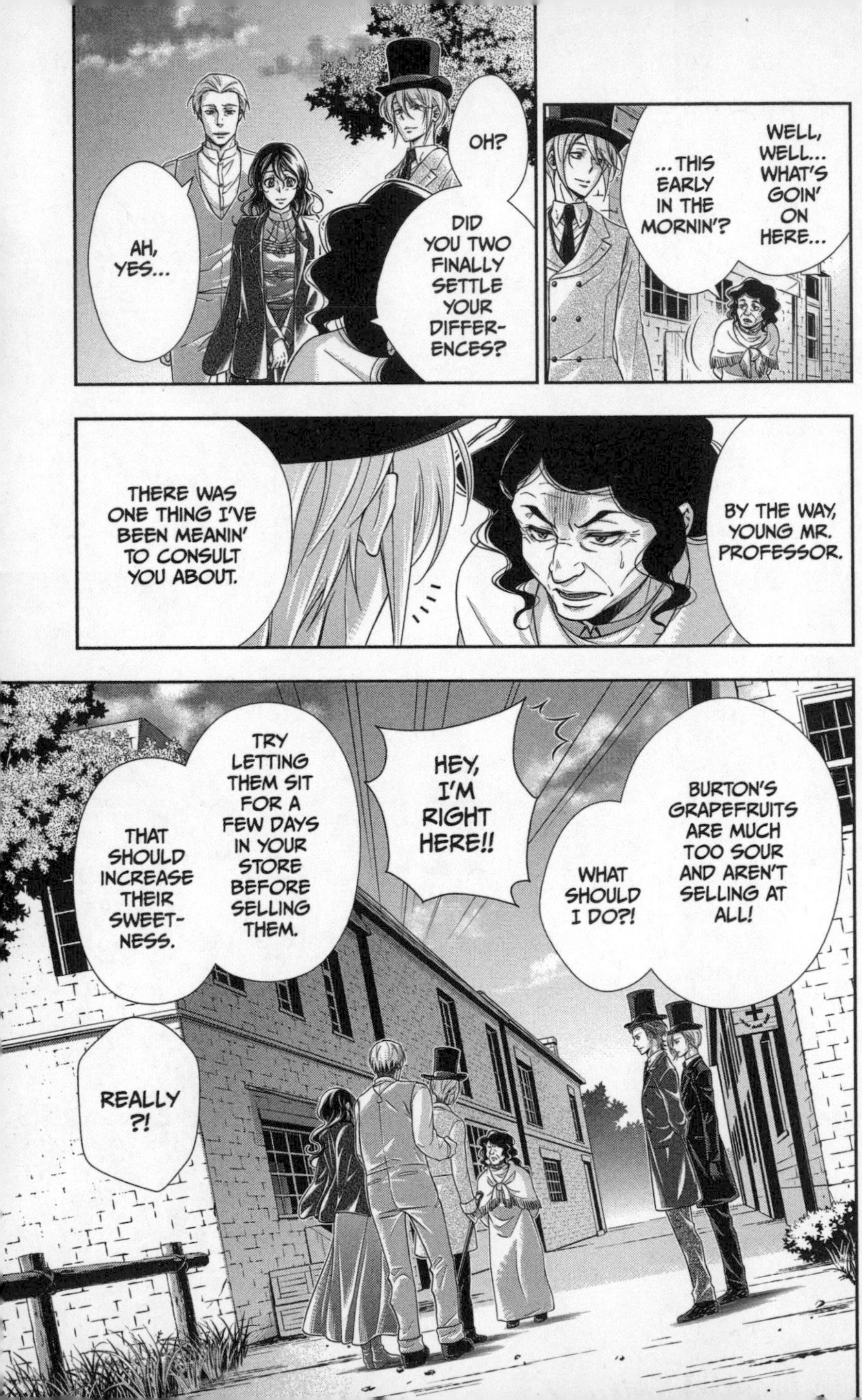
WELL, WELL... WHAT'S GOIN' ON HERE...
...THIS EARLY IN THE MORNIN'?
OH?
DID YOU TWO FINALLY SETTLE YOUR DIFFER-ENCES?
AH, YES...
BY THE WAY, YOUNG MR. PROFESSOR.
THERE WAS ONE THING I'VE BEEN MEANIN' TO CONSULT YOU ABOUT.
BURTON'S GRAPEFRUITS ARE MUCH TOO SOUR AND AREN'T SELLING AT ALL!
WHAT SHOULD I DO?!
HEY, I'M RIGHT HERE!!
TRY LETTING THEM SIT FOR A FEW DAYS IN YOUR STORE BEFORE SELLING THEM.
THAT SHOULD INCREASE THEIR SWEET-NESS.
REALLY?!

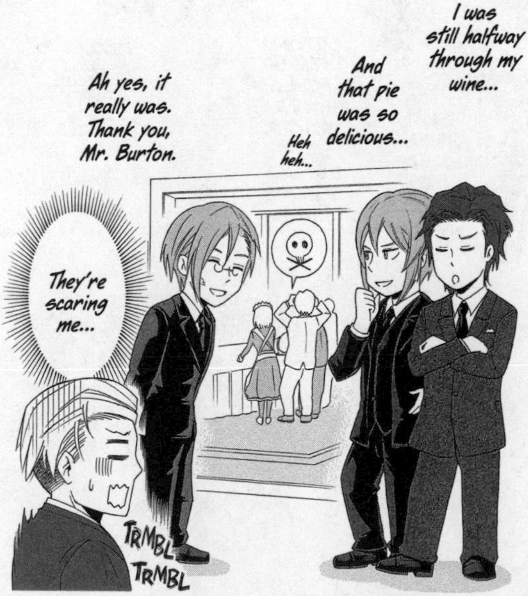
I was still halfway through my wine...
And that pie was so delicious...
Heh heh...
Ah yes, it really was. Thank you, Mr. Burton.
They're scaring me...
TRMBL TRMBL

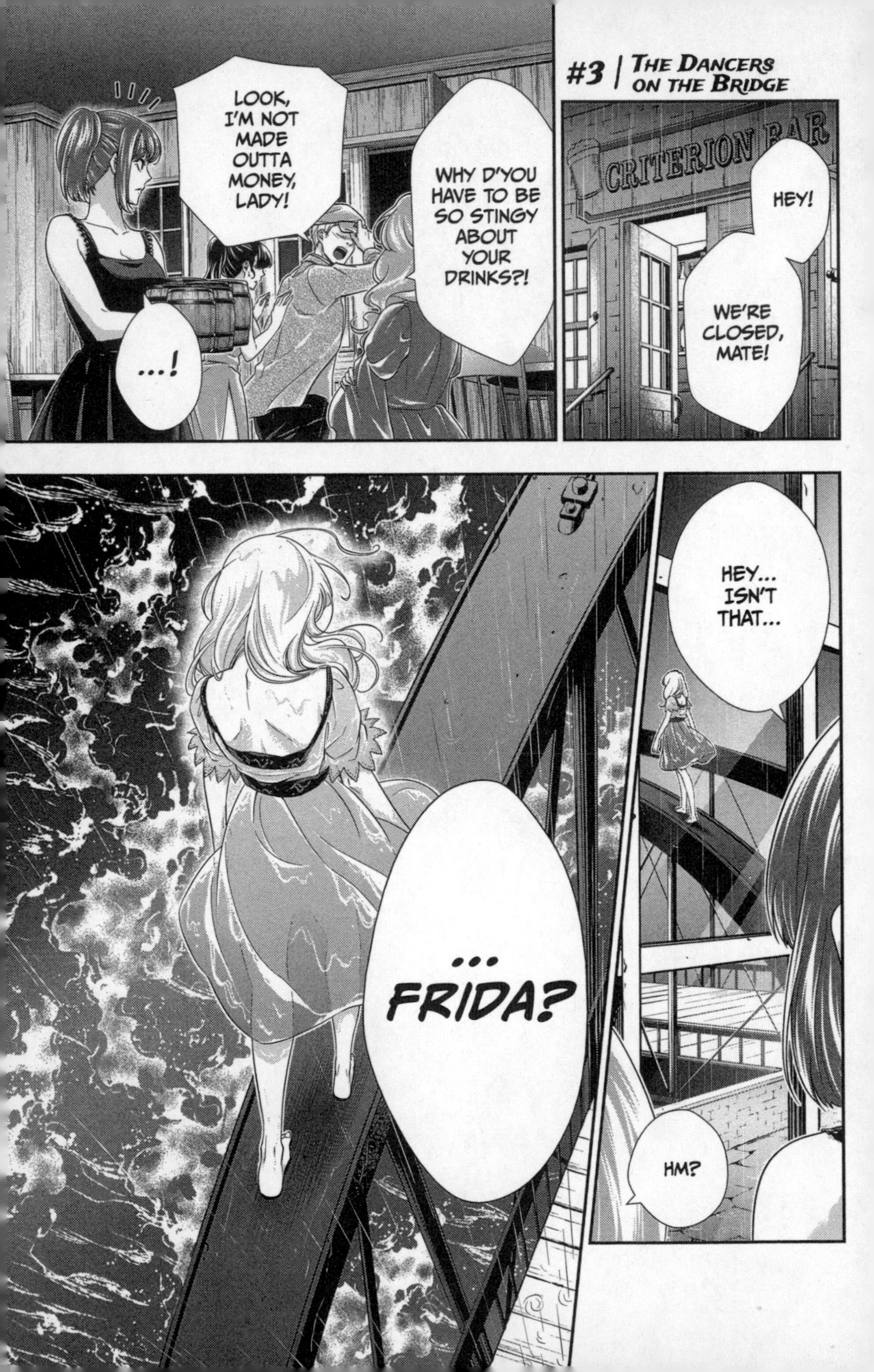
#3 | The Dancers on the Bridge
CRITERION BAR
HEY!
WE'RE CLOSED, MATE!
WHY D'YOU HAVE TO BE SO STINGY ABOUT YOUR DRINKS?!
LOOK, I'M NOT MADE OUTTA MONEY, LADY!
...!
HEY... ISN'T THAT...
HM?
... FRIDA?

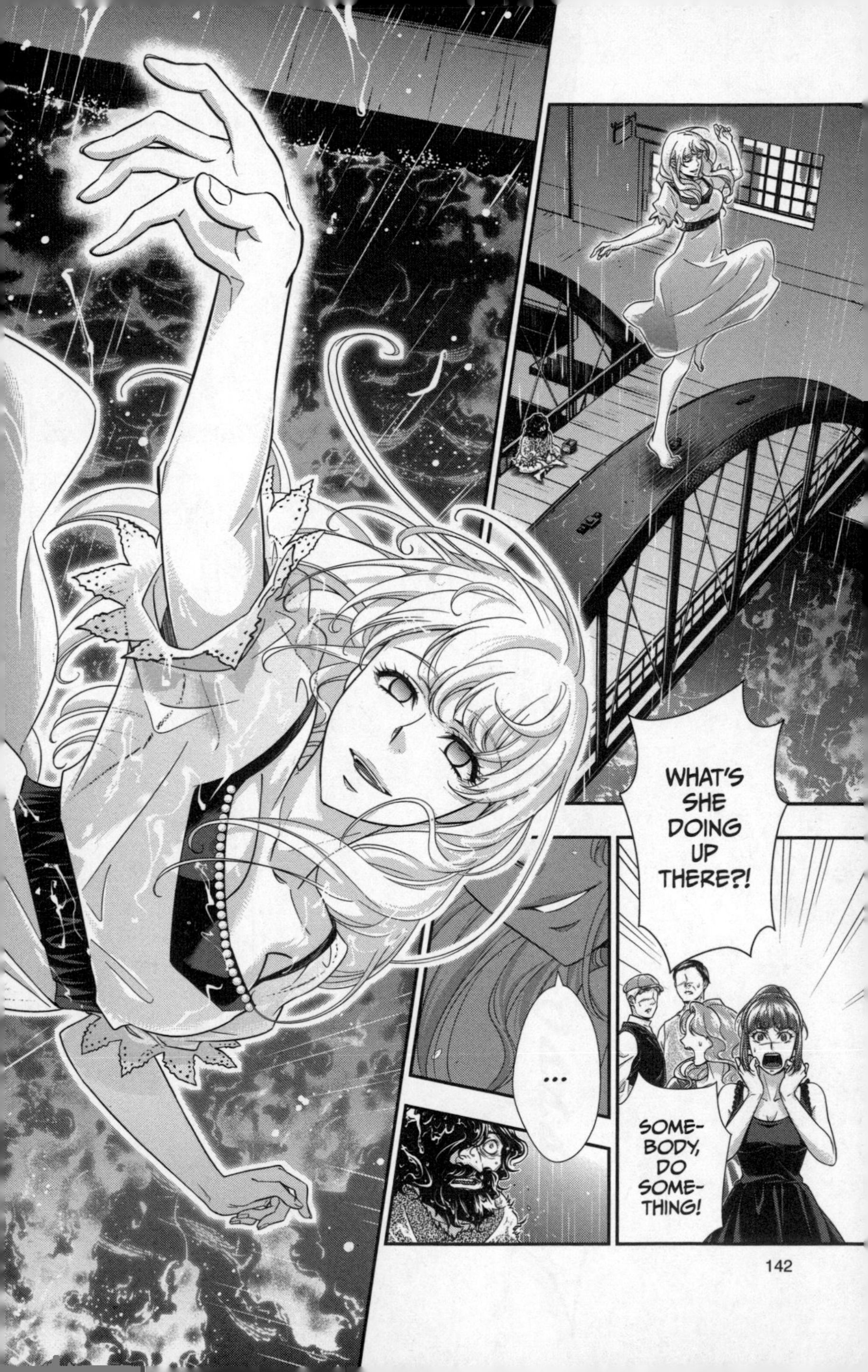
WHAT'S SHE DOING UP THERE?!
SOME-BODY, DO SOME-THING!
...

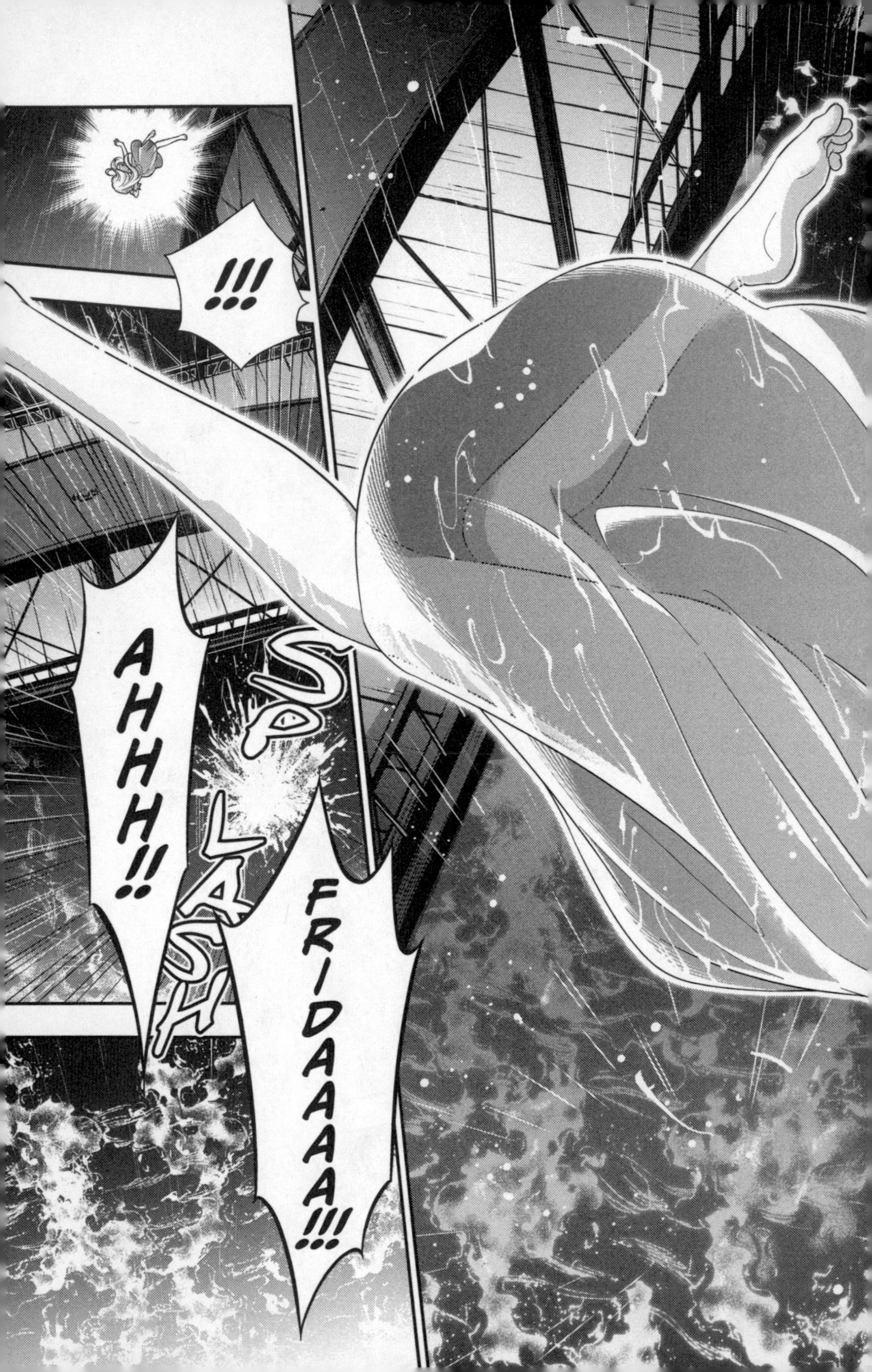
!!!
FRIDAAAAAA!!!
SPLASH
AHHHH!!

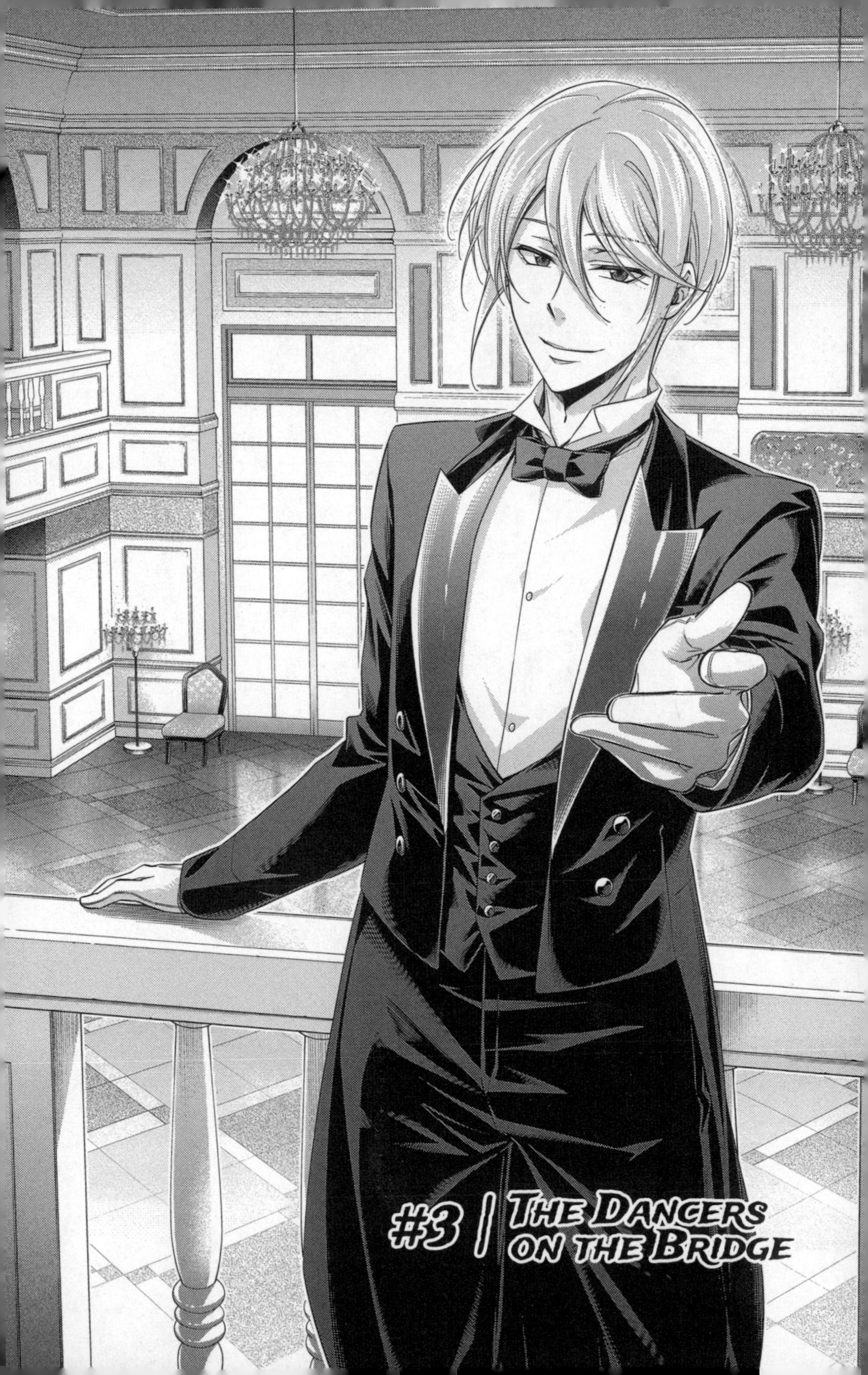
#3 | The Dancers on the Bridge

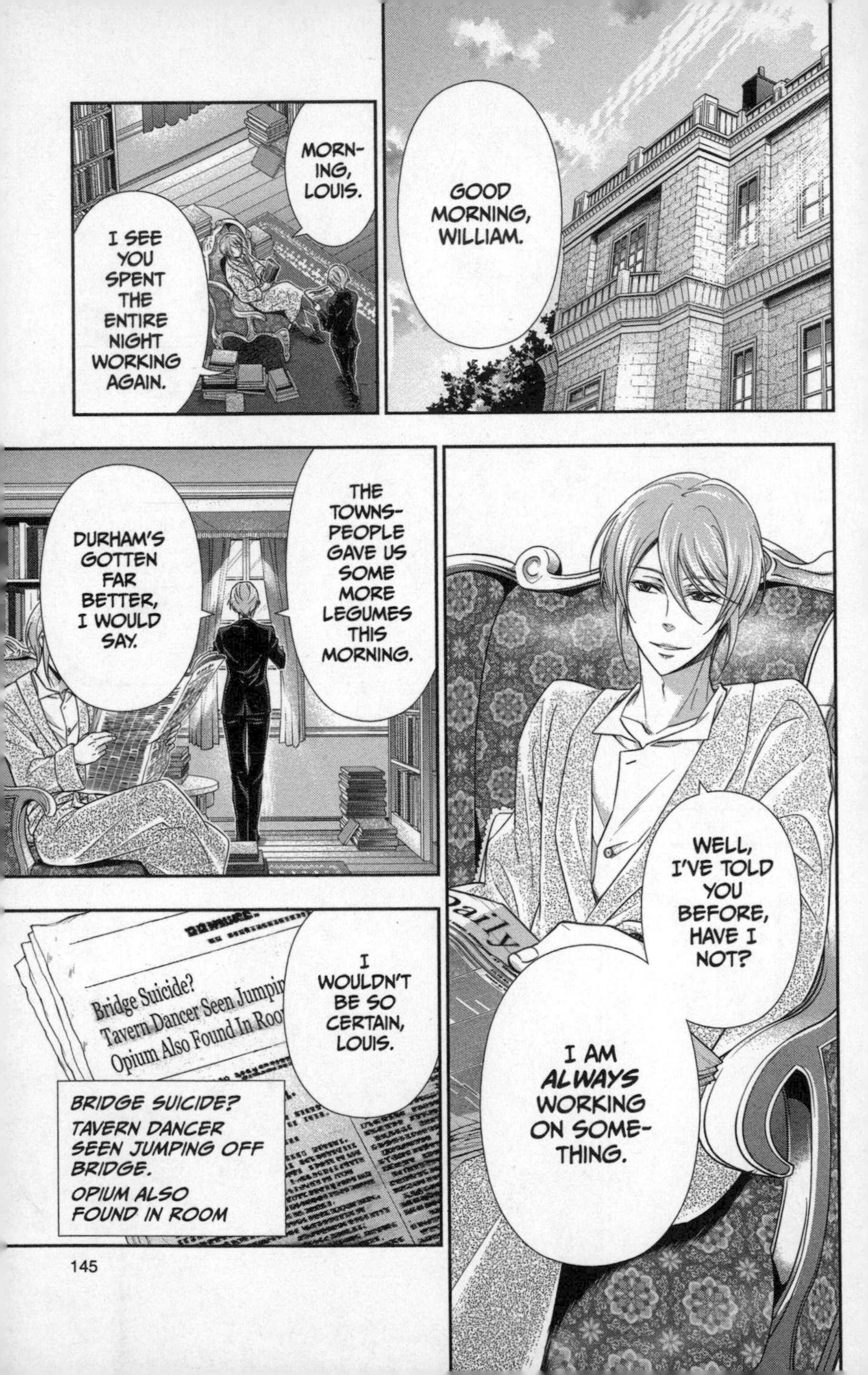
GOOD MORNING, WILLIAM.
MORNING, LOUIS.
I SEE YOU SPENT THE ENTIRE NIGHT WORKING AGAIN.
WELL, I'VE TOLD YOU BEFORE, HAVE I NOT?
I AM *ALWAYS* WORKING ON SOMETHING.
Daily
THE TOWNSPEOPLE GAVE US SOME MORE LEGUMES THIS MORNING.
DURHAM'S GOTTEN FAR BETTER, I WOULD SAY.
Bridge Suicide?
Tavern Dancer Seen Jumpin
Opium Also Found In Roo
I WOULDN'T BE SO CERTAIN, LOUIS.
BRIDGE SUICIDE?
TAVERN DANCER SEEN JUMPING OFF BRIDGE.
OPIUM ALSO FOUND IN ROOM

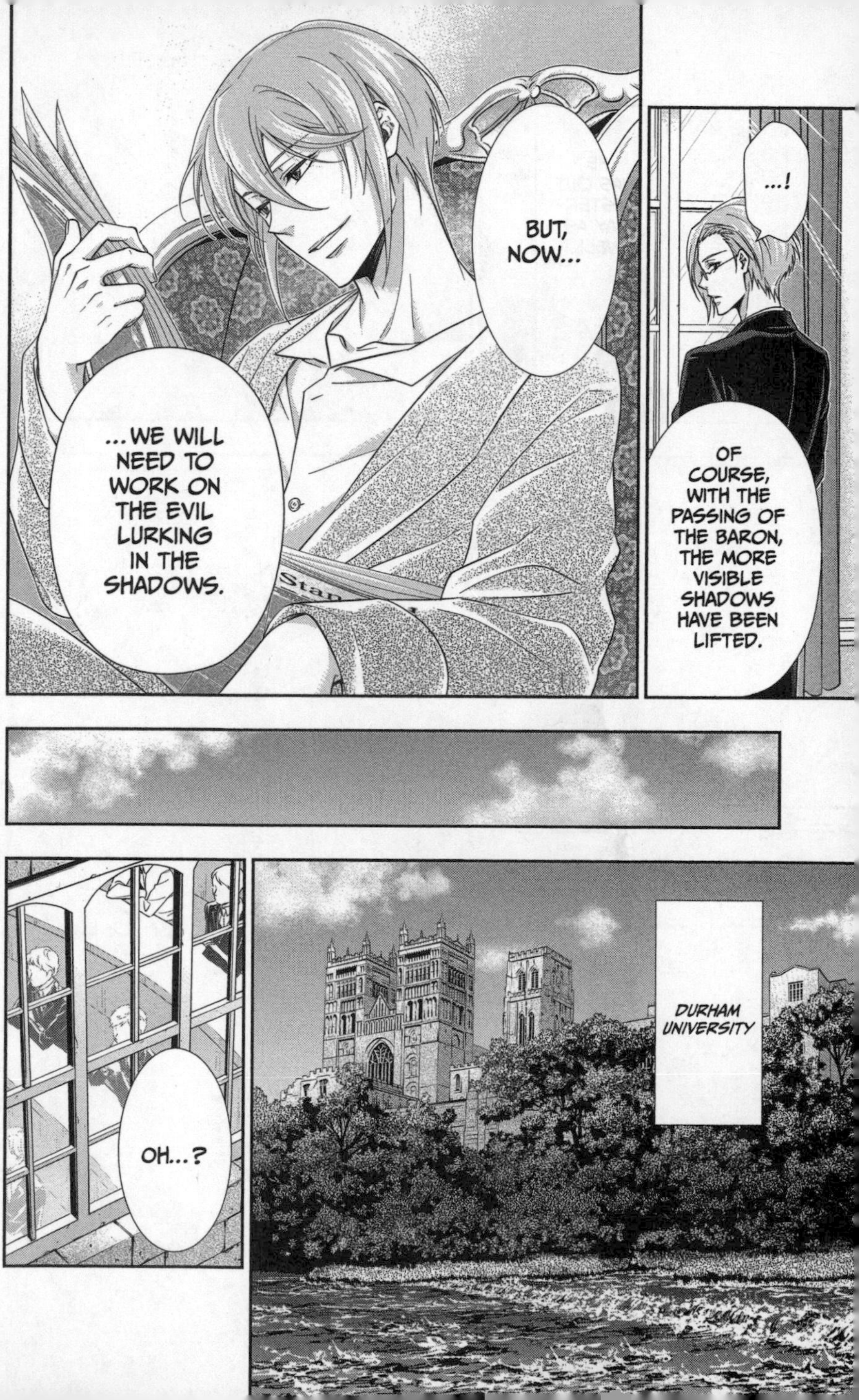
...!
OF COURSE, WITH THE PASSING OF THE BARON, THE MORE VISIBLE SHADOWS HAVE BEEN LIFTED.
BUT, NOW...
...WE WILL NEED TO WORK ON THE EVIL LURKING IN THE SHADOWS.
DURHAM UNIVERSITY
OH...?

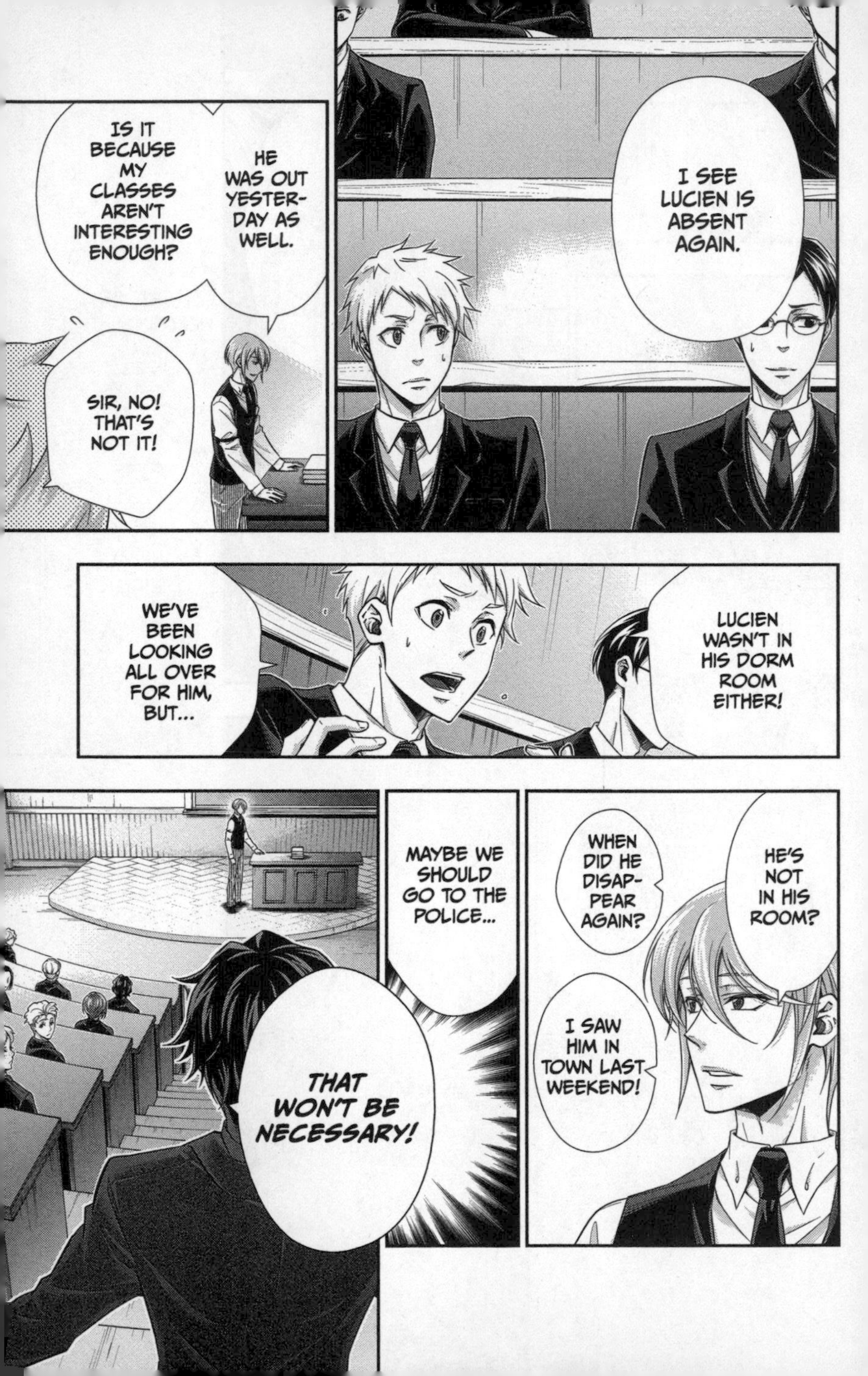
I SEE LUCIEN IS ABSENT AGAIN.
HE WAS OUT YESTERDAY AS WELL.
IS IT BECAUSE MY CLASSES AREN'T INTERESTING ENOUGH?
SIR, NO! THAT'S NOT IT!
LUCIEN WASN'T IN HIS DORM ROOM EITHER!
WE'VE BEEN LOOKING ALL OVER FOR HIM, BUT...
HE'S NOT IN HIS ROOM?
WHEN DID HE DISAPPEAR AGAIN?
I SAW HIM IN TOWN LAST WEEKEND!
MAYBE WE SHOULD GO TO THE POLICE...
THAT WON'T BE NECESSARY!

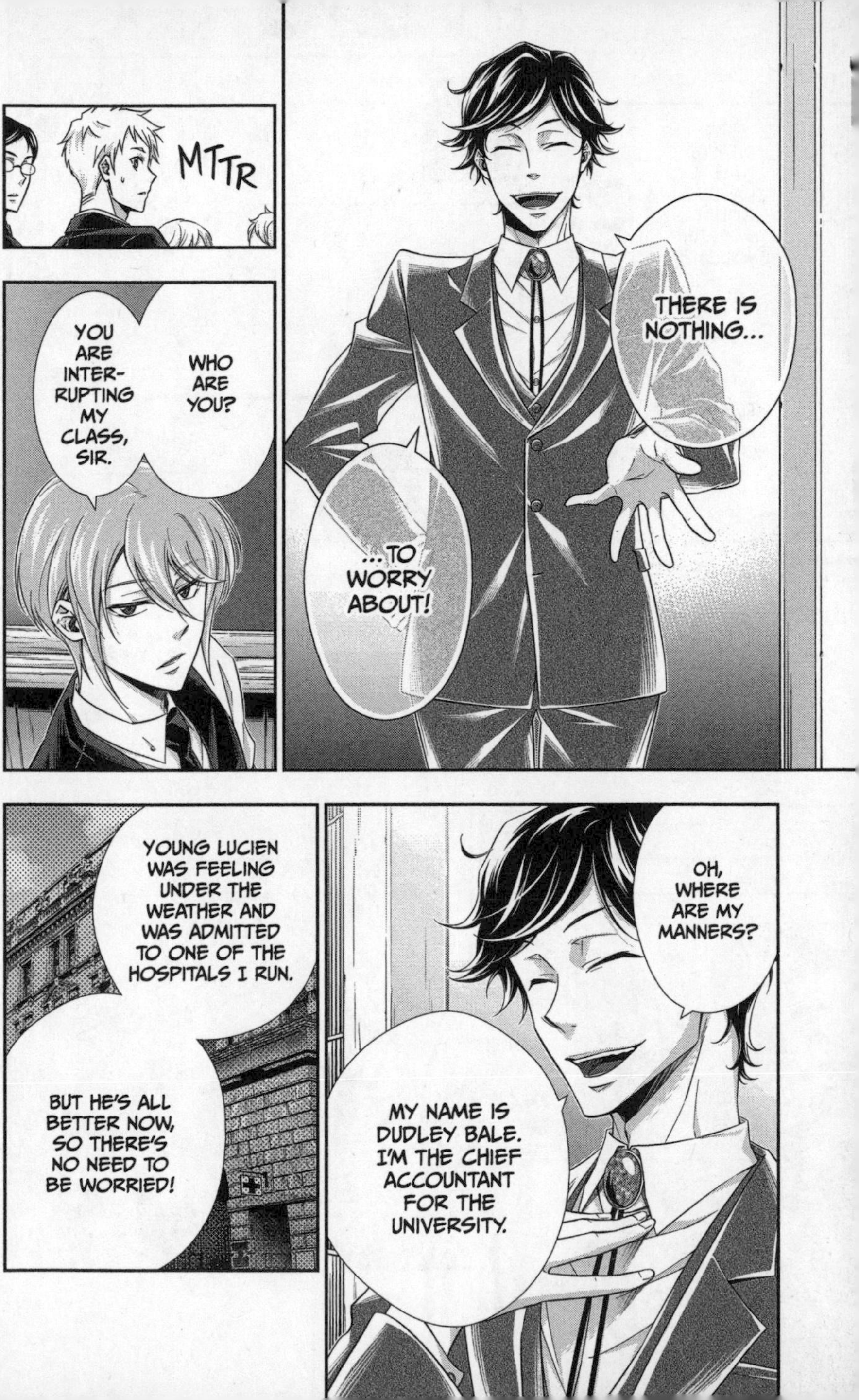
THERE IS NOTHING...
...TO WORRY ABOUT!
MTTR
WHO ARE YOU?
YOU ARE INTERRUPTING MY CLASS, SIR.
OH, WHERE ARE MY MANNERS?
MY NAME IS DUDLEY BALE. I'M THE CHIEF ACCOUNTANT FOR THE UNIVERSITY.
YOUNG LUCIEN WAS FEELING UNDER THE WEATHER AND WAS ADMITTED TO ONE OF THE HOSPITALS I RUN.
BUT HE'S ALL BETTER NOW, SO THERE'S NO NEED TO BE WORRIED!

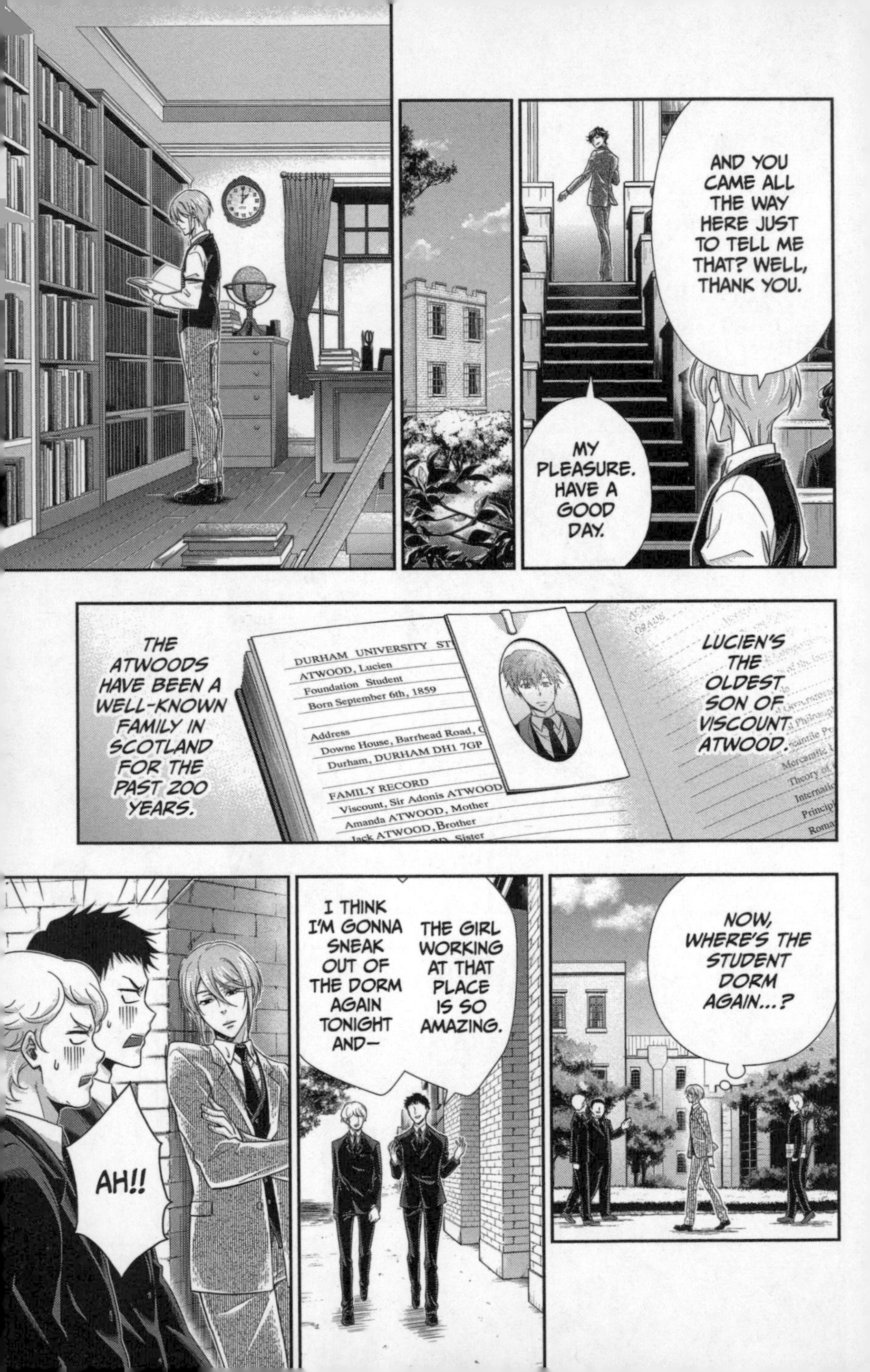
AND YOU CAME ALL THE WAY HERE JUST TO TELL ME THAT? WELL, THANK YOU.
MY PLEASURE. HAVE A GOOD DAY.
LUCIEN'S THE OLDEST SON OF VISCOUNT ATWOOD.
DURHAM UNIVERSITY ST
ATWOOD, Lucien
Foundation Student
Born September 6th, 1859
Address
Downe House, Barrhead Road,
Durham, DURHAM DH1 7GP
FAMILY RECORD
Viscount, Sir Adonis ATWOOD
Amanda ATWOOD, Mother
Jack ATWOOD, Brother
THE ATWOODS HAVE BEEN A WELL-KNOWN FAMILY IN SCOTLAND FOR THE PAST 200 YEARS.
NOW, WHERE'S THE STUDENT DORM AGAIN...?
I THINK I'M GONNA SNEAK OUT OF THE DORM AGAIN TONIGHT AND— THE GIRL WORKING AT THAT PLACE IS SO AMAZING.
AH!!

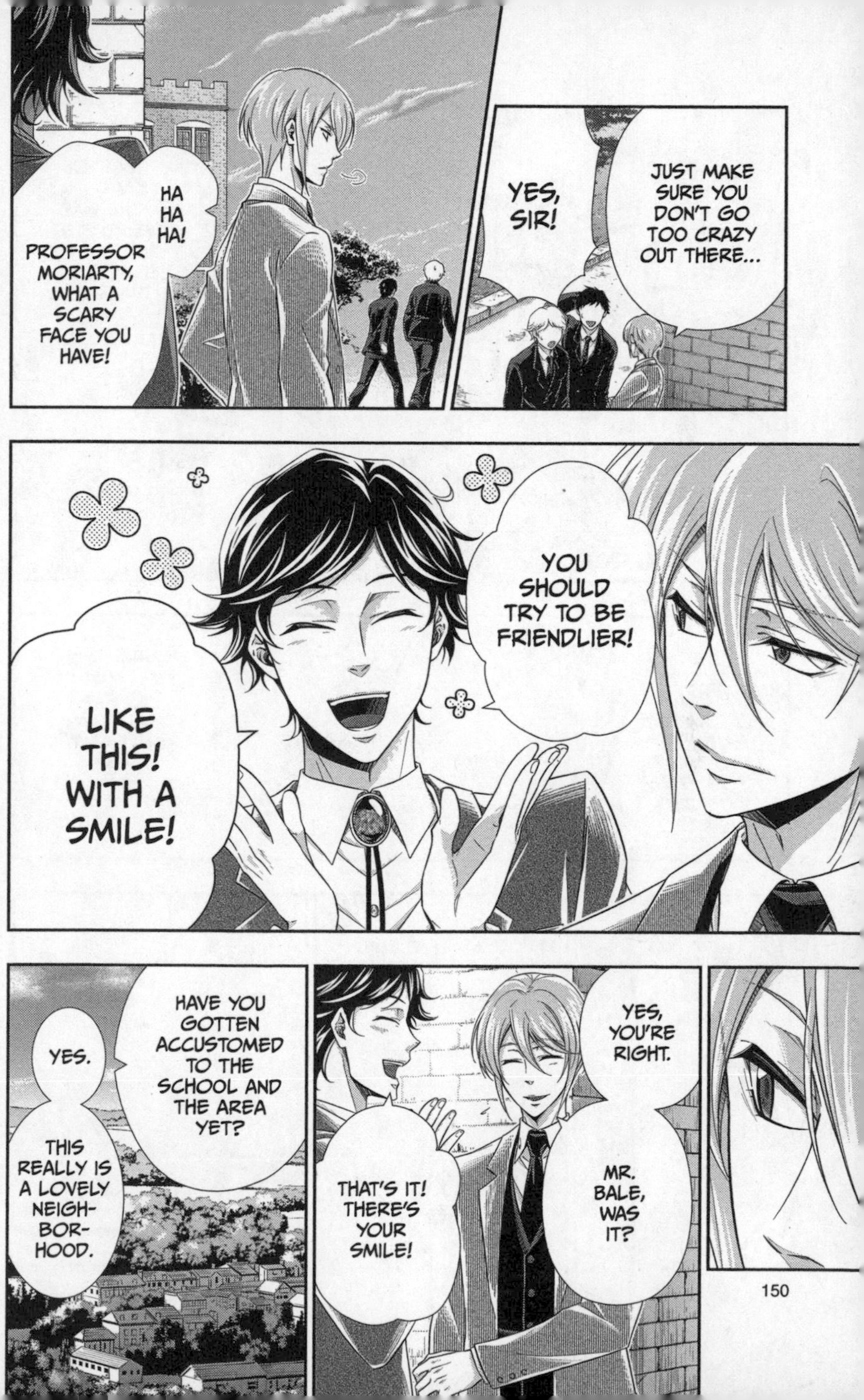
JUST MAKE SURE YOU DON'T GO TOO CRAZY OUT THERE...
YES, SIR!
HA HA HA!
PROFESSOR MORIARTY, WHAT A SCARY FACE YOU HAVE!
YOU SHOULD TRY TO BE FRIENDLIER!
LIKE THIS! WITH A SMILE!
YES, YOU'RE RIGHT.
MR. BALE, WAS IT?
THAT'S IT! THERE'S YOUR SMILE!
HAVE YOU GOTTEN ACCUSTOMED TO THE SCHOOL AND THE AREA YET?
YES.
THIS REALLY IS A LOVELY NEIGH-BOR-HOOD.

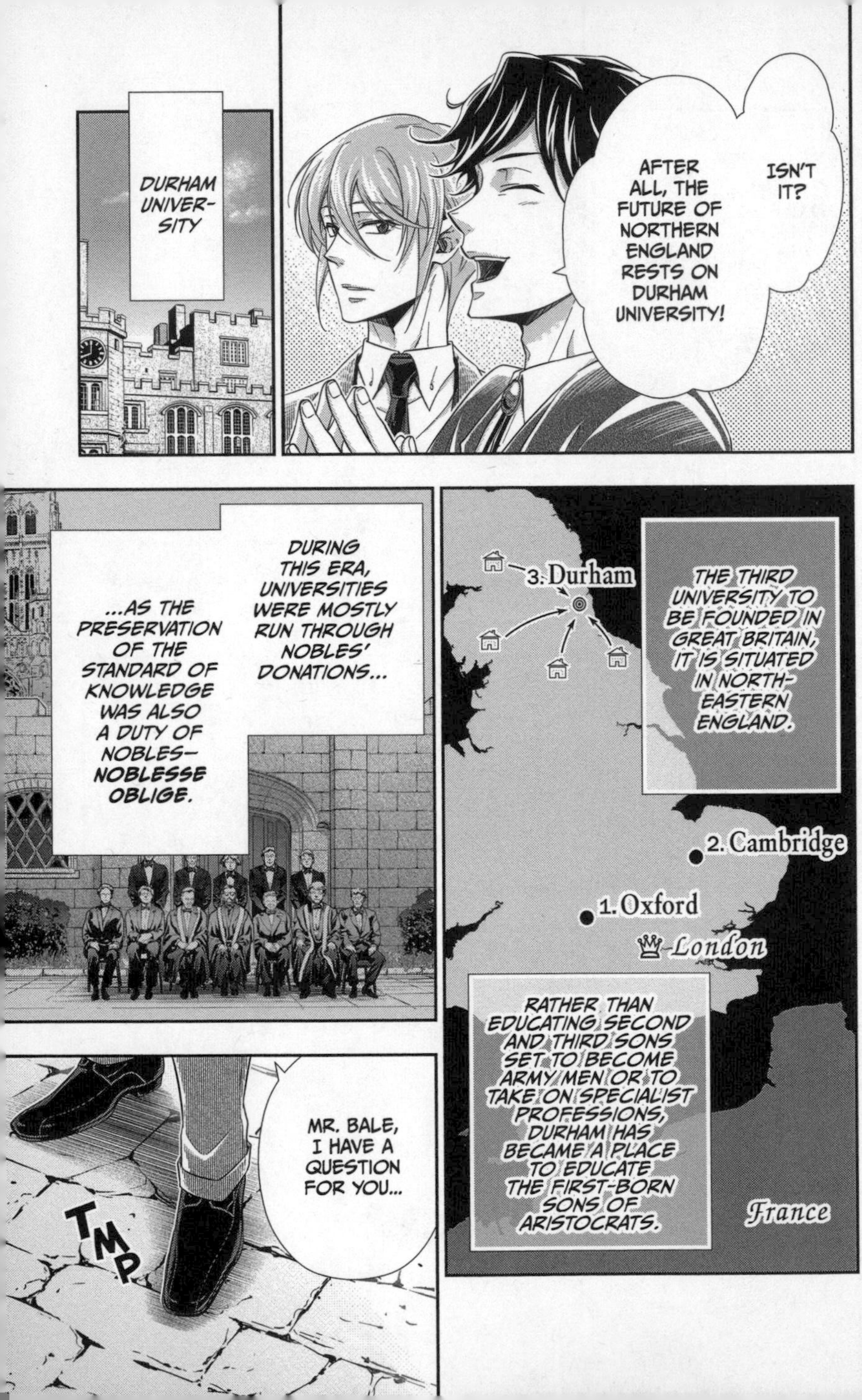
AFTER ALL, THE FUTURE OF NORTHERN ENGLAND RESTS ON DURHAM UNIVERSITY!
ISN'T IT?
DURHAM UNIVER-SITY
3. Durham
THE THIRD UNIVERSITY TO BE FOUNDED IN GREAT BRITAIN, IT IS SITUATED IN NORTH-EASTERN ENGLAND.
2. Cambridge
1. Oxford
London
RATHER THAN EDUCATING SECOND AND THIRD SONS SET TO BECOME ARMY MEN OR TO TAKE ON SPECIALIST PROFESSIONS, DURHAM HAS BECAME A PLACE TO EDUCATE THE FIRST-BORN SONS OF ARISTOCRATS.
France
DURING THIS ERA, UNIVERSITIES WERE MOSTLY RUN THROUGH NOBLES' DONATIONS...
...AS THE PRESERVATION OF THE STANDARD OF KNOWLEDGE WAS ALSO A DUTY OF NOBLES—NOBLESSE OBLIGE.
MR. BALE, I HAVE A QUESTION FOR YOU...
TMP

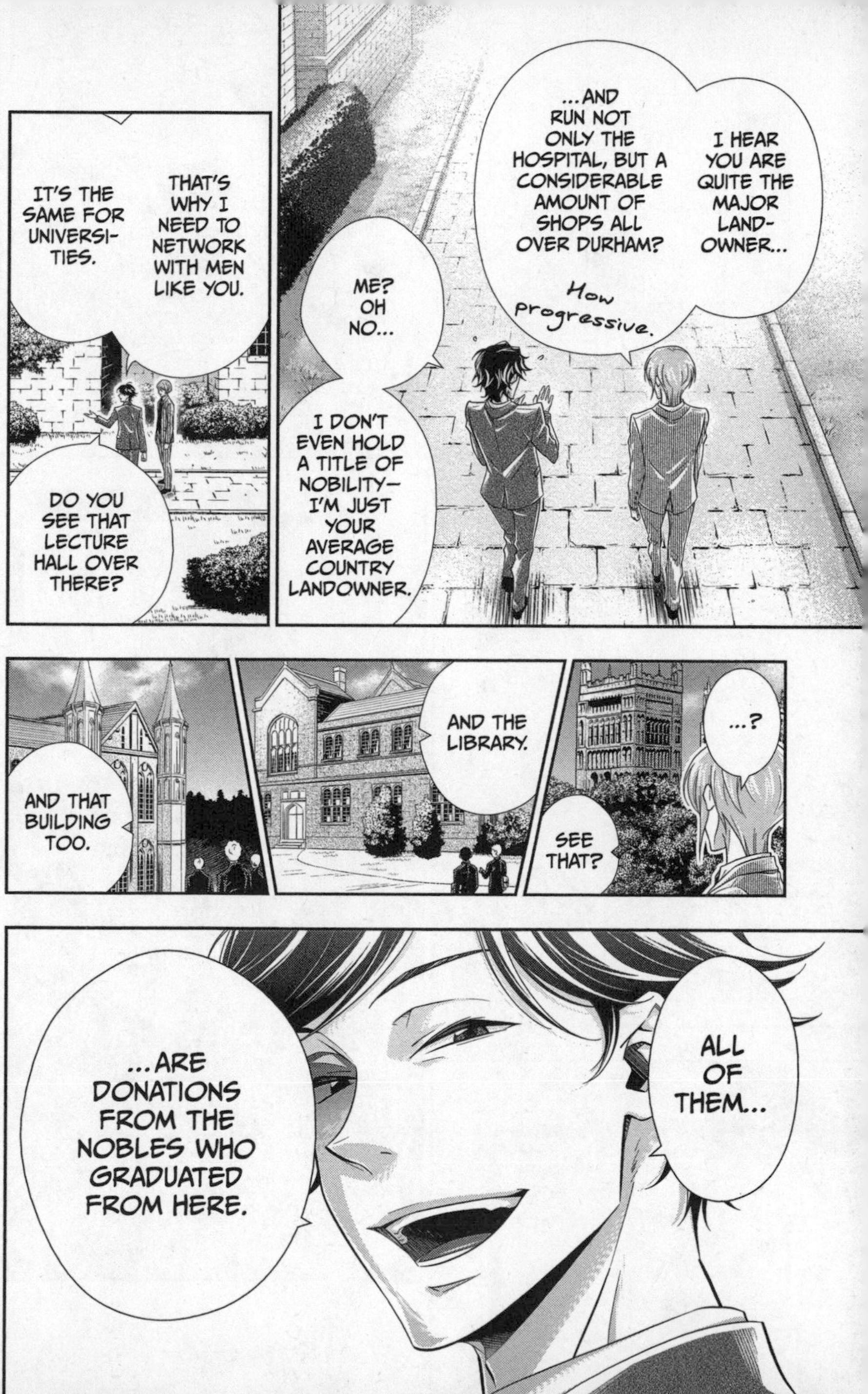
I HEAR YOU ARE QUITE THE MAJOR LAND-OWNER...
...AND RUN NOT ONLY THE HOSPITAL, BUT A CONSIDERABLE AMOUNT OF SHOPS ALL OVER DURHAM?
How progressive.
ME? OH NO...
I DON'T EVEN HOLD A TITLE OF NOBILITY—I'M JUST YOUR AVERAGE COUNTRY LANDOWNER.
THAT'S WHY I NEED TO NETWORK WITH MEN LIKE YOU.
IT'S THE SAME FOR UNIVERSITIES.
DO YOU SEE THAT LECTURE HALL OVER THERE?
...?
SEE THAT?
AND THE LIBRARY.
AND THAT BUILDING TOO.
ALL OF THEM...
...ARE DONATIONS FROM THE NOBLES WHO GRADUATED FROM HERE.

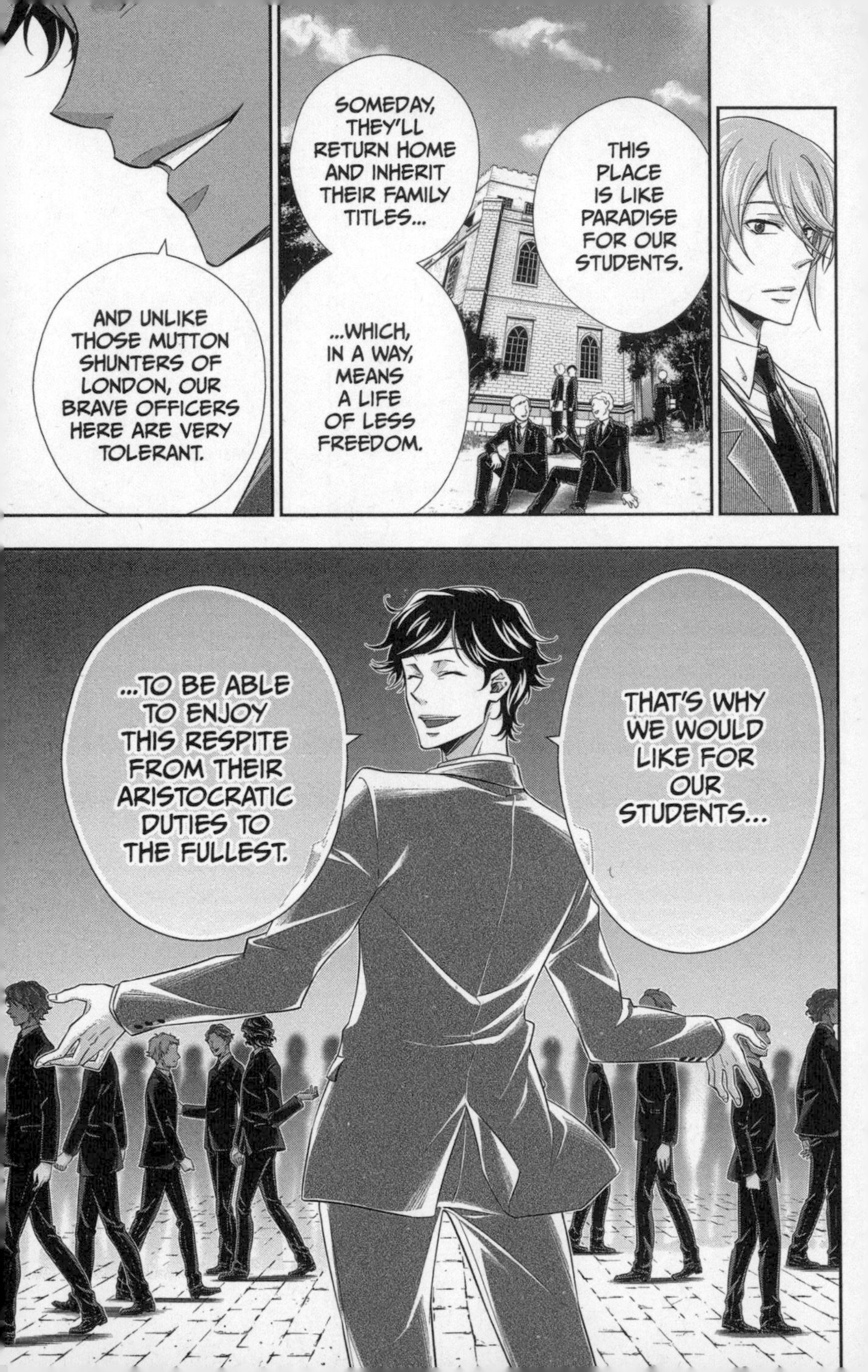
THIS PLACE IS LIKE PARADISE FOR OUR STUDENTS.
SOMEDAY, THEY'LL RETURN HOME AND INHERIT THEIR FAMILY TITLES...
...WHICH, IN A WAY, MEANS A LIFE OF LESS FREEDOM.
AND UNLIKE THOSE MUTTON SHUNTERS OF LONDON, OUR BRAVE OFFICERS HERE ARE VERY TOLERANT.
THAT'S WHY WE WOULD LIKE FOR OUR STUDENTS...
...TO BE ABLE TO ENJOY THIS RESPITE FROM THEIR ARISTOCRATIC DUTIES TO THE FULLEST.

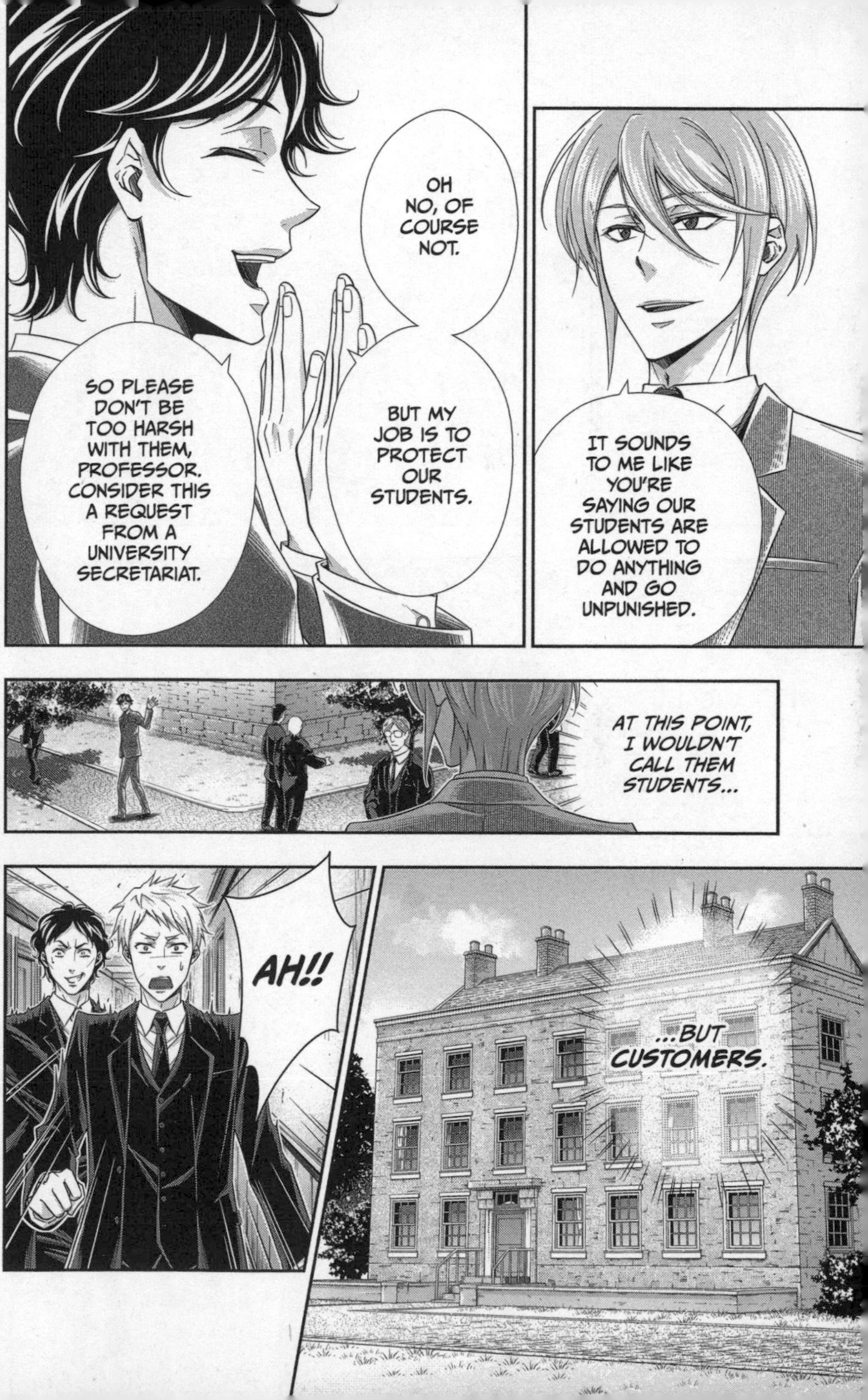
IT SOUNDS TO ME LIKE YOU'RE SAYING OUR STUDENTS ARE ALLOWED TO DO ANYTHING AND GO UNPUNISHED.
OH NO, OF COURSE NOT.
BUT MY JOB IS TO PROTECT OUR STUDENTS.
SO PLEASE DON'T BE TOO HARSH WITH THEM, PROFESSOR. CONSIDER THIS A REQUEST FROM A UNIVERSITY SECRETARIAT.
AT THIS POINT, I WOULDN'T CALL THEM STUDENTS...
...BUT CUSTOMERS.
AH!!

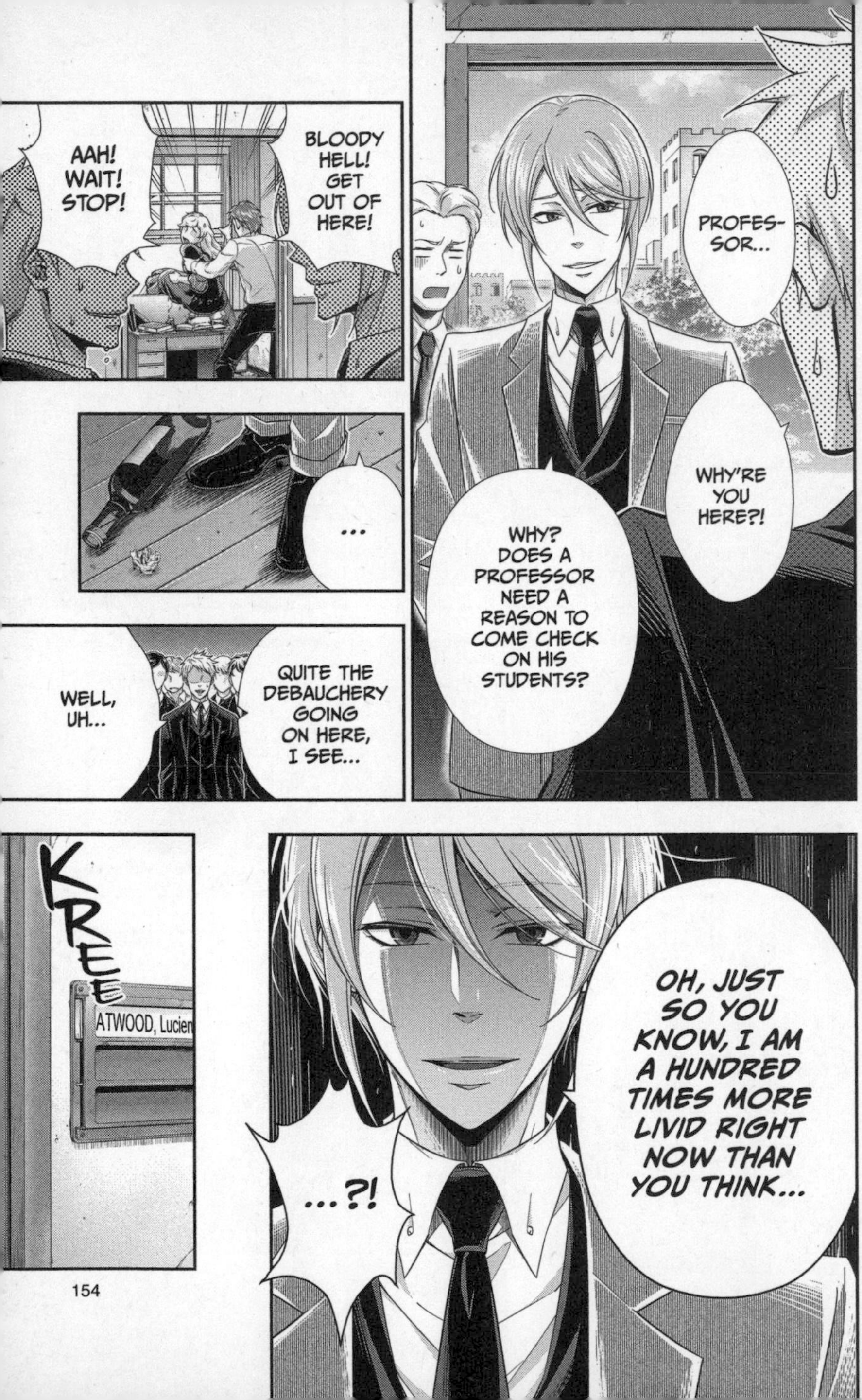
PROFES-SOR...
WHY'RE YOU HERE?!
WHY? DOES A PROFESSOR NEED A REASON TO COME CHECK ON HIS STUDENTS?
BLOODY HELL! GET OUT OF HERE!
AAH! WAIT! STOP!
...
QUITE THE DEBAUCHERY GOING ON HERE, I SEE...
WELL, UH...
OH, JUST SO YOU KNOW, I AM A HUNDRED TIMES MORE LIVID RIGHT NOW THAN YOU THINK...
...?!
KREE
ATWOOD, Lucien

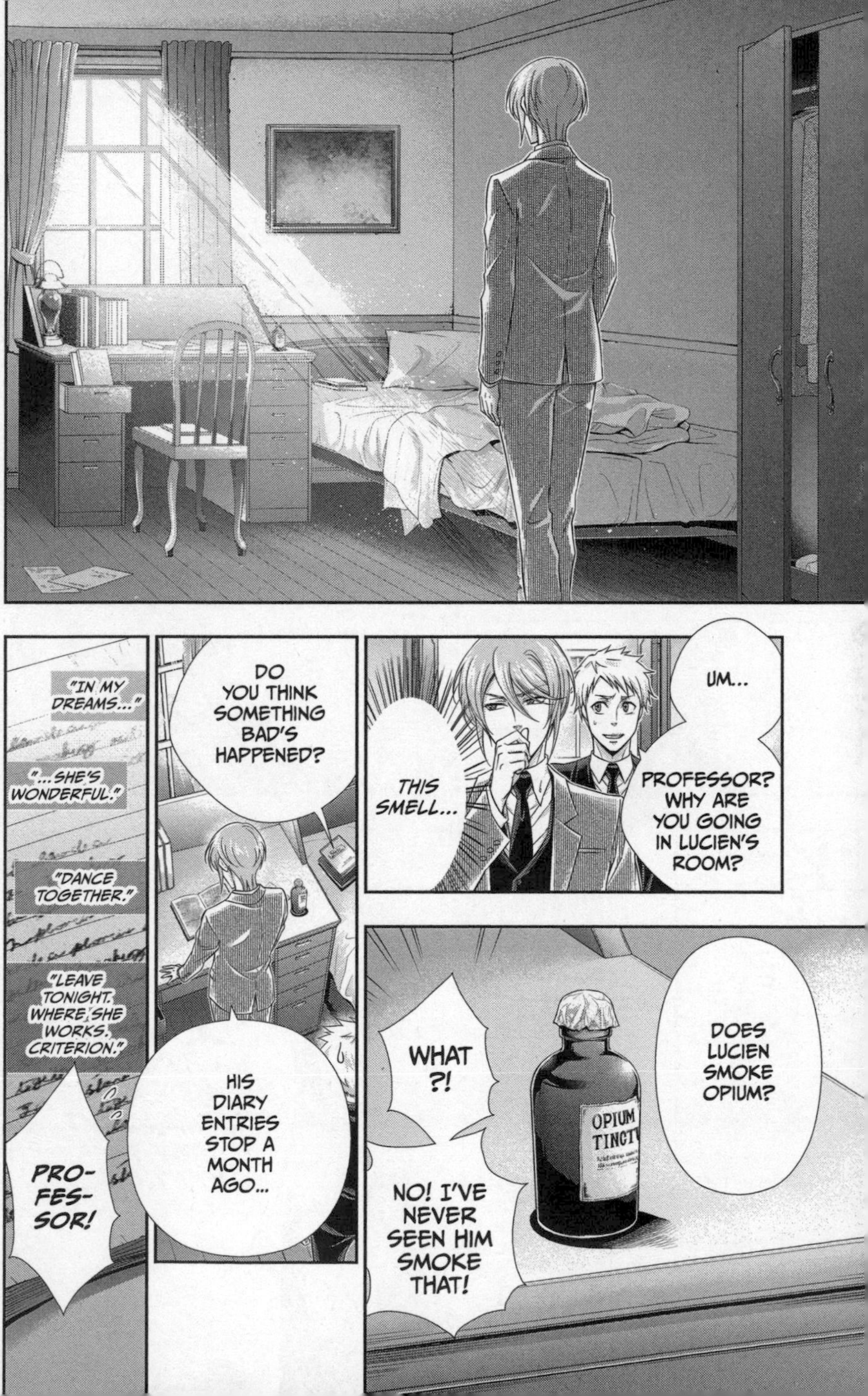
UM...
PROFESSOR? WHY ARE YOU GOING IN LUCIEN'S ROOM?
THIS SMELL...
DOES LUCIEN SMOKE OPIUM?
WHAT?!
NO! I'VE NEVER SEEN HIM SMOKE THAT!
OPIUM TINCTU
DO YOU THINK SOMETHING BAD'S HAPPENED?
HIS DIARY ENTRIES STOP A MONTH AGO...
"IN MY DREAMS..."
"...SHE'S WONDERFUL."
"DANCE TOGETHER."
"LEAVE TONIGHT. WHERE SHE WORKS. CRITERION."
PRO-FES-SOR!

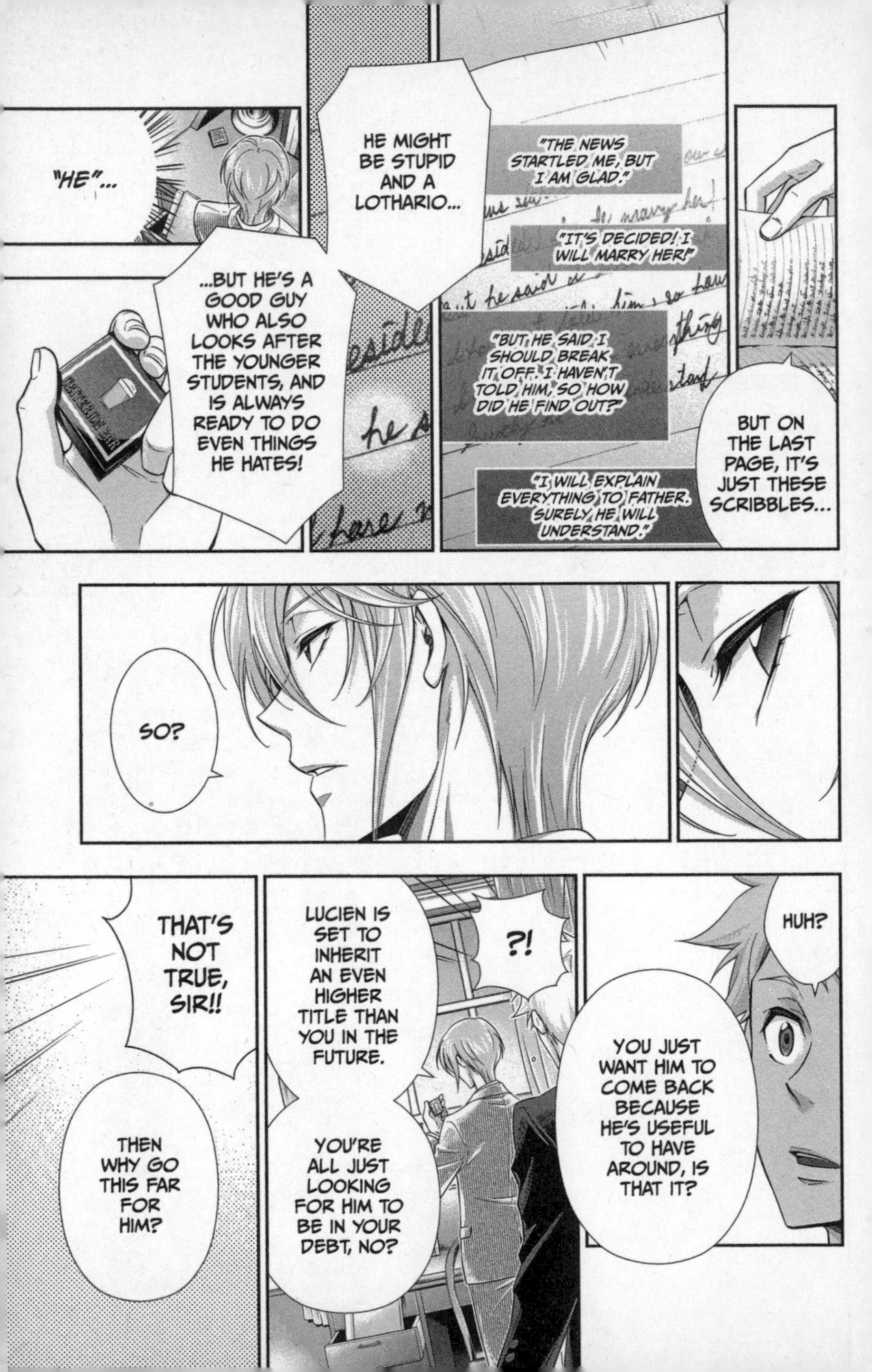
BUT ON THE LAST PAGE, IT'S JUST THESE SCRIBBLES...
"THE NEWS STARTLED ME, BUT I AM GLAD."
"IT'S DECIDED! I WILL MARRY HER!"
"BUT HE SAID I SHOULD BREAK IT OFF. I HAVEN'T TOLD HIM, SO HOW DID HE FIND OUT?"
"I WILL EXPLAIN EVERYTHING TO FATHER. SURELY HE WILL UNDERSTAND."
"HE"...
HE MIGHT BE STUPID AND A LOTHARIO...
...BUT HE'S A GOOD GUY WHO ALSO LOOKS AFTER THE YOUNGER STUDENTS, AND IS ALWAYS READY TO DO EVEN THINGS HE HATES!
SO?
HUH?
YOU JUST WANT HIM TO COME BACK BECAUSE HE'S USEFUL TO HAVE AROUND, IS THAT IT?
?!
LUCIEN IS SET TO INHERIT AN EVEN HIGHER TITLE THAN YOU IN THE FUTURE.
YOU'RE ALL JUST LOOKING FOR HIM TO BE IN YOUR DEBT, NO?
THAT'S NOT TRUE, SIR!!
THEN WHY GO THIS FAR FOR HIM?

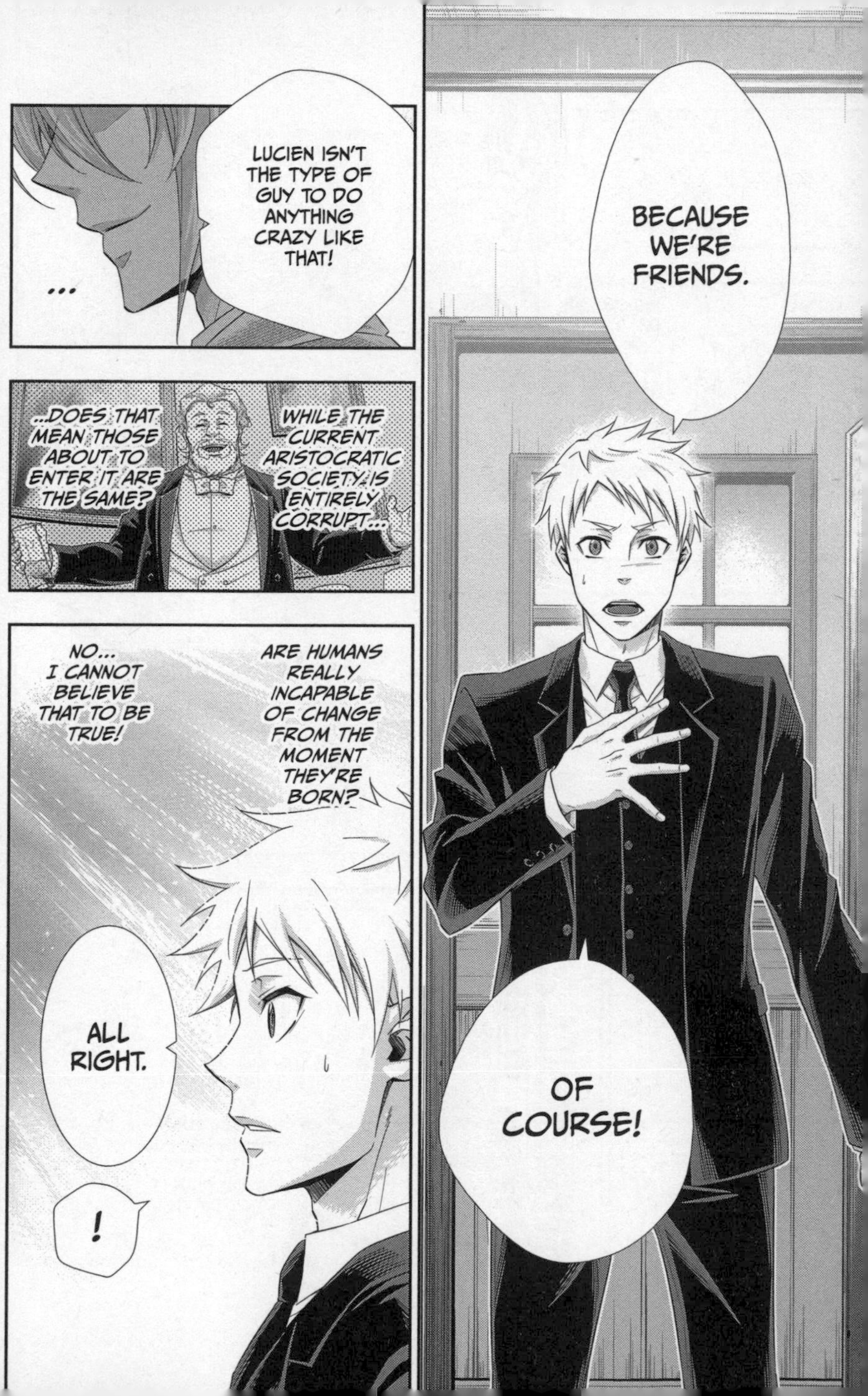
BECAUSE WE'RE FRIENDS.
OF COURSE!
LUCIEN ISN'T THE TYPE OF GUY TO DO ANYTHING CRAZY LIKE THAT!
...
WHILE THE CURRENT ARISTOCRATIC SOCIETY IS ENTIRELY CORRUPT...
...DOES THAT MEAN THOSE ABOUT TO ENTER IT ARE THE SAME?
ARE HUMANS REALLY INCAPABLE OF CHANGE FROM THE MOMENT THEY'RE BORN?
NO... I CANNOT BELIEVE THAT TO BE TRUE!
ALL RIGHT.
!

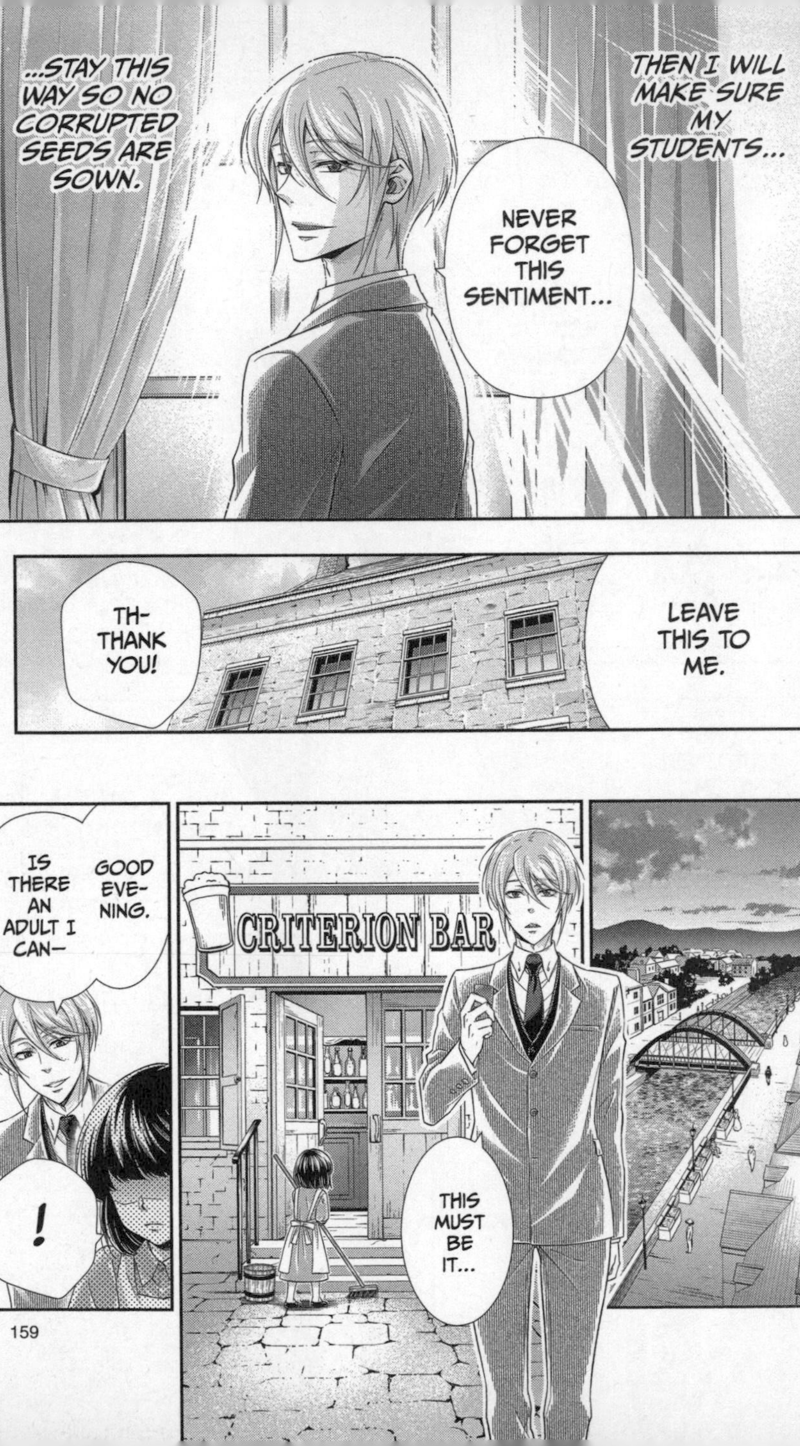
THEN I WILL MAKE SURE MY STUDENTS...
...STAY THIS WAY SO NO CORRUPTED SEEDS ARE SOWN.
NEVER FORGET THIS SENTIMENT...
LEAVE THIS TO ME.
TH- THANK YOU!
CRITERION BAR
THIS MUST BE IT...
GOOD EVE- NING.
IS THERE AN ADULT I CAN—
!

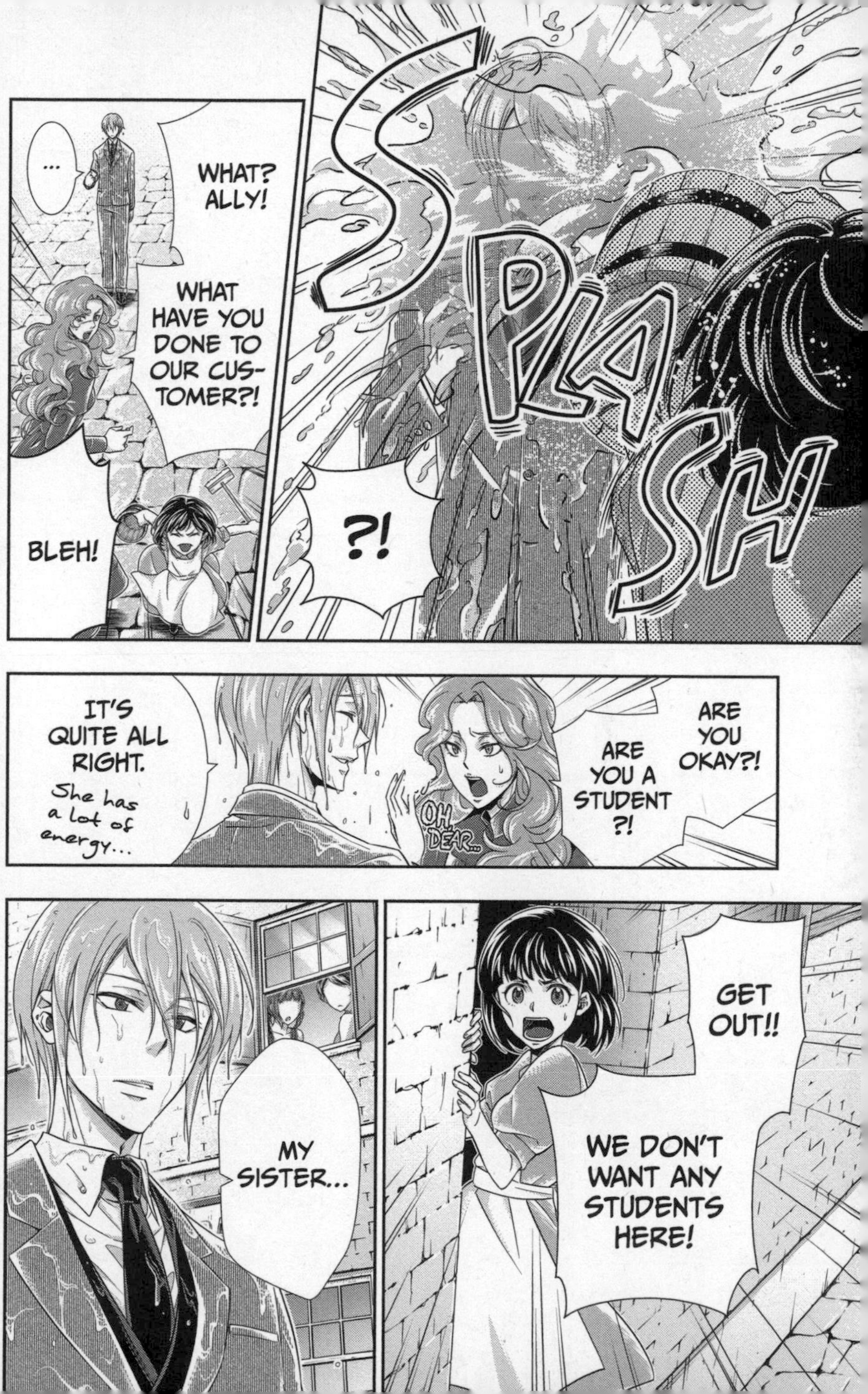
SPLASH
?!
...
WHAT? ALLY!
WHAT HAVE YOU DONE TO OUR CUS-TOMER?!
BLEH!
ARE YOU OKAY?!
ARE YOU A STUDENT ?!
OH, DEAR...
IT'S QUITE ALL RIGHT.
She has a lot of energy...
GET OUT!!
WE DON'T WANT ANY STUDENTS HERE!
MY SISTER...

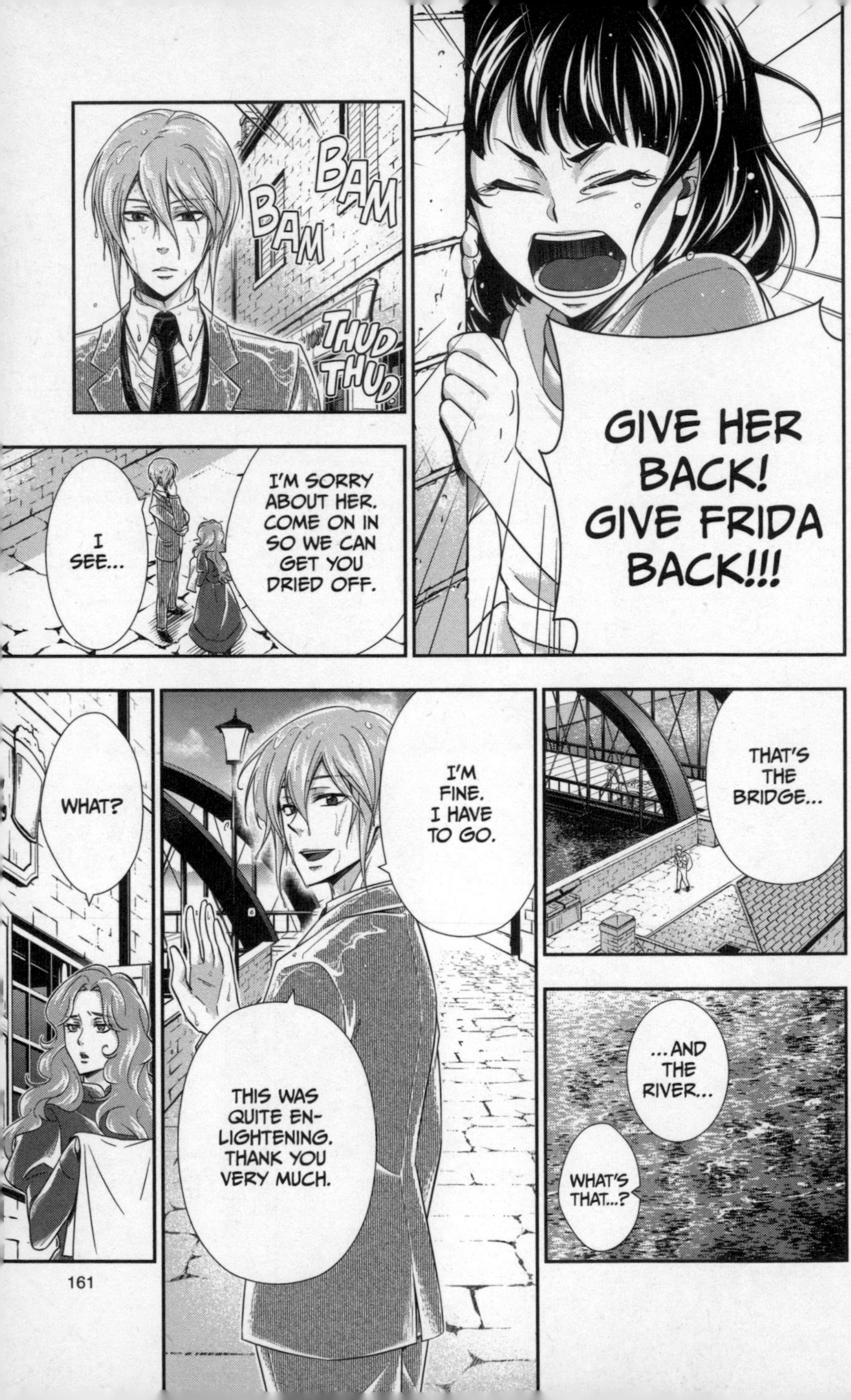
GIVE HER BACK! GIVE FRIDA BACK!!!
BAM
BAM
THUD THUD
I'M SORRY ABOUT HER. COME ON IN SO WE CAN GET YOU DRIED OFF.
I SEE...
THAT'S THE BRIDGE...
...AND THE RIVER...
WHAT'S THAT...?
I'M FINE. I HAVE TO GO.
THIS WAS QUITE EN-LIGHTENING. THANK YOU VERY MUCH.
WHAT?

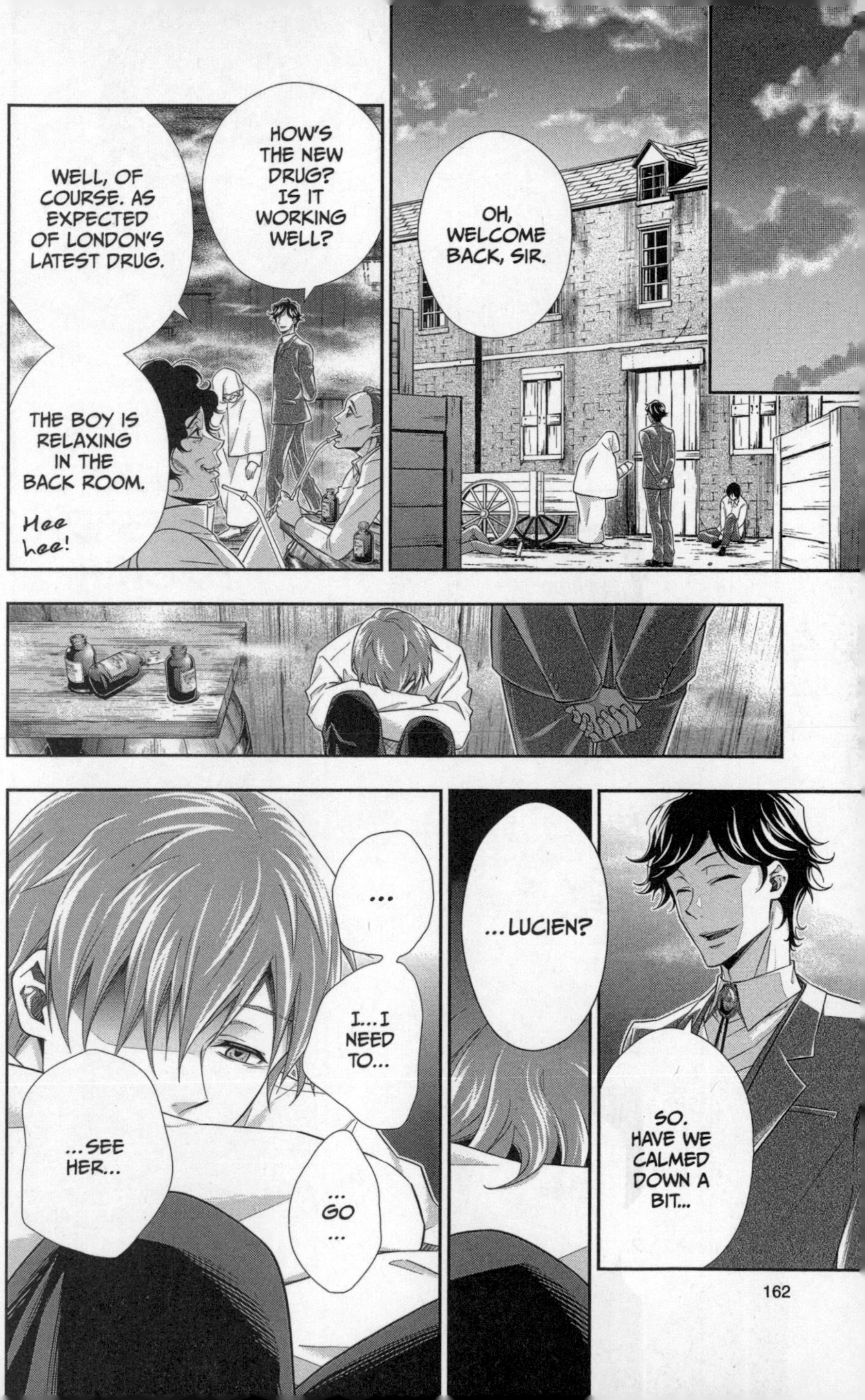
OH, WELCOME BACK, SIR.
HOW'S THE NEW DRUG? IS IT WORKING WELL?
WELL, OF COURSE. AS EXPECTED OF LONDON'S LATEST DRUG.
THE BOY IS RELAXING IN THE BACK ROOM.
Hee hee!
SO. HAVE WE CALMED DOWN A BIT...
...LUCIEN?
...
I...I NEED TO...
...SEE HER...
... GO ...

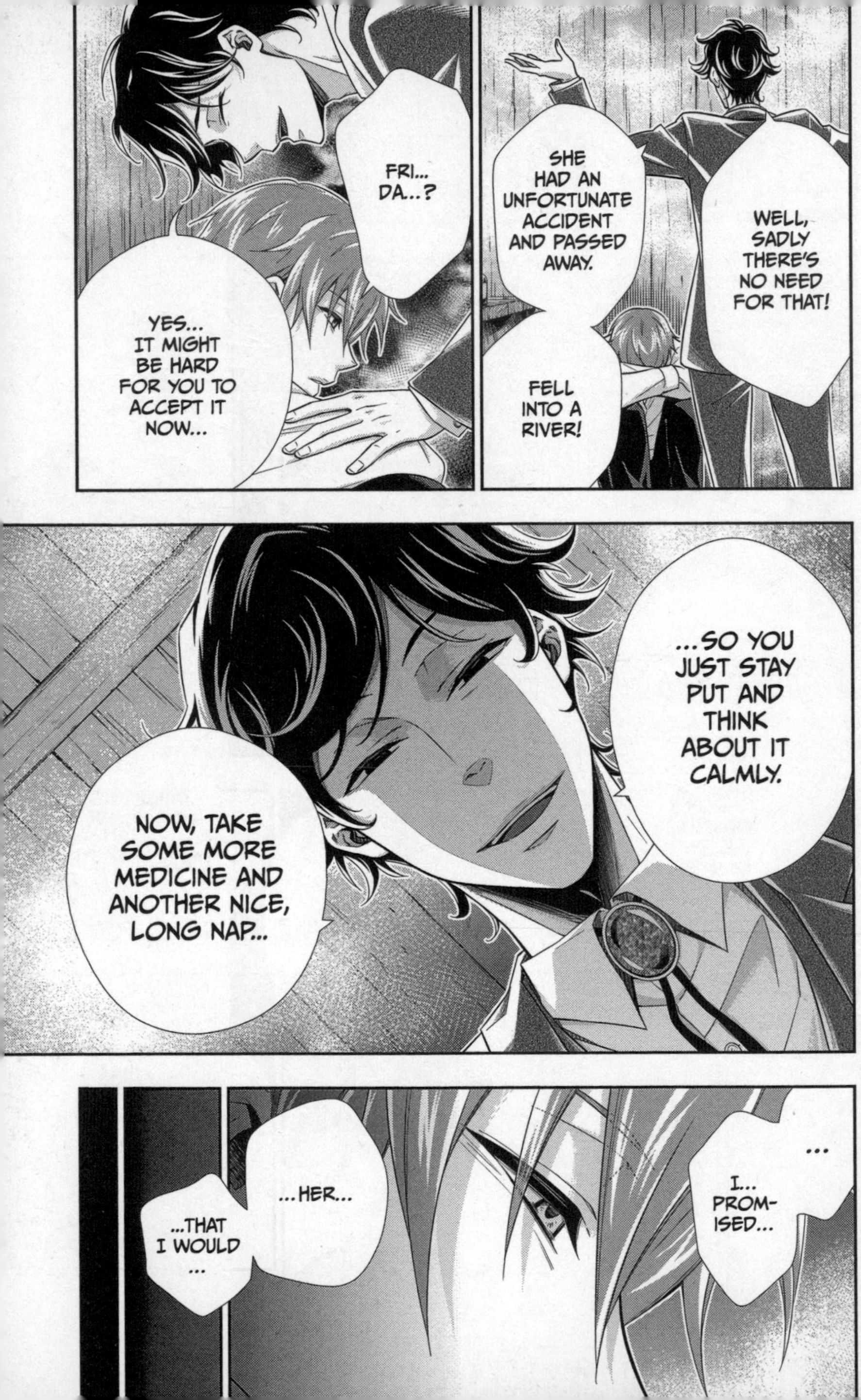
WELL, SADLY THERE'S NO NEED FOR THAT!
SHE HAD AN UNFORTUNATE ACCIDENT AND PASSED AWAY.
FELL INTO A RIVER!
FRI... DA...?
YES... IT MIGHT BE HARD FOR YOU TO ACCEPT IT NOW...
...SO YOU JUST STAY PUT AND THINK ABOUT IT CALMLY.
NOW, TAKE SOME MORE MEDICINE AND ANOTHER NICE, LONG NAP...
...
I... PROM-ISED...
...HER...
...THAT I WOULD ...

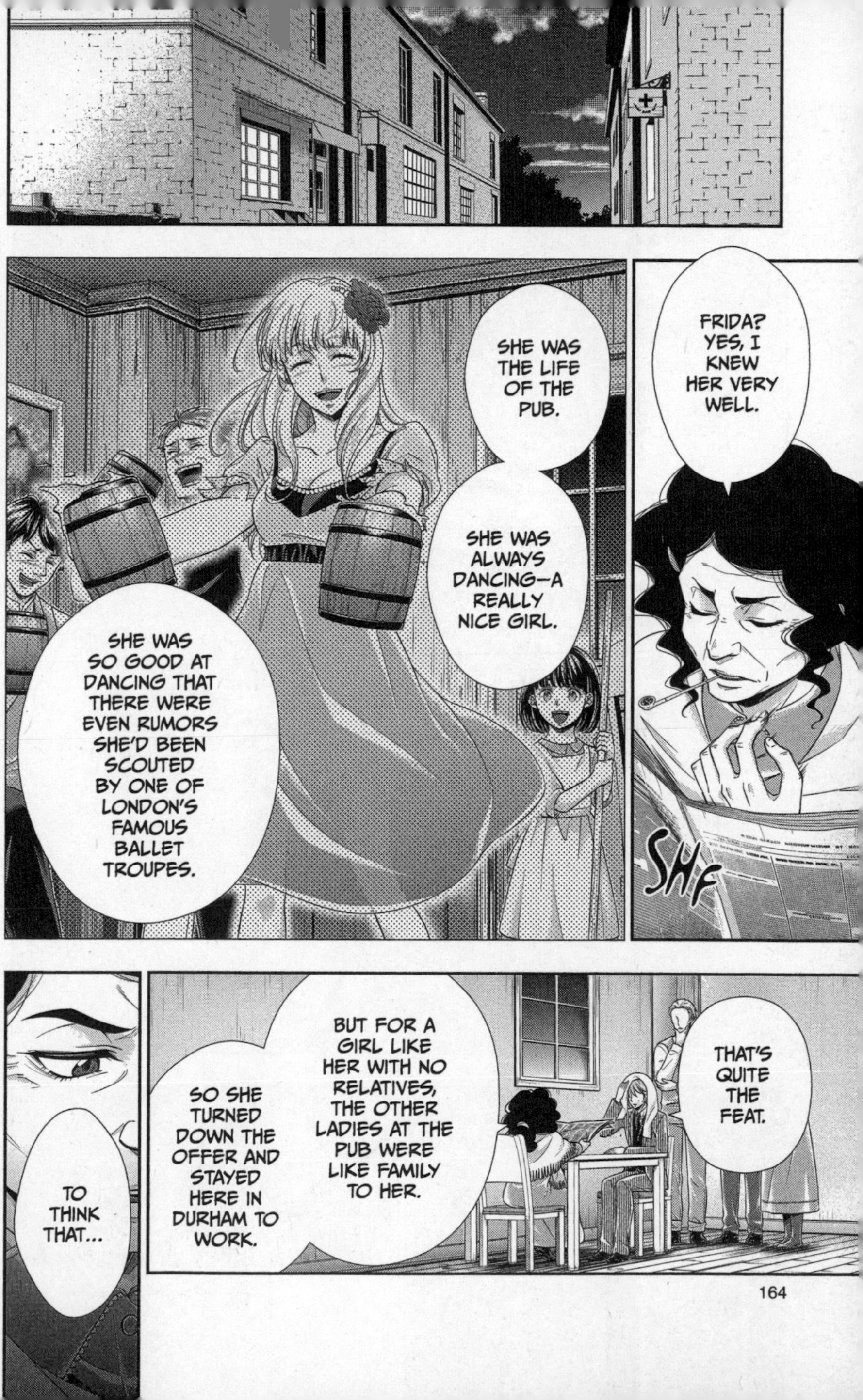
FRIDA? YES, I KNEW HER VERY WELL.
SHF
SHE WAS THE LIFE OF THE PUB.
SHE WAS ALWAYS DANCING—A REALLY NICE GIRL.
SHE WAS SO GOOD AT DANCING THAT THERE WERE EVEN RUMORS SHE'D BEEN SCOUTED BY ONE OF LONDON'S FAMOUS BALLET TROUPES.
THAT'S QUITE THE FEAT.
BUT FOR A GIRL LIKE HER WITH NO RELATIVES, THE OTHER LADIES AT THE PUB WERE LIKE FAMILY TO HER.
SO SHE TURNED DOWN THE OFFER AND STAYED HERE IN DURHAM TO WORK.
TO THINK THAT...

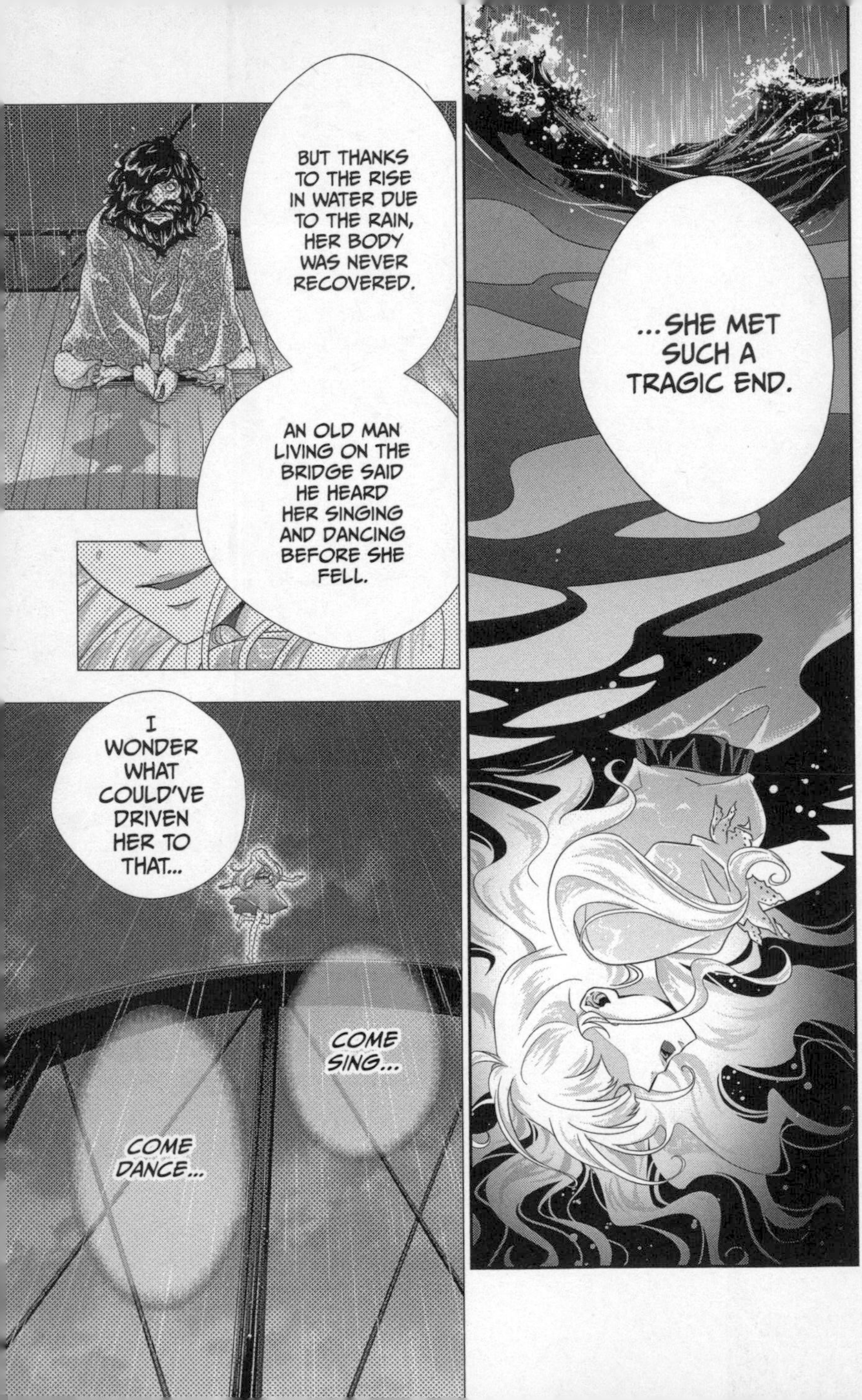
...SHE MET SUCH A TRAGIC END.
BUT THANKS TO THE RISE IN WATER DUE TO THE RAIN, HER BODY WAS NEVER RECOVERED.
AN OLD MAN LIVING ON THE BRIDGE SAID HE HEARD HER SINGING AND DANCING BEFORE SHE FELL.
I WONDER WHAT COULD'VE DRIVEN HER TO THAT...
COME SING...
COME DANCE...

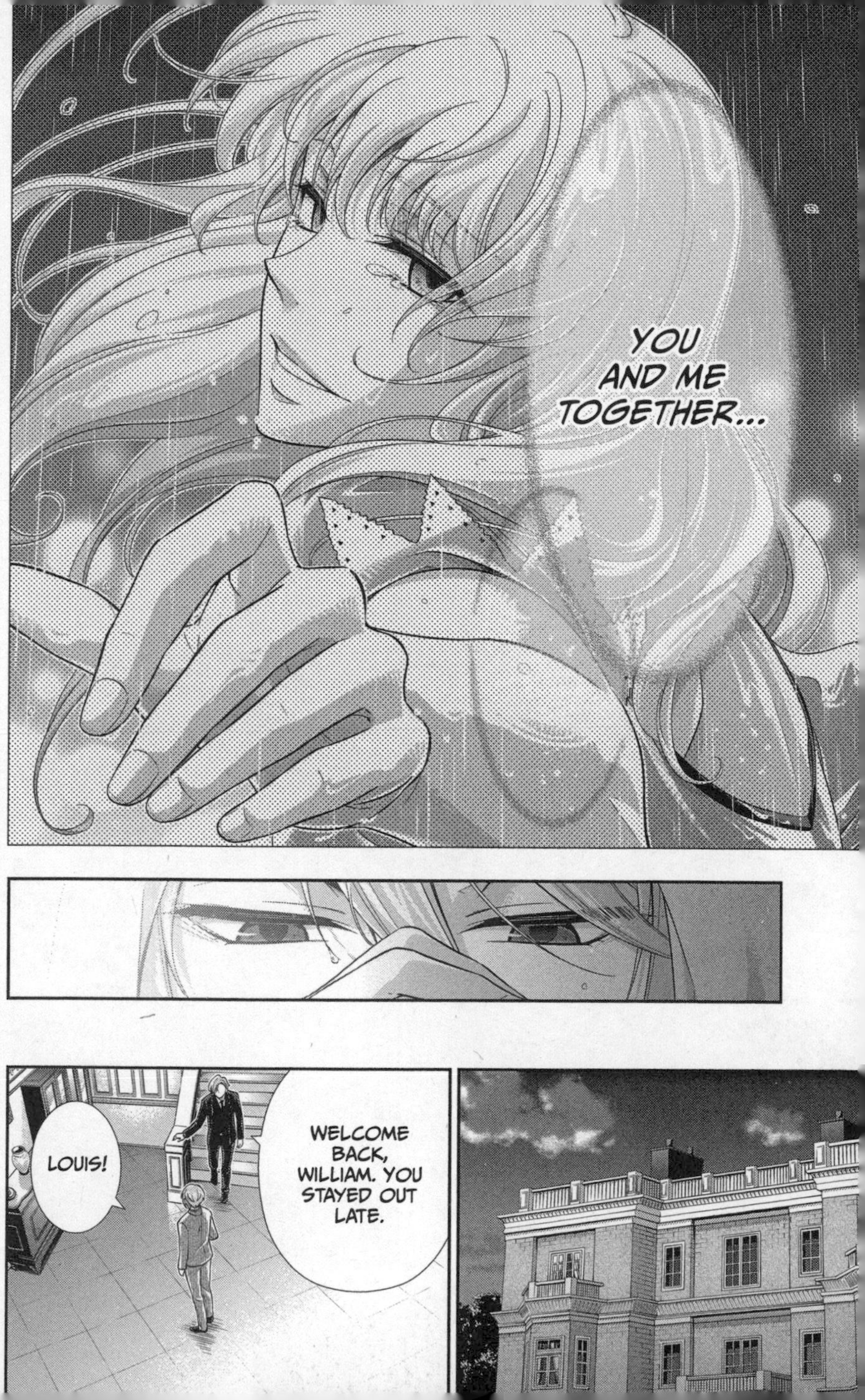
YOU AND ME TOGETHER...
WELCOME BACK, WILLIAM. YOU STAYED OUT LATE.
LOUIS!

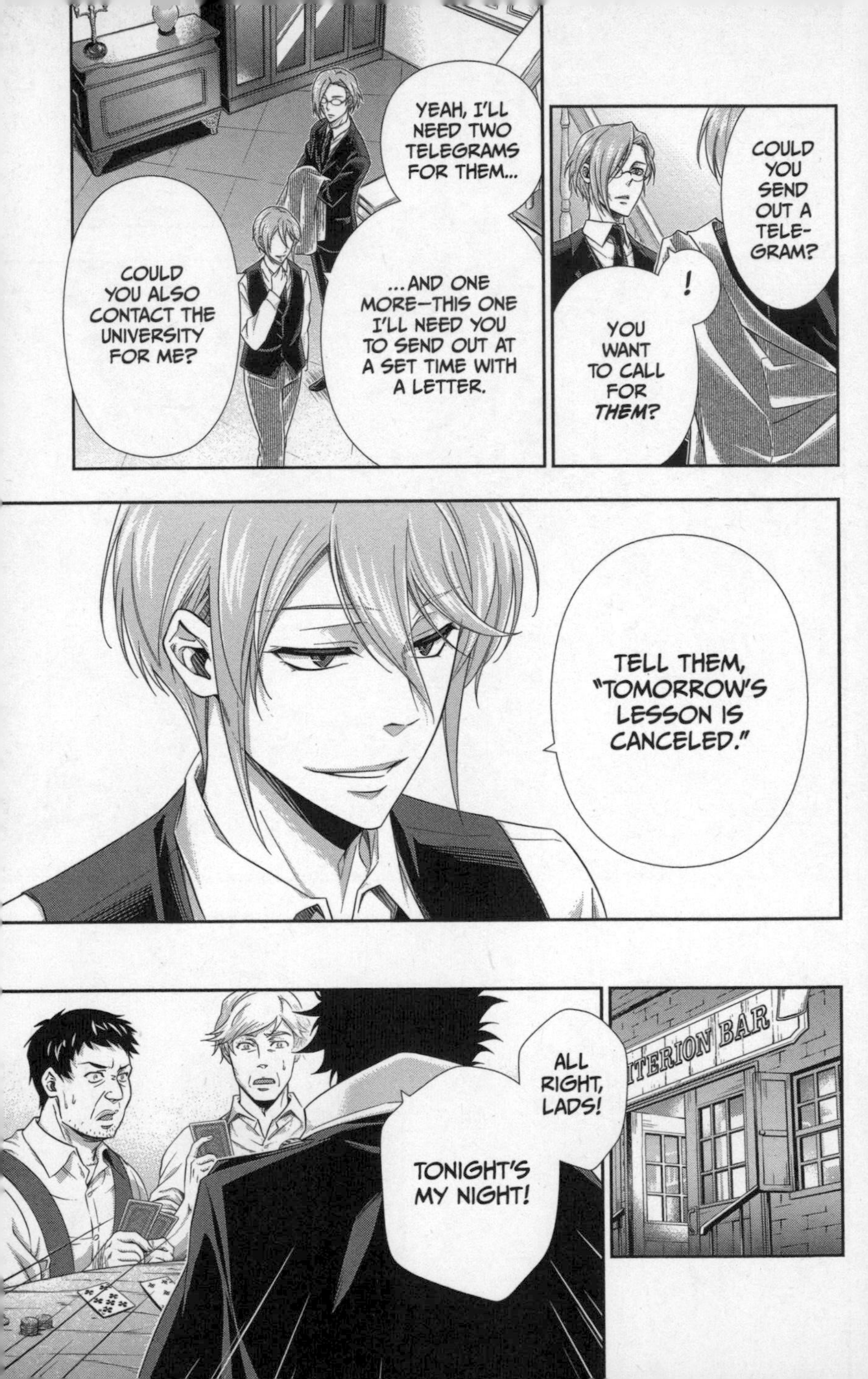
COULD YOU SEND OUT A TELE-GRAM?
!
YOU WANT TO CALL FOR *THEM*?
YEAH, I'LL NEED TWO TELEGRAMS FOR THEM...
...AND ONE MORE—THIS ONE I'LL NEED YOU TO SEND OUT AT A SET TIME WITH A LETTER.
COULD YOU ALSO CONTACT THE UNIVERSITY FOR ME?
TELL THEM, "TOMORROW'S LESSON IS CANCELED."
ITERION BAR
ALL RIGHT, LADS!
TONIGHT'S MY NIGHT!

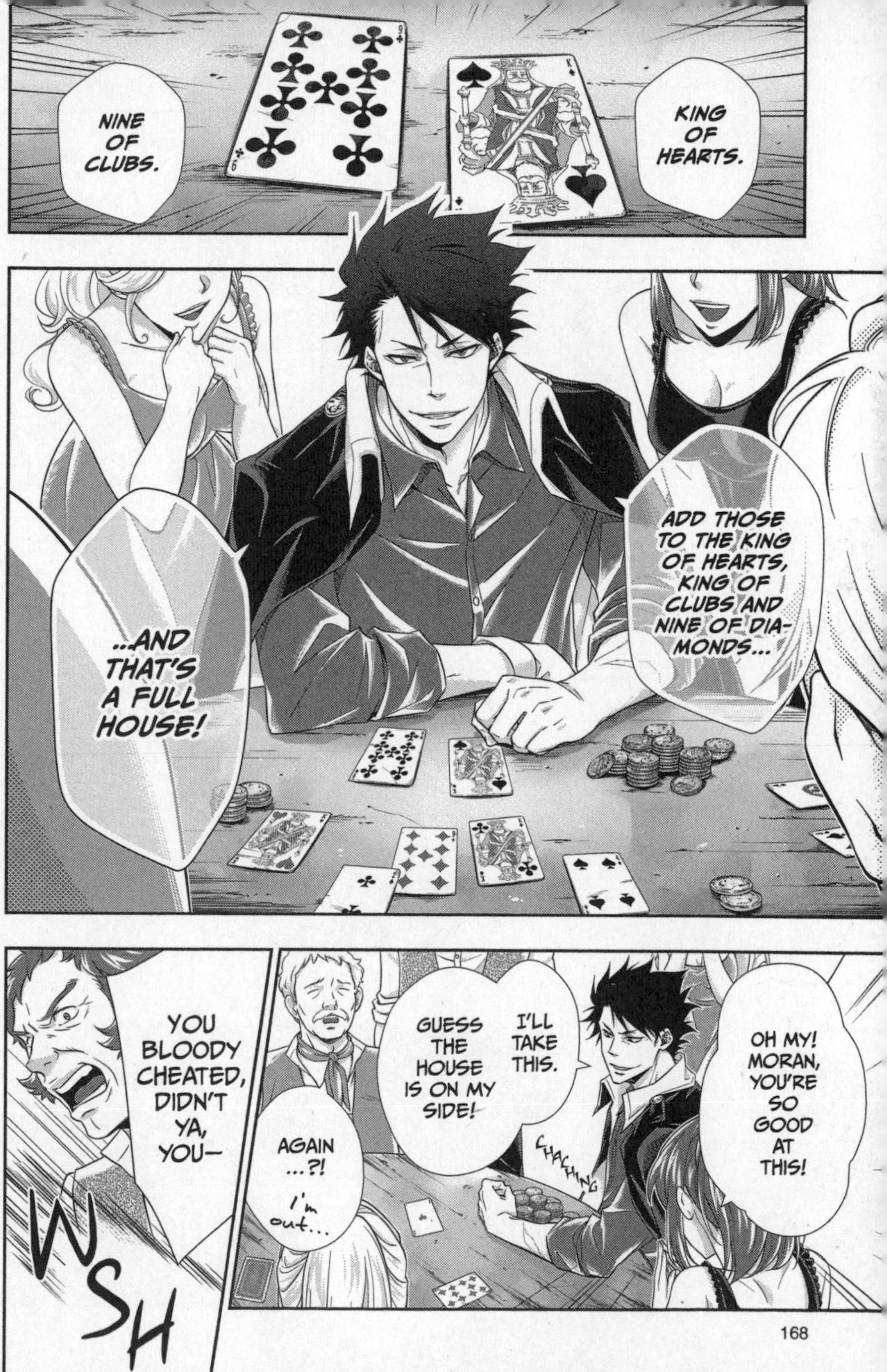
KING OF HEARTS.
NINE OF CLUBS.
ADD THOSE TO THE KING OF HEARTS, KING OF CLUBS AND NINE OF DIAMONDS...
...AND THAT'S A FULL HOUSE!
OH MY! MORAN, YOU'RE SO GOOD AT THIS!
I'LL TAKE THIS.
GUESS THE HOUSE IS ON MY SIDE!
CHACHING
AGAIN ...?!
I'm out...
YOU BLOODY CHEATED, DIDN'T YA, YOU—
WSH

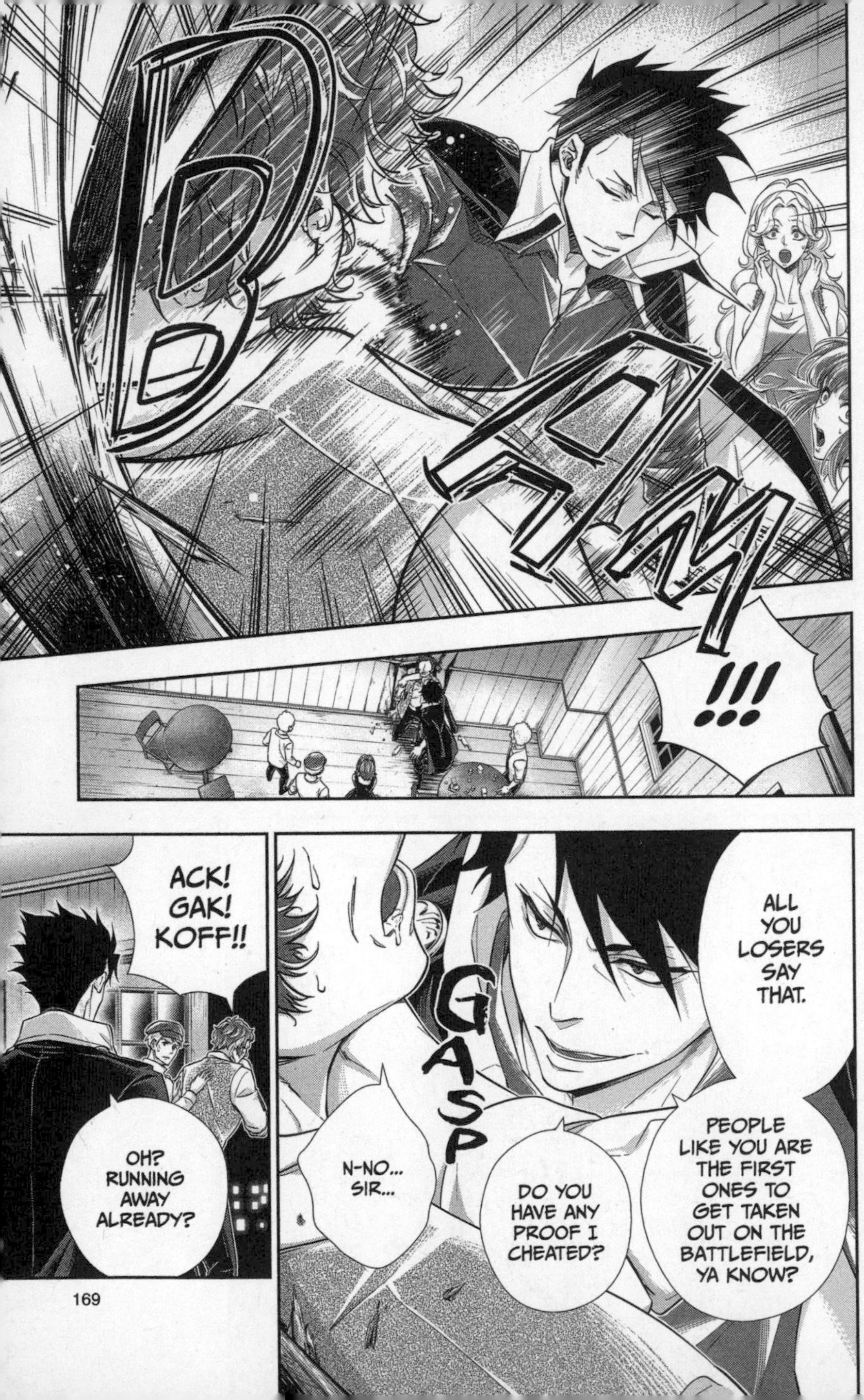
DAM!!!
ALL YOU LOSERS SAY THAT.
GASP
PEOPLE LIKE YOU ARE THE FIRST ONES TO GET TAKEN OUT ON THE BATTLEFIELD, YA KNOW?
DO YOU HAVE ANY PROOF I CHEATED?
N-NO... SIR...
ACK! GAK! KOFF!!
OH? RUNNING AWAY ALREADY?

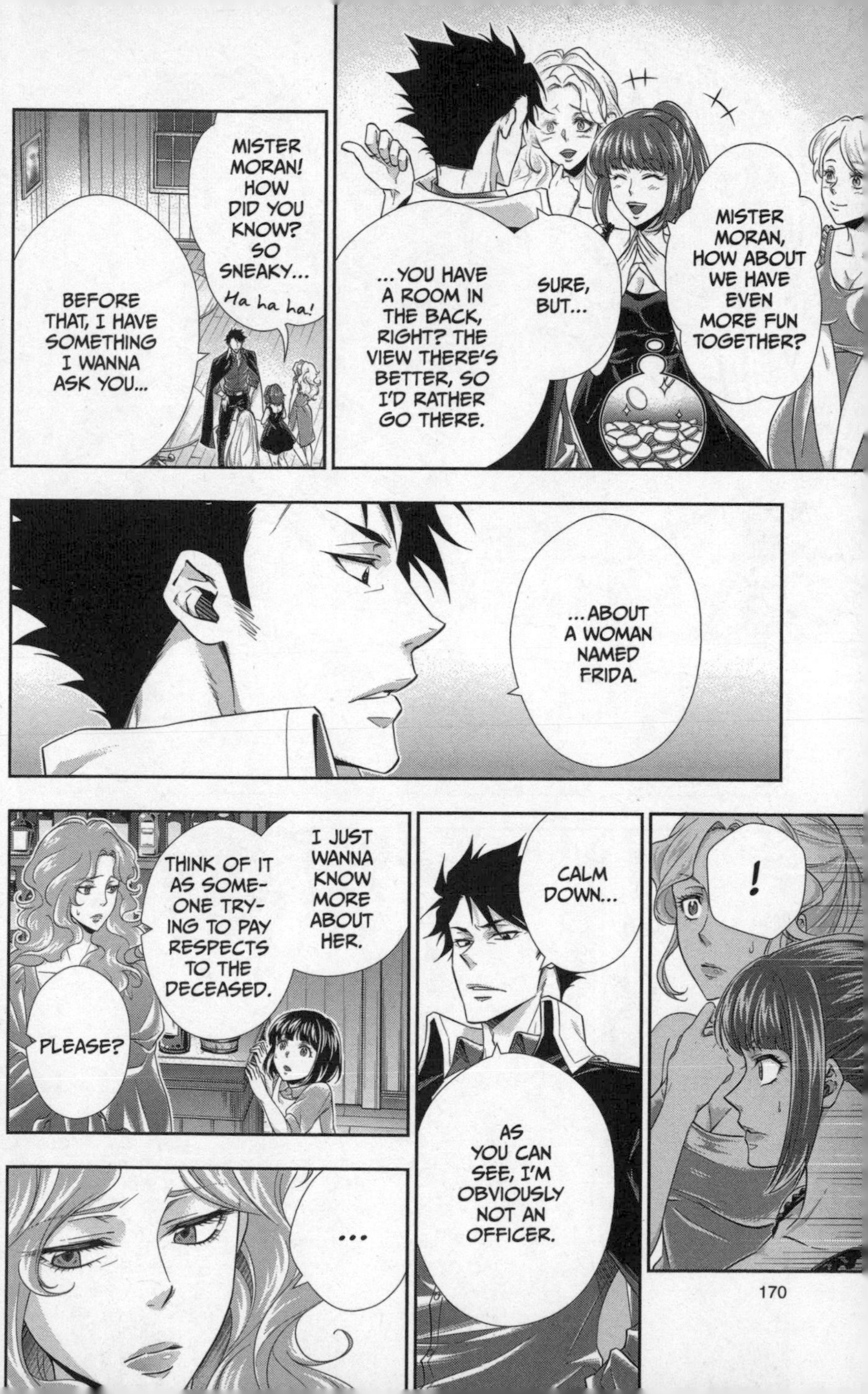
MISTER MORAN, HOW ABOUT WE HAVE EVEN MORE FUN TOGETHER?
SURE, BUT...
...YOU HAVE A ROOM IN THE BACK, RIGHT? THE VIEW THERE'S BETTER, SO I'D RATHER GO THERE.
MISTER MORAN! HOW DID YOU KNOW? SO SNEAKY...
Ha ha ha!
BEFORE THAT, I HAVE SOMETHING I WANNA ASK YOU...
...ABOUT A WOMAN NAMED FRIDA.
!
CALM DOWN...
AS YOU CAN SEE, I'M OBVIOUSLY NOT AN OFFICER.
I JUST WANNA KNOW MORE ABOUT HER.
THINK OF IT AS SOME-ONE TRY-ING TO PAY RESPECTS TO THE DECEASED.
PLEASE?
...

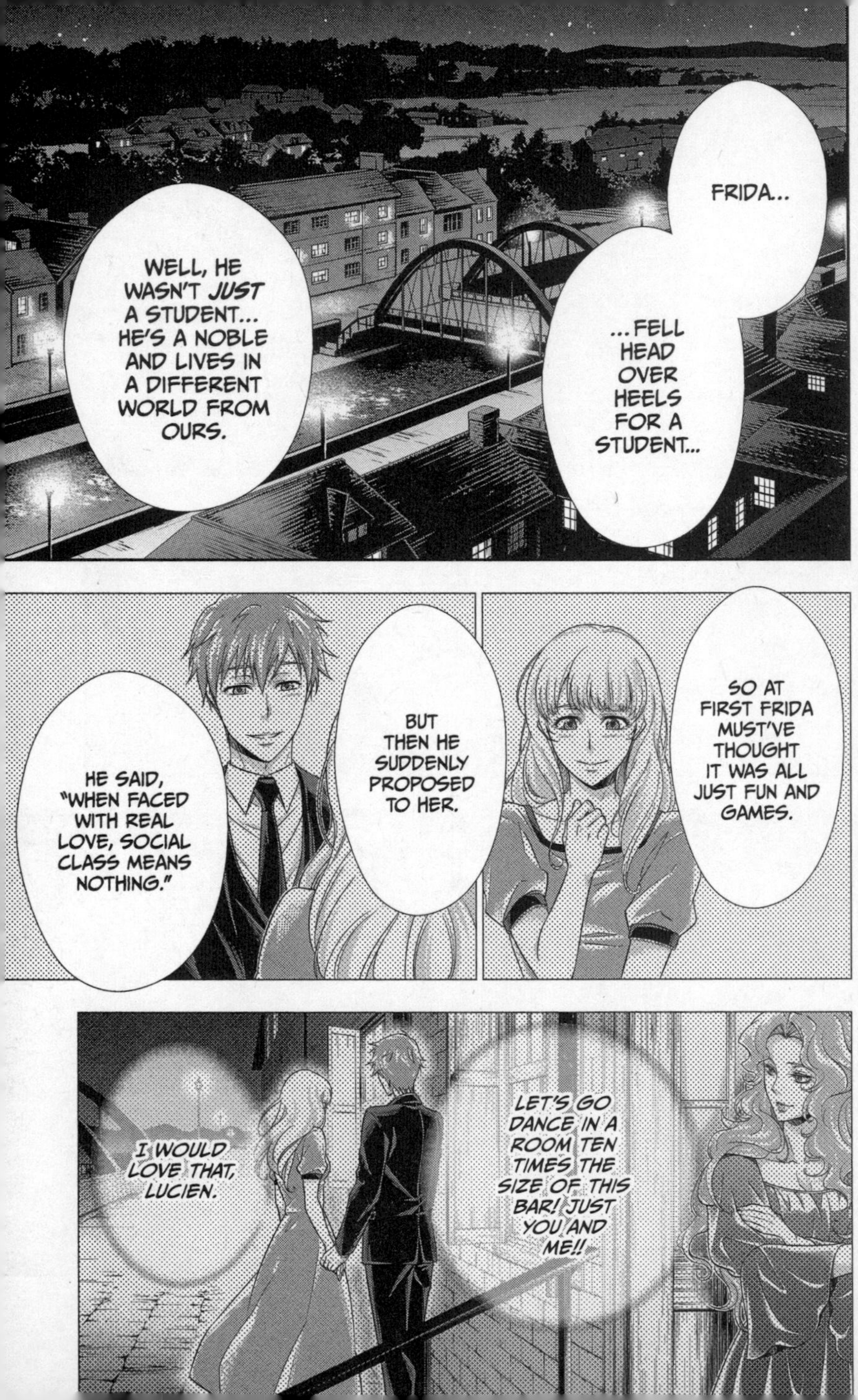
FRIDA...
...FELL HEAD OVER HEELS FOR A STUDENT...
WELL, HE WASN'T JUST A STUDENT... HE'S A NOBLE AND LIVES IN A DIFFERENT WORLD FROM OURS.
SO AT FIRST FRIDA MUST'VE THOUGHT IT WAS ALL JUST FUN AND GAMES.
BUT THEN HE SUDDENLY PROPOSED TO HER.
HE SAID, "WHEN FACED WITH REAL LOVE, SOCIAL CLASS MEANS NOTHING."
LET'S GO DANCE IN A ROOM TEN TIMES THE SIZE OF THIS BAR! JUST YOU AND ME!!
I WOULD LOVE THAT, LUCIEN.

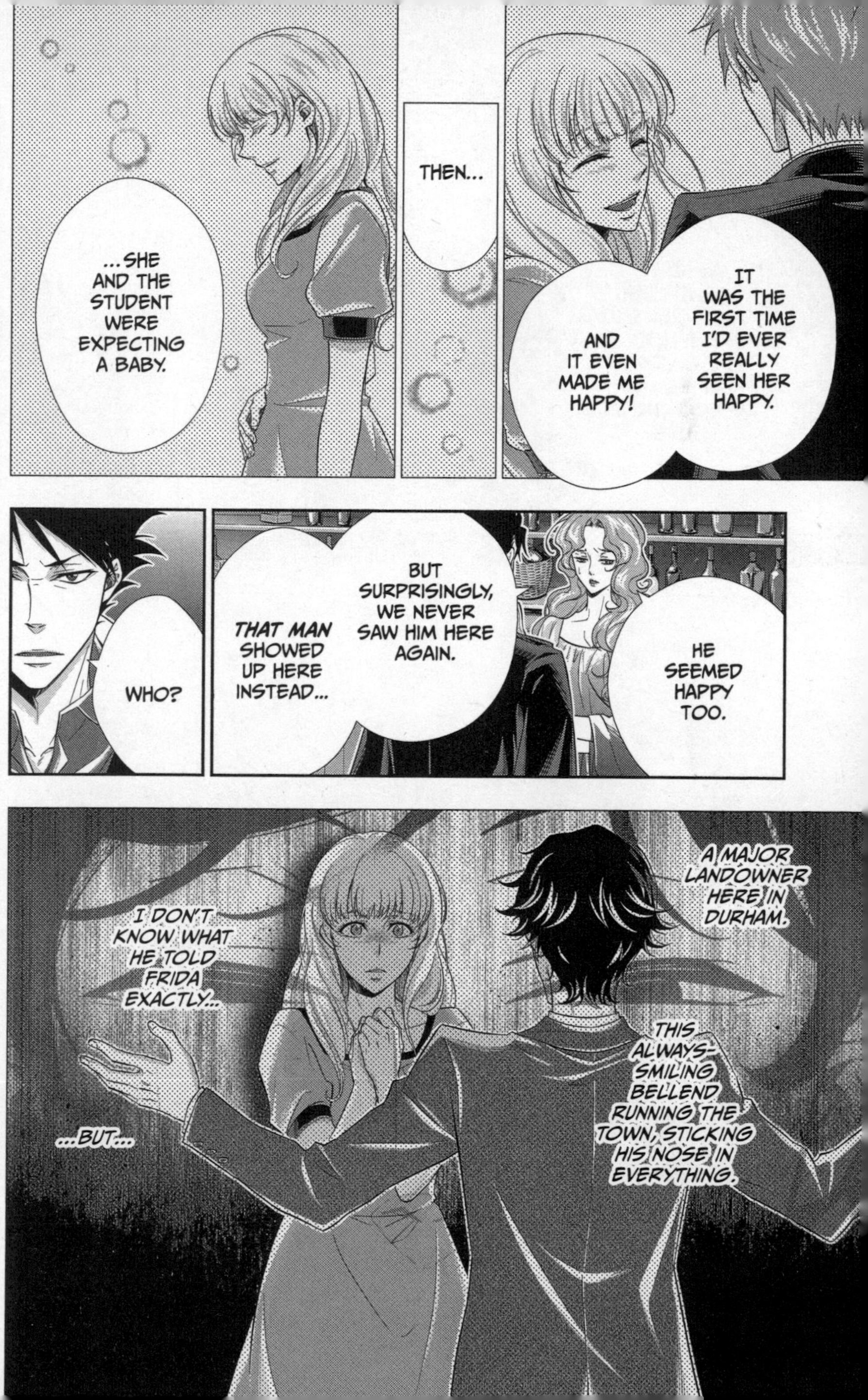
IT WAS THE FIRST TIME I'D EVER REALLY SEEN HER HAPPY.
AND IT EVEN MADE ME HAPPY!
THEN...
...SHE AND THE STUDENT WERE EXPECTING A BABY.
HE SEEMED HAPPY TOO.
BUT SURPRISINGLY, WE NEVER SAW HIM HERE AGAIN.
THAT MAN SHOWED UP HERE INSTEAD...
WHO?
A MAJOR LANDOWNER HERE IN DURHAM.
THIS ALWAYS-SMILING BELLEND RUNNING THE TOWN, STICKING HIS NOSE IN EVERYTHING.
I DON'T KNOW WHAT HE TOLD FRIDA EXACTLY...
...BUT...

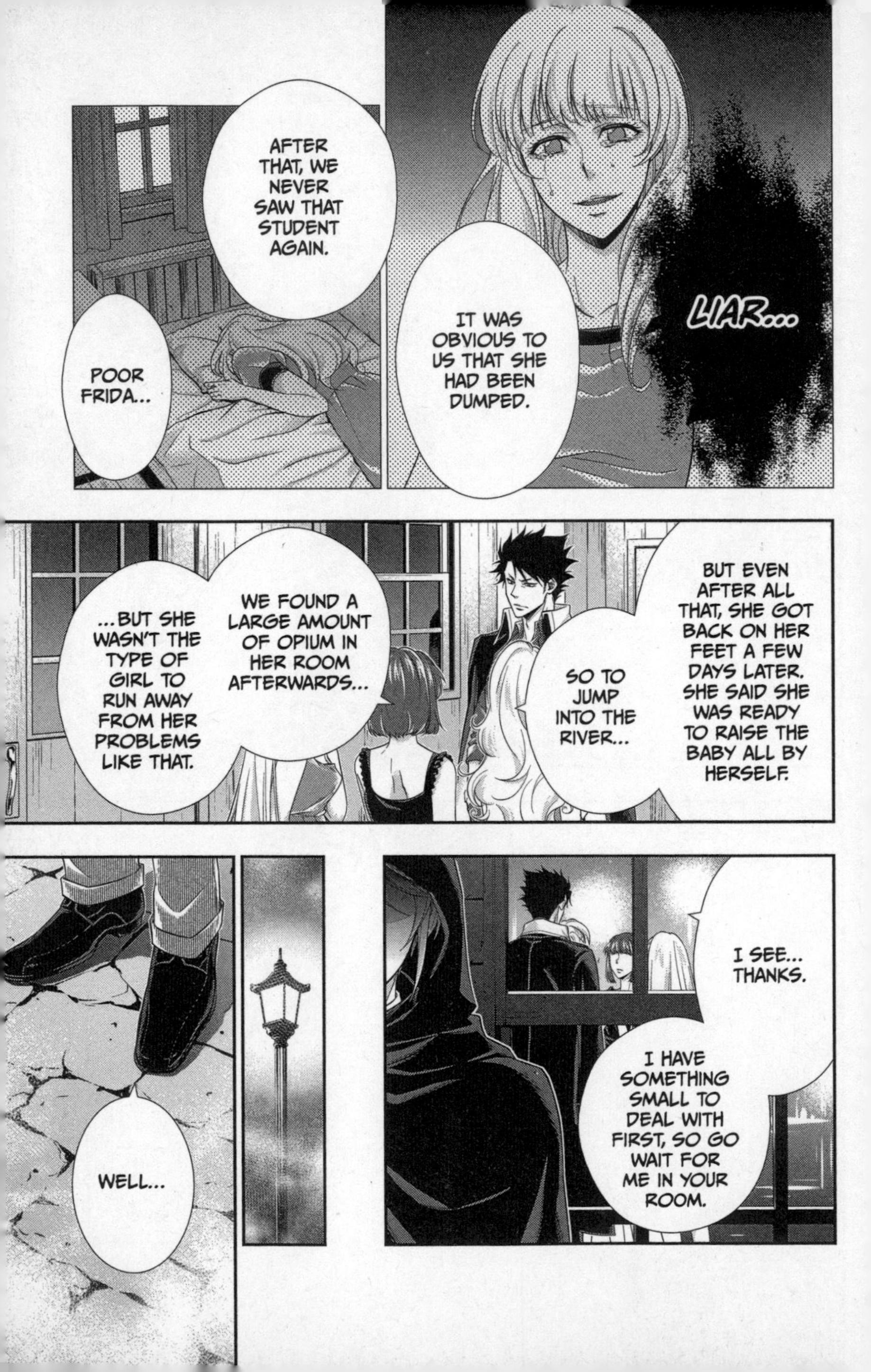
IT WAS OBVIOUS TO US THAT SHE HAD BEEN DUMPED.
LIAR...
AFTER THAT, WE NEVER SAW THAT STUDENT AGAIN.
POOR FRIDA...
BUT EVEN AFTER ALL THAT, SHE GOT BACK ON HER FEET A FEW DAYS LATER. SHE SAID SHE WAS READY TO RAISE THE BABY ALL BY HERSELF.
SO TO JUMP INTO THE RIVER...
WE FOUND A LARGE AMOUNT OF OPIUM IN HER ROOM AFTERWARDS...
...BUT SHE WASN'T THE TYPE OF GIRL TO RUN AWAY FROM HER PROBLEMS LIKE THAT.
I SEE... THANKS.
I HAVE SOMETHING SMALL TO DEAL WITH FIRST, SO GO WAIT FOR ME IN YOUR ROOM.
WELL...

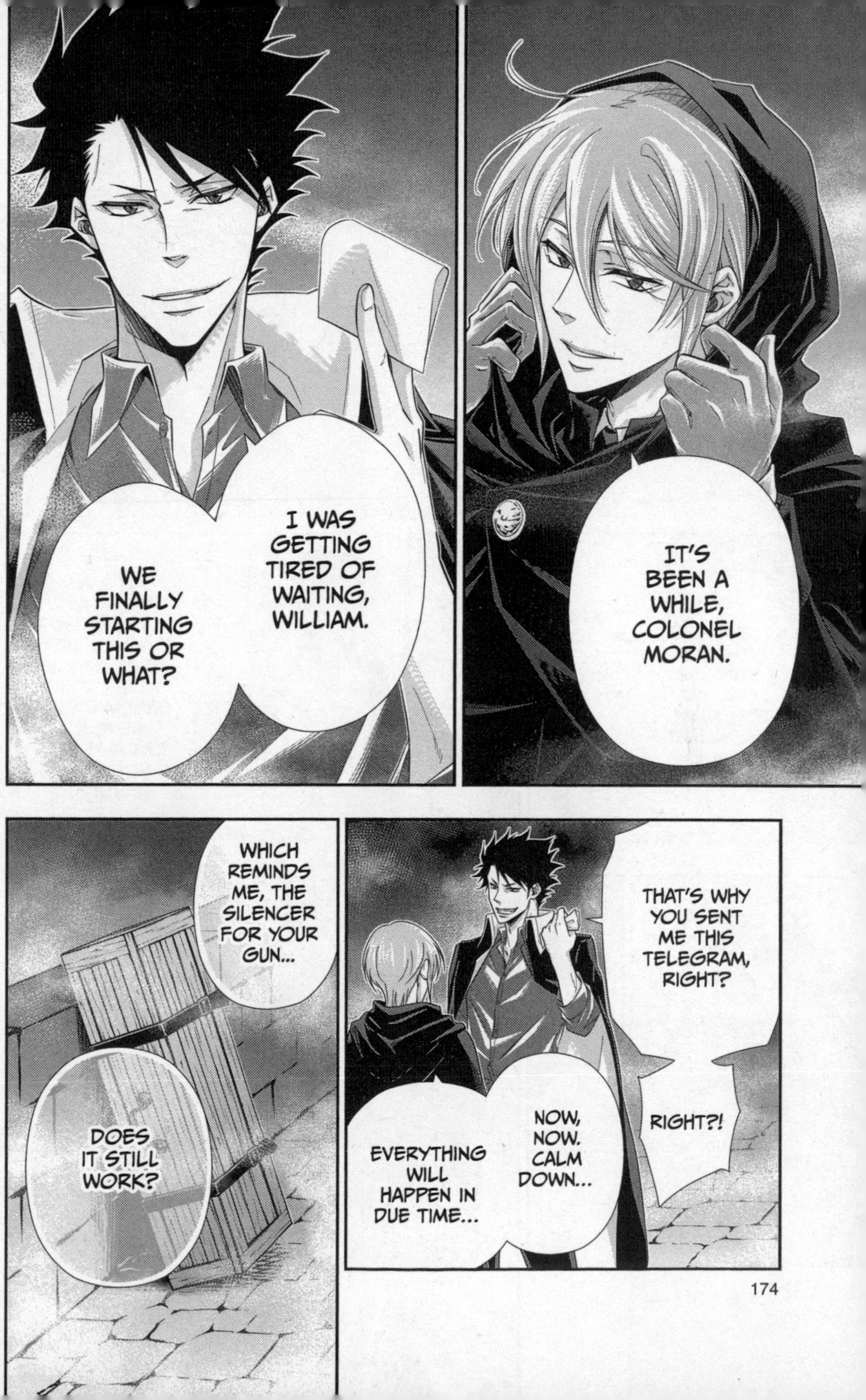
IT'S BEEN A WHILE, COLONEL MORAN.
I WAS GETTING TIRED OF WAITING, WILLIAM.
WE FINALLY STARTING THIS OR WHAT?
THAT'S WHY YOU SENT ME THIS TELEGRAM, RIGHT?
RIGHT?!
NOW, NOW. CALM DOWN...
EVERYTHING WILL HAPPEN IN DUE TIME...
WHICH REMINDS ME, THE SILENCER FOR YOUR GUN...
DOES IT STILL WORK?

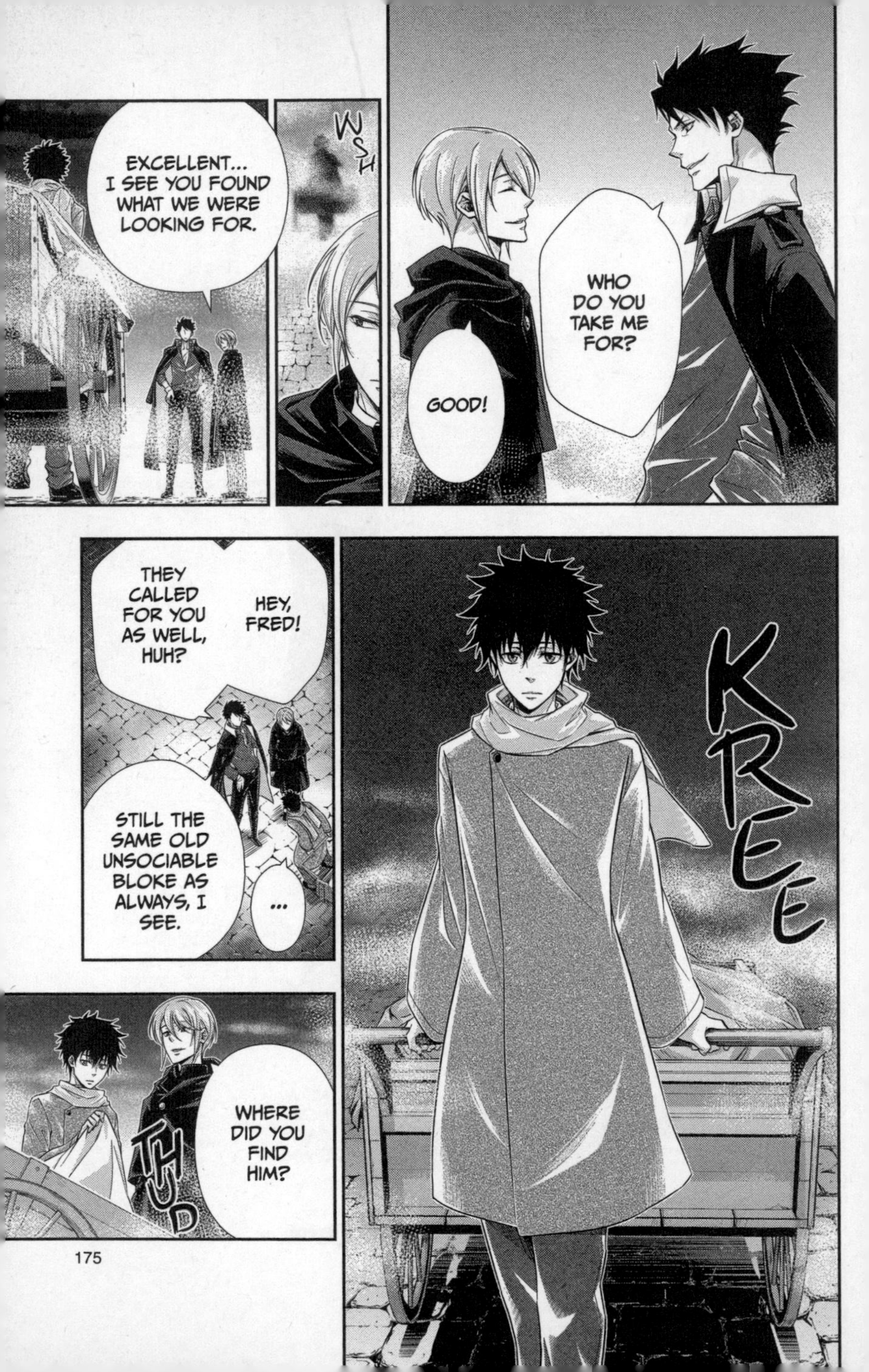
WHO DO YOU TAKE ME FOR?
GOOD!
WSH
EXCELLENT... I SEE YOU FOUND WHAT WE WERE LOOKING FOR.
KREE
HEY, FRED!
THEY CALLED FOR YOU AS WELL, HUH?
STILL THE SAME OLD UNSOCIABLE BLOKE AS ALWAYS, I SEE.
...
WHERE DID YOU FIND HIM?
THUD

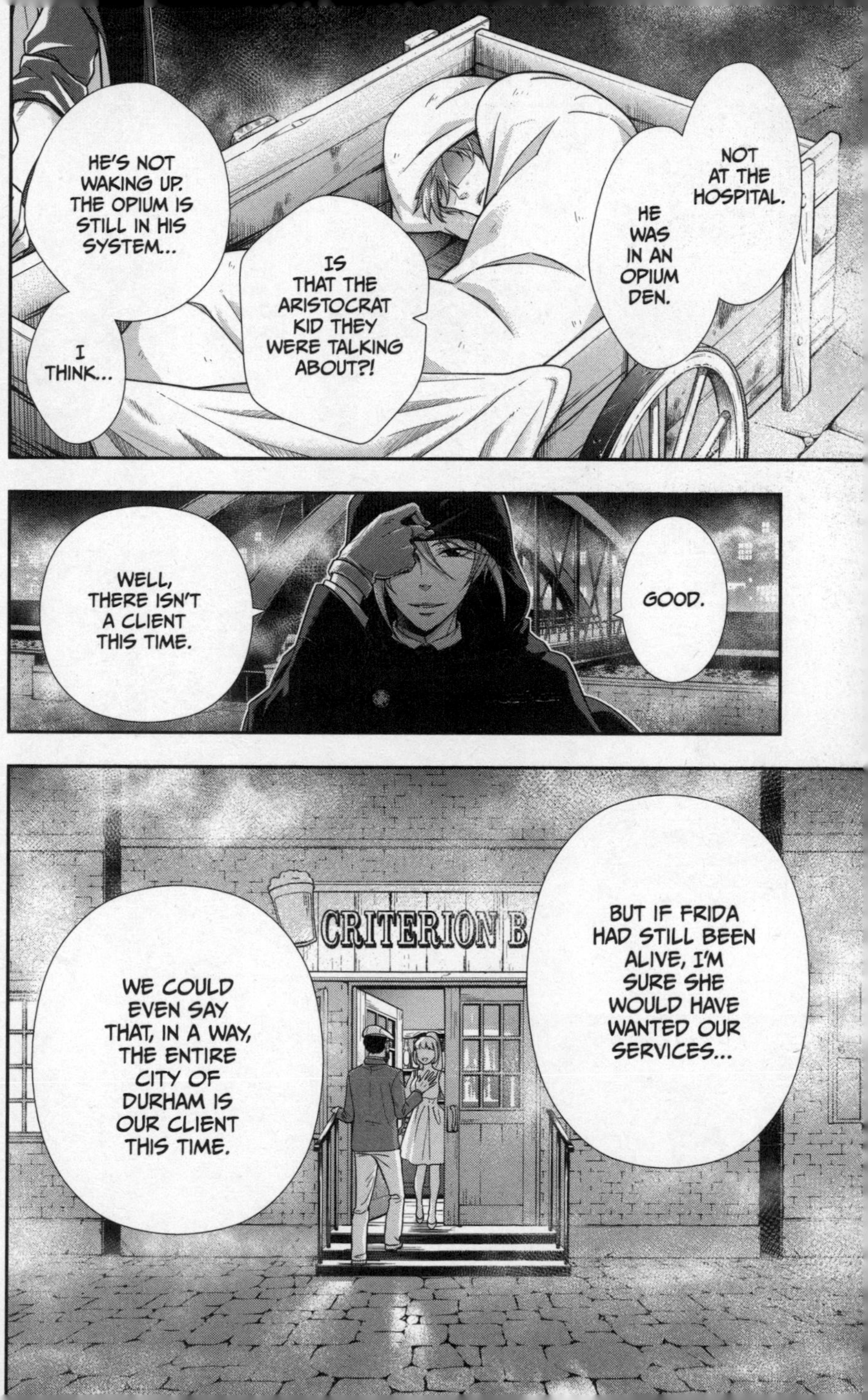
NOT AT THE HOSPITAL.
HE WAS IN AN OPIUM DEN.
IS THAT THE ARISTOCRAT KID THEY WERE TALKING ABOUT?!
HE'S NOT WAKING UP. THE OPIUM IS STILL IN HIS SYSTEM...
I THINK...
GOOD.
WELL, THERE ISN'T A CLIENT THIS TIME.
BUT IF FRIDA HAD STILL BEEN ALIVE, I'M SURE SHE WOULD HAVE WANTED OUR SERVICES...
CRITERION B
WE COULD EVEN SAY THAT, IN A WAY, THE ENTIRE CITY OF DURHAM IS OUR CLIENT THIS TIME.

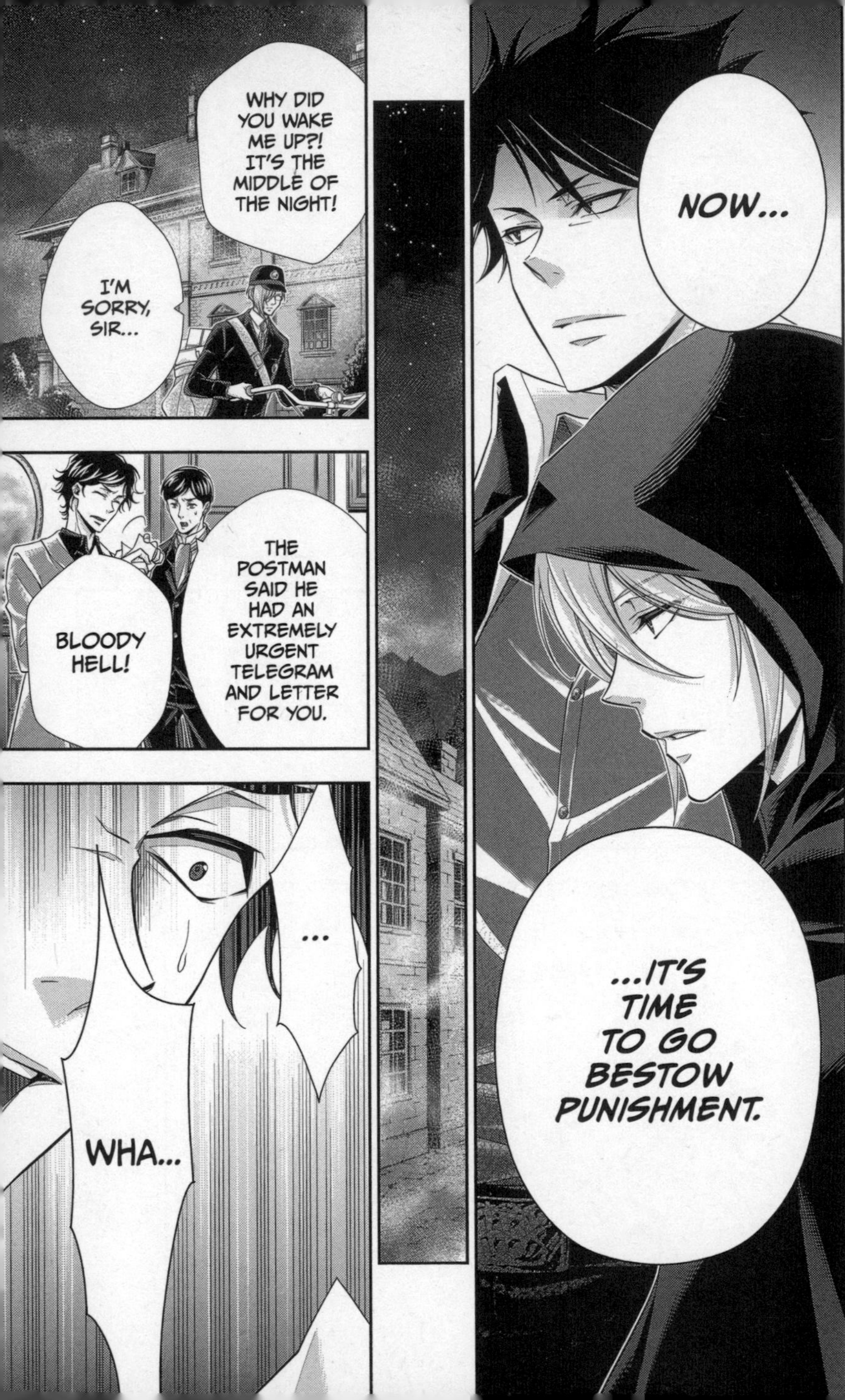
NOW...
...IT'S TIME TO GO BESTOW PUNISHMENT.
WHY DID YOU WAKE ME UP?! IT'S THE MIDDLE OF THE NIGHT!
I'M SORRY, SIR...
THE POSTMAN SAID HE HAD AN EXTREMELY URGENT TELEGRAM AND LETTER FOR YOU.
BLOODY HELL!
...
WHA...

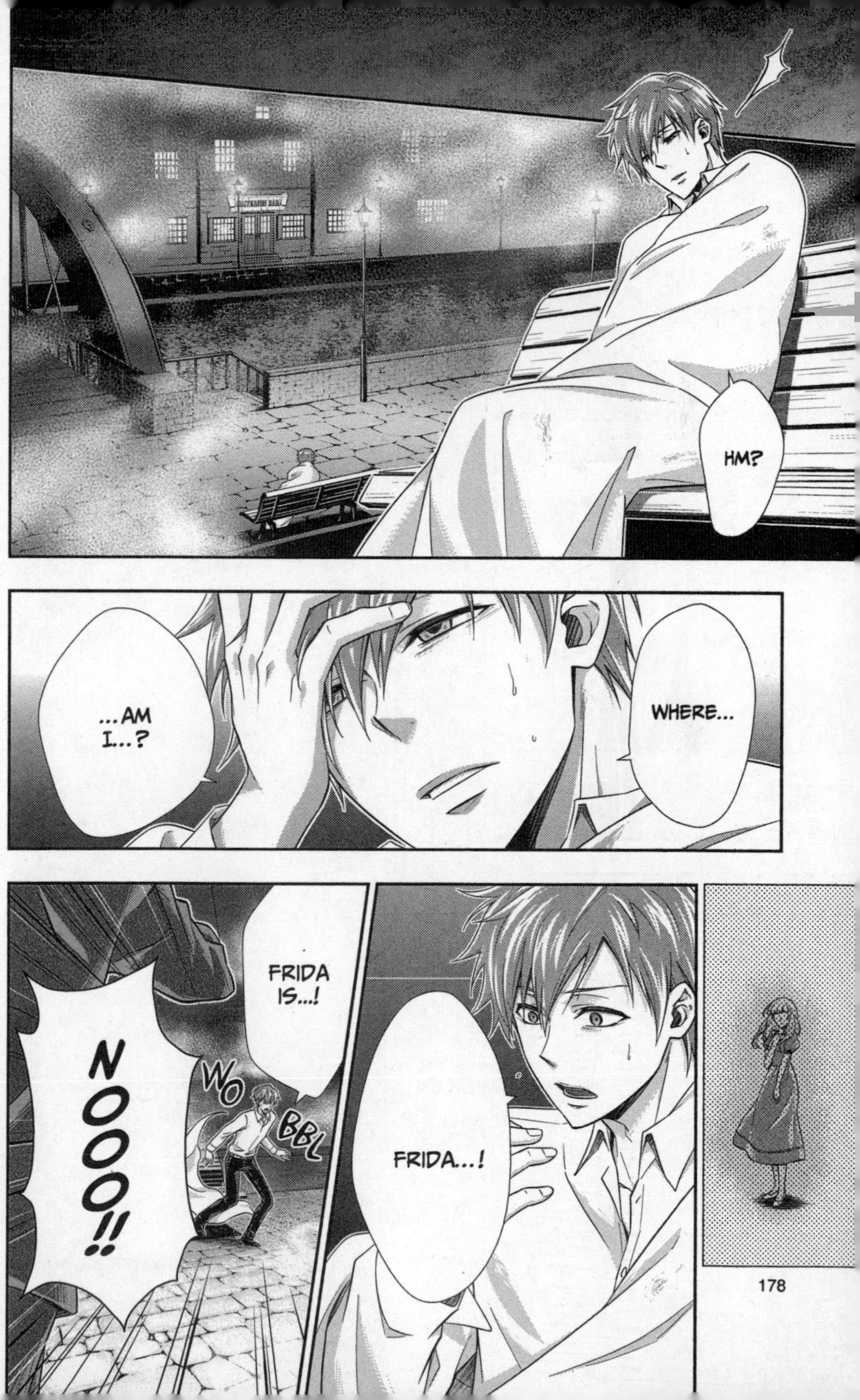
HM?
WHERE...
...AM I...?
FRIDA...!
FRIDA IS...!
WOBBL
NOOOO!!

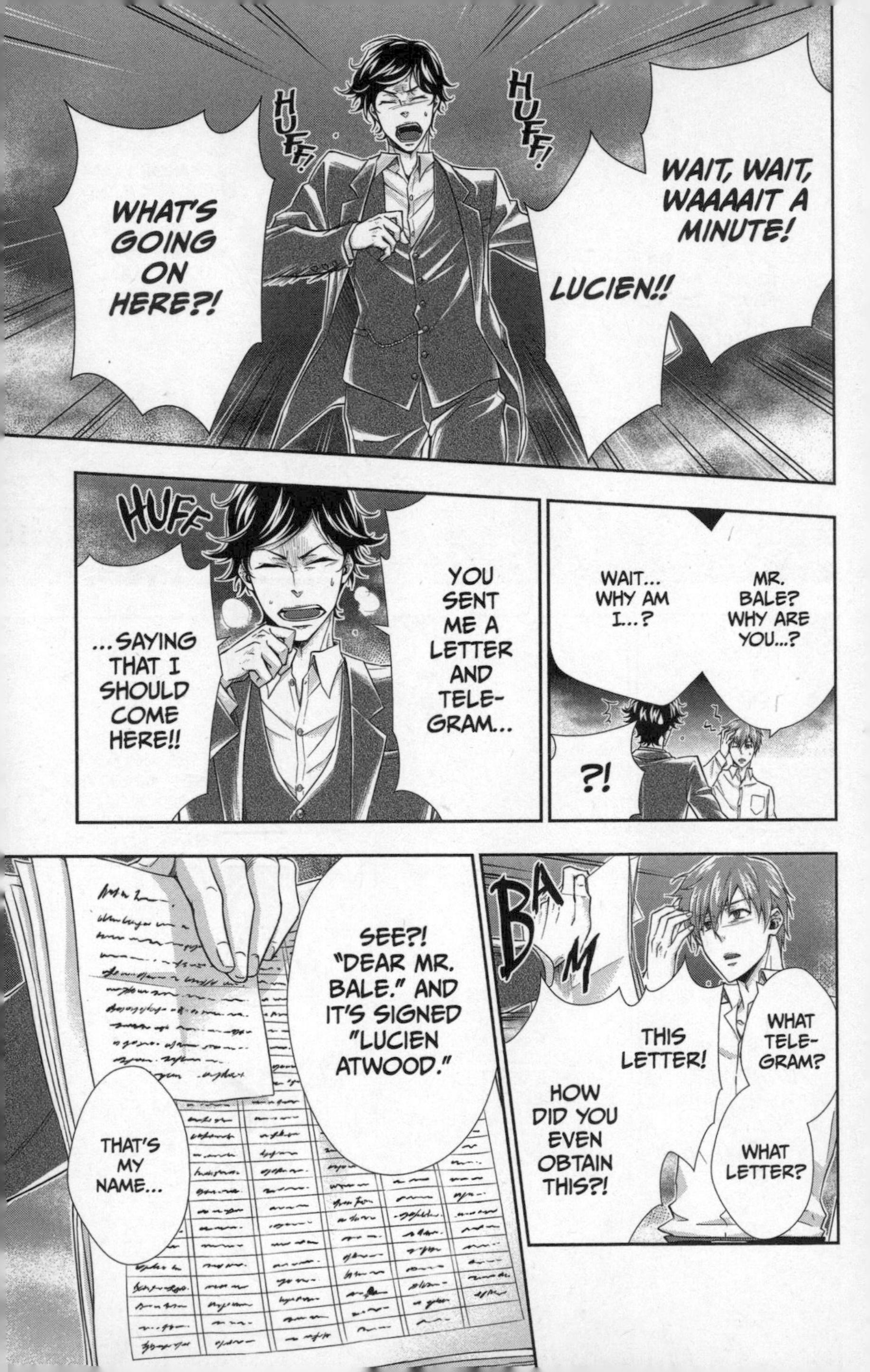
WAIT, WAIT, WAAAAIT A MINUTE!
HUFF!
HUFF!
LUCIEN!!
WHAT'S GOING ON HERE?!
MR. BALE? WHY ARE YOU...?
WAIT... WHY AM I...?
?!
HUFF
YOU SENT ME A LETTER AND TELE-GRAM...
...SAYING THAT I SHOULD COME HERE!!
WHAT TELE-GRAM?
THIS LETTER!
WHAT LETTER?
HOW DID YOU EVEN OBTAIN THIS?!
BAM
SEE?! "DEAR MR. BALE." AND IT'S SIGNED "LUCIEN ATWOOD."
THAT'S MY NAME...

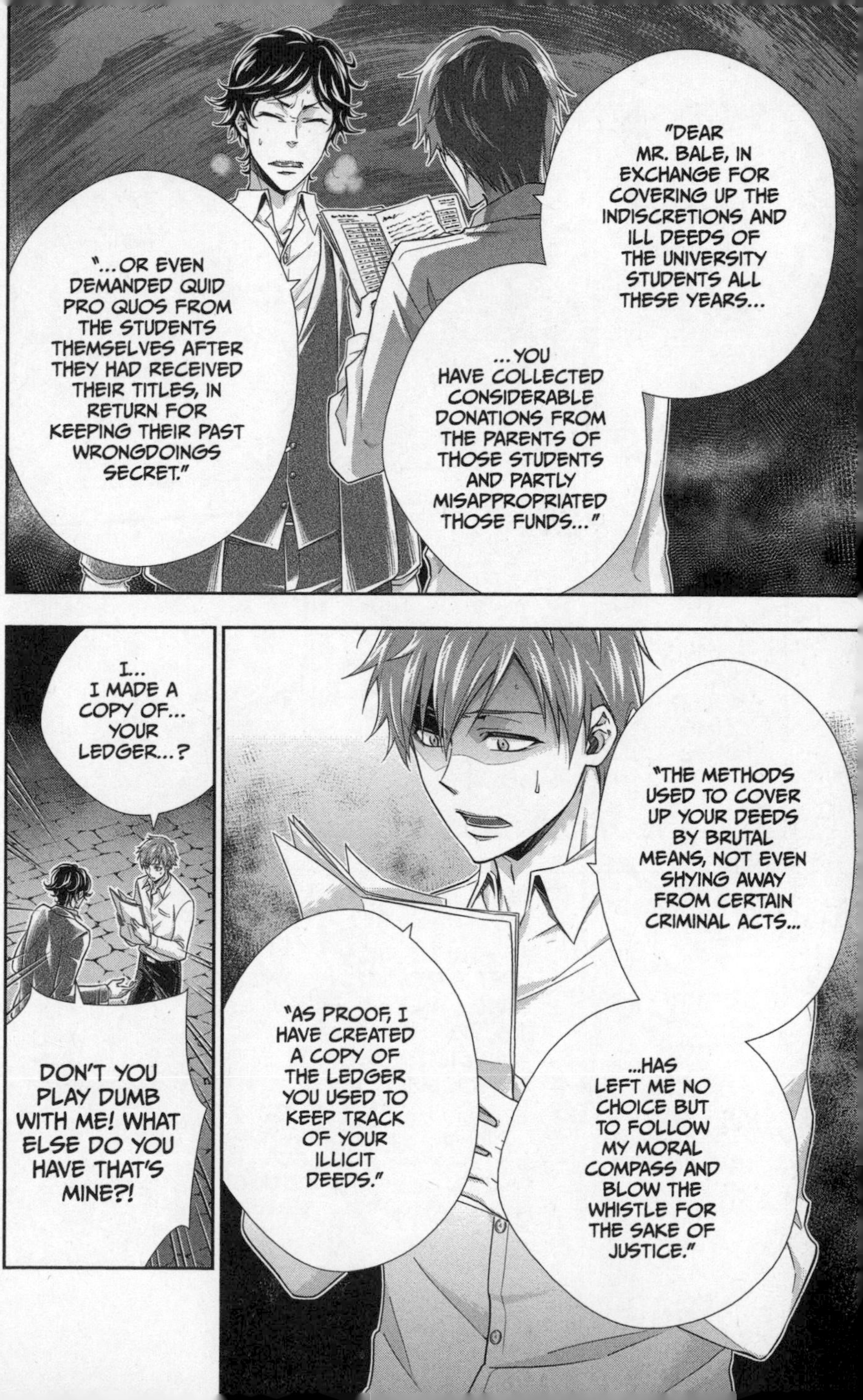
"DEAR MR. BALE, IN EXCHANGE FOR COVERING UP THE INDISCRETIONS AND ILL DEEDS OF THE UNIVERSITY STUDENTS ALL THESE YEARS...
...YOU HAVE COLLECTED CONSIDERABLE DONATIONS FROM THE PARENTS OF THOSE STUDENTS AND PARTLY MISAPPROPRIATED THOSE FUNDS..."
"...OR EVEN DEMANDED QUID PRO QUOS FROM THE STUDENTS THEMSELVES AFTER THEY HAD RECEIVED THEIR TITLES, IN RETURN FOR KEEPING THEIR PAST WRONGDOINGS SECRET."
"THE METHODS USED TO COVER UP YOUR DEEDS BY BRUTAL MEANS, NOT EVEN SHYING AWAY FROM CERTAIN CRIMINAL ACTS...
...HAS LEFT ME NO CHOICE BUT TO FOLLOW MY MORAL COMPASS AND BLOW THE WHISTLE FOR THE SAKE OF JUSTICE."
"AS PROOF, I HAVE CREATED A COPY OF THE LEDGER YOU USED TO KEEP TRACK OF YOUR ILLICIT DEEDS."
I... I MADE A COPY OF... YOUR LEDGER...?
DON'T YOU PLAY DUMB WITH ME! WHAT ELSE DO YOU HAVE THAT'S MINE?!

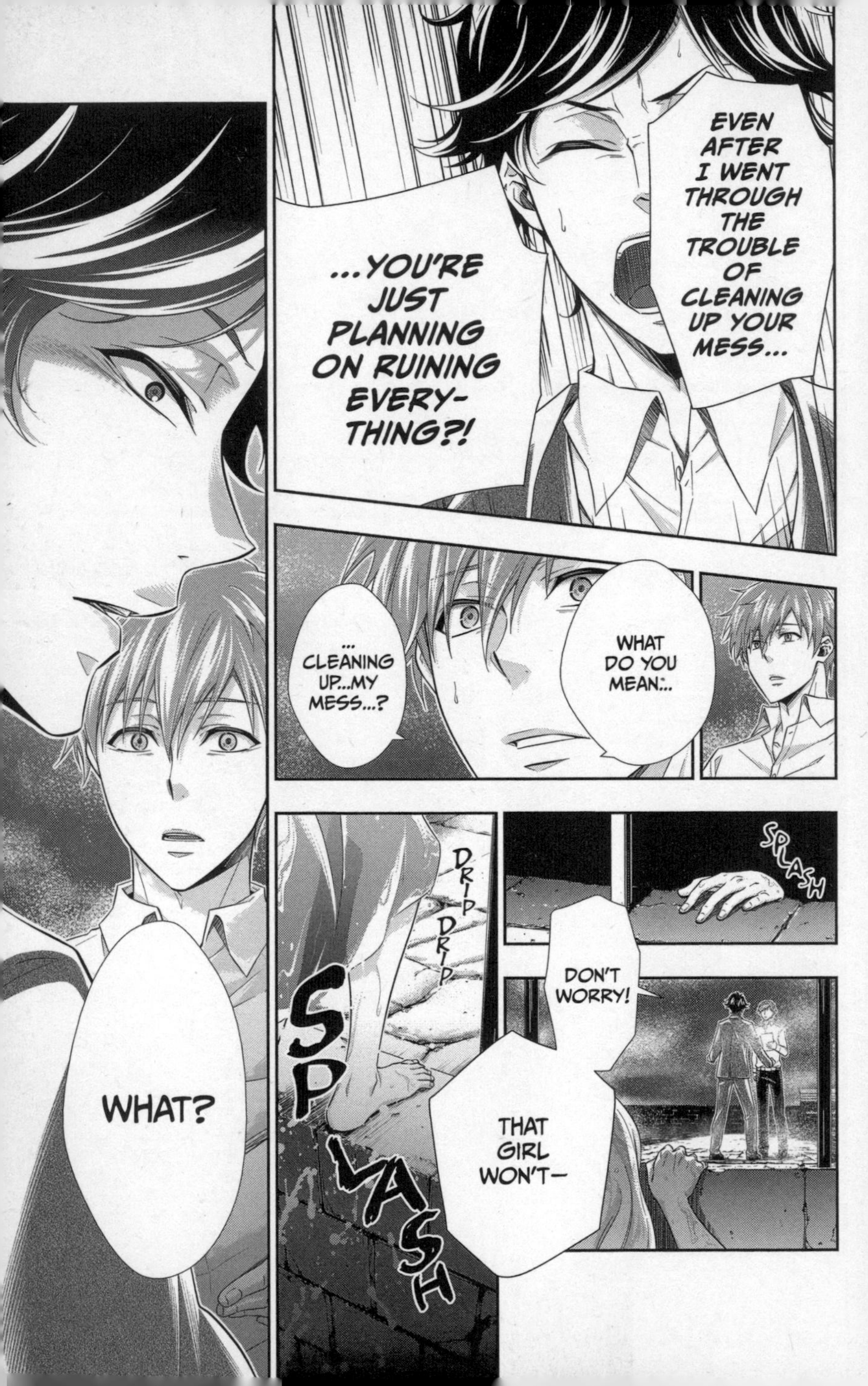
EVEN AFTER I WENT THROUGH THE TROUBLE OF CLEANING UP YOUR MESS...
...YOU'RE JUST PLANNING ON RUINING EVERY-THING?!
WHAT DO YOU MEAN...
...CLEANING UP...MY MESS...?
SPLASH
DON'T WORRY!
THAT GIRL WON'T—
DRIP DRIP DRIP
SPLASH
WHAT?

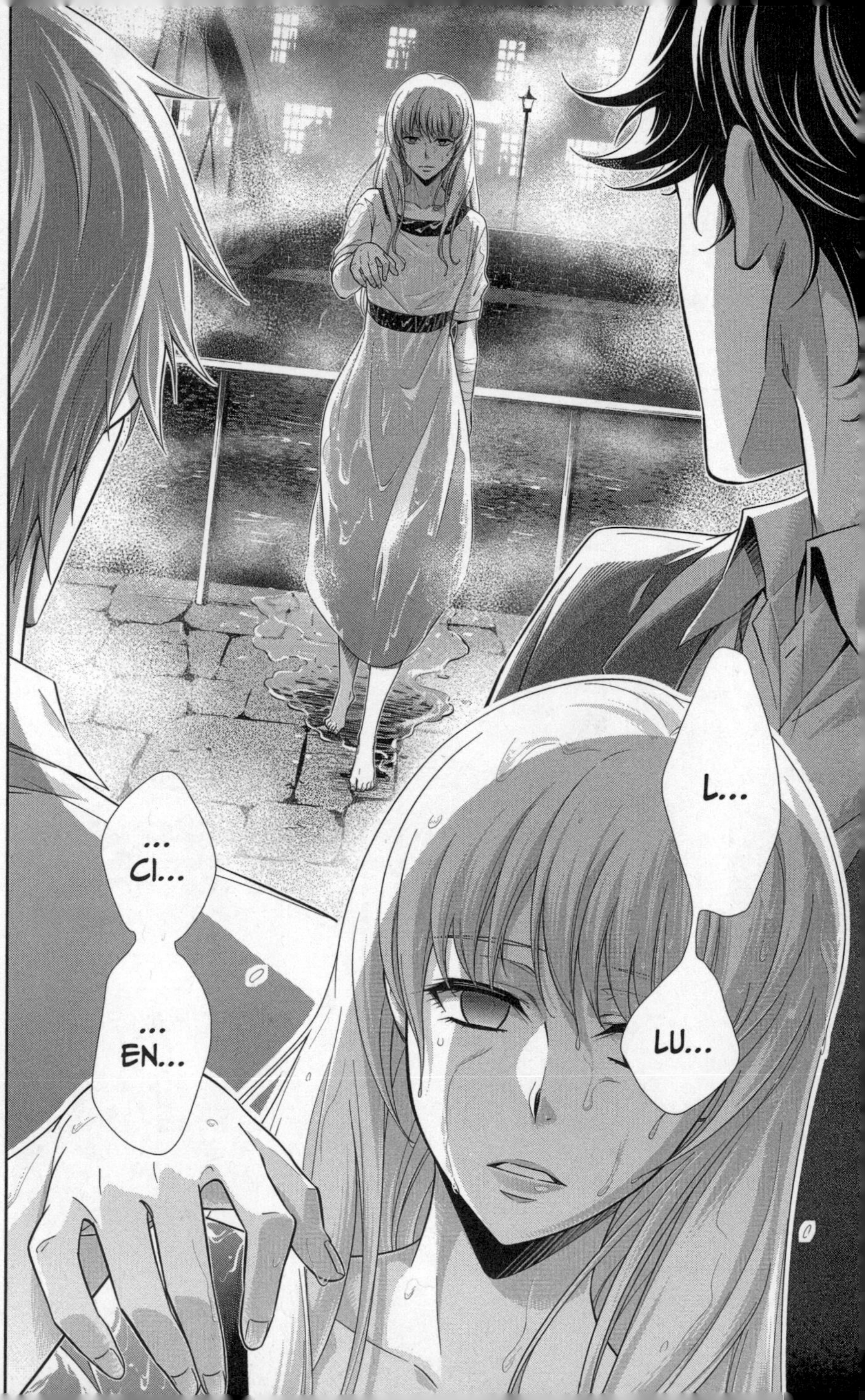
L...
LU...
... CI...
... EN...

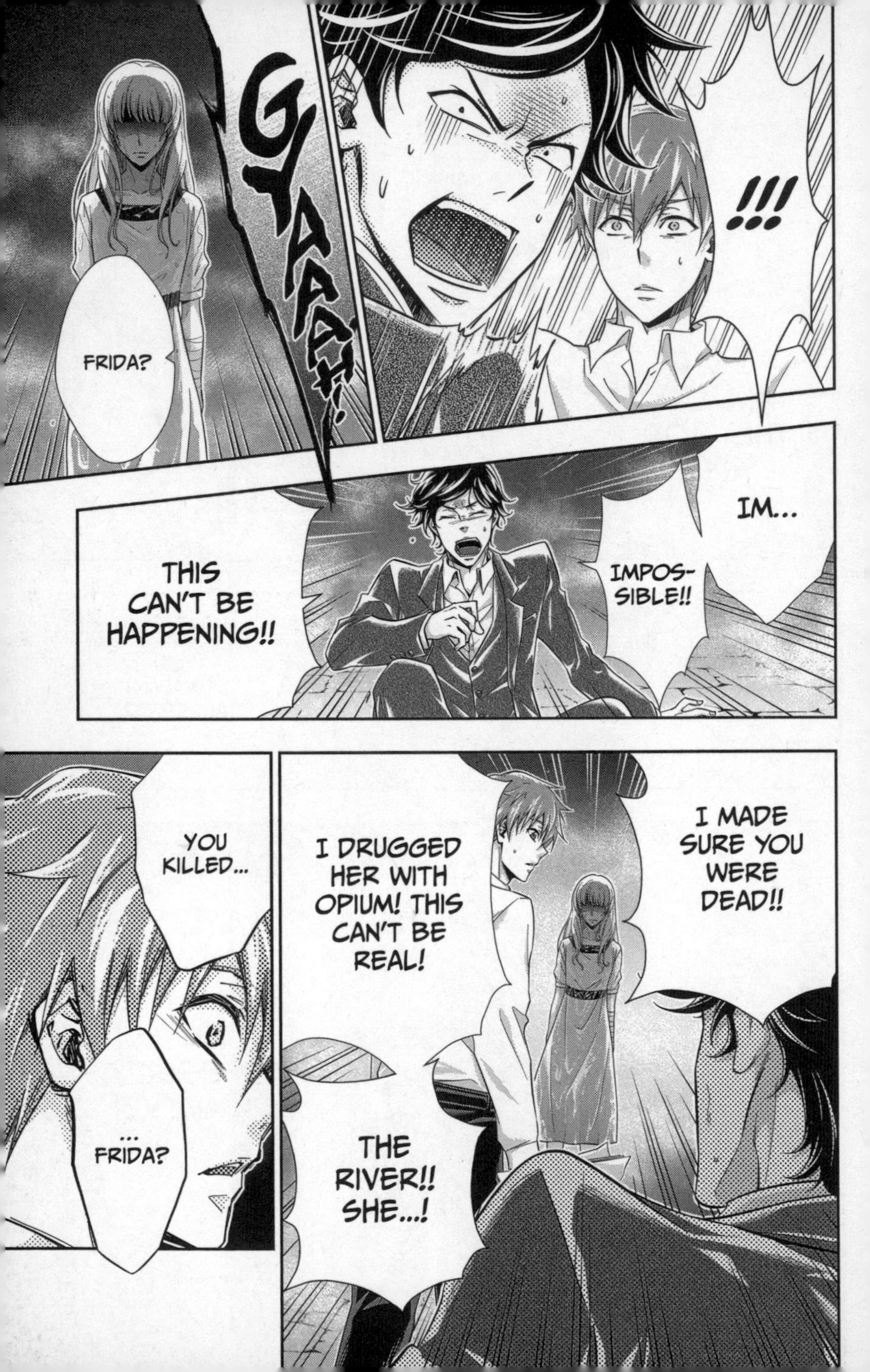
!!!
GYAAAH!
FRIDA?
IM...
IMPOS-
SIBLE!!
THIS CAN'T BE HAPPENING!!
I MADE SURE YOU WERE DEAD!!
I DRUGGED HER WITH OPIUM! THIS CAN'T BE REAL!
THE RIVER!! SHE...!
YOU KILLED...
...FRIDA?

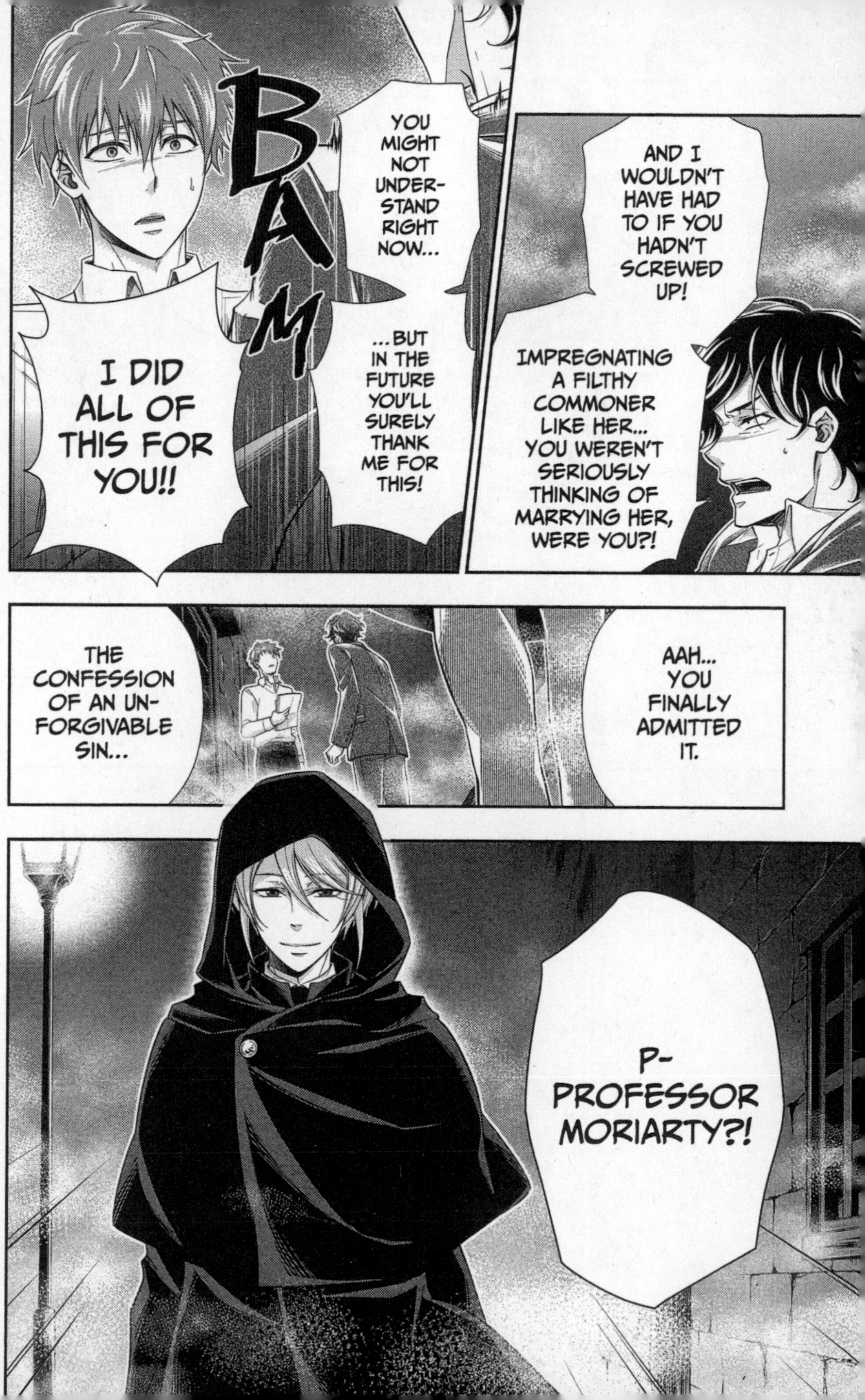
AND I WOULDN'T HAVE HAD TO IF YOU HADN'T SCREWED UP!
IMPREGNATING A FILTHY COMMONER LIKE HER... YOU WEREN'T SERIOUSLY THINKING OF MARRYING HER, WERE YOU?!
YOU MIGHT NOT UNDER-STAND RIGHT NOW...
BAM
...BUT IN THE FUTURE YOU'LL SURELY THANK ME FOR THIS!
I DID ALL OF THIS FOR YOU!!
AAH... YOU FINALLY ADMITTED IT.
THE CONFESSION OF AN UN-FORGIVABLE SIN...
P-PROFESSOR MORIARTY?!

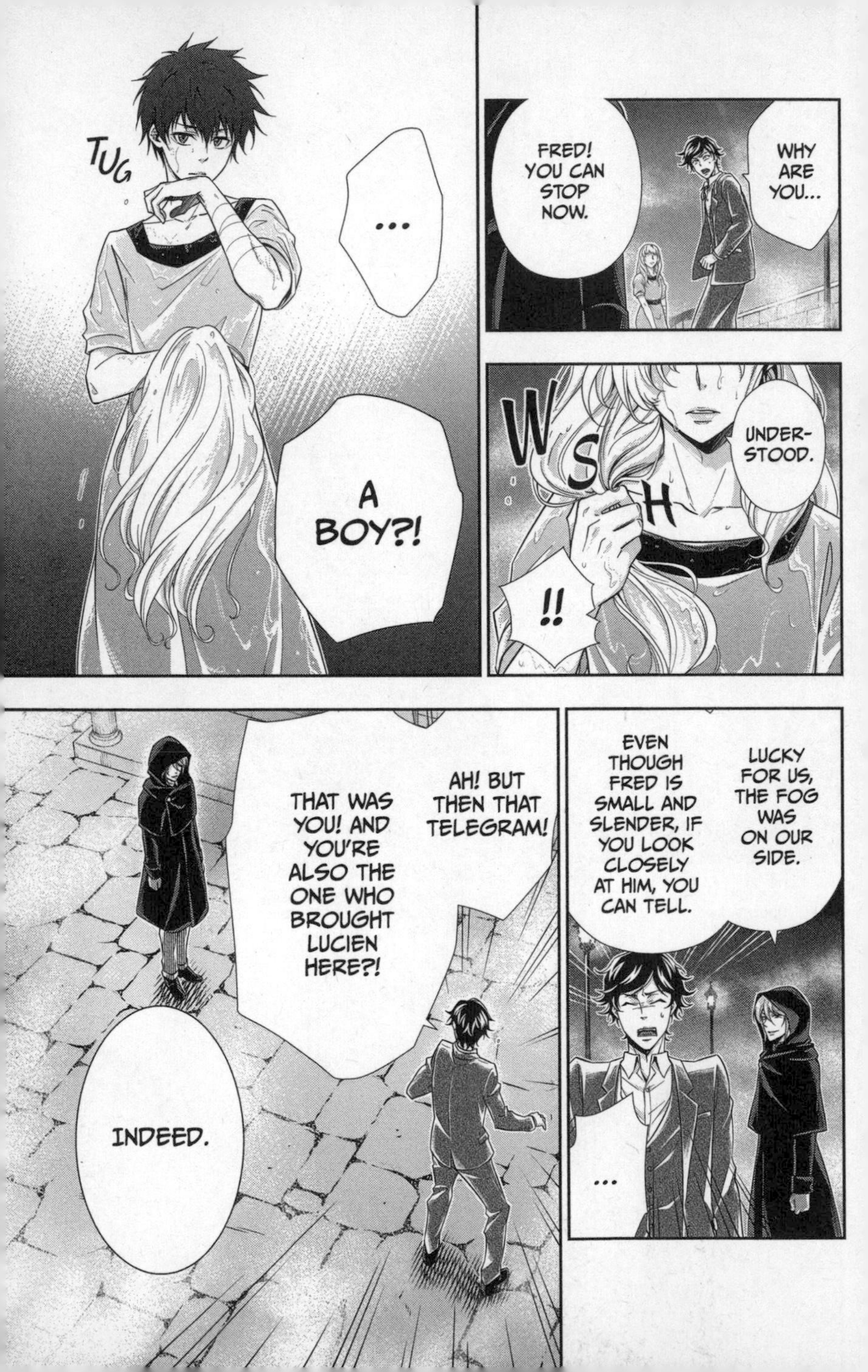
WHY ARE YOU...
FRED! YOU CAN STOP NOW.
WSH
UNDER-STOOD.
!!
...
TUG
A BOY?!
LUCKY FOR US, THE FOG WAS ON OUR SIDE.
EVEN THOUGH FRED IS SMALL AND SLENDER, IF YOU LOOK CLOSELY AT HIM, YOU CAN TELL.
...
AH! BUT THEN THAT TELEGRAM!
THAT WAS YOU! AND YOU'RE ALSO THE ONE WHO BROUGHT LUCIEN HERE?!
INDEED.

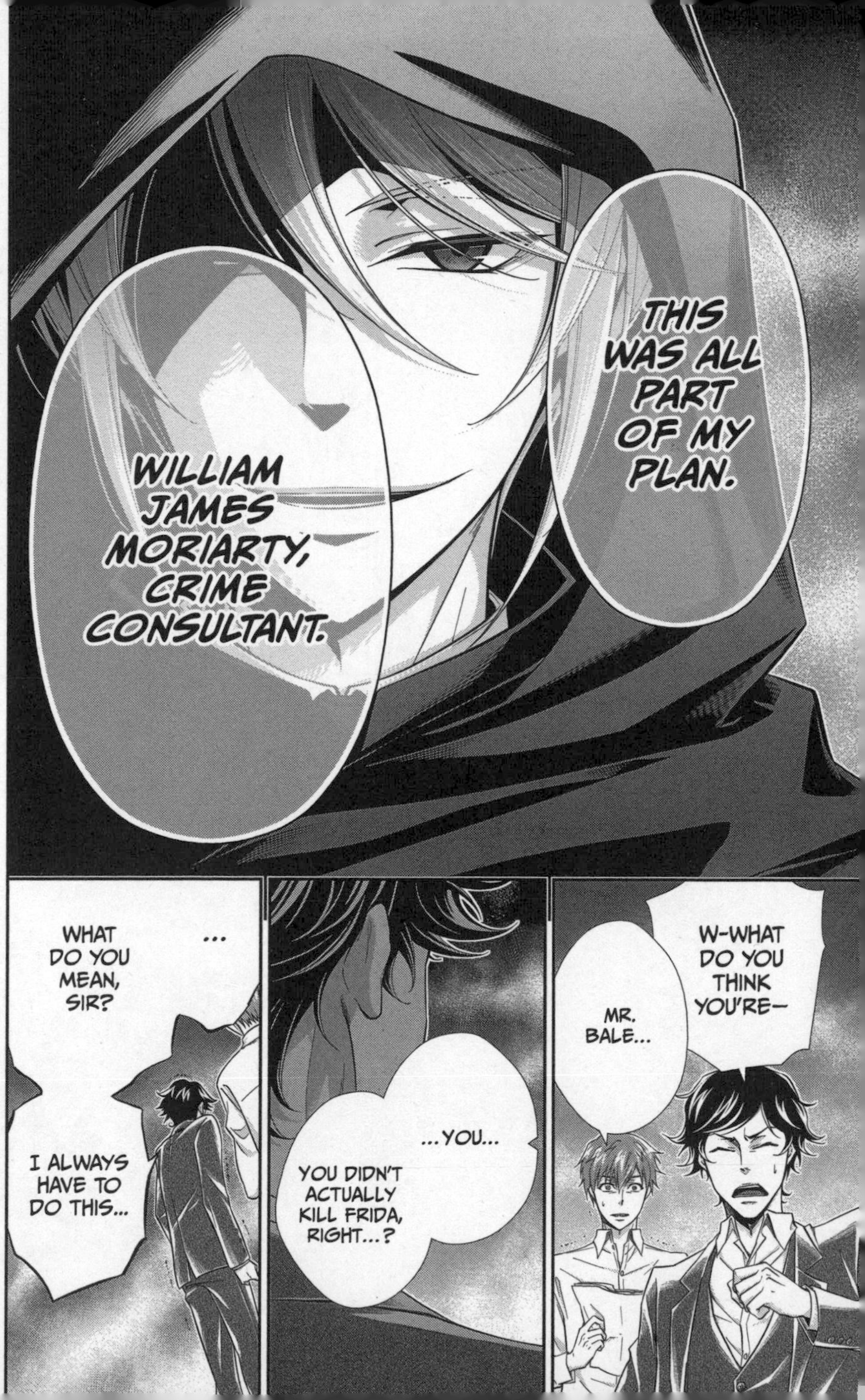
THIS WAS ALL PART OF MY PLAN.
WILLIAM JAMES MORIARTY, CRIME CONSULTANT.
W-WHAT DO YOU THINK YOU'RE—
MR. BALE...
...YOU...
YOU DIDN'T ACTUALLY KILL FRIDA, RIGHT...?
...
WHAT DO YOU MEAN, SIR?
I ALWAYS HAVE TO DO THIS...

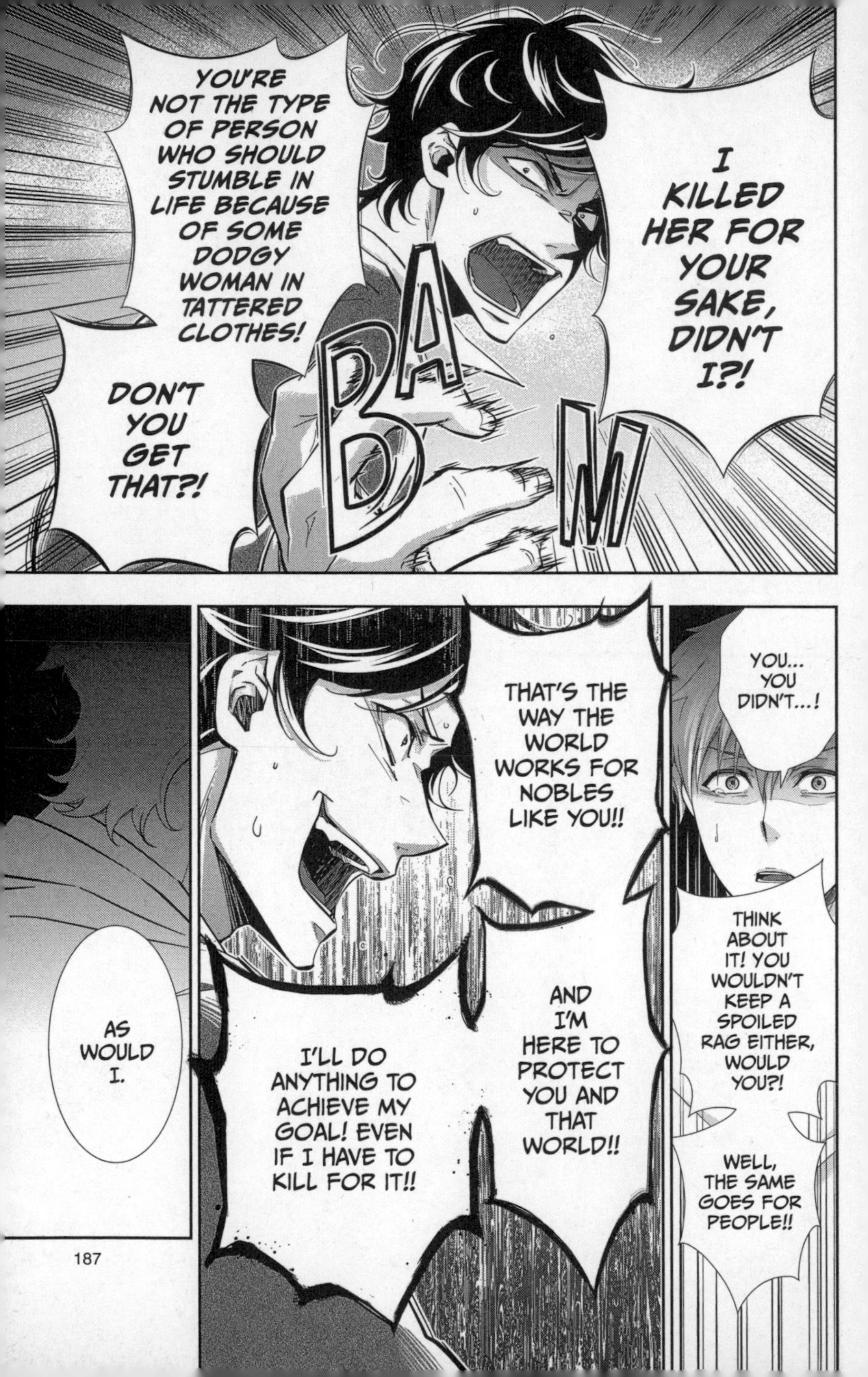
I KILLED HER FOR YOUR SAKE, DIDN'T I?!
YOU'RE NOT THE TYPE OF PERSON WHO SHOULD STUMBLE IN LIFE BECAUSE OF SOME DODGY WOMAN IN TATTERED CLOTHES!
DON'T YOU GET THAT?!
BADAM
YOU... YOU DIDN'T...!
THINK ABOUT IT! YOU WOULDN'T KEEP A SPOILED RAG EITHER, WOULD YOU?!
WELL, THE SAME GOES FOR PEOPLE!!
THAT'S THE WAY THE WORLD WORKS FOR NOBLES LIKE YOU!!
AND I'M HERE TO PROTECT YOU AND THAT WORLD!!
I'LL DO ANYTHING TO ACHIEVE MY GOAL! EVEN IF I HAVE TO KILL FOR IT!!
AS WOULD I.

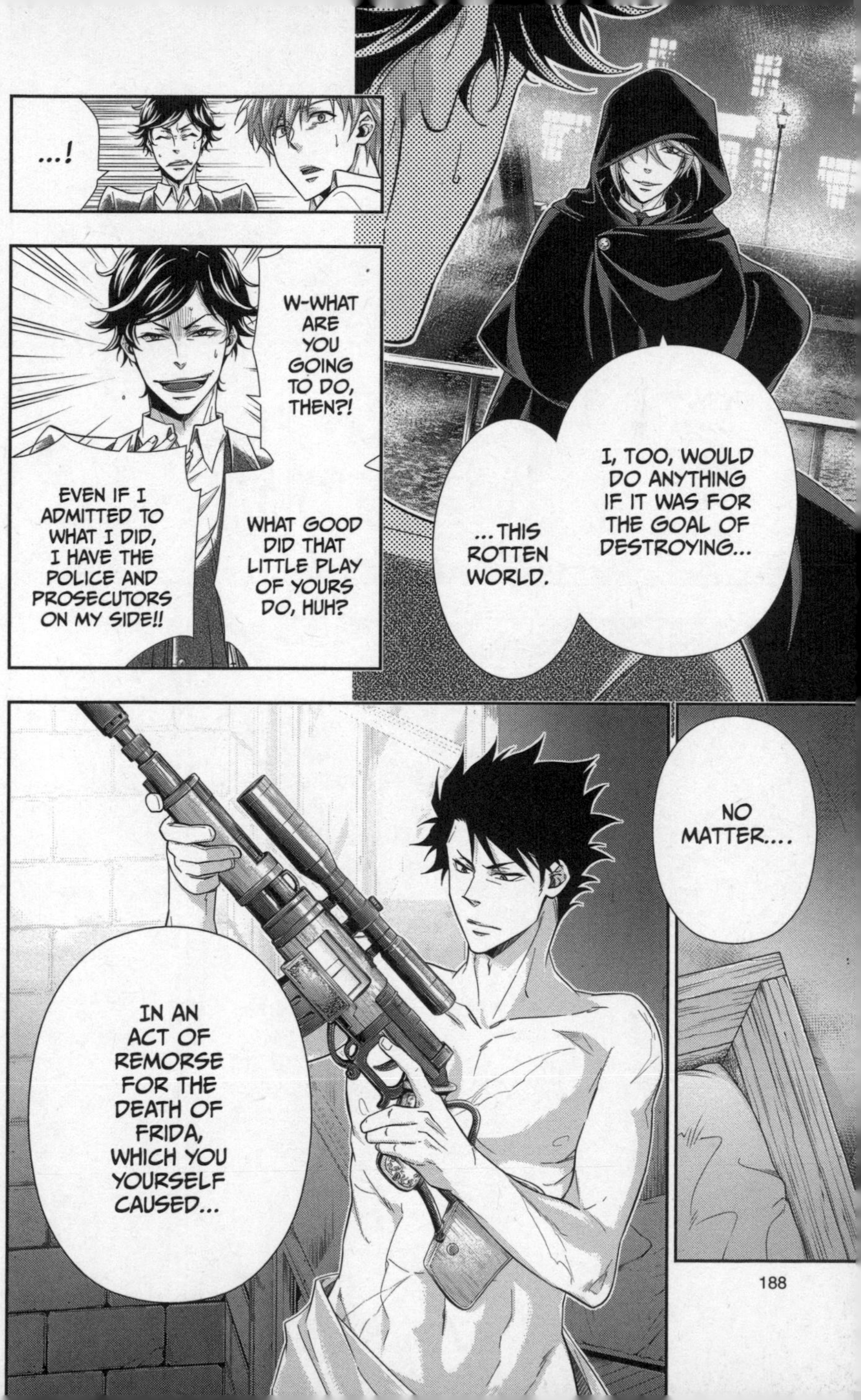
I, TOO, WOULD DO ANYTHING IF IT WAS FOR THE GOAL OF DESTROYING...
...THIS ROTTEN WORLD.
...!
W-WHAT ARE YOU GOING TO DO, THEN?!
WHAT GOOD DID THAT LITTLE PLAY OF YOURS DO, HUH?
EVEN IF I ADMITTED TO WHAT I DID, I HAVE THE POLICE AND PROSECUTORS ON MY SIDE!!
NO MATTER....
IN AN ACT OF REMORSE FOR THE DEATH OF FRIDA, WHICH YOU YOURSELF CAUSED...

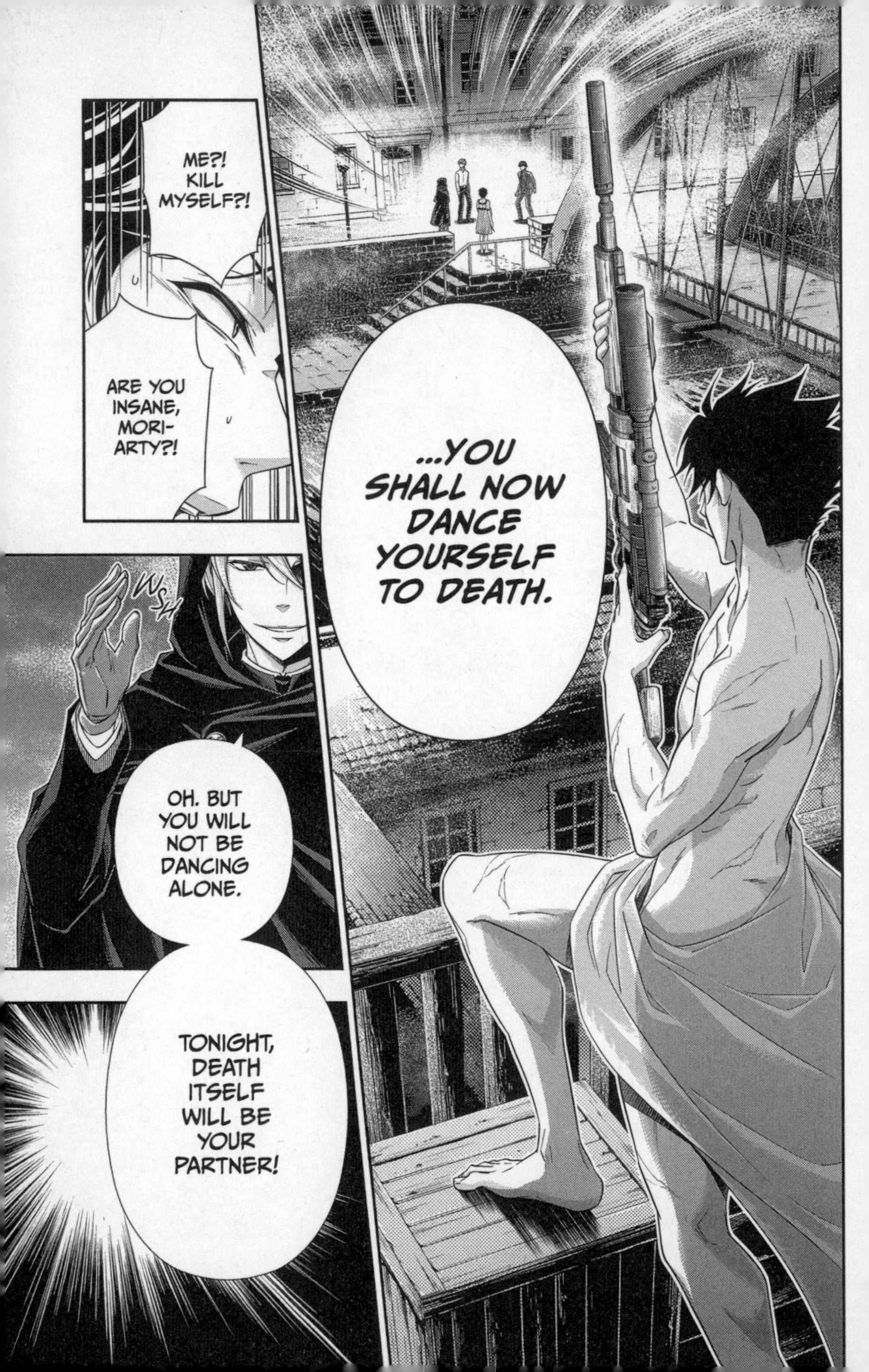
...YOU SHALL NOW DANCE YOURSELF TO DEATH.
ME?! KILL MYSELF?!
ARE YOU INSANE, MORI-ARTY?!
WSH
OH. BUT YOU WILL NOT BE DANCING ALONE.
TONIGHT, DEATH ITSELF WILL BE YOUR PARTNER!

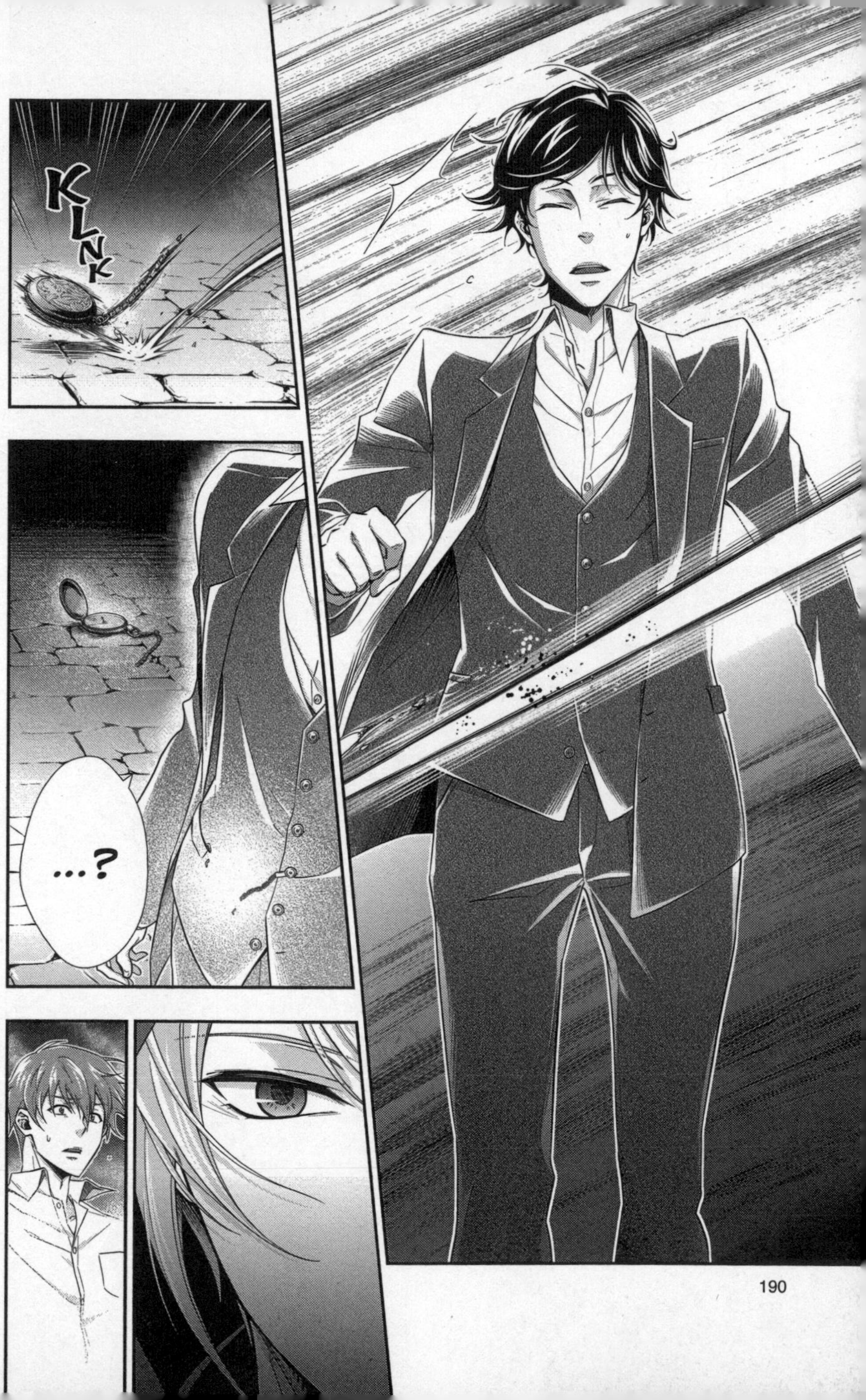
KLNK
...?

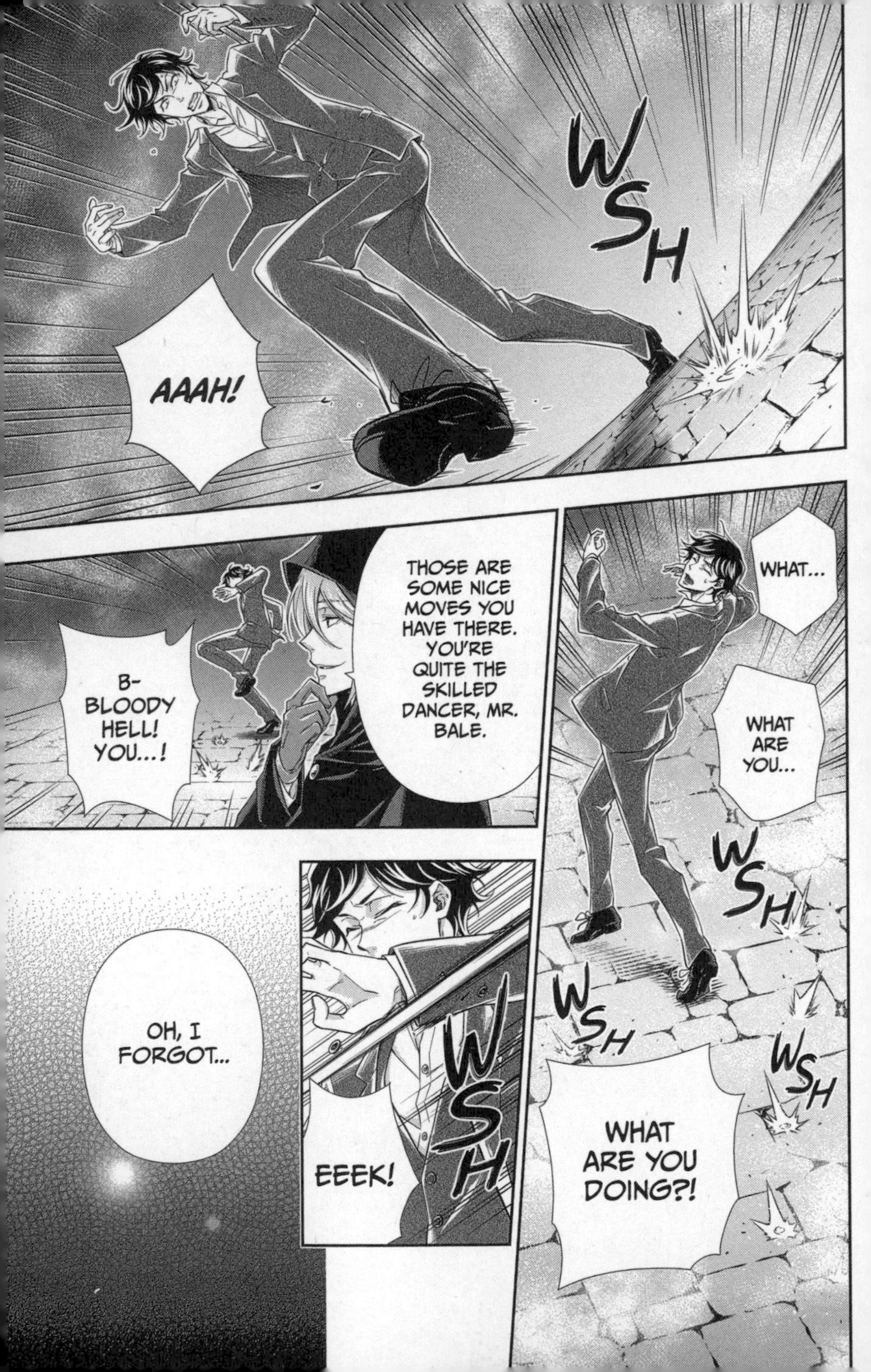
WSH
AAAH!
WHAT...
WHAT ARE YOU...
WSH
WSH
WSH
WHAT ARE YOU DOING?!
THOSE ARE SOME NICE MOVES YOU HAVE THERE. YOU'RE QUITE THE SKILLED DANCER, MR. BALE.
B-BLOODY HELL! YOU...!
WSH
EEEK!
OH, I FORGOT...

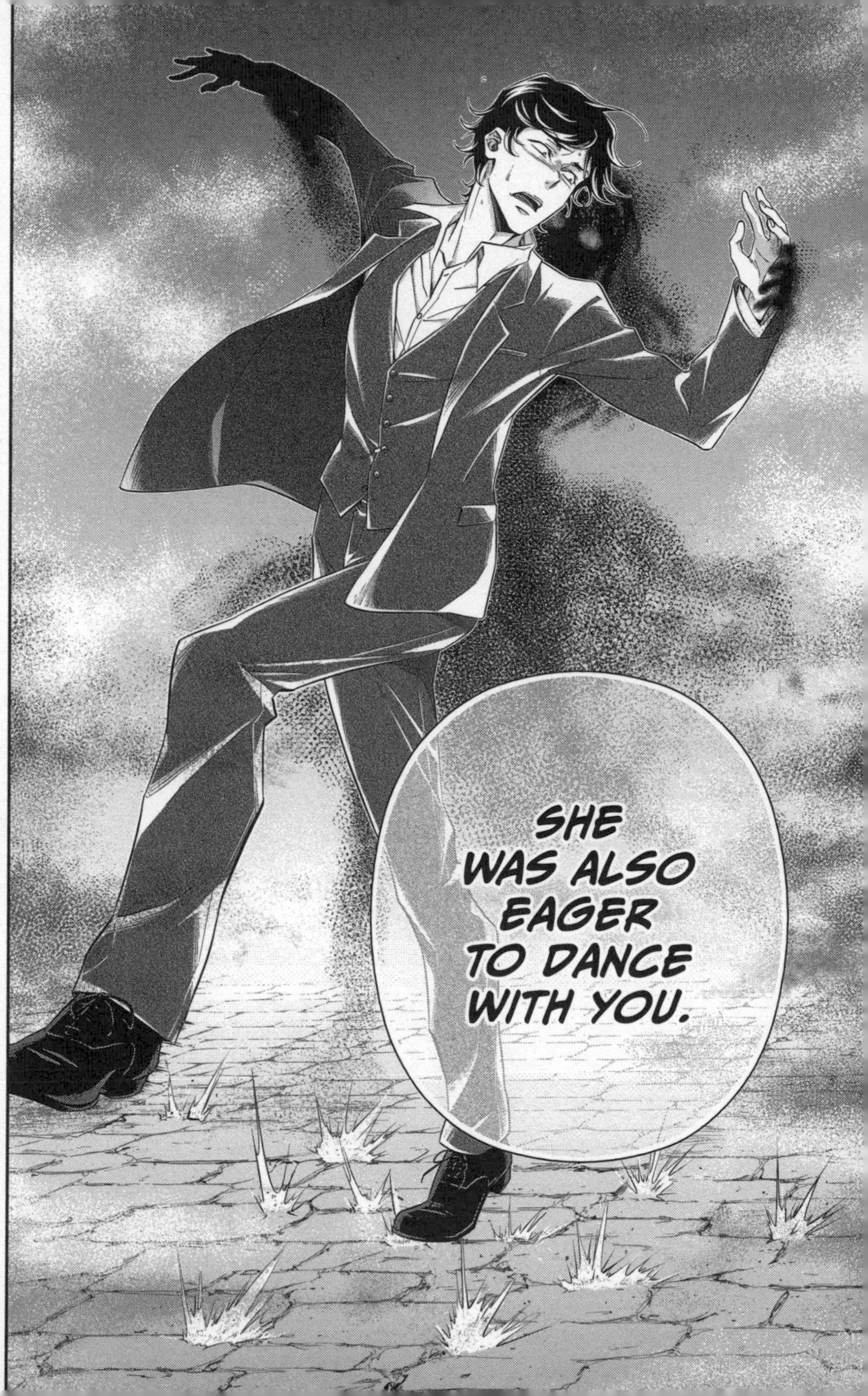
SHE WAS ALSO EAGER TO DANCE WITH YOU.

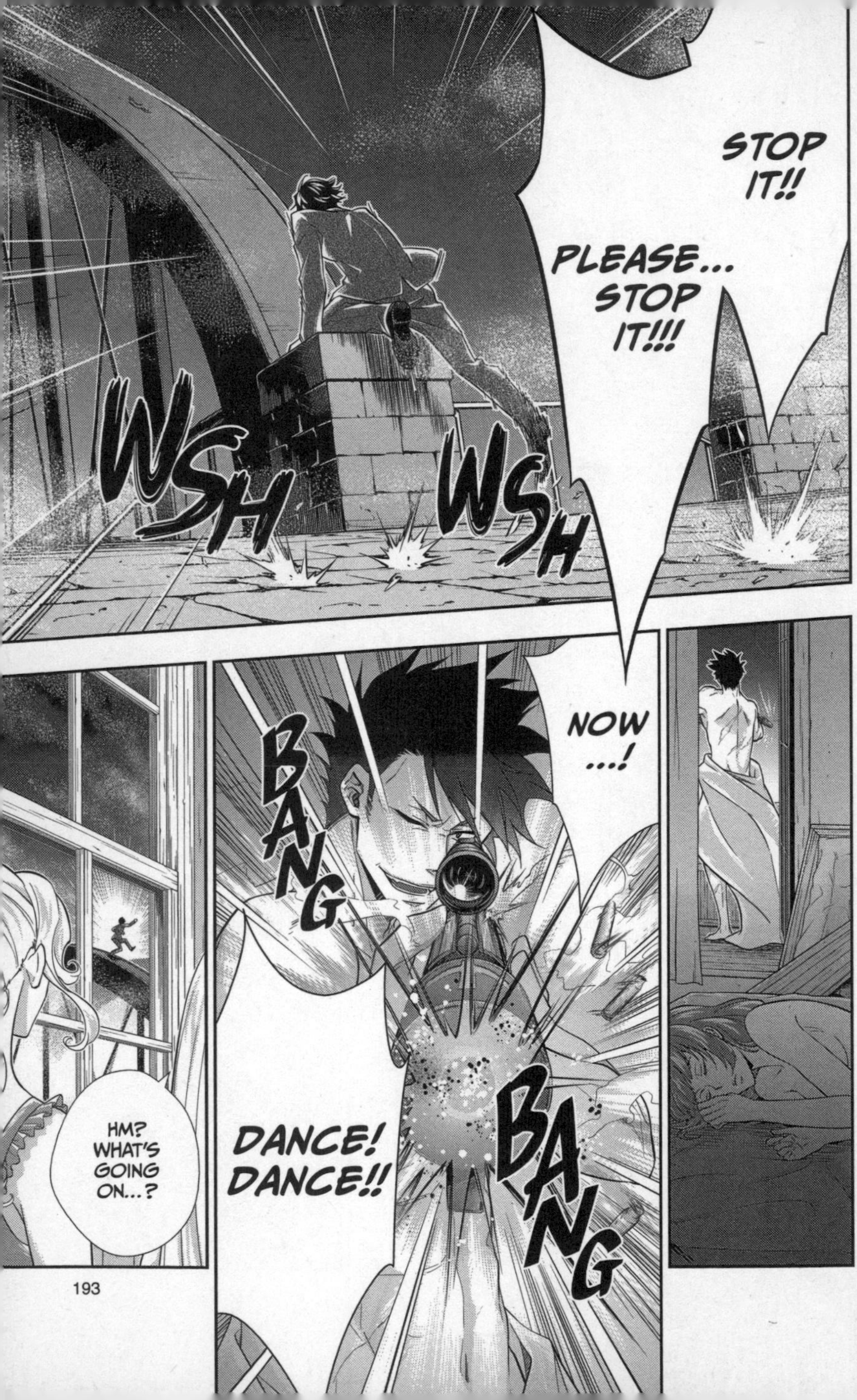
STOP IT!!
PLEASE... STOP IT!!!
WSH
WSH
NOW ...!
BANG
DANCE! DANCE!!
BANG
HM? WHAT'S GOING ON...?

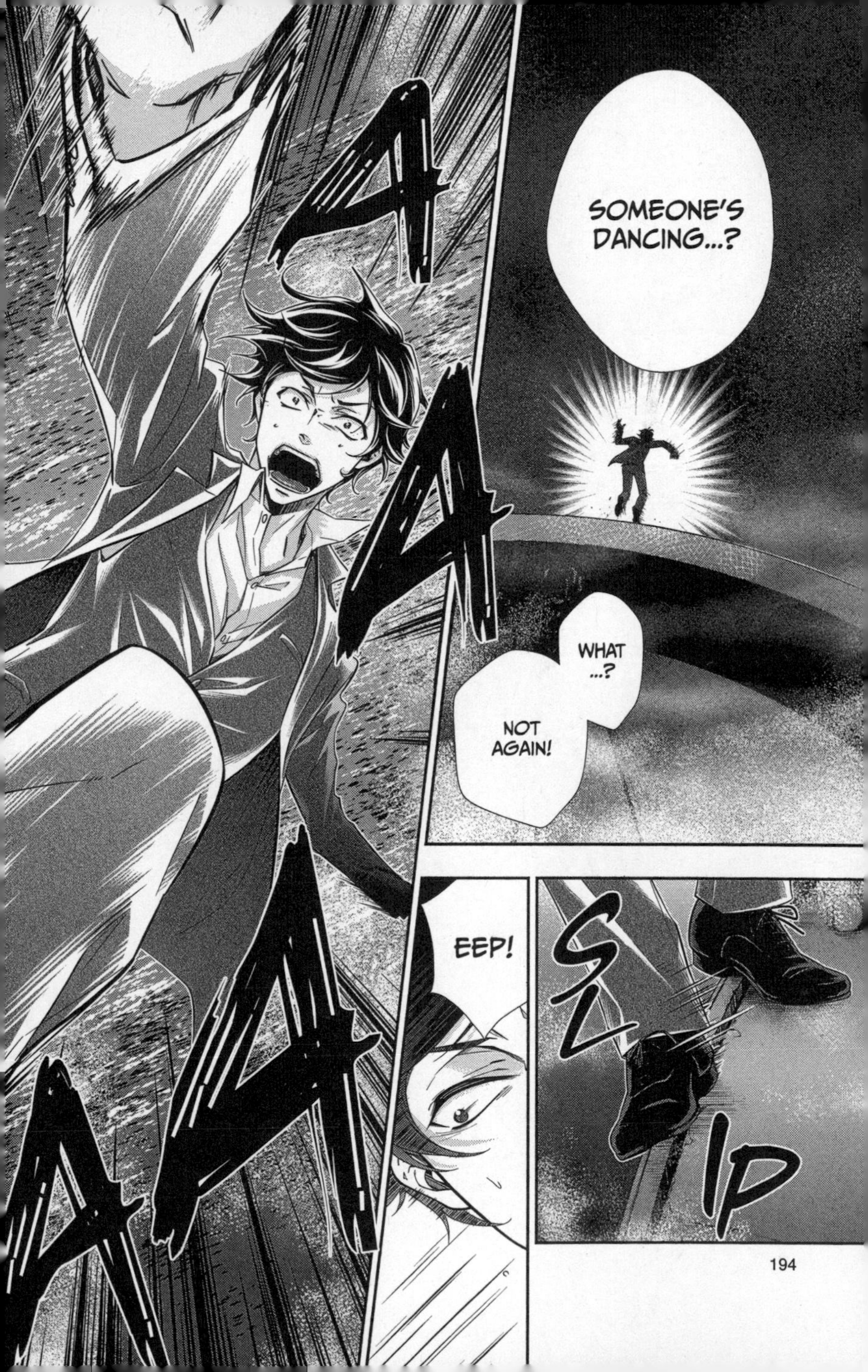
SOMEONE'S DANCING...?
WHAT ...?
NOT AGAIN!
SLIP
EEP!

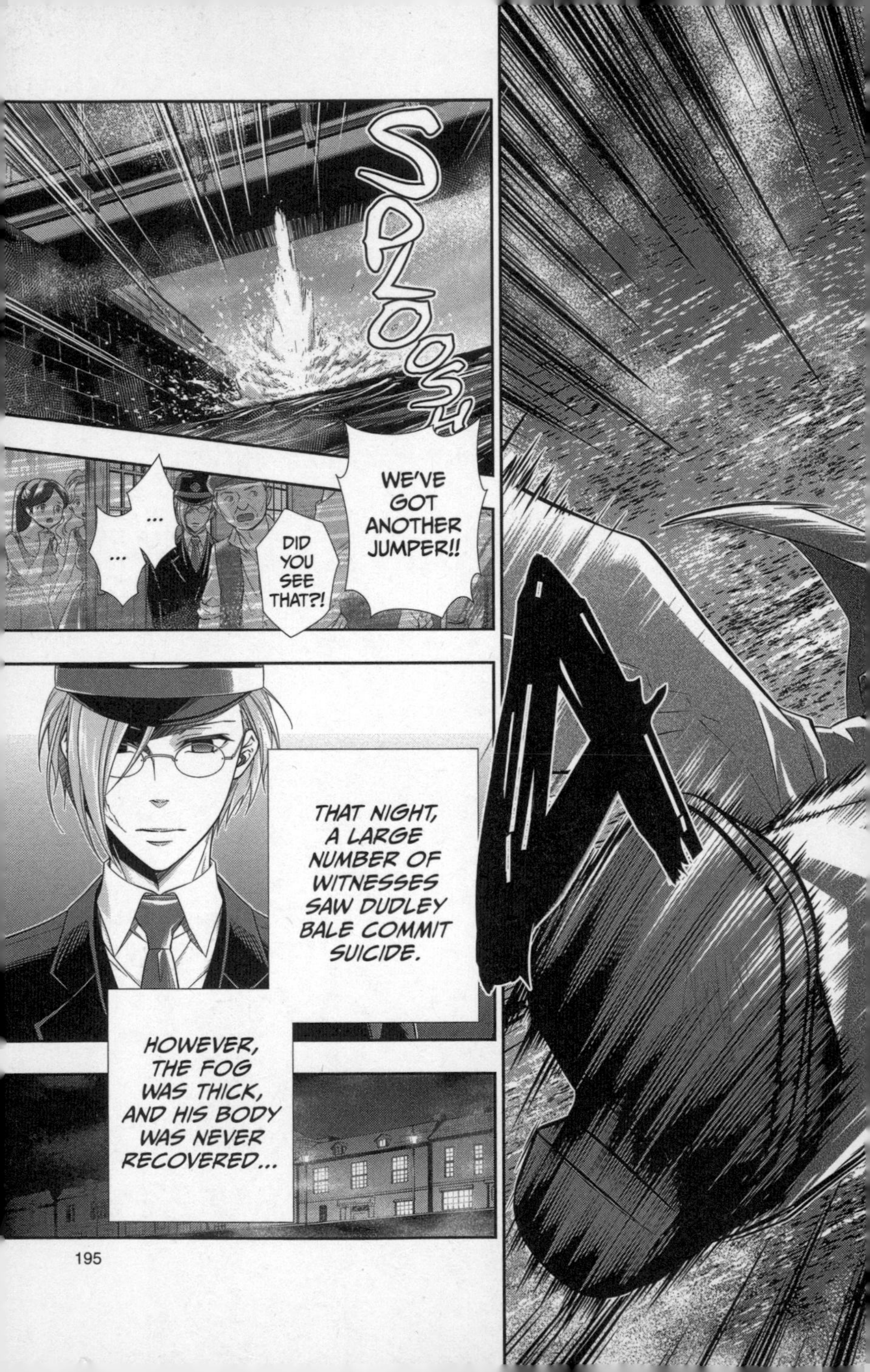
SPLOOSH
WE'VE GOT ANOTHER JUMPER!!
DID YOU SEE THAT?!
...
...
THAT NIGHT, A LARGE NUMBER OF WITNESSES SAW DUDLEY BALE COMMIT SUICIDE.
HOWEVER, THE FOG WAS THICK, AND HIS BODY WAS NEVER RECOVERED...

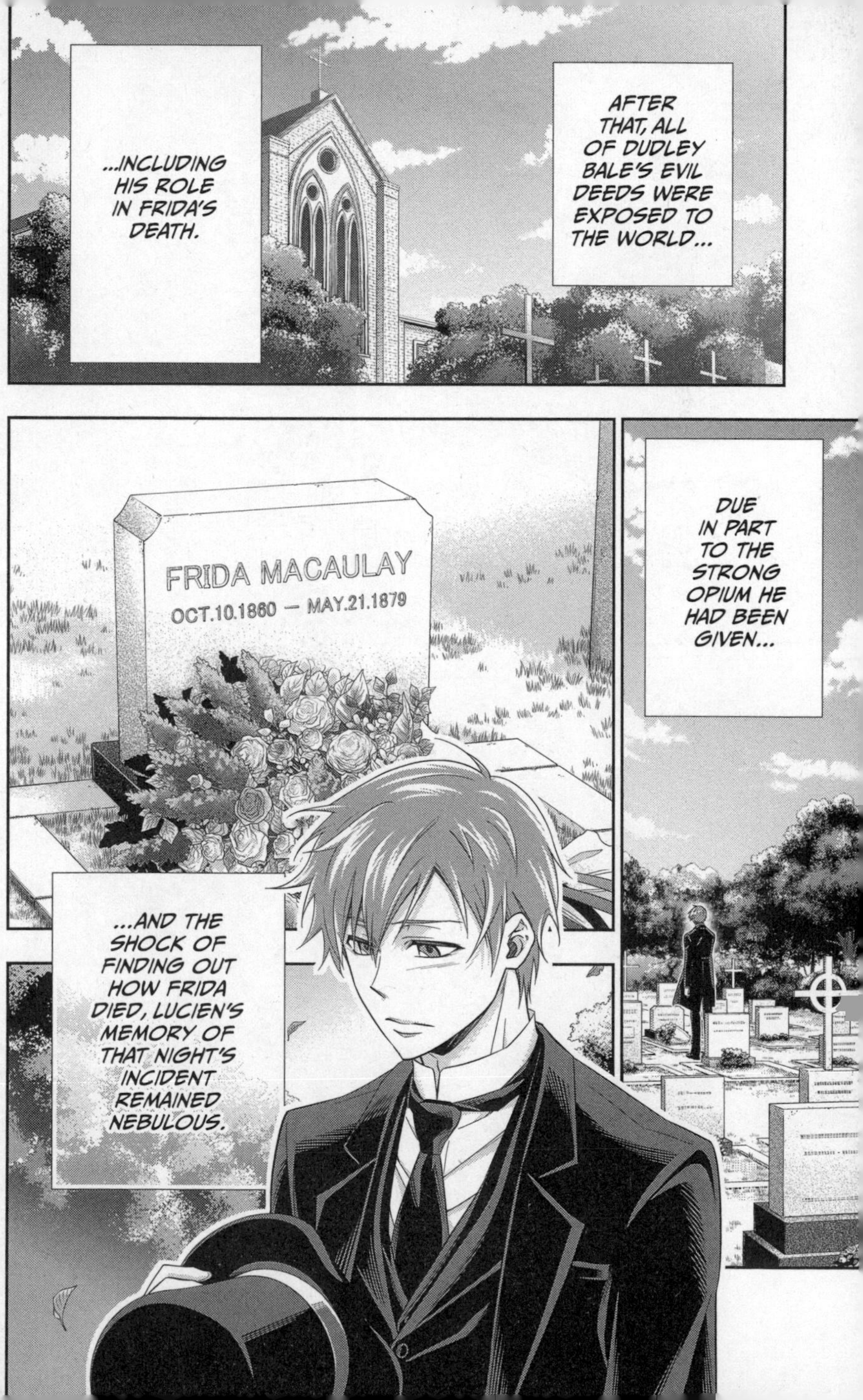
AFTER THAT, ALL OF DUDLEY BALE'S EVIL DEEDS WERE EXPOSED TO THE WORLD...
...INCLUDING HIS ROLE IN FRIDA'S DEATH.
DUE IN PART TO THE STRONG OPIUM HE HAD BEEN GIVEN...
FRIDA MACAULAY
OCT.10.1860 — MAY.21.1879
...AND THE SHOCK OF FINDING OUT HOW FRIDA DIED, LUCIEN'S MEMORY OF THAT NIGHT'S INCIDENT REMAINED NEBULOUS.

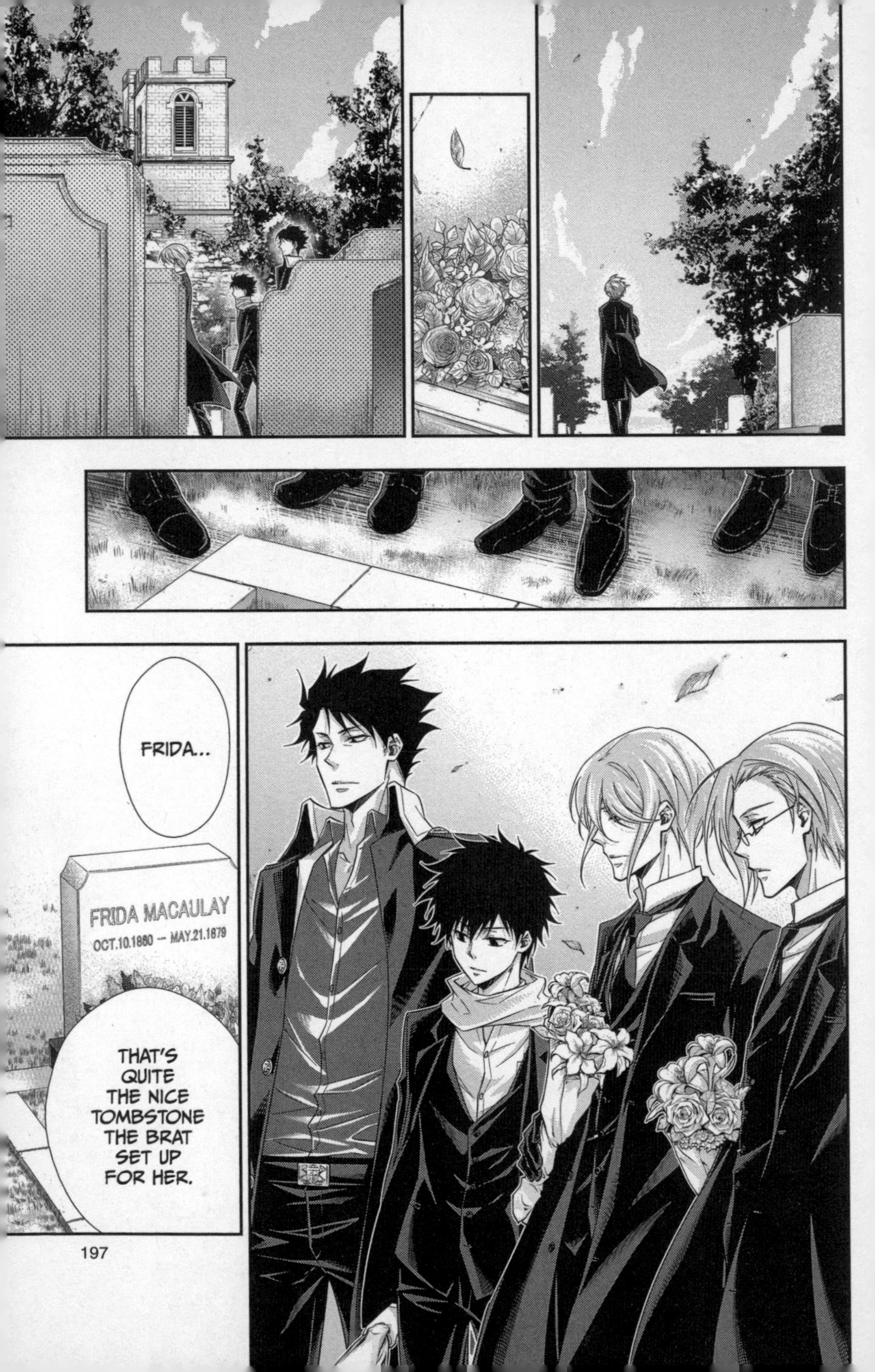
FRIDA...
THAT'S QUITE THE NICE TOMBSTONE THE BRAT SET UP FOR HER.
FRIDA MACAULAY
OCT.10.1860 – MAY.21.1879

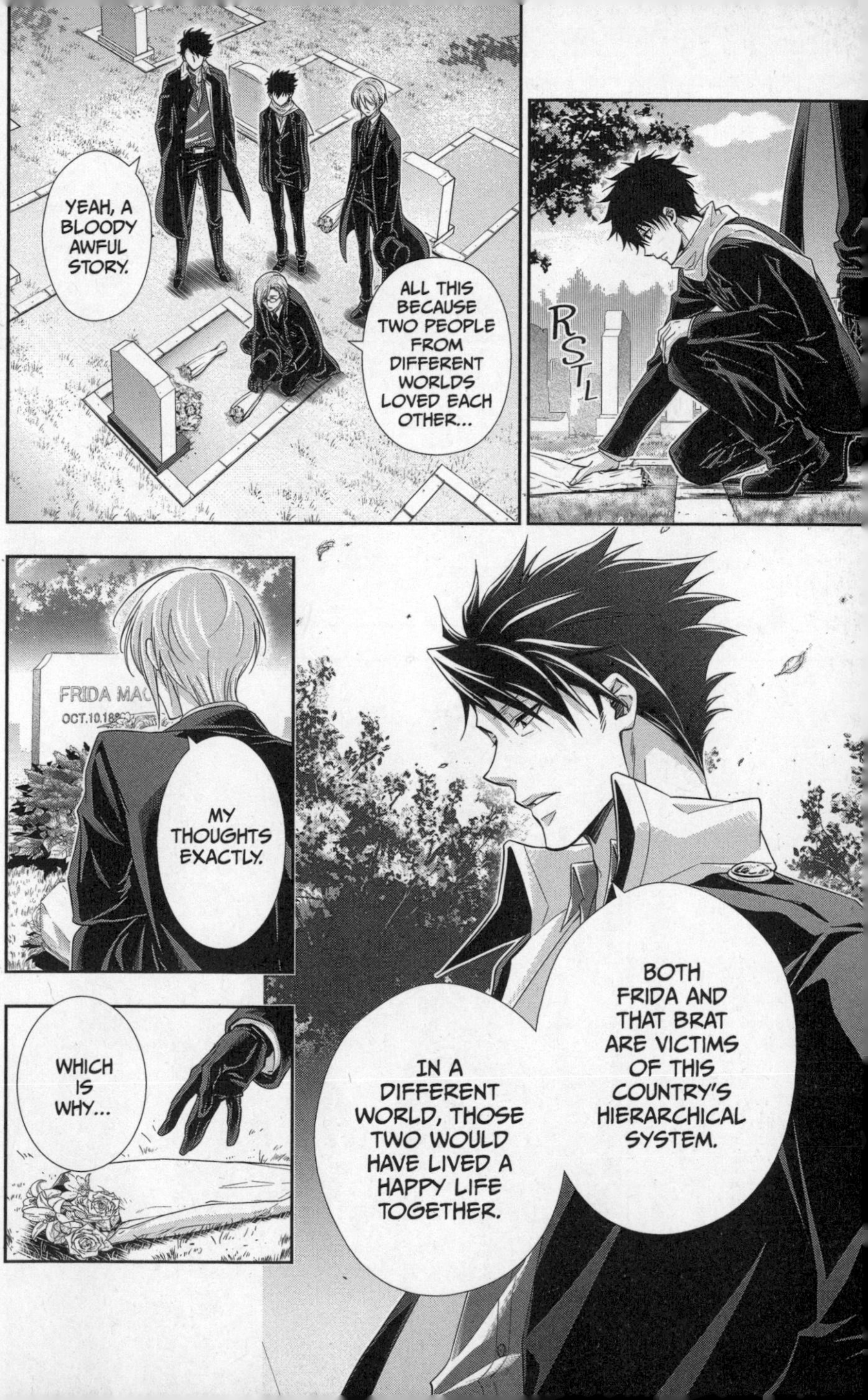
RSTL
ALL THIS BECAUSE TWO PEOPLE FROM DIFFERENT WORLDS LOVED EACH OTHER...
YEAH, A BLOODY AWFUL STORY.
BOTH FRIDA AND THAT BRAT ARE VICTIMS OF THIS COUNTRY'S HIERARCHICAL SYSTEM.
IN A DIFFERENT WORLD, THOSE TWO WOULD HAVE LIVED A HAPPY LIFE TOGETHER.
FRIDA MAC
OCT.10.18
MY THOUGHTS EXACTLY.
WHICH IS WHY...

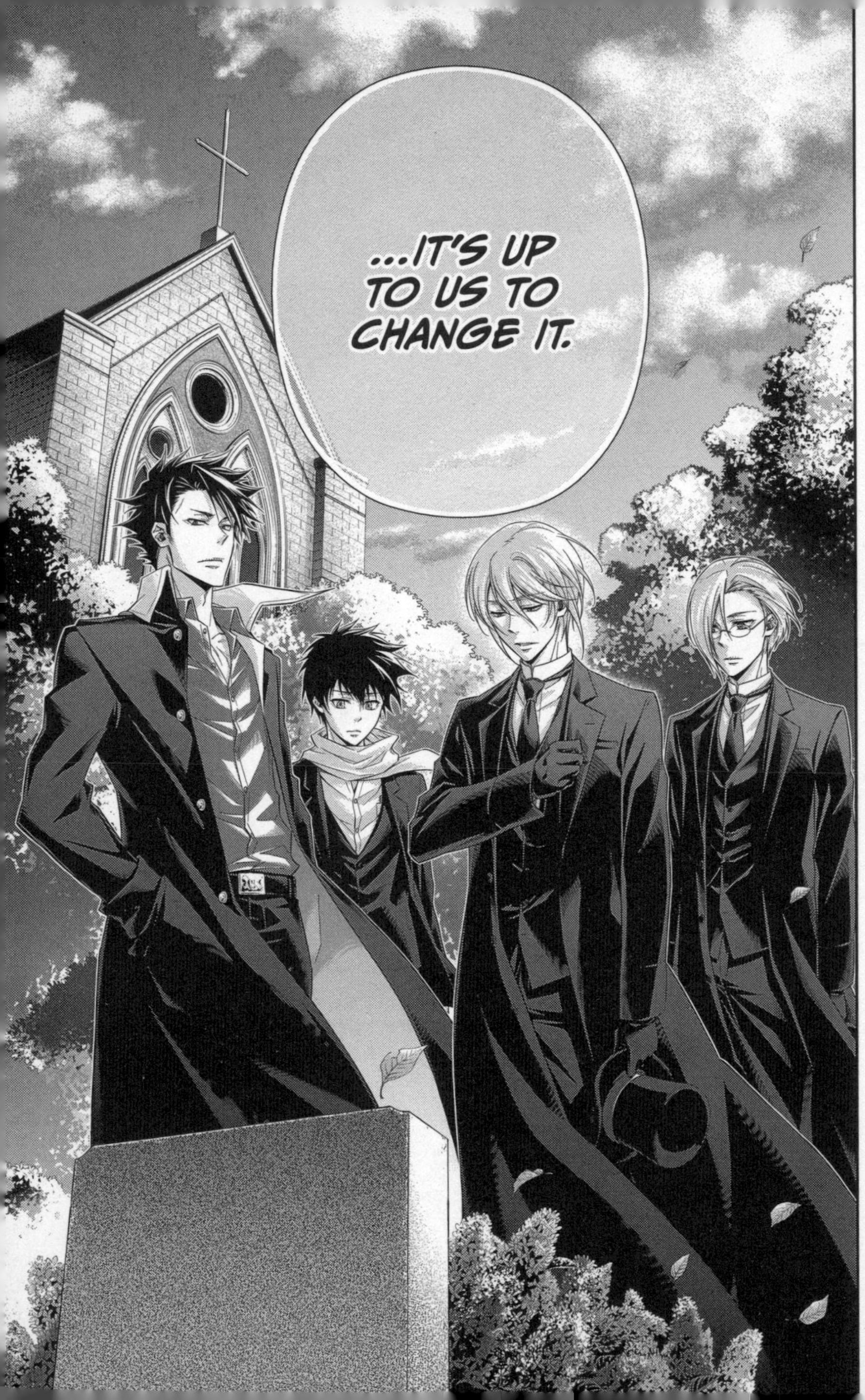
...IT'S UP TO US TO CHANGE IT.

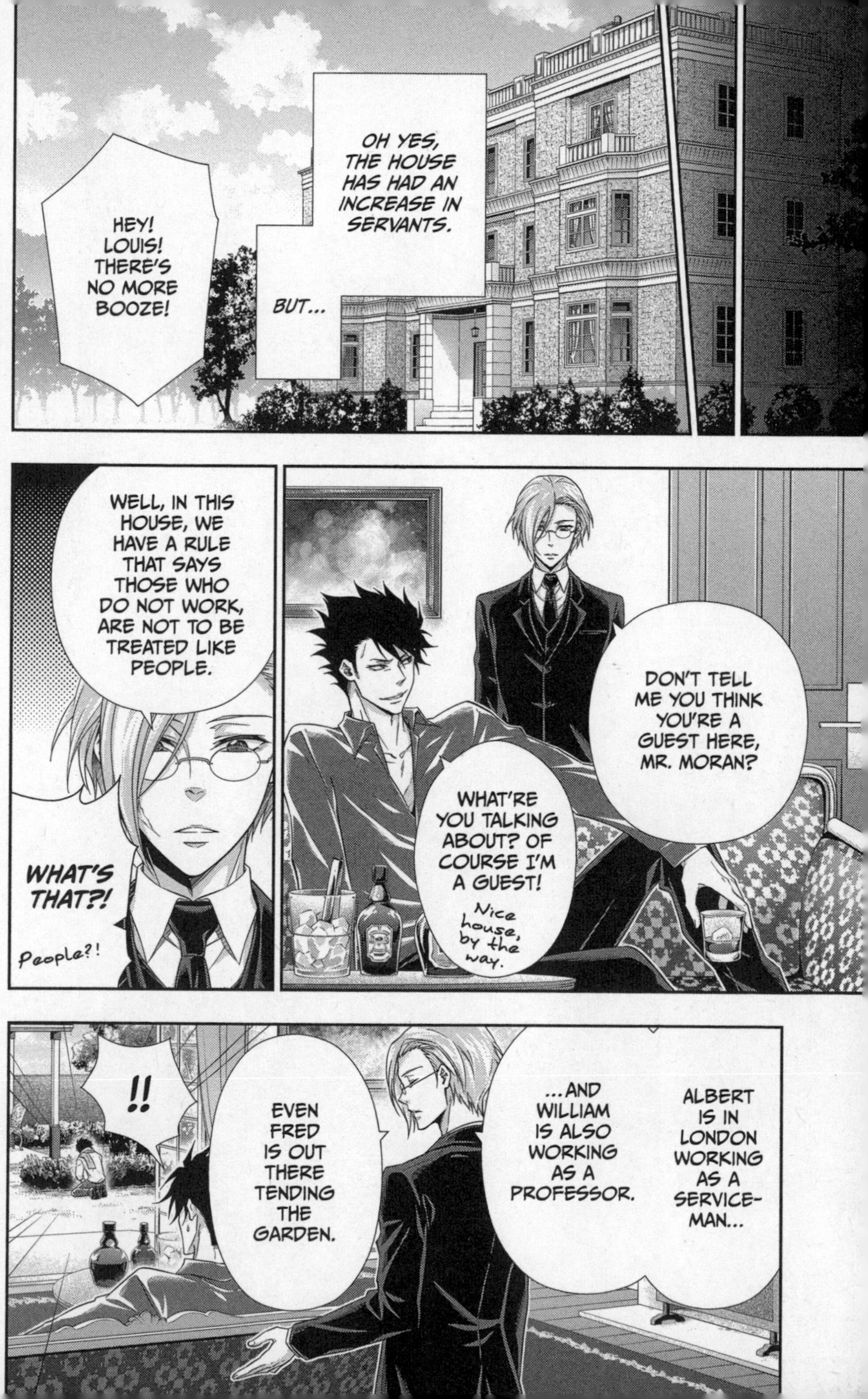
OH YES, THE HOUSE HAS HAD AN INCREASE IN SERVANTS.
BUT...
HEY! LOUIS! THERE'S NO MORE BOOZE!
DON'T TELL ME YOU THINK YOU'RE A GUEST HERE, MR. MORAN?
WHAT'RE YOU TALKING ABOUT? OF COURSE I'M A GUEST!
Nice house, by the way.
WELL, IN THIS HOUSE, WE HAVE A RULE THAT SAYS THOSE WHO DO NOT WORK, ARE NOT TO BE TREATED LIKE PEOPLE.
WHAT'S THAT?!
People?!
ALBERT IS IN LONDON WORKING AS A SERVICE-MAN...
...AND WILLIAM IS ALSO WORKING AS A PROFESSOR.
EVEN FRED IS OUT THERE TENDING THE GARDEN.
!!

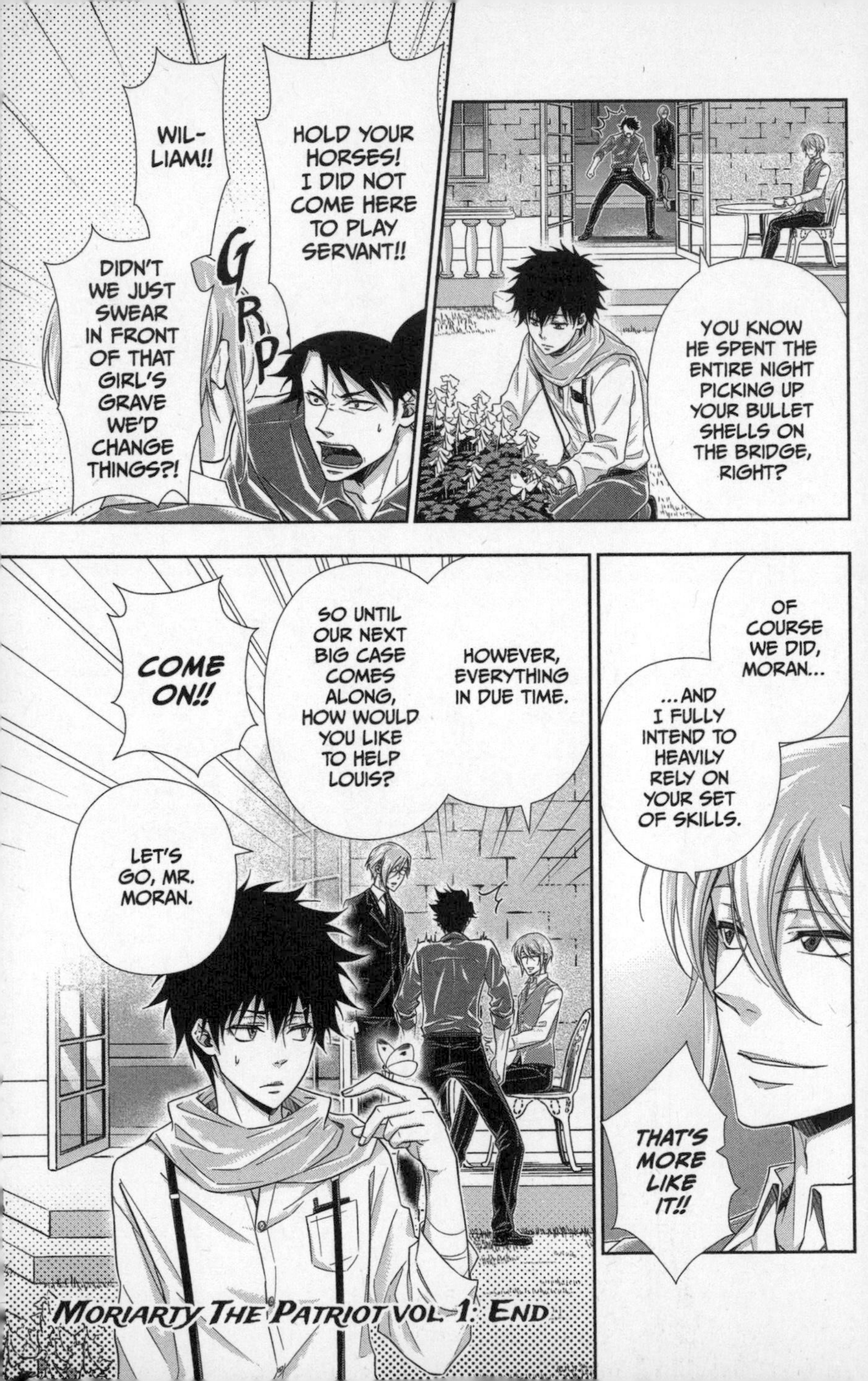
YOU KNOW HE SPENT THE ENTIRE NIGHT PICKING UP YOUR BULLET SHELLS ON THE BRIDGE, RIGHT?
HOLD YOUR HORSES! I DID NOT COME HERE TO PLAY SERVANT!!
WIL-LIAM!!
GRP
DIDN'T WE JUST SWEAR IN FRONT OF THAT GIRL'S GRAVE WE'D CHANGE THINGS?!
OF COURSE WE DID, MORAN...
...AND I FULLY INTEND TO HEAVILY RELY ON YOUR SET OF SKILLS.
THAT'S MORE LIKE IT!!
HOWEVER, EVERYTHING IN DUE TIME.
SO UNTIL OUR NEXT BIG CASE COMES ALONG, HOW WOULD YOU LIKE TO HELP LOUIS?
COME ON!!
LET'S GO, MR. MORAN.
MORIARTY THE PATRIOT VOL. 1: END

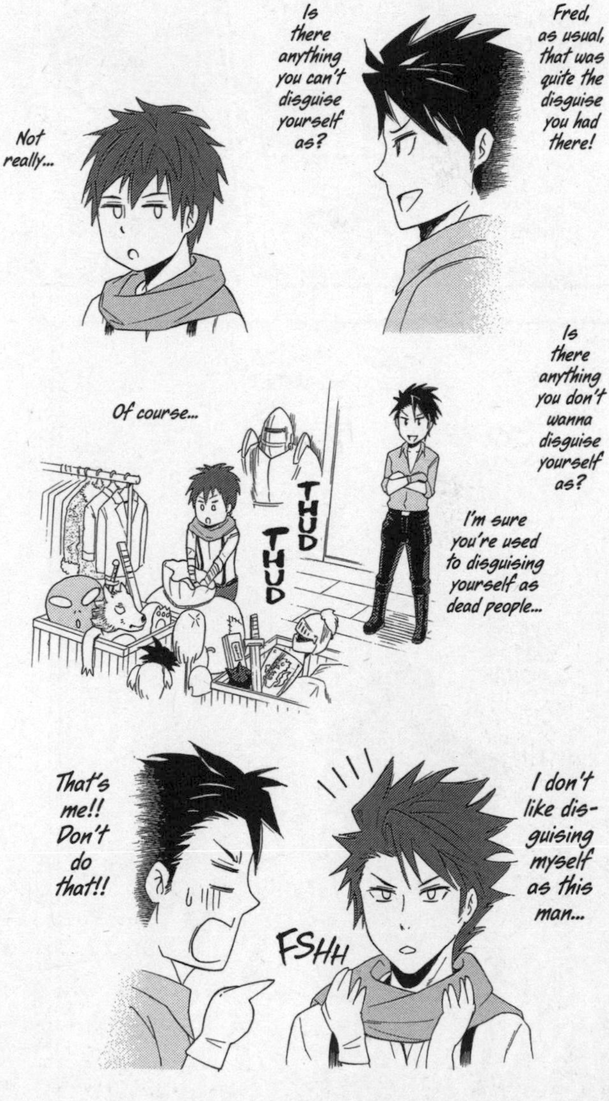
Fred, as usual, that was quite the disguise you had there!
Is there anything you can't disguise yourself as?
Not really...
Is there anything you don't wanna disguise yourself as?
I'm sure you're used to disguising yourself as dead people...
THUD
THUD
Of course...
I don't like dis-guising myself as this man...
FSHH
That's me!! Don't do that!!

MORIARTY
THE PATRIOT

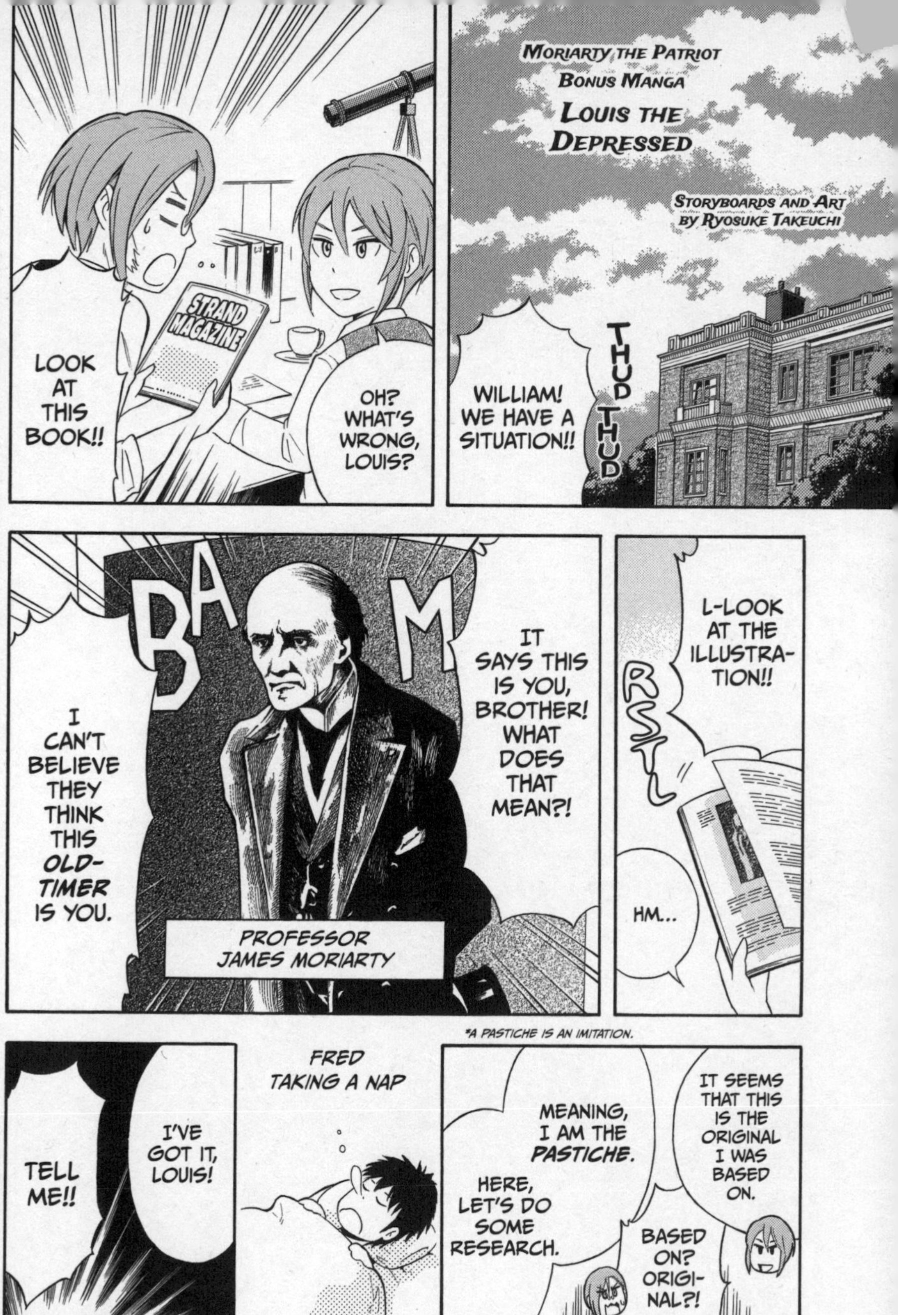
MORIARTY THE PATRIOT
BONUS MANGA
LOUIS THE DEPRESSED
STORYBOARDS AND ART BY RYOSUKE TAKEUCHI
THUD THUD
WILLIAM! WE HAVE A SITUATION!!
OH? WHAT'S WRONG, LOUIS?
LOOK AT THIS BOOK!!
STRAND MAGAZINE
L-LOOK AT THE ILLUSTRATION!!
RSTL
HM...
IT SAYS THIS IS YOU, BROTHER! WHAT DOES THAT MEAN?!
BAM
PROFESSOR JAMES MORIARTY
I CAN'T BELIEVE THEY THINK THIS *OLD-TIMER* IS YOU.
IT SEEMS THAT THIS IS THE ORIGINAL I WAS BASED ON.
MEANING, I AM THE *PASTICHE*.
BASED ON? ORIGINAL?!
HERE, LET'S DO SOME RESEARCH.
FRED TAKING A NAP
I'VE GOT IT, LOUIS!
TELL ME!!

*A PASTICHE IS AN IMITATION.

60 STORIES

A STUDY IN SCARLET | THE SIGN OF FOUR | THE HOUND OF THE BASKERVILLES | THE VALLEY OF FEAR

4 LONG STORIES

IT SEEMS THAT THERE WERE IN TOTAL 60 STORIES THAT THE GREAT ENGLISH LITERARY MASTER SIR CONAN DOYLE WROTE IN THE SAME SERIES.

TH... MU... | THE FIVE ORANGE PIPS | THE 'GLORIA SCOTT' | A SCANDAL IN BOHEMIA | SILVER BLAZE | THE NAVAL TREATY

56 SHORT STORIES

AND THOSE CAN BE FURTHER DIVIDED INTO FOUR LONG STORIES AND 56 SHORT STORIES.

SIXTY?!

*CANON REFERS TO THE ORIGINAL 60 STORIES ARTHUR CONAN DOYLE WROTE. SECONDARY STORIES ARE CALLED APOCRYPHA.

IT'S FINE! REALLY! IT'S THE CANON, AFTER ALL!

DARN YOU, ARTHUR CONAN DOYLE!! EVEN IF YOU WROTE THE ORIGINAL, HOW DARE YOU NOT SEE WILLIAM'S TRUE VALUE!

GRRRR

...IN ONLY SIX STORIES TOTAL.

IN ALL OF THOSE, THE ORIGINAL "JAMES MORIARTY" IS MENTIONED...

?!

IT JUST MEANS...

YOU SHOULD THINK OF IT LIKE THIS, LOUIS.

WHAT?! ONLY SIX? THAT'S TOO LITTLE!!!

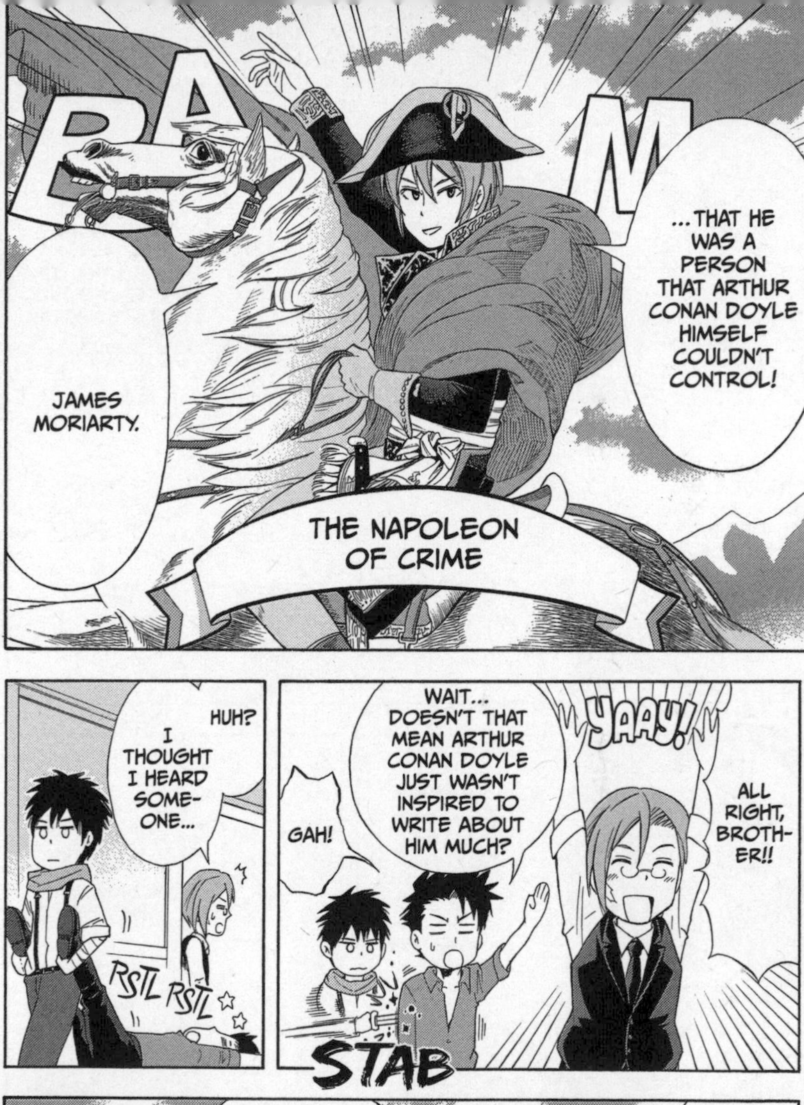
...THAT HE WAS A PERSON THAT ARTHUR CONAN DOYLE HIMSELF COULDN'T CONTROL!
BAM
JAMES MORIARTY.
THE NAPOLEON OF CRIME
YAAY!
ALL RIGHT, BROTHER!!
WAIT... DOESN'T THAT MEAN ARTHUR CONAN DOYLE JUST WASN'T INSPIRED TO WRITE ABOUT HIM MUCH?
GAH!
STAB
HUH?
I THOUGHT I HEARD SOME-ONE...
RSTL RSTL
SURELY YOUR IMAGINA-TION, LOUIS...
NOW GIVE ME TIME TO THINK OF MY NEXT PLAN.
AND YOU CAN COUNT ON ME TO CONTINUE TO FOLLOW YOU WHEREVER YOU GO, BIG BROTHER!

BONUS MANGA: THE END

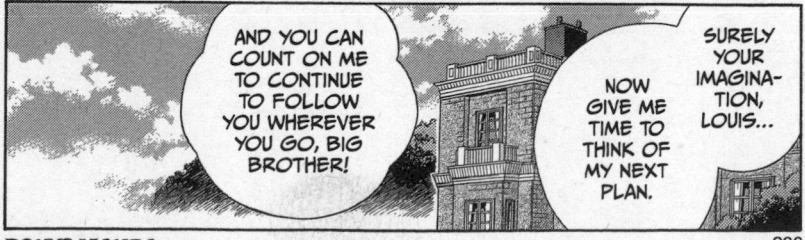